India and Bilateral Investment Treaties

'India has become an influential player in the investment treaty regime. Ranjan's excellent and balanced book traces the evolution of India's investment policy. This book is the first port of call for policymakers and academics who wish to learn more about India's BIT programme in its broader context.'

—Michael Waibel, University Senior Lecturer,
University of Cambridge, United Kingdom

'I have been waiting for a book like this for some time. Given the rising importance of India's economy and the unique path India has taken to investment treaty reform, this book provides an extremely useful guide to India's investment treaty law and policy that is both comprehensive and critical.'

—Anthea Roberts, Professor, *Australian National University*

'Scholarship is very good; presentation is very engaging and well-organized.'

—P.S. Rao, Former Judge AD HOC *International Court of Justice*

'After refusing to sign investment treaties during the Cold War, India jumped on the BIT-bandwagon in the 1990s. In recent years, the pendulum of India's investment treaty policy has swung back towards scepticism and backlash. Few have thought longer and harder about this development than Prabhash Ranjan. His book documents the historical twists and turns of India's investment treaty policy and combines legal analysis with critical reflections on the broader socio-economic context in which the treaties operate. It is a required reading for anyone trying to make sense of the past, present, and possible futures of India's investment protection policy,'

—Lauge N. Skovgaard Poulsen, Associate Professor,
University College London, United Kingdom

India and Bilateral Investment Treaties

Refusal, Acceptance, Backlash

PRABHASH RANJAN

OXFORD
UNIVERSITY PRESS

OXFORD
UNIVERSITY PRESS

Oxford University Press is a department of the University of Oxford. It furthers the University's objective of excellence in research, scholarship, and education by publishing worldwide. Oxford is a registered trademark of Oxford University Press in the UK and in certain other countries.

Published in India by
Oxford University Press
2/11 Ground Floor, Ansari Road, Daryaganj, New Delhi 110 002, India

First Edition published in 2019

ISBN-13 (print edition): 978-0-19-949374-6
ISBN-10 (print edition): 0-19-949374-X

ISBN-13 (eBook): 978-0-19-909707-4
ISBN-10 (eBook): 0-19-909707-0

Typeset in Adobe Garamond Pro 11/13
by The Graphics Solution, New Delhi 110 092
Printed in India by Nutech Print Services India

To My late grandfather, Shri Kedar Nath Sandilya

A secular patriot who fought the British rule for India's independence, and taught me that speaking truth to power is the task of every nationalist and intellectual.

Contents

Table of Cases

International Cases

- *ADF Group Inc.* v. *United States of America*, ICSID Case No ARB (AF)/00/1, Award, 9 January 2003
- *AES Corporation* v. *Argentina*, ICSID Case No ARB/02/17, Decision on Jurisdiction, 26 April 2005
- *AES Summit Generation Limited and AES-Tisza Erömü Kft* v. *The Republic of Hungary*, ICSID Case No. ARB/07/22, Award, 23 September 2010
- *Alex Genin, Eastern Credit Limited, Inc and AS Baltoil (US)* v. *Republic of Estonia*, ICSID Case No ARB/99/2, Award, 25 June 2001
- *Alps Finance and Trade AG* v. *The Slovak Republic*, UNCITRAL, Adhoc Arbitration Award, 5 March 2011
- *American Manufacturing and Trading Inc (AMT)* v. *Republic of Zaire*, ICSID Case No ARB/93/1, Award, 21 February 1997
- *Ampal-American Israel Corp., EGI-Fund (08-10) Investors LLC, EGI-Series Investments LLC, BSS-EMG Investors LLC and David Fischer* v. *Arab Republic of Egypt*, ICSID Case No ARB/12/11, Decision on Liability and Heads of Loss, 21 February 2017

- *Anglia Auto Accessories Ltd* v. *The Czech Republic*, SCC Case No 2014/181, Final Award, 10 March 2017
- *Anrak Aluminium Ltd. & Ors.* v. *State Bank of India &Ors*, CP(IB) No. 127/10/HDB/2017
- *Asian Agricultural Products* v. *Sri Lanka*, ICSID Case No ARB/87/3, Final Award, 27 June 1990
- *AWG Group Limited* v. *Argentine Republic*, ICSID Case No ARB/03/19, Decision on Liability, 30 July 2010
- *Azinian* v. *Mexico*, ICSID Case No. ARB (AF)/97/2, Final Award, 1 November 1999
- *Azurix Corp* v. *Argentina*, ICSID Case No ARB/01/12, Award, 14 July 2006
- *Barcelona Traction Light and Power Company (Belgium* v. *Spain)*, (New Application: 1962, Second Phase), 1970 ICJ REP.3
- *Bayindir Insaat Turizm Ticaret Ve Sanayi A.Ş* v. *Islamic Republic of Pakistan*, ICSID Case No ARB/03/29, Decision on Jurisdiction, 14 November 2005
- *Beijing Urban Construction Group Co Ltd* v. *Republic of Yemen*, ICSID Case No ARB/14/30, Decision on Jurisdiction, 31 May 2017
- *Bilcon of Delaware, William Ralph Clayton, William Richard Clayton, Douglas Clayton and Daniel Clayton* v. *Government of Canada*, PCA Case No 2009-04, Award on Jurisdiction and Liability, 17 March 2015
- *Biwater Gauff Ltd* v. *United Republic of Tanzania*, ICSID Case No. ARB/05/22, Award, 24 July 2008
- *Blusun SA, Jean-Pierre Lecorcier and Michael Stein* v. *Italian Republic*, ICSID Case No ARB/14/3, Award, 27 December 2016
- *Brazil—Measures Affecting Imports of Retreaded Tyres, Appellate Body Report*, WT/DS332/AB/R, 17 December 2007
- *Burlington Resources Inc.* v. *Republic of Ecuador*, ICSID Case No ARB/08/5, Decision on Liability, 14 December 2014
- *Cairn Energy PLC and Cairn UK Holdings Limited* v. *The Republic of India*, PCA Case No. 2016–7
- *Cairn UK Holdings Limited* v. *Deputy Commissioner of Income Tax*, Income Tax Appellate Tribunal, ITA No. 1669 /Del/2016, 9 March 2017

- *Capital India Power Mauritius I and Energy Enterprises (Mauritius) Company* v. *Maharashtra Power Development Corporation Limited, Maharashtra State Electricity Board and the State of Maharashtra*, ICC Case No 12913/MS, Award, 27 April 2005
- *Cargill* v. *Mexico*, ICSID Case No. ARB(AF)/05/2, Award, 18 September 2009
- *Case Concerning Elettronica Sicula S.p.A. (ELSI) (U.S.* v. *Italy)*, Judgement, 1989 I.C.J. Rep. 1989
- *CC/Devas (Mauritius) Ltd, Devas Employees Mauritius Private Limited, and Telcom Devas Mauritius Limited* v. *Republic of India*, PCA Case No. 2013-09, Award, 25 July 2016
- *Cervin Investissements SA and Rhone Investissements SA* v. *Republic of Costa Rica*, ICSID Case No ARB/13/2, Award, 7 March 2017
- *Ceskoslovenska Obchodni Banka, AS* v. *The Slovak Republic*, ICSID Case No ARB/97/4, Decision on Jurisdiction, 24 May 1999
- *Chemtura Corporation (formerly Crompton Corporation)* v. *Government of Canada*, PCA Case No 2008-01, Award, 2 August 2010
- *Chevron Corporation and Texaco Petroleum Corporation* v. *Ecuador*, UNCITRAL, Partial Award on Merits, 30 March 2010
- *CME Czech Republic BV* v. *The Czech Republic*, UNCITRAL, Partial Award, 13 September 2001; Final Award, 14 March 2003
- *CMS Gas Transmission Co* v. *Argentine Republic*, ICSID Case No ARB/01/8, Award, 12 May 2005
- *Continental Casualty Company* v. *Argentine Republic*, ICSID Case No ARB/03/9, Award, 5 September 2008
- *Copper Mesa Mining Corporation* v. *Republic of Ecuador*, PCA No 2012-2, Award, 15 March 2016
- *Corn Products International* v. *Mexico*, ICSID Case No ARB (AF)/04/01, (NAFTA), Decision on Responsibility, 15 January 2008
- *Deutsche Telekom AG* v. *Republic of India*, PCA Case No 2014-10, 13 December 2017

- *Dominican Republic—Measures Affecting the Importation and Internal Sale of Cigarettes* WT/DS320/AB/R, adopted 19 May 2005
- *Duke Energy* v. *Republic of Ecuador* (ICSID Case No ARB/04/19), Award, 18 August 2008
- *El Paso Energy International Company* v. *The Argentine Republic*, ICSID Case No. ARB/03/15, Award, 31 October 2011
- *Elettronica Sicula SpA* (ELSI) (*U.S.* v. *Italy*), [1989] ICJ Rep. 15, 20 July 1989
- *Eli Lilly and Company* v. *The Government of Canada*, ICSID Case No UNCT/14/2, Award, 16 March 2017
- *Emilio Augustine Mafezzini* v. *Spain*, ICSID Case No ARB/97/7, Award, 13 November 2000
- *EnCana Corporation* v. *Republic of Ecuador*, LCIA Case No UN3481, Award, 3 February 2006
- *Enron Corporation and Ponderosa Assents, LP* v. *The Argentine Republic*, ICSID Case No ARB/01/3, Award, 22 May 2007
- *Enron Creditors Recovery Corp* v. *Argentina*, ICSID Case No ARB/01/3, Decision on the Argentine Republic's Application for Annulment of the Award, 30 July 2010
- *Eureko BV* v. *Republic of Poland*, Ad Hoc, Partial Award, 19 August 2005
- *Fedax NV* v. *Venezuela*, ICSID Case No ARB/96/3, Decision on Jurisdiction, 11 July 1997
- *Flemingo Duty Free Shop Private Limited* v. *Republic of Poland*, PCA, Award, 12 August 2016
- *Gami Investments, Inc.* v. *The Government of the United Mexican States*, UNCITRAL Final Award, 15 November 2004
- *Gas Natural SDG SA* v. *Argentine Republic*, ICSID Case No ARB/03/10, Decision of the Tribunal on Preliminary Questions on Jurisdiction, 17 June 2005
- *Generation Ukraine Inc* v. *Ukraine*, ICSID Case No ARB/00/9, Award, 16 September 2003
- *Glamis Gold Ltd* v. *The United States of America*, UNCITRAL, Award, 8 June 2009
- *Goetz and others* v. *Burundi*, ICSID Case No ARB/95/3, Award, 10 February 1999

- *Gold Reserve Inc.* v. *Bolivarian Republic of Venezuela*, ICSID Case No ARB (AF)/09/1, Award, 22 September 2014
- *Hassan Awdi, Enterprise Business Consultants Inc. and Alfa El Corporation* v. *Romania*, ICSID Case No ARB/10/13, Award, 2 March 2015
- *Helnan International Hotels A/S* v. *Arab Republic of Egypt*, ICSID Case No ARB/05/19, Decision on Annulment, 14 June 2010
- *Hulley Enterprises Limited (Cyprus)* v. *The Russian Federation*, PCA Case No AA 226, Final Award, 18 July 2014
- *Içkale Insaat Limited Sirketi* v. *Turkmenistan*, ICSID Case No ARB/10/24, Award, 8 March 2016
- *Impregilo S.p.A.* v. *Argentine Republic, ICSID Case No. ARB/07/17*, Award, 21 June 2011
- *Int'l Thunderbird Gaming Corp. v. United Mexican States*, UNCITRAL, Arbitral Award, 26 January 2006
- *Interhandel Case (Switzerland* v. *U.S.)*, Judgment, 1959 I.C.J. Rep. 1959, Mar. 21
- *Italian Republic* v. *Republic of Cuba*, Ad hoc State-State Arbitration, Final Award, 15 January 2008
- *Jan de Nul NV and Dredging International NV* v. *Arab Republic of Egypt*, ICSID Case No ARB/04/13, Decision on Jurisdiction, 16 June 2006
- *Joy Mining Machinery Limited* v. *Arab Republic of Egypt*, ICSID Case No. ARB/03/11, Award on Jurisdiction, 6 August 2004
- *Korea—Measures Affecting Imports of Fresh, Chilled and Frozen Beef*, WT/DS 161 and WT/DS169/AB/R adopted 11 December, 2000
- *Lemire* v. *Ukr.*, ICSID Case No. ARB/06/18, Decision on Jurisdiction and Liability, 14 January 2010
- *LESI SpA et Astaldi SpA* v. *Algeria*, ICSID Case No. ARB/05/3, Decision on Jurisdiction, 12 July 2006
- *LFH Neer and PE Neer* v. *United Mexican States* (Docket No 136), General Claims Commission – United States and Mexico, 4 UNRIAA 60, 15 October 1926
- *LG&E Energy Corp., LG&E Capital Corp., and LG&E International, Inc.* v. *Argentine Republic*, ICSID Case No.

ARB/02/1, Decision on Liability, 3 October 2006, Award, 25 July 2007

- *Loewen* v. *United States*, ICSID Case No. ARB(AF)/98/3, Award, 26 June 2003
- *Malaysian Historical Salvors* v. *Malaysia*, ICSID Case No. ARB/05/10, Award on Jurisdiction, 17 May 2007
- *Malaysian Historical Slavors, SDN, BHD* v. *Malaysia*, ICSID Case No ARB/05/10, Award, 17 May 2007; Decision on Application for Annulment, 16 April 2009
- *Mamidoil Jetoil Greek Petroleum Products Societe Anonyme S.A.* v. *Republic of Albania*, ICSID Case No. ARB/11/24, Award, 30 March 2015
- Marvin Roy Feldman *Karpa* v. *United Mexican States*, ICSID Case No ARB(AF)/99/1, Award, 16 December 2002
- *Merrill and Ring Forestry LP* v. *Canada* (ICSID Case No UNCT/07/1), Award, 31 March 2010
- *Mesa Power Group LLC* v. *Government of Canada*, PCA Case No 2012-17, Award, 24 March 2016
- *Metalclad Corporation* v. *United Mexican States*, ICSID Case No ARB(AF)/97/1, Award, 30 August 2000
- *Metaplar* v. *The Argentine Republic*, ICSID Case No. ARB/03/5, Award, 6 January 2008
- *Methanex Corporation* v. *United States of America*, NAFTA-UNCITRAL, Award, 3 August 2005
- *Methanex* v. *United States*, NAFTA Ch. 11/UNCITRAL Arb. Trib, Jurisdiction and Merits, 3 August 2005
- *Middle East Shipping Cement Ltd* v. *Egypt*, 7 ICSID Rep 178
- *Millicom International Operations B.V. and Sentel GSM SA* v. *The Republic of Senegal, ICSID Case No. ARB/08/20*, Decision on Jurisdiction, 16 July 2010
- *Mondev International Ltd.* v. *United States* (ICSID Case No ARB (AF)/99/2), Award, 11 October 2002
- *Mondev International Ltd.* v. *United States of America*, ICSID Case No. ARB(AF)/99/2, Award, 11 October 2002
- *Mr. Patrick Mitchell* v. *The Democratic Republic of Congo*, ICSID Case No. ARB/99/7, Annulment proceeding, 9 February 2004

- *MTD Equity SDN BHD and MTD Chile SA* v. *Republic of Chile*, ICSID Case No ARB/01/7, Award, 25 May 2004; Decision on Annulment, 21 March 2007
- *National Grid Plc* v. *Argentine Republic*, UNCITRAL, Award, 3 November 2008
- *Occidental Exploration & Production Co.* v. *Republic of Ecuador*, LCIA Case No. UN3467, Final Award, 1 July 2004
- *Parkerings Compagniet AS* v. *Republic of Lithuania*, ICSID Case No ARB/05/8, Award, 11 September 2007
- *Philip Morris Asia Ltd.* v. *The Commonwealth of Australia*, UNCITRAL, PCA Case No. 2012-12, Award on Jurisdiction and Admissibility, 17 December 2015
- *Philip Morris Brand Sàrl (Switzerland), Philip Morris Products S.A. (Switzerland) and Abal Hermanos S.A. (Uruguay)* v. *Oriental Republic of Uruguay*, ICSID Case No. ARB/10/7, Award, 8 July 2016
- *Phoenix Action Ltd.* v. *Czech Republic* (ICSID Case No ARB/06/5), Award, 15 April 2009
- *PL Holdings S.à.r.l.* v. *Republic of Poland*, SCC Case No. V 2014/163, Partial Award, 28 June 2017
- *Plama Consortium Limited* v. *Republic of Bulgaria*, ICSID Case No ARB/03/24, Award, 27 August 2008
- *Pope and Talbot Inc.* v. *The Government of Canada*, UNCITRAL, Award on the Merits of Phase 2, 10 April 2001
- *Pope and Talbot* v. *Canada*, Ad hoc Tribunal (UNCITRAL), Interim Award, 26 June 2000
- *PSEG Global Inc., The North American Coal Corporation, and Konya Ingin Electrik Üretim ve Ticaret Limited Sirketi* v. *Republic of Turkey*, ICSID Case No ARB/02/5, Award, 19 January 2007
- *RAKIA* v. *India* 2016, *Ras-AI-Khaimah Investment Authority (RAKIA)* v. *India* (2016), UNCTAD
- *Romak SA (Switzerland)* v. *Uzbekistan*, PCA Case No AA280, Award, 26 November 2009
- *Ronald S Lauder* v. *The Czech Republic*, UNCITRAL, Final Award, 3 September 2001
- *Rumeli Telekom* v. *Republic of Kazakhstan*, ICSID Case No ARB/05/16, Award, 29 July 2008

- *S.S. Lotus (France* v. *Turkey)*, 1927 P.C.I.J. (ser. A) No. 10
- *Saipem SpA* v. *People's Republic of Bangladesh*, ICSID Case No ARB/05/07, Decision on Jurisdiction, 21 March 2007
- *Salini Costruttori SpA and Italstrade SpA* v. *Kingdom of Morocco*, ICSID Case No ARB/00/4, Decision on Jurisdiction, 23 July 2001
- *Saluka Investments BV* v. *The Czech Republic*, UNCITRAL, Partial Award, 17 March 2006
- *Sempra Energy International* v. *The Argentine Republic*, ICSID Case No ARB/02/16, Award, 28 September 2007
- *SGS Société Générale de Surveillance SA* v. *Islamic Republic of Pakistan*, ICSID Case No. ARB/01/13, Decision on Jurisdiction, 6 August 2003
- *SGS Société Générale de Surveillance SA* v. *Republic of the Philippines*, ICSID Case No ARB/02/6, Decision of the Tribunal on Objections to Jurisdiction, 29 January 2004
- *Siemens AG* v. *Argentine Republic*, ICSID Case No ARB/02/8, Decision on Jurisdiction, 3 August 2004; Award, 6 February 2007
- *Spyridon Roussalis* v. *Romania*, ICSID Case No. ARB/06/1, Award, 7 December 2011
- *Starrett Housing Corporation* v. *Islamic Republic of Iran*, 4 Iran-US CTR 122, 154 (1983)
- *Suez, Sociedad General de Aguas de Barcelona SA and Vivendi Universal SA* v. *Argentine Republic*, ICSID Case No ARB/03/19, Decision on Jurisdiction, 3 August 2006
- *Técnicas Medioambientales Tecmed SA* v. *The United Mexican States*, ICSID Case No ARB (AF)/00/2), Award 29 May 2003
- *TECO Guatemala Holdings LLC* v. *Republic of Guatemala*, ICSID Case No ARB/10/23, Award, 19 December 2013
- *Telenor Mobile Communications A.S.* v. *Republic of Hungary*, ICSID Case No. ARB/04/15, Award, 13 September, 2006
- *International Thunderbird Gaming Corporation* v. *The United Mexican States*, UNCITRAL, Award, 26 January 2006
- *Tippetts, Abbett, McCarthy, Stratton and TAMS-AFFA Consulting Engineers of Iran* v. *Islamic Republic of Iran*, 6 Iran-US CTR 219, 225 (1984)
- *Tokios Tokelés* v. *Ukraine*, ICSID Case No. ARB/02/18, Award, 26 July 2007

- *Total S.A.* v. *The Argentine Republic*, ICSID Case No. ARB/04/01, Decision on Liability, 27 December 2010
- *Union of India* v. *Vodafone Group Plc United Kingdom & Anr, Delhi High Court*, CS(OS) 383/2017, Order, 22 August 2017
- *Urbaser SA and Consorcio de Aguas Bilbao Biskaia, Bilbao Biskaia Ur Partzuergoa* v. *Argentine Republic* (ICSID Case No ARB/07/26), Award, 8 December 2016
- *Urbaser SA and Consorcio de Aguas Bilbao Bizkaia, Bilbao Biskaia Ur Partzuergoa* v. *The Argentine Republic*, ICSID Case No. ARB/07/26, Decision on the Claimant's Proposal to Disqualify Professor Campbell McLachlan, Arbitrator, 12 August 2010
- *US—Measures Affecting the Cross-Border Supply of Gambling and Betting*, WT/DS/285/AB/R, Appellate Body Report, adopted 20 April 2005
- *Vattenfall AB and others* v. *Federal Republic of Germany (II)*, ICSID Case No ARB/12/12, Decision on the Achmea Issue, 31 August 2018
- *Veteran Petroleum Limited (Cyprus)* v. *The Russian Federation*, PCA Case No AA 228, Final Award, 18 July 2014
- *Vladimir Berschader and Moïse Berschader* v. *The Russian Federation*, SCC Case No 080/2004, Award, 21 April 2006
- *Vodafone International Holdings BV* v. *India*, PCA Case No. 2016-35, UNCTIRAL, 17 April 2014
- *White Industries Australia Limited* v. *Republic of India*, UNCITRAL, Final Award, 30 November 2011
- *Wintershall Aktiengesellschaft* v. *The Argentine Republic*, ICSID Case No ARB/04/14, Award, 8 December 2008
- *WNC Factoring Ltd (WNC)* v. *The Czech Republic*, PCA Case No. 2014-34, Award, 22 February 2017
- *Yukos Universal Limited (Isle of Man)* v. *The Russian Federation*, PCA Case No AA 227, Final Award, 18 July 2014

Domestic Cases

- *Bayer Corp.* v. *Natco Pharma. Ltd.*, Order No. 45/2013 (Intellectual Property Appellate Board, Chennai, 2013)
- *Bayer Corporation* v. *Union of India*, Petition for Special Leave to Appeal (C) NO (S). 30145/2014, 12 December 2014

- *Centre for Public Interest Litigation and Others* v. *Union of India and others*, Writ Petitions (C) No. 423 Of 2010 With No. 10 Of 2011
- *Commissioner of Income Tax, New Delhi* v. *M/S Eli Lilly & Company (India) Pvt. Ltd.*, (2009) 3 TMI 33 (SC)
- *D K Basu* v. *State of West Bengal*, 1997 1 SCC 416
- *DIT (International Taxation)* v. *Morgan Stanley & Co Inc.*, (2007) 292 ITR 416 (SC)
- *E-Funds IT Solutions* v. *DIT*, Civil Appeal 6082 of 2015, 24 October 2017 (SC)
- *Formula One World Championship Ltd.* v. *CIT*, (2017) SCC Online SC 474
- *H H Maharajadhiraja Madhav Rao* v. *Union of India*, 1971 AIR 530
- *Hindustan Vegetable Oils* v. *Progressive Industries and Ors.*, 1995 SCC (6) 174
- *ITO v Right Florists Limited*, ITA No 1336/Kol/2011; [2013] 143 ITD 445 (Kol)
- *Mahindra and Mahindra Ltd* v. *Union of India (UOI) and another*, (1979) 2 SCC 529
- *MI Patel* v. *Union of India*, (1970) 3 SCC 400
- *Minerva Mills Ltd. & others* v. *Union Of India and others*, 1980 AIR 1789
- *National Textiles Corporation (South Maharashtra) Limited* v. *Tamil Nadu Co-operative Marketing Federation Ltd.*, AIR 1998 SC 2658
- *P Vajravelu Mudaliar* v. *Special Deputy Collector, Madras*, AIR 1965 SC 1017
- *Rosiline George* v. *Union of India*, (1994) 2 SCC 80
- *Rustom Cavasjee Cooper* v. *Union of India*, AIR 1970 SC 564
- *Sanjeev Coke Manufacturing* v. *Bharat Coking Coal Ltd*, 1983 AIR 239
- *SP Gupta* v. *President of India and others*, AIR 1982 SC 149
- *State of Gujarat* v. *Shri Shantilal Mangaldas and others*, AIR 1969 SC 634

- *State of Madras* v. *D Namasivaya Mudaliar*, AIR 1965 SC 190
- *State of West Bengal* v. *Bella Banerjee*, AIR 1954 SC 170
- *Supreme Court Advocates-on-Record - Association and another* v. *Union of India*, Writ Petition (Civil) No 13 OF 2015, 16 October 2015 (SC)
- *Supreme Court Advocates-records- Association* v. *Union of India*, (1993) 4 SCC 441
- *Tata Engineering and Locomotive Co Ltd* v. *The Registrar of the Restrictive Trade Agreement*, (1977) 2 SCC 55
- *Union of India* v. *Metal Corporation of India*, AIR 1967 SC 637
- *Union of India* v. *Sankal Chand Himmatlal Sheth*, AIR 1977 SC 2328; (1977) 4 SCC 193
- *Union of India* v. *Azadi Bachao Andolan*, (2003) 263 ITR 706 (SC)
- *Vodafone International Holdings B.V.* v. *Union of India (3 December 2008). Writ Petition No 2550 of 2007*
- *Vodafone International Holdings BV* v. *Union of India*, Civil Appeal No 733 of 2012, 20 January, 2012
- *Vodafone International Holdings BV* v. *Union of India*, (2012) 6 SCC 613

Foreword

Studies on the investment treaty practices and policies of individual states have been a recurrent feature in the scholarship on international investment law over the past few decades. The reason for this is simple. It is the practice of specific states, or groups of states, that has influenced the field and shaped the content of the international legal instruments used to govern international investment relations. For most of its history, it has been capital-exporting states that have had the greatest influence on present-day international investment law. European states, spearheaded by the Federal Republic of Germany, have developed, endorsed, and promoted the use of bilateral investment treaties (BITs) since the late 1950s under what came to be known as the 'European model', a set of narrowly tailored treaty commitments focused exclusively on the protection of foreign investment post-establishment. The 'European model' influenced investment treaty practices worldwide and made European capital-exporting states into the dominant rule-makers in international investment law well into the 2000s.

The United States, building on its programme of friendship, commerce, and navigation treaties, joined the league of BIT users in the early 1980s and developed a distinctly 'American model' that added market access commitments to the European approach, turning BITs into instruments of investment liberalization. While this approach remained the exception on a global scale for a long time, the United States became the dominant rule-maker in international investment law from the mid-2000s onwards. The approach taken in the North American Free Trade Agreement (NAFTA) to integrate investment and trade commitments and the 2004 US Model BIT, which recalibrated investment treaty commitments in reaction to arbitral awards that have been perceived as striking an inadequate balance between investment protection and competing public concerns, heralded a 'NAFTA-ization' or 'Americanization' of international investment law. Countries the world over, as well as regional integration associations, like the European Union (EU) or the Association of South East Asian Nations (ASEAN), moulded their investment treaties after the NAFTA and the recalibrated US Model BIT.

With European and North-American states having served as the predominant rule-makers in international investment law for decades, much scholarly attention has focused on the approaches taken by these actors. In fact, the investment treaty practices and policies of European states, above all that of Germany, as well as that of the United States and NAFTA have been documented and analysed almost ad nauseam in international investment law scholarship. A painful gap exists, however, when it comes to the practices and policies of non-European actors, with China being so far a notable exception. This gap is painful for a number of reasons. First, it is highly relevant to analyse the trajectory of a legal field not only from the perspective of rule-makers, but also to assess the engagement of rule-takers with the law in question. What effects—positive and negative—does international investment law have on affected countries? Does it meet their needs and interests as well? Or does it cause economic, political, social, environmental, or other disruptions and tensions?

Second, realities in international investment relations are changing fundamentally. Investor–state dispute settlement, long dormant, has started to bite, both developed and developing countries, and led to a reassessment of whether the conventional norms and institutional arrangements strike an appropriate balance between investment protection and competing concerns. Meanwhile, this reassessment has led to a heated struggle for a global reform of international investment law and investor–state dispute settlement. Of note, in this context, is that economic realities have shifted quite fundamentally. Many countries in the developing world, which have qualified until recently almost exclusively as capital-importers, are now significant sources of foreign investment flows, both into developed and other developing countries. Conversely, developed countries are suddenly at the receiving end of investment disputes as incoming foreign investment now, unlike before, is often enough covered by an investment treaty. These shifts have an impact on the relative weighing of offensive and defensive interests and the individual foreign investment policies countries adopt. But they also change the global landscape, with traditional capital-importers gaining political clout and bargaining power in relation to the former rule-makers from the West.

India is an important case in point in this context. Until recently, it has been among the countries with the largest number of BITs and, in reaction to investment treaty arbitrations against it, has started to reevaluate its approach to international investment protection. With its new 2016 Model BIT, India has departed fundamentally from the European model followed earlier, not only by including duties for foreign investors, but above all by scaling down the substantive protections and procedural recourses available both for foreign investors in India and Indian investors abroad. Moreover, the new 2016 Model BIT represents an approach that is now widely discussed among the leading models to shape the future of international investment law, together with the approaches of Brazil and those contained in mega-regionals, in particular the Comprehensive and Progressive Agreement for Trans-Pacific Partnership (CPTPP) concluded between 11 Pacific Rim countries and the Comprehensive Economic and Trade Agreement (CETA) concluded between Canada and the EU. At the same time, India's emerging role as a capital-exporter and the involvement of Indian firms as claimants in investment treaty arbitration raise the question of whether India's new Model BIT is suitable both for its own (offensive) economic and political interests and attractive as a global model for governing international investment relations.

Despite the importance India has assumed for the future of international investment law, so far no comprehensive analysis of India's engagement with international investment law and investment treaties has been presented. The present book, which is based on Prabhash Ranjan's PhD dissertation at King's College London, therefore, undertakes pioneering work of outstanding importance. What is of particular note is that, in his book, he not only engages in a mapping exercise of the content of India's BITs and investment chapters in free trade agreements that make us understand what commitments India has undertaken in its investment agreements. His monograph does much more. It analyses the development of India's foreign investment policy and practice over time, starting with India's independence post-World War II up to the present day. The strength of his analysis of the origins, evolution, and current state of play of India's investment policy is the thick contextualization he provides, explaining the country's stance on foreign investment and international investment protection as a function of the country's shifting political ideologies and its repercussions on its internal economic and foreign policy.

Prabhash Ranjan convincingly shows how India's position vis-à-vis investment treaties developed from 'refusal' up until 1980, first reflecting Nehru's position of economic nationalism, which was nevertheless open for foreign investment, and later Indira Gandhi's socialist policies, which included large-scale nationalization, to 'acceptance' between 1980 and 2010. This was catalysed not least by the need for integration into the global economy following the country's economic difficulties in the 1970s and 1980s, to 'backlash' after the award in *White Industries* v. *India* was handed down in 2010. It is this latter event that triggered a review process in India of its foreign investment policies, which ultimately resulted in its 2016 Model BIT, one of the most restrictive models for governing international investment relations that is currently around.

The long-term, evolutionary perspective Ranjan adopts shows in an exemplary fashion how country studies of foreign investment law and policy should today be conducted, combining a focus on the law in force, paying attention to its evolution over time, and providing explanations for this evolution by taking into account the economic and foreign policies of the country in question. Moreover, he does not shy away from criticizing India's current approach. He provides a detailed and strong criticism of India's 2016 Model BIT as unworkable for investors and neither reflecting India's offensive foreign policy interests nor providing an approach that represents a globally attractive model. He also takes on the TWAIL approaches that have been forged to a large extent by Indian scholars and criticizes them for having stirred India's international investment policy in a direction that is at odds with the vision he pleads India to take, namely, that of a global rule-maker and standard-setter in the field of international investment law. This, Ranjan holds, is the appropriate role the world's most populous democracy and long-term voice of developing countries should take rather than sliding back into a position of refusal and disengagement. Constructive engagement in reforming international investment law would, he argues, not only align with India's own economic and foreign policy interests, but demonstrate India's commitment to a stable global economic order under the rule of law that produces benefits for all countries, developed and developing, and their citizens alike.

In the current debates about the future of international investment law, in fact potentially a turning point in the field's history, I commend the reading of this book on India's engagement with international investment law. It is a lucid, insightful, and informative study of one of the major players in international investment law and governance that will, without doubt, leave its mark on the future of the field, but whose role has long been underappreciated and ignored. This book brings the long overdue closure of a crucial gap in the literature on international investment and does so by setting standards for how country-specific studies of international investment law and policy should be conducted.

Stephan W. Schill
Professor of International Economic Law and Governance,
Amsterdam Center for International Law, University of Amsterdam;
Editor, *The Journal of World Investment and Trade*

Acknowledgements

My interest in this topic first arose when I was an LLM student at School of Oriental and African Studies (SOAS) in London in 2006. My constant interactions with my LLM dissertation supervisor, Professor Peter Muchlinski at SOAS, played a vital role in generating interest in international investment law and bilateral investment treaties (BITs). Professor Muchlinski encouraged me to work on Indian BITs as very little research had been done on Indian investment treaties. I shall always remain grateful to him for this suggestion that had a huge positive impact on my academic career. Later, I did research on Indian BITs as part of my PhD at King's College London. This book is a thoroughly upgraded and comprehensively revised version of my doctoral thesis. I am indebted to my supervisors at King's, Dr Federico Ortino and Dr Racheal Walsh. Dr Ortino, in particular, supported me throughout my PhD studies and provided excellent research supervision. I am also grateful to my PhD thesis examiners, Professor Asif Qureshi and Professor Jansen Calamita, whose comments proved to be immensely useful.

I wish to thank the anonymous reviewers of OUP for their very helpful comments on the manuscript. I would like to thank many outstanding scholars and practitioners, from whom I have learnt so much over the years: Stephan Schill, Luke Nottage, Julien Chaisse, Chester Brown, P.S. Rao, B.S. Chimni, Jurgen Kurtz, Tania Voon, Jansen Calamita, Mahdev Mohan, Michael Waibel, Lauge

Poulsen, Mavluda Sattorova, Romesh Weeramantry, Olga Boltenko, Aniruddha Rajput, Kabir Duggal, Christian Tams, Piet Eeckhout, Prabhakar Singh, James Nedumpara, Shreyas Jayasimha, R.V. Anuradha, Martins Paparinskis, Anthea Roberts, Leila Choukroune, Andrew Newcombe, and Esme Shirlow. I express my gratitude to Stephan Schill for writing a very encouraging Foreword for the book and also to Michael Waibel, Anthea Roberts, and Lauge Poulsen for endorsing the book.

Many of my current and former students and others have helped me in this project and I record my sincere gratitude to all of them: Digvijay Dam, Tania Singla, Sparsha Janardhan, Dhruv Sharma, Aratrika Choudhuri, Varsha Singh, Samarth Trigunayat, and Tanya Thakur. I also thank Pushkar Anand who has been my co-author in some of my writings on international investment law. I owe a particular debt of gratitude to all my students whom I have taught over the years, in different universities. Their probing questions challenging my knowledge, deep affection and love has always inspired me.

Special thanks to the South Asian University (SAU) and to all my colleagues at SAU for their support and encouragement. Some minor parts of this book have been previously published in the *Northwestern Journal of International Law and Business* (2017), in an article titled 'The 2016 Model Indian Bilateral Investment Treaty: A Critical Deconstruction', and in the chapter titled 'Investor State Dispute Settlement in the 2016 Indian Model Bilateral Investment Treaty: Does it Go Too Far?' in *International Investment Treaties and Arbitration Across Asia* (edited by Julien Chaisse and Luke Nottage, published by Brill, 2017). I am grateful to the respective publishers for their permission to reproduce some parts of my published work.

I also wish to thank Professor Mahendra Pal Singh, one of the finest constitutional law scholars India has produced. I started my academic career in 2007 at the National University of Juridical Sciences (NUJS), Kolkata, where Professor Singh was the Vice Chancellor. His academic scholarship and vision for higher education in India has left an indelible mark on my mind. I express my sincere gratitude to him for his constant support and encouragement throughout my career. I express my gratitude to Oxford University Press and its staff for their very professional help and support.

This book wouldn't have been possible without the love, sacrifice, and support of my family. I couldn't have completed this book without the blessings of my beloved parents, Shashi Ranjan and Prabha Ranjan. I thank them for their unconditional love and innumerable sacrifices. I express my gratitude to my father-in-law, R.N. Sharma, and mother-in-law, Gyan Sheela Sharma, for their blessings and love.

I also would like to express my deep gratefulness to my brother, Shashank Ranjan, my sister-in-law, Malti Ranjan, and my lovely niece Sakshi Ranjan. My thanks to Vivek Anand, Shilpi Rai, Sujit Rai, and Supriya Sharma for their support.

On this day, I also remember my late grandfather, Kedar Nath Sandilya, who fought the British rule for India's independence. His patriotism has been a constant source of inspiration for everyone in my family. His indomitable nationalist spirit and belief in Indian Constitutional values has surely been a very strong guiding force behind this book and behind all my professional endeavours. Hence I dedicate this book to him.

Last, but surely not the least, I am indebted to my wonderful wife, Shweta, for her unwavering support and sacrifices. She is my friend, philosopher, and guide and my pillar of strength and source of constant motivation. She has always, patiently heard all my trials and tribulations. For all this, and many other reasons, this book is as much hers as it is mine. I hope my eight-year-old son, Aanjnay, one day would read his father's book and write a critique of it!

Prabhash Ranjan
1 February 2019

Abbreviations

AALCO	Asian-African Legal Consultative Organization
A&C	Act Arbitration and Conciliation Act
ALCC	Asian Legal Consultative Committee
ASEAN	Association of Southeast Asian Nations
BIPA	Bilateral Investment Promotion Agreement
BIT	Bilateral Investment Treaty
BoP	Balance of Payment
CAC	Capital Account Convertibility
CCS	Cabinet Committee on Security
CECA	Comprehensive Economic Cooperation Agreement
CEPA	Comprehensive Economic Partnership Agreement
CERDS	Charter of Economic Rights and Duties
CIHL	Cairn India Holdings Limited
CIL	Customary International Law
DPC	Dabhol Power Company
EU	European Union
FCN	Friendship, Commerce, and Navigation
FDI	Foreign Direct Investment
FET	Fair and Equitable Treatment
FEMA	Foreign Exchange Management Act
FERA	Foreign Exchange Regulation Act
FII	Foreign Institutional Investment

FIPB	Foreign Investment Promotion Board
FPS	Full Protection and Security
FTA	Free Trade Agreement
FTC	Free Trade Commission
GATS	General Agreement on Trade in Services
GATT	General Agreements on Tariffs and Trade
GDP	Gross Domestic Product
GE	General Electric
HC	High Court
HEL	Hutchison Essar Ltd
HDI	Human Development Index
HTIL	Hutchison Telecommunications International Ltd
ICC	International Chamber of Commerce
ICJ	International Court of Justice
ICSID	International Centre for Settlement of Investment Disputes
IGA	Investment Guarantee Agreement
ILC	International Law Commission
IMF	International Monetary Fund
IMS	International Minimum Standard
ISRO	Indian Space Research Organisation
ISDS	Investor State Dispute Settlement
IIA	International Investment Agreement
ITAT	Income Tax Appellate Authority
KHML	Khaitan Holdings Mauritius Limited
LCIA	London Centre of International Arbitration
LDC	Least Developed Country
MAI	Multilateral Agreement on Investment
MFN	Most-Favoured Nation
MIGA	Multilateral Investment Guarantee Agreement
MRTP	Monopolies and Restrictive Trade Practice Act
MSEB	Maharashtra State Electricity Board
MTP	Monetary Transfer Provision
NAFTA	North American Free Trade Agreement
NGO	Non-Governmental Organization
NIEO	New International Economic Order
NPM	Non-Precluded Measures

OECD	Organization for Economic Cooperation and Development
OPIC	Overseas Private Investment Corporation
PCA	Permanent Court of Arbitration
PCIJ	Permanent Court of International Justice
PSNR	Permanent Sovereignty over Natural Resources
RBI	Reserve Bank of India
SEZ	Special Economic Zone
SSDS	State State Dispute Settlement
TCC	Transnational Capitalist Class
TOC	Transnational Oppressed Class
TWAIL	Third World Approaches to International Law
UAE	United Arab Emirates
UK	United Kingdom
UN	United Nations
UNDP	United Nations Development Programme
UNGA	United Nations General Assembly
UNCITRAL	United Nations Commission on International Trade Law
UNCTAD	United Nations Conference on Trade and Development
US	United States of America
VCLT	Vienna Convention on the Law of Treaties
WTO	World Trade Organization

1

Introduction

Bilateral Investment Treaties (BITs) are treaties between two countries aimed at protecting investments made by investors of both countries.[1] The BITs protect investments by imposing conditions on the regulatory behaviour of the host state and thus prevent undue interference with the rights of the foreign investor.[2] These conditions include restricting host state from expropriating investments, barring for public interest with adequate compensation and following due process; imposing obligations on host states to accord fair and equitable treatment (FET) to foreign investment and not to discriminate against foreign investment; allowing for repatriation of profits subject to conditions agreed to between the two countries. Bilateral Investment Treaties also specify what constitutes an 'investment' and who qualifies as an 'investor'. This ensures that

[1] For a general discussion on BITs, see R. Dolzer and C. Schreuer. 2012. *Principles of International Investment Law*. Oxford: Oxford University Press (hereinafter Dolzer and Schreuer. *Principles of International Investment* Law); A. Newcombe and L. Paradell. 2009. *Law and Practice of Investment Treaties*. Bedfordshire: Kluwer Law International, pp. 1–73 (hereinafter Newcombe and Paradell *Law and Practice of Investment Treaties*); Jeswald Salacuse. 2015. *The Law of Investment Treaties*. Oxford: Oxford University Press (hereinafter Salacuse *The Law of Investment Treaties*).

[2] Dolzer and Schreuer. *Principles of International Investment* Law, p. 13.

BITs protect only such investments and investors. Today, BITs are the most important source of international investment law.[3]

A very important feature of BITs is that they give rights to individual investors to bring cases to settle investment disputes against the host state's sovereign regulatory measures that breach the BIT, for monetary compensation. This is known as investor–state dispute settlement (ISDS).[4] The ISDS provision in BITs exists along with the State–State dispute settlement (SSDS) provisions that allows contracting parties, that is, the states to bring cases against each other concerning 'interpretation or application' of the treaty.[5] The ISDS and SSDS have different mandates. While ISDS focusses on resolving investment disputes between the foreign investor and the host state, SSDS is concerned about interpretation or application of the treaty.[6]

As part of the ISDS provisions, most BITs allow foreign investors to bring claims against the host state even without exhausting local remedies.[7] In the large majority of BITs, these ISDS clauses offer unequivocal consent to arbitration to foreign investors.[8] The ISDS

[3] Dolzer and Schreuer. *Principles of International Investment Law*, p. 13.

[4] In the book, ISDS and ISDS system are used interchangeably. While ISDS refers to just the dispute settlement system between the investor and the state, 'ISDS system' means not just the dispute settlement system but the entire universe of BITs and investment treaty arbitration.

[5] See Article 10 of India-UK BIT. 1994. https://investmentpolicyhub.unctad.org/Download/TreatyFile/1613; Article 27 of the Energy Charter Treaty. 1994. https://energycharter.org/fileadmin/DocumentsMedia/Legal/ECTC-en.pdf.

[6] A. Roberts. 2014. 'State to State Investment Treaty Arbitration: A Hybrid Theory of Independent Rights and Shared Interpretative Authority' *Harvard International Law Journal* 55(1): 5. Also see *Republic of Italy* v. *Republic of Cuba*, Final Award, Ad Hoc Tribunal, 15 January 2008.

[7] Dolzer and Schreuer. *Principles of International Investment Law*, p. 265. Also see *Helnan International Hotels A/S* v. *Arab Republic of Egypt*, ICSID Case No ARB/05/19, Decision on Annulment, 14 June 2010, paras 43–57; *Generation Ukraine, Inc* v. *Ukraine*, ICSID Case No. ARB/00/9, Award, 16 September 2003, para 13.4.

[8] Christoph Schreuer. 2008. 'Consent to Arbitrate', in *The Oxford Handbook of International Investment Law* Peter Muchlinski, Federico Ortino, and Christoph Schreuer (eds), pp. 835–6. Oxford: Oxford University Press.

system in BITs ensures that states can be held accountable for the exercise of their public power by a third party, that is, an international tribunal, which will have the power to review the action of the host state—whether executive, judicial, or legislative.[9]

1.1 Global Developments and Growth of BITs

Although roots of the contemporary treaty rules on protection of foreign investment can be traced back to 1796 when the United States (US) negotiated the first Friendship, Commerce and Navigation treaty with France,[10] the era of current investment treaties began when Germany and Pakistan signed a BIT in 1959 that came into force in 1962. As Salacuse has written, the reason behind Germany taking this initiative was that it had lost all of its foreign investment due to its defeat in World War II and thus wanted to enter into bilateral treaties governing and protecting foreign investment.[11] Furthermore, various European countries felt the need to protect the investment of their nationals in their erstwhile political colonies that started gaining political independence in the 1950s and 1960s.[12] Consequently, European countries such as the UK, Belgium, France, and Netherlands and also other countries that had no colonies, such as Switzerland and Austria, started entering into BITs.[13] Deficiencies of customary international law on foreign investment also triggered

---

Also see, K. Vandevelde. 2010. *Bilateral Investment Treaties: History, Policy and Interpretation*. Oxford: Oxford University Press, pp. 433–9. (hereinafter Vandevelde, *Bilateral Investment Treaties*).

[9] Andreas Kulick. 2012. *Global Public Interest in International Investment Law*. Cambridge: Cambridge University Press, p. 93. See also, S.W. Schill. 2009. *Multilateralization of International Investment Law*. Cambridge: Cambridge University Press (hereinafter Schill, *Multilateralization of International Investment Law*).

[10] Dolzer and Schreuer. *Principles of International Investment Law*, p. 1.

[11] Salacuse, *The Law of Investment Treaties*, p. 100.

[12] Salacuse, *The Law of Investment Treaties*, p. 101. Also see F. Mann. 1981. 'British Treaties for the Promotion and Protection of Investments', *British Yearbook of International Law*, 52: 241.

[13] Salacuse, *The Law of Investment Treaties*, p. 101.

countries to enter into BITs.[14] For instance, as Salacuse writes, customary international law offered very little guidance about the right of foreign investors to make monetary transfers from a host country.[15] Likewise, while customary international law required payment of compensation on nationalization of foreign investment, the exact principles as to how this compensation shall be calculated had not crystalized.[16] Bilateral Investment Treaties intended to write down the rules on all these issues clearly so that ambiguities over protection of foreign investment under international law could be addressed.

From 1959 till the end of 1989, the total number of BITs signed were 385[17]—an average of around 13 BITs per year. Most BITs were signed between a developed country—typically a capital-exporting country and a developing country—typically a capital-importing country.[18] This started to change from early 1990s. In just 10 years, this number, from 385, jumped to 1,857 by the end of 1999[19]—an average of around 147 treaties per year. Moreover, out of 1,857 BITs, 737 (40 per cent) were signed between developed and developing countries, as against 260 in the period from 1959 to 1989.[20] In other words, along with the exponential rise in BITs signed between developed and developing countries, there was also an increase in BITs signed between developing countries, also known as South–South BITs.[21] The number of BITs continued to increase in the 2000s although the rate of increase was not the same as 1990s

[14] Salacuse, *The Law of Investment Treaties*, p. 85.

[15] Salacuse, *The Law of Investment Treaties*, p. 85.

[16] Salacuse, *The Law of Investment Treaties*, p. 85.

[17] United Nations Conference on Trade and Development (UNCTAD). 2000. 'Bilateral Investment Treaties: 1959-1999',UNCTAD/ITE/IIA/2, http://unctad.org/en/docs/poiteiiad2.en.pdf, accessed 12 March 2018. (hereinafter UNCTAD. 'Bilateral Investment Treaties: 1959-1999')

[18] UNCTAD. 'Bilateral Investment Treaties: 1959-1999'.

[19] UNCTAD. 'Bilateral Investment Treaties: 1959-1999'.

[20] UNCTAD. 'Bilateral Investment Treaties: 1959-1999'.

[21] On South–South BITs, see L.N. Poulsen. 2010. 'The Significance of South-South BITs for the International Investment Regime: A Quantitative Analysis', *Northwestern Journal of International Law and Business* 30: 101.

(see Figure 1.1). Till the end of 2017, more than 3,322 BITs had been signed.[22]

Beginning from late 1970s till early 1990s, the world saw major changes in the global economy and global politics, which created the right conditions for the proliferation of BITs. This period was characterized by the collapse of communism in many countries and a universal acknowledgment that 'capitalism and private ordering are superior to socialism and state ownership of means of production'.[23]

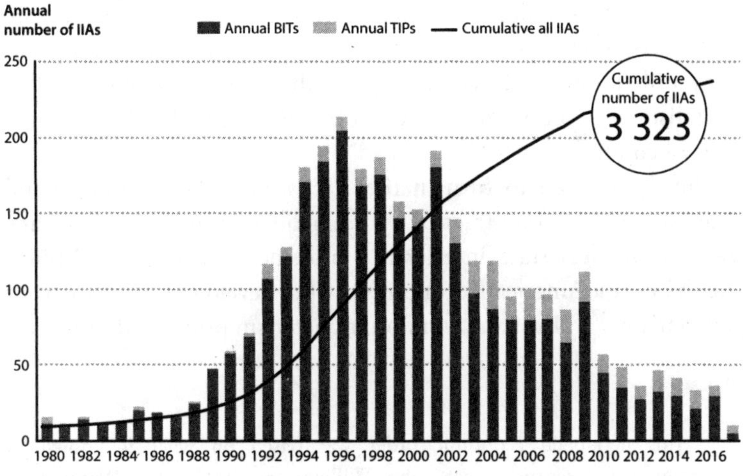

Figure 1.1 Investment Treaties Signed from 1980 to 2017
Source: United Nations Conference on Trade and Development (UNCTAD). 2018. 1, IIA Issues Note. Geneva.

[22] This includes 2,946 standalone investment treaties and 376 Treaties with Investment Provisions (TIPs) or investment chapters in FTAs. See UNCTAD. 2018. 'World Investment Report – Investor Nationality: Policy Challenges', http://unctad.org/en/PublicationsLibrary/wir2018_en.pdf, p. 88, accessed 12 June 2018.

[23] Jonathan R. Macey and Geoffrey P. Miller. 1992. 'The End of History and the New World Order: The Triumph of Capitalism and the Competition between Liberalism and Democracy', *Cornell International Law Journal* 25 (275): 283.

This period saw the rise and almost universal acceptance of a neoliberal political and economic order.[24]

The intellectual origins of neo-liberalism can be traced back to the work of Friedrich August von Hayek. Hayek, in his book, *The Road to Serfdom*,[25] published during World War II, tried to revive classical or laissez-faire liberalism of the nineteenth century that believed the state should have a minimal role in a society mainly to uphold public order.[26] This went against the dominant narrative of the post-World War II years of modern liberalism shaped by the work of scholars like John Maynard Keynes. Modern liberalism challenged the belief of classical liberals that market mechanisms had the ability to autocorrect its failures, thus advocating a greater role for the state in the economy. From 1945 to 1970, the world witnessed what is commonly known as Keynesian-ism or the 'golden age of controlled capitalism'—a compromise between free market and welfare obligations of countries.

The tide started to turn in the 1970s when Hayek's neoliberal ideas started gaining traction. The neoliberal principles of free markets and less state interference informed the work of Milton Friedman, an American economist, who developed his theory of monetarism.[27] Friedman's work on monetarism prioritized monetary

[24] This neoliberal economic order was based on what is known as 'Washington Consensus' – see John Williamson. 2004. 'The Washington Consensus as Policy Prescription for Development'. https://piie.com/publications/papers/williamson0204.pdf, 13 January. Also see David Harvey. 2007. *A Brief History of Neoliberalism*. Oxford: Oxford University Press. (hereinafter Harvey. *A Brief History of Neoliberalism*)This has also been described as market fundamentalist version of economic liberalism – see Suzzane Spears. 2010. 'The Quest for Policy Space in a New Generation of International Agreements', *Economic Law* 13(4): 1037–75.

[25] Bruce Caldwell (ed.). 2007. *The Road to Serfdom: Text and Documents—The Definitive Edition (The Collected Works of F. A. Hayek, Volume 2)*. Chicago: The University of Chicago Press.

[26] Look at the world of classical liberals such as John Locke and Adam Smith.

[27] See Milton Friedman. 2002. *Capitalism and Freedom, 40th Anniversay Edition*. Chicago: The University of Chicago Press.

policies over the policies of taxation and redistribution followed by a big Keynesian-style government based on welfare-ism. These neo-liberal ideas received political endorsement with the rise of Margaret Thatcher in the UK and Ronald Reagan in the US in the late 1970s and early 1980s.[28]

The neoliberal order was based on principles that included deregulation of markets, privatization of public sector undertakings, trade liberalization, liberalization of the foreign investment regime, and legal security for private property rights, which collectively came to be known as the Washington consensus—the policy advice rendered by Washington-based international institutions like the International Monetary Fund (IMF) and the World Bank.[29] By the end of the Cold War, developing countries no longer perceived foreign investment as a threat to their national sovereignty.[30] Francis Fukuyama, an American political scientist, described these momentous developments in the world as 'the end of history': 'that is the end point of mankind's ideological evolution and the universalization of Western liberal democracy as the final form of human government'.[31] This was also the period that saw the rise of legal liberal internationalism with the formation of the World Trade Organization (WTO) in 1995 being a very important development.[32]

[28] See Manfred B. Steger and Ravi K. Roy. 2010. *Neoliberalism: A Very Short Introduction*. Oxford: Oxford University Press; Harvey, *A Brief History of Neoliberalism*.

[29] See John Williamson, 'The Washington Consensus as Policy Prescription for Development', https://piie.com/publications/papers/williamson0204.pdf. Also see Harvey. *A Brief History of Neoliberalism*.

[30] J. Bonnithca, L. Paulsen, and M. Waibel. 2017. *The Political Economy of the Investment Treaty Regime*. Oxford. Oxford University Press. (hereinafter-Bonnitcha, Poulsen, and Waibel. *The Political Economy of the Investment Treaty Regime*).

[31] Francis Fukuyama. 1989. 'The End of History?', *The National Interest* 16 (3):4. Also see Francis Fukuyama. 1992. *The End of History and the Last Man*. New York: Free Press.

[32] See generally, R. Hoswe. 1999. 'The House That Jackson Built: Restructuring the GATT System', *Michigan Journal of International Law* 20(2): 107. Also see Chapter 3.

Since the late 1980s and early 1990s, many countries saw BITs as a commitment to liberal economic policies[33] and as instruments that could further the objectives of a liberal foreign investment regime and lead to greater investment flows especially into developing countries.[34] Bilateral Investment Treaties signed during this period followed a neoliberal template that favoured a minimalist state. Thus, these treaties (also known as the first generation BITs) contained very broad and substantive guarantees to foreign investors with limited or no provisions recognizing the host state's right to regulate in public interest.[35] The host state's right to regulate here and in this book means the state's legal right that exceptionally allows a host state to regulate in derogation of international obligations assumed by means of an investment treaty (such as a BIT), without incurring a duty to compensate the aggrieved foreign investors.[36]

Interestingly, BITs signed before the spread of the neoliberal economic order also followed the same laissez-faire liberalism template.[37] This aspect is especially significant because the normativity of 'embedded liberalism' that guided the international economic order in general and trade law regime in particular like the General Agreement on Tariffs and Trade (GATT) in the post-World War II period was seemingly absent when it came to investment treaties.[38] John Gerad Ruggie, an American political scientist, conceptualized

[33] J. Kurtz. 2016. 'The WTO and International Investment Law: Converging Systems'. Cambridge: Cambridge University Press, pp. 55–61. (hereinafterKurtz. 'The WTO and International Investment Law').

[34] Bonnitcha, Poulsen, and Waibel. *The Political Economy of the Investment Treaty Regime.*

[35] Also see Chapters 3, 4, and 5.

[36] Catherine Titi. 2014. *The Right to Regulate in International Investment Law*. Oxford: Nomos and Hart Publishing, pp. 33–4 (hereinafter Titi. *The Right to Regulate in International Investment Law*).

[37] See K. Vandevelde. 2018. 'IIA Provisions, Properly Interpreted, are Fully Consistent with a Roboust Regulatory State', Columbia FDI Perspectives. No 216.http://ccsi.columbia.edu/files/2016/10/No-216-Vandevelde-FINAL.pdf; K. Daniel. 2010. 'Investment Treaties and Public Goods'. *Transnational Dispute Management Journal* 7:1 (hereinafter Daniel. 'Investment Treaties and Public Goods'); Titi, *The Right to Regulate in International Investment Law*, p. 56.

[38] See Daniel. 'Investment Treaties and Public Goods'; Titi, *The Right to Regulate in International Investment Law* p. 56.

the post-World War II international economic order as a case of 'embedded liberalism'[39]—a multilateral economic order predicated upon domestic interventionism.[40] Ruggie argued that the post-World War II international economic order shows how 'power and legitimate social objectives become fused to project political authority into the international system'.[41] 'Embedded liberalism' represented compromise between free market and the state intervening in favour of political and social stability.[42] In ways it represented modern liberalism of the post-World War II era as mentioned before.

This was different from the laissez-faire liberalism of the international economic order in the nineteenth century that was disembedded from the social systems.[43] In context of GATT, 'embedded liberalism' meant liberalization of trade embedded against much flexibility that comprised a subset of shared social purposes.[44] Thus, the GATT legal text talked of tariff liberalization to boost international trade, and also contained many safeguards and exceptions designed to protect a variety of domestic social policies of participating countries.[45]

[39] J.G. Ruggie. 1982. 'International Regimes, Transactions, and Change: Embedded Liberalism and the Postwar Economic Order', *International Organization* 36 (2): 379. (hereinafter Ruggie, 'International Regimes, Transactions, and Change').

[40] Ruggie, 'International Regimes, Transactions, and Change', p. 393.

[41] Ruggie, 'International Regimes, Transactions, and Change', p. 382.

[42] Harvey, *A Brief History of Neoliberalism*. Also see, Ruggie, 'International Regimes, Transactions, and Change', pp. 379–415.

[43] K. Polanyi. 1944. *The Great Transformation: The Political and Economic Origins of our Time*. Boston: Beacon Press, p. 71.

[44] J. Ruggie (ed.). 1998. 'Embedded Liberalism and Postwar Economic Regimes', *Constructing the World Polity: Essays on International Institutionalisation.* London: Routledge, pp. 62–84. Also see,R. Howse. 2002. 'From Politics to Technocracy – And Back Again: The Fate of the Multilateral Trading Regime', *American Journal of International Law* 95(94): 97; Kurtz, 'The WTO and International Investment Law', p. 4.

[45] Ruggie, 'International Regimes, Transactions, and Change', p. 396. Also see, A.T.F. Lang. 2006. 'Reconstructing Embedded Liberalism: John Gerard Ruggie and Constructivist Approaches to the Study of the International Trade Regime', *Journal of International Economic Law* 9: 81; A.T.F. Lang. 2011. *World Trade Law after Neoliberalism. Re-imagining the Global Economic Order*. Oxford: Oxford University Press.

1.2 Global Debate on BITs and ISDS

The increasing mass of BITs with ISDS provisions, over the years, has led to significant increase in investor–state disputes in international investment law.[46] From a negligible number in early 1990s, the total number of known treaty-based ISDS cases rose to 904 as of 31 July 2018.[47] Over the years, foreign investors have used the ISDS provision in BITs to challenge a wide array of sovereign regulatory measures, such as environmental policy;[48] regulatory issues related to supply of drinking water;[49] monetary policy;[50] laws and policies related to taxation;[51] regulations related

[46] United Nations Conference on Trade and Development (UNCTAD), n.d. 'Investment Dispute Settlement Navigator', http://investmentpolicyhub.unctad.org/ISDS, accessed 12 March 2018 (hereinafter UNCTAD, 'Investment Dispute Settlement Navigator').

[47] UNCTAD, ISDS Trends: Cases Initiated in first 7 Months of 2018, https://investmentpolicyhub.unctad.org/News/Database/Home/1604, 28 November 2018.

[48] *Metalclad Corporation* v. *United Mexican States*, ICSID Case No. ARB(AF)/97/1, Award, 30 August 2000; *Methanex Corporation* v. *United States of America*, NAFTA-UNCITRAL, Award, 3 August 2005 (hereinafter *Methanex* v. *USA*). An important ISDS claim in the area of environment policy has arisen because of Germany's decision to phase out nuclear power plants by 2022—*Vattenfall AB and others* v. *Federal Republic of Germany* (II), ICSID Case No. ARB/12/12, Decision on the Achmea Issue, 31 August 2018.

[49] *Biwater Gauff Ltd* v. *United Republic of Tanzania*, ICSID Case No. ARB/05/22, Award, 24 July 2008.

[50] *CMS Gas Transmission Co.* v. *Argentina*, ICSID Case No. ARB/01/8, Award, 12 May 2005; *Enron Corporation and Ponderosa Assents, L.P.* v. *The Argentine Republic*, ICSID Case No ARB/01/3, Award, 22 May 2007 (hereinafter 'Enron Award'); *Enron Creditors Recovery Corp* v. *Argentina*, ICSID Case No ARB/01/3, Decision on the Argentine Republic's Application for Annulment of the Award, 30 July 2010 (hereinafter 'Enron Annulment'); *Sempra Energy International* v. *The Argentine Republic*, ICSID Case No ARB/02/16, Award, 28 September 2007 (hereinafter 'Sempra Award').

[51] *Occidental Exploration & Production Co.* v. *Republic of Ecuador*, LCIA Case No.UN3467, Final Award, 1 July 2004 (hereinafter *Occidental Exploration* v. *Ecuador*); *EnCana Corporation* v. *Republic of Ecuador*, LCIA Case No.UN3481, Award, 3 February 2006; Marvin Roy Feldman *Karpa* v. *United Mexican States*,

to health[52] as potential breaches of BITs. Also, a successful ISDS claim means awarding damages to foreïgn investors, that is, diversion of tax payer's money to foreign investors.[53]

This is not to suggest that foreign investors have been successful in all these claims against host states. In fact, according to the United Nations Conference on Trade and Development (UNCTAD), as of 31 July 2017, out of 530 ISDS proceedings that have been concluded, 37 per cent were in favour of the State and 27 per cent were in favour of the investor, with 23 per cent of disputes being mutually settled.[54] In other words, states have won more disputes than investors. However, when one looks at the statistics of cases decided

---

ICSID Case No. ARB(AF)/99/1, Award, 16 December 2002; *Burlington Resources, Inc.* v. *Republic of Ecuador*, ICSID Case No. ARB/08/5, Decision on Liability, 14 December 2014.

[52] *Philip Morris Asia Ltd.* v. *The Commonwealth of Australia,* UNCITRAL, PCA Case No. 2012-12, Award on Jurisdiction and Admissibility, 17 December 2015; *Philip Morris Brands Sàrl (Switzerland), Philip Morris Products S.A. and AbalHermanos S.A. (Uruguay)* v. *Oriental Republic of Uruguay*, ICSID Case No. ARB/10/7, 8 July 2016 (hereinafter *Philip Morris* v. *Uruguay*).

[53] See *Hulley Enterprises Limited (Cyprus)* v. *The Russian Federation*, PCA Case No. AA 226, Final Award, 18 July 2014; *Yukos Universal Limited (Isle of Man)* v. *The Russian Federation*, PCA Case No.AA 227, Final Award, 18 July 2014; *Veteran Petroleum Limited (Cyprus)* v. *The Russian Federation*, PCA Case No. AA 228, Final Award, 18 July 2014; See also, Martine Dietrich Brauch. 2014. 'Yukos v. Russia: Issues and Legal Reasoning Behind US$50 Billion Awards', *Investment Treaty News*, https://www.iisd.org/itn/2014/09/04/yukos-v-russia-issues-and-legal-reasoning-behind-us50-billion-awards/, accessed 12 March 2018. Important to bear in mind again, as UNCTAD reports, 'on average, successful claimants were awarded about 40 per cent of the amounts they claimed'— In cases decided in favour of foreign investors, the average amount claimed was US$1.35 billion and the median US$113 million. The average amount awarded was US$522 million and the median US$19 million. See UNCTAD. 2017. 'Special Update on Investor State Dispute Settlement: Facts and Figures', http://investmentpolicyhub.unctad.org/Upload/Documents/diaepcb2017d7_en.pdf.

[54] UNCTAD. 2017. 'Special Update On Investor–State Dispute Settlement: Facts And Figures', http://unctad.org/en/PublicationsLibrary/diaepcb2017d7_en.pdf, p. 4, accessed 12 March 2018. (hereinafter UNCTAD. 'Special Update On Investor–State Dispute Settlement: Facts And Figures').

on merits (that is, cases where the tribunal ruled it had the jurisdiction and then went on to examine whether the state has breached its BIT obligations), the numbers change in favour of the investor—investors have won 59 per cent cases whereas States have won 41 per cent cases.[55]

Nonetheless, adjudication of such wide gamut of sovereign regulatory measures by ISDS tribunals as potential breaches of BITs has given rise to a global debate on BITs and ISDS. Before we deal with Indian BITs (which is the focus of this book), an understanding of the global debate on BITs and ISDS is critical. Such discussion will provide a useful backdrop against which we study India's approach to BITs.

This global debate has many facets such as the debate on the relationship between BITs and host state's right to regulate and other shortcomings of BITs and ISDS; the reaction of states against BITs and ISDS as evidenced in state practice; critique of BITs based on critique of globalization and the alleged colonial character of international law; and justifications for BITs and ISDS based on public interest and rule of law. We discuss each of these facets briefly.

1.2.1 The Relationship Between BITs and the Host State's Regulatory Power

Since BITs impose certain limits on the exercise of the host state's public power for the protection of foreign investment, at times, the rights of foreign investors and host state's right to regulate come face-to-face. For instance, if a state adopts a regulatory measure for protection of public health which adversely impacts the interests of a foreign investor, the investor may potentially challenge the regulatory measure as a breach of State's BIT obligations.[56] Scenarios such as this have given rise to a debate as to whether BITs encroach upon a host state's right to regulate.[57] It has been argued that the ISDS system in BITs interferes

[55] UNCTAD. 'Special Update On Investor–State Dispute Settlement: Facts And Figures', p. 4.

[56] See *Philip Morris* v. *Uruguay* as an example.

[57] Titi, *The Right to Regulate in International Investment Law*; L.T. Wells. 2010. 'Backlash to Investment Arbitration: Three Causes', in *The Backlash Against Investment Arbitration* M. Waibel, Asha Kaushal, Kyo-Hwa Chung, and

with the rights of sovereign states to regulate investment in public interest such as adopting measures for the protection of environment and public health.[58] This has been conceptualized as 'regulatory chill'—the failure of host states to regulate in public interest in a timely and effective manner due to concerns of ISDS.[59] Tienhara

---

Claire Balchin (eds), p. 341. Berdfordshire: Kluwer Law International (hereinafter Wells, 'Backlash to Investment Arbitration'); See also, Stephan W. Schill. 2011. 'Enhancing International Investment Law's Legitimacy: Conceptual and Methodological Foundations of a New Public Law Approach,' *Virginia Journal of International Law* 52:69 (hereinafter Schill, 'Enhancing International Investment Law's Legitimacy'), who states, 'the extent to which investment treaties limit a state's regulatory powers and subject the exercise of such powers to liability claims by foreign investors may become the litmus test for the future viability of the system'; See also, Susan D. Franck. 2005. 'The Legitimacy Crisis in Investment Treaty Arbitration: Privatizing Public International Law through Inconsistent Decisions,' Fordham Law Review 73:1521; G. Harten. 2008. *Investment Treaty Arbitration and Public Law.* Oxford: Oxford University Press; B. Choudhary. 2008. 'Recapturing Public Power: Is Investment Arbitration's Engagement of the Public Interest Contributing to the Democratic Deficit,' *Vanderbilt Journal of Transnational Law* 41:775; David Schneiderman. 2018. *Constitutionalizing Economic Globalization: Investment Rules and Democracy's Promise.* Cambridge: Cambridge University Press; Sornarajah Muthucumaraswamy. 2015. *Resistance and Change in the International Law on Foreign Investment.* Cambridge: Cambridge University Press.

58 K. Tienhaara. 2011. 'Regulatory Chill and the Threat of Arbitration: A View from Political Science', in *Evolution in Investment Treaty Law and Arbitration,* C. Brown and K. Miles (eds), pp. 606–28, at 615. Cambridge: Cambridge University Press (hereinafter Tienhaara, 'Regulatory Chill and the Threat of Arbitration'); K. Tienhaara. 2017. 'Regulatory Chill in a Warming World: The Threat to Climate Policy Posed by Investor-State Dispute Settlement', *Transnational Environmental Law* 7(2): 229–50.

59 Tienhaara, 'Regulatory Chill and the Threat of Arbitration', p. 615. Also see, Jonathan Bonnitcha. 2011, 'A Framework for Understanding the Political Economy of International Investment Interpretation', in *International Investment Law and Arbitration,* C. Brown and K. Miles (eds), pp. 133–7, Cambridge: Cambridge University Press. K. Miles. 2013. *The Origins of International Investment Law: Empire, Environment and the Safeguarding of Capital.* Cambridge: Cambridge University Press, p. 187. Schill, 'Enhancing

has developed the broad concept of 'regulatory chill' by dividing it into three different types[60]—internalization chill (policymakers take into account potential ISDS disputes and thus accordingly modify the regulatory measure),[61] threat chill (chilling of specific regulatory measures after the threat of an ISDS arbitration), and cross-border chill.[62] Cross-border chill is pursued by investors when a state adopts a policy that 'affects a form of investment common to many jurisdictions, is easily transferable, and is highly likely to be emulated by other governments'.[63] Arguably, this chill is induced by actually launching an ISDS case in one or more jurisdictions.[64]

The contestation against BITs and ISDS has been further fuelled by instances where a similar set of facts[65] or the same provision of a BIT[66]

International Investment Law's Legitimacy' p. 69 states, 'the extent to which investment treaties limit a state's regulatory powers and subject the exercise of such powers to liability claims by foreign investors may become the litmus test for the future viability of the system'. Also see S. Schill. 2007. 'Do Investment Treaties Chill Unilateral State Regulation to Mitigate Climate Change?' *Journal of International Arbitration* 24(5): 469–77.

[60] Tienhara, 'Regulatory Chill in a Warming World', p. 5.

[61] See C. Côté. 2014. 'A Chilling Effect? The Impact of International Investment Agreements on National Regulatory Autonomy in the Areas of Health, Safety and the Environment', PhD thesis, London School of Economics, February; G. Van Harten and D.N. Scott. 2016. 'Investment Treaties and the Internal Vetting of Regulatory Proposals: A Case Study from Canada', *Journal of International Dispute Settlement* 7(1): 1–25.

[62] Tienhara, 'Regulatory Chill in a Warming World', p. 10.

[63] Tienhara, 'Regulatory Chill in a Warming World', p. 10.

[64] Tienhara, 'Regulatory Chill in a Warming World', p. 10. The ISDS cases brought against tobacco regulations by Philip Morris against Australia and Uruguay are cited as examples to prove 'cross-border' chill.

[65] The most commonly stated example of this is the *Lauders* case where two arbitration tribunals gave different decisions to essentially the same set of facts for disputes brought under two different BITs. The cases are: *CME Czech Republic BV* v. *The Czech Republic*, UNCITRAL, Partial Award, 13 September 2001; Final Award, 14 March 2003 and *Ronald S. Lauder* v. *The Czech Republic*, UNCITRAL, Final Award, 3 September 2001.

[66] The Argentine cases on Article XI of the Treaty between United States of America and the Argentine Republic Concerning the Reciprocal Encouragement

has been interpreted differently by tribunals. This has given rise to inconsistent awards, adding to the uncertainity of the regime—both for foreign investors and host states.

One of the chief reasons for the wide range of sovereign decisions of host states being caught in the broad net of ISDS is the vague and broad language of BITs.[67] For example, most BITs obligate states to treat foreign investors in a fair and equitable manner (the FET standard). However, the normative content of FET is missing in most BITs. Consequently, imprecise provisions like FET become suitable candidates for broad and inconsistent treaty interpretations.[68] The textual indeterminacy of BITs has resulted in divergent and inconsistent legal conclusions.[69] Such indeterminacy in treaty drafting gives a

---

and Protection of Investment (signed 14 November 1991, entered into force 20 October 1994) [hereinafter US–Argentina BIT], are a good example of such inconsistency. Different arbitration tribunals interpreted the defence of necessity given in Article XI differently.

[67] See Schill, 'Enhancing International Investment Law's Legitimacy', pp. 67–8; Wells, 'Backlash to Investment Arbitration', n. 32, p. 342; Suzanne Spears. 2010. 'The Quest for Policy Space in a New Generation of International Investment Agreements,' *Journal of International Economic Law* 13: 1040; Jose E. Alvarezand K. Khamsi. 2009. 'The Argentine Crisis and Foreign Investors', in *Yearbook on International Investment Law and Policy 2008-09*, Karl P. Sauvant (ed.), pp. 472–8. Oxford: Oxford University Press (hereinafter Alvarez and Khamsi, 'The Argentine Crisis and Foreign Investors'); M.A. Clodfelter. 2009. 'The Adaptation of States to the Changing World of Investment Protection through Model BITs,' *ICSID Review of Foreign Investment Law* 24:165. Also see Chapters 4 and 5.

[68] For example, Vandevelde, writing on the FET provision, states: 'because the language by its terms can apply to virtually any instance of host-state conduct, it is potentially a basis for recovery in any situation'. Vandevelde, *Bilateral Investment Treaties*, p. 203.

[69] For a detailed discussion on such inconsistent decisions, see Franck, 'The Legitimacy Crisis in Investment Treaty Arbitration: Privatizing Public International Law through Inconsistent Decisions', n.32, pp. 1558–82.; See also August Reinisch. 2009. 'The Future of Investment Arbitration', in *International Investment Law for the 21st Century: Essays in Honour of Christoph Schreuer*, Christina Binder, Ursula Kriebaum, August Reinisch, and Stephan Wittich (eds), pp. 905–8. Oxford: Oxford University Press.

fair degree of discretion to ISDS tribunals to interpret the terms occurring in BITs and hence indulge in 'law-making' activity.[70] Such lawmaking by ISDS tribunals is problematic because states create international law while international tribunals are only supposed to interpret and apply it.[71] Nonethless, important to bear in mind that since treaty parties delegate interpretative power to ISDS tribunals, some level of law creation through interpretation is inherent in the adjudication process.[72]

Another major issue of concern is regarding the alleged lack of independence and impartiality of the ISDS mechanism in BITs.[73] For example, it has been argued that the appointment of arbitrators is influenced by the positions taken by them in other arbitrations and in academic writings.[74] In this regard, concerns such as 'issue conflict' become important. An 'issue conflict' has been defined as a conflict that stems from the arbitrator's relationship to the subject matter of the dispute, rather than the arbitrator's relationship with the parties to the dispute.[75] A notable way in which 'issue conflicts'

[70] Stephan W. Schill. 2011. 'System-Building in Investment Treaty Arbitration and Lawmaking', *German Law Journal* 12(5): 1092–3.

[71] Anthea Roberts. 2010. 'Power and Persuasion in Investment Treaty Interpretation', *American Journal of International Law* 14: 188–9 (hereinafter Roberts, 'Power and Persuasion in Investment Treaty Interpretation').

[72] Roberts, 'Power and Persuasion in Investment Treaty Interpretation', p. 189; Martin Shapiro and Alec Stone Sweet. 2002. *On Law, Politics, And Judicialization*. Oxford: Oxford University Press, pp. 90–135; David D. Caron. 2006. 'Towards a Political Theory of International Courts and Tribunals', *Berkeley Journal of International Law* 24:408.

[73] G. Van Harten. 2007. *Investment Treaty Arbitration, Procedural Fairness, and the Rule of Law.* Oxford: Oxford University Press. (hereinafter Van Harten, *Investment Treaty Arbitration, Procedural Fairness, and the Rule of Law*).

[74] B. Pirker. 2011. 'Seeing the Forest Without the Trees – The Doubtful Case for Proportionality Analysis in International Investment Arbitration', https://papers.ssrn.com/sol3/papers.cfm?abstract_id=1926166, accessed 12 March 2018. Also see Ajay Sharma. 2016. 'Arbitrators Appointed In The ICSID Cases Commencing Since 2011: Data Compilation And Analysis', *Asian International Arbitration Journal* 12(2): 107–35.

[75] Nassib G. Ziadé. 2009. 'How Many Hats Can a Player Wear: Arbitrator, Counsel and Expert?', *ICSID Review - Foreign Investment Law Journal* 24(1):49.

arise is when an arbitrator concomitantly acts as a counsel in another case relating to similar issues.[76] In such situations there is an apprehension that the arbitrator can shape the interpretation of a legal principle in a manner that may benefit her in the case where she is appearing as the counsel.[77]

Also, important to bear in mind that ISDS tribunals adjudicate upon investor–state disputes using the adjudicative process of commercial arbitration.[78] Consequently, the procedural aspects of commercial arbitration, such as party-appointed arbitrators, secrecy in arbitral proceedings, lack of access to arbitral documents including non-availability of arbitral awards (at times), have become characteristics of ISDS as well[79] leading to confidentiality and secrecy.[80] Thus concerns are expressed about lack of transparency in ISDS.[81]

[76] Sundaresh Menon. 2015. 'The Transnational Protection of Private Rights', in *Practising Virtue: Inside International Arbitration,* David D. Carron, Stephan W. Schill, Abby Cohen Smutny, and Epaminontas E. Triantafilou (eds), p. 17. Oxford: Oxford University Press (hereinafter Menon, 'The Transnational Protection of Private Rights').

[77] Menon, 'The Transnational Protection of Private Rights', p. 17.

[78] See Zachary Douglas. 2003. 'The Hybrid Foundations of Investment Arbitration', *British Yearbook of International Law* 74:151; G. Van Harten. 2007. *Investment Treaty Arbitration as Public Law.* Oxford: Oxford University Press, pp. 46–50; Loukas Mistelis, 'Confidentiality and Third Party Participation: UPS v Canada and Methanex Corp. v USA', in *International Investment Law and Arbitration,* Todd Weiler (ed.), p. 169. London: Cameron May.

[79] See Organisation for Economic Co-operation and Development (OECD). 2005. 'Transparency and Third Party Participation in Investor-State Dispute Settlement Procedures', *OECD Working Papers on International Investment,* OECD Publishing. 2005/01, https://www.oecd.org/daf/inv/investment-policy/WP-2005_1.pdf, accessed 12 March 2018 (hereinafter OECD, 'Transparency and Third Party Participation in Investor-State Dispute Settlement Procedures').

[80] See generally, Cindy Buys. 2003. 'The Tensions between Confidentiality and Transparency in International Arbitration', *American Review of International Arbitration* 14:121; Emilie M. Hafner-Burtonand David G. Victor. 2016. 'Secrecy in International Investment Arbitration', *Journal of International Dispute Settlement* 7:161–82.

[81] See K. Tienhaara. 2007. 'Third Party Participation in Investment-Environment Disputes: Recent Developments', *Review of European Community*

1.2.2 National Contestation against BITs and ISDS As Evidenced in State Practice

For reasons discussed earlier and due to increased exposure to ISDS claims many countries, developing and developed, have started contesting BITs and ISDS. This contestation against BITs is evident in state practice.[82] This state practice can be classified into two categories.[83] The first category is of states that have completely denounced the ISDS system. For example, countries such as Bolivia, Ecuador, and Venezuela have denounced the International Centre for Settlement of Investment Disputes (ICSID) convention (that provides for ISDS mechanism) in 2007, 2009, and 2012, respectively[84]

---

and International Environmental Law 16(2):230–42; Joachim Delaneyand D.B. Magraw. 2008. 'Procedural Transparency', in *Oxford Handbook of International Investment Law,* Peter Muchlinski, Federico Ortino and Christoph Schreuer (eds), p. 721. Oxford: Oxford University Press; D. Magraw and N. Amerasinghe. 2009. 'Transparency and Public Participation in Investor-State Arbitration' *ILSA Journal International & Comparative Law* 15(2):341–2; J. Atik. 2004. 'Legitimacy, Transparency and NGO Participation in the NAFTA Chapter 11 Process', in *NAFTA Investment Law and Arbitration: Past Issues, Current Practice and Future Prospects,* T. Weiler (ed.), p. 142. Ardsley: Transnational Publications; OECD, 'Transparency and Third Party Participation in Investor-State Dispute Settlement Procedures'.

[82] O.E. Garcia-Bolivar. 2009. 'Sovereignty vs. Investment Protection: Back to Calvo?' *ICSID Review of Foreign Investment Law Journal* 24:464–88; See also Prabhash Ranjan. 2016. 'National Contestation of International Investment Law and International Rule of Law', in *Rule of Law at National and International Levels: Contestations and Deference*, M. Kanetake and A. Nollkaemper (eds), pp. 115–42. Oregon: Hart Publishing.

[83] Anthea Roberts has classified the reaction of countries to ISDS in four different categories: loyalists, reformists, revolutionaries, and undecideds. See Anthea Roberts. 2017. The Shifting Landscape of Investor-State Arbitration: Loyalists, Reformists, Revolutionaries and Undecideds,' *EJIL Talk* (15 June 2017), https://www.ejiltalk.org/the-shifting-landscape-of-investor-state-arbitration-loyalists-reformists-revolutionaries-and-undecideds/, accessed 12 March 2018.

[84] See Tania Voon and Andrew D. Mitchell. 2016. 'Denunciation, Termination and Survival: The Interplay of Treaty Law and International Investment Law', *ICSID Review of Foreign Investment Law Journal* 31(2):413–33.

and also terminated their respective BITs.[85] Similarly, South Africa has terminated BITs,[86] and has also repudiated the ISDS mechanism.[87] A more nuanced approach in this category is of countries like Australia that, as a response to the Philip Morris dispute,[88] initially stated in 2011 that it would not have the ISDS provision in its treaties;[89] however, they changed their position in 2013 by stating that it would negotiate for ISDS on a case-by-case basis.[90]

The second category is of states who are contesting the ISDS system, not by taking the extreme step of denouncing BITs, but

[85] Bolivia has terminated its 10 BITs out of total 23 BITs; Venezuela has terminated its BIT with Netherlands; Ecuador has terminated its 11 BITs out of total 29 BITs; Indonesia has terminated 26 BITs out of total 71 BITs. See Anthony Crockett. 2015. 'Indonesia's Bilateral Investment Treaties: Between Generations?', *ICSID Review of Foreign Investment Law Journal* 30(2):437–48.

[86] South Africa has terminated its 9 BIT out of total 49 BITs most of which are not yet in force.

[87] For more on South Africa's BIT practice, see Engela C. Schlemmer. 2016. 'An Overview of South Africa's Bilateral Investment Treaties and Investment Policy', *ICSID Review of Foreign Investment Law Journal* 31(1):167. See also, Michael Webb. 2016. 'New Treatment of Foreign Investors in South Africa', http://isds.bilaterals.org/?new-treatment-of-foreign-investors&lang=en, 26 March, accessed 12 March 2018. Some scholars support countries denouncing the ISDS system. See Sornarajah, *Resistance and Change in International Law on Foreign Investment*.

[88] *Philip Morris Asia Ltd.* v. *The Commonwealth of Australia,* UNCITRAL, PCA Case No. 2012-12, Award on Jurisdiction and Admissibility, 17 December 2015.

[89] Australian Government, Department of Foreign Affairs and Trade. 2011. 'Gillard Government Trade Policy Statement: Trading Our Way to More Jobs and Prosperity', http://blogs.usyd.edu.au/japaneselaw/2011_Gillard%20Govt%20Trade%20Policy%20Statement.pdf, accessed 12 March 2018; Luke Nottage. 2013. 'Throwing the Baby out with the Bathwater: Australia's New Policy on Treaty Based Investor State Arbitration and its impact on Asia', *Asian Studies Review* 37(2):253–72; Jürgen Kurtz. 2012. 'Australia's Rejection of Investor–State Arbitration: Causation, Omission and Implication', *ICSID Review of Foreign Investment Law Journal* 27(1):65.

[90] Leon Trakman and David Musayelyan. 2016. 'The Repudiation of Investor–State Arbitration and Subsequent Treaty Practice: The Resurgence of Qualified Investor–State Arbitration', *ICSID Review of Foreign Investment Law Journal* 31(1):194–218.

by developing a new BIT practice aimed at balancing investment protection and host state's right to regulate through precise drafting of the substantive provisions of these treaties[91] or by reasserting their right to regulate within these treaties. A good example of this is the investment chapter in the recently signed European Union-Canada Comprehensive Economic and Trade Agreement (CETA),[92] where Article 8.9 specifically mentions that the countries reaffirm 'their right to regulate within their territories to achieve legitimate policy objectives, such as the protection of public health, safety, the environment or public morals'.[93] Similarly, countries wish to amend the existing ISDS system by either making it more transparent[94] or by bringing about other kinds of reforms such as introducing an appellate mechanism[95] or even developing a world investment court system.[96]

[91] The US and Canadian Model BITs are examples of countries trying to define substantive provisions. See 2012. 'U.S. Model BIT', https://ustr.gov/sites/default/files/BIT%20text%20for%20ACIEP%20Meeting.pdf, accessed 12 March 2018. [hereinafter 2012 US Model BIT]; 2004. 'Canadian Model BIT', http://www.italaw.com/documents/Canadian2004-FIPA-Model-en.pdf, accessed 12 March 2018. [hereinafter 2004 Canadian Model BIT]; See also, Caroline Henckels. 2016. 'Protecting Regulatory Autonomy through Greater Precision in Investment Treaties: The TPP, CETA, and TTIP', *Journal of International Economic Law* 19:27–50. herein.

[92] Comprehensive Economic and Trade Agreement Between Canada, of the one Part, and the European Union and its Member States, of the Other Part, Chapter 8 C 'Investment' (30 October 2016) [hereinafter Canada–E.U. CETA].

[93] Canada–E.U. CETA, Art. 8.9.

[94] On the issue of reforms to the ISDS system, see Jean E.Kalicki and Anna Joubin-Bret. 2014. 'Introduction - TDM Special Issue on "Reform of Investor-State Dispute Settlement: In Search of a Roadmap"', *Transnational Dispute Management* 11, and other contributions in the special issue.

[95] Eun Young Park. 2015. 'Appellate Review in Investor State Arbitration', in *Reshaping the Investor-State Dispute Settlement System* Jean E. Kalicki and Anna Joubin-Bret (eds), pp. 443–54. Leiden: Koninklijke Brill NV.

[96] See Free Trade Agreement Between the European Union and The Socialist Republic of Vietnam, Chapter II (Investment), section 3, art. 15 (Agreed text as of January 2016); See also, Piero Bernardini. 2017. 'Reforming Investor State Dispute Settlement: The Need to Balance Both Party's Interest', *ICSID Review of Foreign Investment Law Journal* 32(1): 38–57.

A term often associated with the contestation against BITs and ISDS as described earlier is 'backlash'.[97] However, the term 'backlash' is often not defined. As Caron and Shirlow argue, a large range of decisions taken by States such as the decision to terminate BITs to the decision to renegotiate BITs; or a change in the approach of States towards BIT negotiations, are all termed as 'backlash'.[98] Caron and Shirlow argue that the term 'backlash' refers to an 'intense, sustained and aggressive calls for the abandonment of a system or for the adoption of a radically alternative structure'.[99] Understood this way, termination of BITs or walking out of the ICSID convention might qualify as backlash. However, state actions aimed at renegotiating BITs so to reconcile investment protection with State's right to regulate will not qualify as backlash. Nonetheless, in this book, the term 'backlash' and 'contestation' are used interchangeably and refers to voices that are critical of BITs and ISDS fully recognising that while some are critical with the aim of abandoning the system whereas some are critical so as to improve the system.

1.2.3 Critique of BITs as part of critique of globalization and of the alleged colonial character of international law

The critique or contestation of BITs discussed earlier is specific to the actual working of BITs and ISDS. However, contestation against BITs and ISDS is also a result of backlash against globalization, especially economic globalization. Joseph Stiglitz has described the concept of globalization as '*the closer integration of the countries and peoples of the world which has been brought about by the enormous reduction of costs of transportation and communication, and the*

[97] M. Waibel, Asha Kaushal, Kyo-Hwa Chung, and Claire Balchin (eds). 2009. *The Backlash against Investment Arbitration*. Berdfordshire: Kluwer Law International.

[98] D. Caron and E. Shirlow. 2018. 'Dissecting Backlash: The Unarticulated Causes of Backlash and its Unintended Consequences', in *The Judicialisation of International Law: A Mixed Blessing?*, A. Follesdal and G. Ulfstein (eds), p. 161. Oxford: Oxford University Press (hereinafter Caron and Shirlow, 'Dissecting Backlash').

[99] Caron and Shirlow, 'Dissecting Backlash', p. 162.

breaking down of artificial barriers to the flow of goods, services, capital, knowledge, and (to a lesser extent) people across borders'.[100] The process of economic globalization is often accompanied by creation of trade and investment treaties. For instance, Stiglitz argues that increase in cross-border investment and capital flows—very important facets of globalization—were accompanied by a growth in investment treaties.[101] As explained earlier, these treaties impose certain limits on the sovereign power of the nation states. These treaties lead to some of the state's regulatory powers being transferred to international institutions[102] in the anticipation of larger global good that would benefit all. For instance, if a member state of the WTO adopts a law or a regulation, this has to pass muster with the WTO agreements. If such a regulation is challenged, the dispute settlement body of the WTO, not the country's judiciary or the parliament, will be the final arbiter of whether the regulation is consistent with the WTO treaty obligations. In simpler terms, globalization has pushed many things outside the sovereign control of nation states.[103] Based on this, Dani Rodrik has argued that globalization leads to a political trilemma where democracy, national sovereignty, and global economic integration become mutually incompatible.[104] According to Rodrik, any two of the three can be combined but one cannot have all three simultaneously and in full.[105]

[100] J. Stiglitz. 2002. *Globalisation and its Discontents*.London: Penguin, p. 9.

[101] Joseph E. Stiglitz. 2017. *Globalisation and its Discontents: Revisited*. London: Penguin, p. 35 (hereinafter Stiglitz, *Globalisation and its Discontents: Revisted*).

[102] See B. Choudhary. 2008. 'Recapturing Public Power: Is Investment Arbitration's Engagement of the Public Interest Contributing to the Democratic Deficit?', *Vanderbilt Journal of Transnational Law* 41:775.

[103] See Jost Delbrlck. 1993. 'Globalization of Law, Politics, and Markets-Implications for Domestic Law-A European Perspective', *Indiana Journal of Global Legal Studies* 1(9): 10–11.

[104] D. Rodrik. 2007. 'The Inescapable Trilemma of the World Economy', http://rodrik.typepad.com/dani_rodriks_weblog/2007/06/the-inescapable.html (hereinafter Rodrik, 'The Inescapable Trilemma of the World Economy').

[105] Rodrik, 'The Inescapable Trilemma of the World Economy'. Also see D. Rodrik. 2011. *The Globalisation Paradox*. Oxford: Oxford University Press. A. Stein. 2016. 'The Great Trilemma: Are Globalization, Democracy, and

There is a concern that globalization has gone too far (a term used for this is 'hyper globalization') constraining democracy within nation states.[106] Stiglitz argues that unfettered globalization and the overselling of trade globalization has contributed to growing inequality; to frequent crisis such as the 2008 global financial crisis; and contributed to the growthof powerful multinational corporations.[107]

Since there is no clear agent or face of globalization, the anger is often directed at global economic institutions like the WTO,[108] or at economic treaties like trade treaties, BITs or ISDS. These treaties are often in the firing line of the vociferous critics of globalization because these treaties transfer democratic power of nation states to international institutions and to international tribunals like ISDS[109] Thus, it is argued that by precluding individual states from taking a range of political decisions and by taking many policy areas effectively out of democratic contestation, these treaties become part of a global ecosystem that could be described as undemocratic liberalism or rights without democracy.[110] Stiglitz argues that the intent of investment treaties is to 'discourage governments from taking actions like passing regulations that would hurt corporate profits, period'.[111]

Very important critiques of investment treaties are civil society organizations. For instance, a declaration from the People's Convention

---

Sovereignty Compatible?',International Theory 8(2): 297–340 (hereinafter Rodrik, *The Globalisation Paradox*).

[106] Rodrik, *The Globalisation Paradox*, pp. 199–201.

[107] Stiglitz, *Globalisation and its Discontents: Revisted*, p. 4.

[108] Anti-globalization protestors protested against the WTO in 1999 at the WTO's Seattle ministerial conference—see Noah Smith. 2014. 'The Dark Side of Globalization: Why Seattle's 1999 Protesters Were Right', 6 January, https://www.theatlantic.com/business/archive/2014/01/the-dark-side-of-globalization-why-seattles-1999-protesters-were-right/282831/.

[109] See generally Cory Adkins and David Grewal. 2016. 'Democracy and Legitmacy in Investor-State Arbitration', *Yale Law Journal* 126: 57; Lorenzo Cotula. 2017. 'Democracy and International Investment Law', *Leiden Journal of International Law* 33: 351.

[110] See Yascha Mounk. 2018. *The People Vs. Democracy: Why our Freedom is in Danger and How to Save It*. Harvard. Harvard University Press, pp. 73–7.

[111] Stiglitz, *Globalisation and its Discontents: Revisted*, p. 37.

against free trade agreements (FTA) and the Regional Comprehensive Economic Partnership (RCEP) agreement[112] states, 'we strongly oppose the onslaught of corporate globalization by which policies and laws of the country are being made to suit the interests of multinational corporations. We want democratic governments to retain the sovereignty to make laws and policies in the interests of the citizens, particularly the more vulnerable sections—whether it is import tariffs, subsidies, minimum wages or protections for its people and environment'.[113] Likewise, many Indian non-governmental organizations (NGOs) are signatories to a statement issued by 95 such organizations urging member states to reject ISDS.[114] The statement states that foreign investors can sue countries 'for unlimited cash damages and compound interest'.[115] Further, the statement says that 'if the proposals are accepted, this investor-to-state dispute settlement (ISDS) would allow foreign investors to sue RCEP governments if they regulate in ways that disadvantages the foreign investor, for example, by reducing its profits, including by introducing new laws/policies or changing their laws/policies, even if it is for public interest reasons'.[116]

Consequently, in order to placate the concerns pertaining to hyper globalization, some argue that ambitions for global economic integration may be downgraded.[117] One way to do so, as some argue, is to question international agreements that tightly constrain the state's regulatory discretion in the interests of existing corporations.[118]

[112] RCEP is a proposed free trade agreement involving 10 ASEAN countries and China, India, Australia, Korea, Japan and New Zealand—Regional Comprehensive Economic Partnership—http://asean.org/?static_post=rcep-regional-comprehensive-economic-partnership.

[113] Declaration from the People's Convention against FTAs and RCEP, http://itforchange.net/statement-against-the-RCEP.

[114] Civil society groups say No to investors suing States in RCEP, https://www.tni.org/en/article/civil-society-groups-say-no-to-investors-suing-states-in-rcep.

[115] Civil society groups say No to investors suing States in RCEP, https://www.tni.org/en/article/civil-society-groups-say-no-to-investors-suing-states-in-rcep.

[116] Civil society groups say No to investors suing States in RCEP, https://www.tni.org/en/article/civil-society-groups-say-no-to-investors-suing-states-in-rcep.

[117] Rodrik, 'The Inescapable Trilemma of the World Economy'.

[118] M. Wolf. 2016. 'Capitalism and Democracy: The Strain is Showing', https://www.ft.com/content/e46e8c00-6b72-11e6-ae5b-a7cc5dd5a28c.

Thus, BITs and ISDS become visible sites for downgrading ambitious economic globalization.

While concerns about globalization have merit, these generic concerns do not fully capture the nuances of how BITs and ISDS function.[119] In the enthusiasm to criticize globalization, these critiques overstate and also oversimplify the problems with investment treaties. For instance, Stiglitz's generalist critique about investment agreements, in the course of identifying the discontents of globalization, is a classic example of a one-sided description of how these treaties have operated.[120] Stiglitz gives an impression that foreign investors have been using BITs to sue states left, right, and centre, and have been successful in their endeavours.[121] These claims are not backed by any empirical evidence, which, as mentioned earlier, shows that states have fared better at ISDS forums in comparison to foreign investors. On numerous occasions, ISDS tribunals have upheld the state's sovereign right to regulate. Moreover, the tendency to paint every state action as an innocuous effort to regulate in public interest without even considering the fact that states may abuse their public power is equally problematic.[122] Stiglitz's one-sided critique of BITs is consistent with the pattern of critics of globalization who confuse between problems pertaining to globalization in general and issues surrounding BITs and ISDS in particular.[123]

Also see L. Summers. 2016. 'Voters Deserve Responsible Nationalism not Reflex Globalism', https://www.ft.com/content/15598db8-4456-11e6-9b66-0712b3873ae1.

[119] Also see Caron and Shirlow, 'Dissecting Backlash', pp.162–5.

[120] Stiglitz, *Globalisation and its Discontents:Revisited*, pp. 35–8.

[121] Stiglitz, *Globalisation and its Discontents: Revisited*, pp. 35–8.

[122] See Chapter 6 for examples on abuse of public power by India in dealing with foreign investors.

[123] Stern Brigete. 2011. 'The Future of International Investment Law: A Balance Between the Protection of Investors and the States's Capacity to Regulate', in *The Evolving International Investment Regime: Expectations, Realities, Options* Alvarez (ed), p. 175. Oxford: Oxford University Press. Also see Spears, 'The Quest for Policy Space in a New Generation of International Investment Agreements', p. 1074.

Apart from these non-legal generalist and specialist critics of globalization, the other set of people who critique BITs and ISDS are critical international lawyers[124] and scholars who subscribe to the third world approaches to international law (TWAIL).[125] TWAIL, in broader terms, represents an endeavour to comprehend the history, structure, and process of international law from the perspective of Third World countries that includes not just Third World governments but also the people of these countries.[126] Scholars of TWAIL view many regimes of international law like international investment law as contemporary forms of neo-colonialism.[127] They look at modern international law as not being neutral law formed between sovereign equals but as law imposed by the First World on

[124] For a discussion on critical legal studies see M. Tushnet. 1990–1. 'Critical Legal Studies: A Political History', *Yale Law Journal* 100:1515; D. Kennedy. 1988–9. 'A New Stream of International Legal Scholarship', *Wisconsin International Law Journal* 7: 1.

[125] B.S. Chimni. 2003. 'Third World Approaches to International Law: A Manifesto', in *The Third World and International Order: Law, Politics and Globalization*Antony Anghie, Bhupinder Chimni, Karin Mickelson, and Obiora C. Okafor (eds), p. 47. Leiden: Brill/Nijhoff.

[126] B.S. Chimni. 2007. 'The Past, Present and Future of International Law: A Critical Third World Perspective', *Melbourne Journal of International Law* 8(2): 499 (hereinafter Chimni, 'The Past, Present and Future of International Law'). Often a distinction is made between TWAIL I and TWAIL II scholarship. TWAIL I scholarship refers to the scholarship produced by the first generation of postcolonial international lawyers like R.P. Anand whereas TWAIL II refers to second generation of postcolonial international lawyers like B.S. Chimni and Antony Anghie who are critical of many tenets of TWAIL I scholarship—see B.S. Chimni and A. Anghie. 2003. 'Third World Approaches to International Law and Individual Responsibility in Internal Conflicts', *Chinese Journal of International Law* 2(1): 77–103. Also see J.T. Gathi. 2000. 'Rejoinder Twailing International Law', *Michigan Law Review* 98:2066. Also important to bear in mind that TWAIL scholarship is not a monolith but a 'chorus of voices' comprising of Marxists (B.S. Chimni), feminists, post-structuralists—see K. Mickelson. 1998. 'Rhetoric and Rage: Third World Voices in International Legal Discourse', *Wisconsin International Law Journal* 16: 353 (hereinafter Mickelson, 'Rhetoric and Rage'.

[127] See O.C. Okafor. 2005. 'Newness, Imperialism, and International Legal Reform in Our Time: A TWAIL Perspective', *Osgoode Hall Law Journal* 43: 171.

the Third World to further its imperial and neoliberal project.[128] Chimni, for example, argues that since the end of the Cold War, international law has been shaped by the transnational capitalist class (TCC)[129] to realize its own interests as universal interests that collide with the interests of the subaltern class.[130] In other words, some kind of nefarious motives are attributed to the TCC and the entire narrative is presented as if it is part of some global elitist conspiracy against the poor of the world. Specifically in the context of international investment law, TWAIL scholars like Anghie allude to the colonial origins of international investment law as a discipline.[131] Likewise, Chimni describes BITs and international investment laws as instruments to achieve the objectives of global

[128] See U. Mattei. 2003. 'A Theory of Imperial Law: A Study on U.S. Hegemony and the Latin Resistance', *Indiana Journal of Global Legal Studies* 10: 383; B.S. Chimni. 2004. 'International Institutions Today: An Imperial Global State in the Making', *European Journal of International Law* 15:1. M. Sornarajah. 2015. *Resistance and Change in the International Law on Foreign Investment.* Cambridge. Cambridge University Press (hereinafter Sornarajah, *Resistance and Change in the International Law on Foreign Investment*).

[129] Broadly, it is argued that the TCC consists of Transnational Corporations (TNC), globalizing state, globalizing professionals including academics, merchants and media. See L. Sklair. 2002. *Globalisation: Capitalism and Its Alternatives.* Oxford. Oxford University Press; B.S. Chimni. 2012. 'Capitalism, Imperialism and International Law in the Twenty-First Century', *Oregon Review of International Law* 14:17 (hereinafter Chimni, 'Capitalism, Imperalism and International Law in the Twenty-First Century').

[130] B.S. Chimni. 2007. 'A Just World Under Law: A View from the South', *American University International Law Review* 22:199 at 200; Chimni, 'Capitalism, Imperalism and International Law in the Twenty-First Century', p. 17. Philip Alston critiques some of Chimni's arguments such as the failure to precisely identify what is third world and also the tendency to attribute nefarious goals to the TCC—see P. Alston. 2007. 'Remarks on Professor B.S. Chimni's A Just World under Law: A View From the South', *American University International Law Review* 22:222.

[131] A. Anghie. 2004. *Imperialism, Sovereignty, and the Making of International Law.* Cambridge: Cambridge University Press. Also see K. Miles. 2013. *The Origins of International Investment Law: Empire, Environment and the Safegaruding of Capital.* Cambridge: Cambridge University Press, pp. 17–69.

imperialism.[132] Borrowing from David Harvey, Chimni argues that BITs are being used by global capitalism for 'accumulation by dispossession'[133] at the expense of the subaltern class and ignoring societal and environmental concerns.[134] He also argues that BITs are being used to free transnational capital of 'spatial and temporal constraints'[135] and that powerful nations are using investment treaties to seek capital account liberalization[136] in the Third World countries.[137] Likewise, Sornarajah argues that US hegemonic power and ideological dominance of neo-liberalism are responsible for the current manifestations of international investment law.[138]

Three points need to be made about these critiques of BITs. First, these critiques are a reflection of the larger critique of the so-called colonial and neo-imperial character of international law aimed at legitimizing colonialism.[139] Many TWAIL-ers like Chimni extend this critique to international economic law[140] including international trade law and international monetary law. These TWAIL critiques especially by Marxist scholars like Chimni are not critiques specific

[132] B.S. Chimni. 2017. *An Integrated Marxist Approach to International Law*. Cambridge: Cambridge University Press, 510–11 (hereinafter Chimni, *An Integrated Marxist Approach to International Law*).

[133] For more on 'accumulation by dispossesion', see David Harvey. 2003. *The New Imperialism*. New York: Oxford University Press.

[134] Chimni, 'Capitalism, Imperialism and International Law in the Twenty-First Century', p. 30.

[135] B.S. Chimni. 2006. 'Third World Approaches to International Law: A Manifesto', *International Community Law Review* 8(3): 9.

[136] For a debate on capital account convertibility in India see Chapters 3 and 5.

[137] Chimni, *An Integrated Marxist Approach to International Law*, p. 509

[138] Sornarajah, *Resistance and Change in the International Law on Foreign Investment*.

[139] See J. Kangave. 2008. 'Taxing TWAIL: A Preliminary Inquiry into TWAIL's Application to the Taxation of Foreign Direct Investment', *International Community Law Review* 10(4): 389–90.

[140] See Mickelson, 'Rhetoric and Rage', p. 362; J.T. Gathi. 2008. 'Third World Approaches to International Economic Governance', in *International Law and the Third World: Reshaping Justice* R. Falk, Balakrishnan Rajagopal, and Jacqueline Stevens (eds), pp. 255, at 256–7. London: Routledge.

to the working of BITs and ISDS. In the TWAIL project, critiquing BITs and ISDS are short-term goals in fighting a bigger ideological battle against the capitalist modes of production; and to sell a one-sided narrative of international law being a tool to pursue the goals of global capitalism and imperialism by the TCC. Given the strong ideological underpinnings of TWAIL, this project will continue unabated even if all BITs were terminated[141]

Second, these critiques, while true to some extent, are misleading because they are often not based on the actual working of BITs, ISDS, case laws, and empirical evidence. While there is no denying the fact that emergence of BITs was aimed at protecting the investment of capital-exporting countries (western Europe and the US) in developing or Third World countries, presenting BITs in a one-sided manner does not adequately reflect many nuances. For instance, while it is true that the first-generation BITs didn't contain provisions for protection of environment, this does not mean that foreign investors have always been successful in an ISDS claim challenging a host state's environment-related regulatory measures. There have been many instances where ISDS tribunals have upheld the host state's right to regulate for environmental[142] and public health concerns.[143] Likewise, arguing that powerful countries are using BITs to seek capital account liberalization is an oversimplified description. The reality is much more nuanced. While it is true that first generation BITs contain broad monetary transfer provisions (MTPs) that give foreign investors almost unfettered freedom to transfer funds,[144] these BITs do not impose a positive obligation on states to liberalize their

[141] Also see D. Krishan. 2011. 'Thinking About BITs and BIT Arbitration: The Legitimacy Crisis that Never Was', in *New Directions in International Economic Law: In Memoriam Thomas Walde* Todd Weiler and Freya Baetens (eds), p. 107 at 136. Leiden. Martinus Nijhoff.

[142] See *Methanex* v. *USA*; *Chemtura* v. *Canada*.

[143] See *Philip Morris* v. *Uruguay*; *Eli Lily* v. *Canada*.

[144] See M. Waibel. 2009. 'BIT by BIT: The Silent Liberalisation of the Capital Account', in *International Investment Law for the 21st Century: Essays in Honour of Christoph Schreuer* Christina Binder, Ursula Kriebaum, August Reinisch, and Stephan Wittich (eds), p. 498. Oxford: Oxford University Press.

capital account.[145] Moreover, many new-generation BITs, signed by both developed and developing countries, specifically recognize the right of countries to impose controls on movement of capital across borders.[146]

Third, interestingly, the TWAIL critique even in 2017 sounds exactly the same as early 2000, almost as if the world hasn't changed. As a result, the critique ignores today's reality that is much more complex and nuanced. The one-sided and generic critiques of TWAILers do not take into account the countervailing forces that act against developed countries like the US.[147] For instance, US today, unlike the past, is not just an exporter of capital but also an importer of capital.[148] Quite a few ISDS claims have been brought against the US under NAFTA. Thus, US cannot look at BITs in a manner that only reflects the perspective of a capital-exporting country.[149] These factors explain US's changed approach towards investment treaties as reflected in the US 2012 Model BIT. The 2012 Model is quite different from the US 1984 Model BIT. The 2012 Model tries to provide a better textual balance between the rights of investors and host state's right to regulate.

Likewise, many developing countries today such as India have become huge exporters of capital—India is the fourth-largest investor in the UK.[150] Thus, India cannot look at the investment regime purely from a capital-importing country perspective—something that it could do two decades back. Since 1990, the share of the G7

[145] See Chapter 5.

[146] See Article 94(1) of the India–Japan FTA. Also see Chapter 5 for description of MTPs in new generation Indian BITs.

[147] See J. Alvraez. 2009. 'Contemporary International Law: An "Empire of Law" or the "Law of Empire"', *American University International Law Review* 24(5): 811, 832–6 (hereinafter Alvarez, 'Contemporary International Law').

[148] See A. Kullick. 2016. 'Narrating Narratives of International Investment Law: History and Epistemic Forces', in *International Investment Law and History*, Rainer Hoffman, Stephan W. Schill, and Christian J. Tams (eds). Cheltenham/Northampton: Edward Elgar, p. 20 at 21.

[149] Alvarez, 'Contemporary International Law', pp. 832–3.

[150] 'India Slips to be 4th Largest Investor into UK', 6 July2017, https://economictimes.indiatimes.com/news/politics-and-nation/india-slips-to-be-4th-largest-investor-into-uk/articleshow/59473832.cms.

group—Canada, France, Germany, Italy, Japan, the UK, and the US—in the global GDP has fallen from 50 per cent to 30.9 per cent in 2016 and share of countries like India, in the global GDP, over the same period has doubled to an estimated 7.3 per cent from 3.6 per cent.[151] This shows that the engine of world economy is moving from the First World to the Third World—a fact that hopefuly should help TWAIL-ers update their somewhat dated North–South analytical framework.

These factors have impacted the shape and design of international investment law in ways that TWAIL-ers have not been able to fully comprehend. Also, ever since developed countries have become targets of ISDS, newer opportunities have emerged to re-engage with many principles of international investment law that were earlier considered settled.[152] However, the use of Marxist vocabulary like 'class struggle' and bringing in notions of imperialism and colonialism dampens the scope for a constructive engagement and thus dilutes the emancipatory potential of international investment law for developing countries—to use BITs as a tool to attract foreign investment and as a commitment to international rule of law without excessively compromising on the sovereign right to regulate.[153]

Even if TWAIL has succeeded in making detailed and specific critiques of BITs and ISDS,[154] it has failed to offer pragmatic suggestions for the improvement of the regime. Asking for the abrogation of the entire regime (countries terminating investment treaties and walking out of arbitral institutions like ICSID), as Sornarajah argues[155] is not

151 M. Chakravarty. 2017. 'Which Countries have Benefitted the Most from Globalisation', https://www.livemint.com/Money/cNmmQJZdnMhbk3Ydbs26wI/Which-countries-have-benefited-the-most-from-globalization.html.

152 See I.T. Odumosu. 2007. 'The Law and Politics of Engaging Resistance in Investment Dispute Settlement', *Penn State International Law Review* 26: 251 (hereinafter Odumosu, 'The Law and Politics of Engaging Resistance in Investment Dispute Settlement').

153 See Chapter 9.

154 For instance see Sornarajah, *Resistance and Change in the International Law on Foreign Investment*; Odumosu, 'The Law and Politics of Engaging Resistance in Investment Dispute Settlement'.

155 Sornarajah, *Resistance and Change in the International Law on Foreign Investment*, p. 408.

quite helpful. Absence of investment treaty obligations would mean that a very important check on potential abuse of the host state's regulatory behaviour towards foreign investors will cease to exist. This will create a vacuum as regards protection of foreign investment in international law.

1.2.4 In defence of BITs and ISDS

Along with the above voices that are critical of BITs and ISDS, those who defend the international investment law regime occupy an important space in the global debate. But this camp is also not homogenous. There are some who appear to be unabashed cheerleaders of the international investment law regime refusing to see problems.[156] Instances of ISDS tribunals upholding the state's sovereign right to regulate in the interest of public health and environment[157] are often cited as proof of the fact that the system is working fine.

Between the virulent critics and unabashed cheerleaders of BITs and ISDS, there are those who support the regime, but, at the same time, also recognize the flaws in the system such as broad and indeterminate language of BITs and lack of transparency in ISDS and advocate for reforms.[158] Proposals to reform BITs and ISDS range from improving the language of BITs, that is, moving away from brief BITs;[159] to reconceptualizing international investment law as

[156] See Krishan, 'Thinking About BITs and BIT Arbitration: The Legitimacy Crisis that Never Was'; C.N. Brower and S. Blanchard. 2014. 'What's in a Meme? The Truth about Investor State Arbitration: Why It Need Not, and Must Not, Be Repossessed by States', *Columbia Journal of Transnational Law* 52:689.

[157] See *Philip Morris* v. *Uruguay*; *Methanex* v. *USA*.

[158] See S. Schill. 2016. 'In Defense of International Investment Law', in *European Yearbook of International Economic Law, vol. 7*, Marc Bungenberg, Christoph Herrmann, Markus KrajewskiJörg, and Philipp Terhechte (eds), pp. 309–41. Cham: Springer. P. Ranjan. 2014. 'Using Public Law Concept of Proportionality to Balance Investment Protection with Regulation in International Investment Law—A Critical Appraisal', *Cambridge International Law Journal* 3: 853.

[159] See Section 1.1.2. Also see A. Roberts. 2013. 'Clash of Paradigms: Actors and Analogies Shaping the Investment Treaty System', *American Journal of International Law* 107(45): 78–83.

part of a global economic governance system;[160] to putting greater onus on arbitrators to interpret BITs in a manner that balance investment protection and the host state's right to regulate;[161] to reforming the ISDS system by bringing in greater amount of transparency;[162] to even arguing for the creation of a multilateral investment court.[163] Some scholars adopting a legal realist perspective contend that the international investment system should not simply rely on ISDS or on a single multilateral investment court system replacing the ISDS.[164] Instead, Puig and Shaffer argue that there should be flexibility that allows countries, facing different challenges, to choose from a menu of imperfect international alternatives.[165]

[160] J. Frank Garcia, Lindita Ciko, Apurv Gaurav, and Kirrin Hough. 2015. 'Reforming the International Investment Regime: Lessons from International Trade Law', *Journal of International Economic Law* 18:861.

[161] B. Kingsbury and S.W. Schill. 2010. 'Public Law Concepts to Balance Investors' Rights with State Regulatory Actions in the Public Interest—the Concept of Proportionality', in *International Investment Law and Comparative Public Law* S.W. Schill (ed.), p. 75. Oxford, Oxford University Press; Caroline Henckels. 2012. 'Indirect Expropriation and the Right to Regulate: Revisiting Proportionality Analysis and the Standard of Review in Investor-State Arbitration', *Journal of International Economic Law* 15(1):223; Andreas Kulick. 2012. *Global Public Interest in International Investment Law*.Cambridge, New York: Cambridge University Press, pp. 168–224; Ursula Kriebaum. 2007. 'Regulatory Takings: Balancing the Interests of the Investor and the State', *Journal of World Investment and Trade* 8: 717.

[162] For an overview over the recent reform debates, see the contributions in Andreas Kulick (ed). 2016. *Reassertion of Control over the Investment Treaty Regime*. Cambridge: Cambridge University Press (hereinafter Kulick, *Reassertion of Control over the Investment Treaty Regime*); Steffen Hindelang and Markus Krajewski (eds). 2016. *Shifting Paradigms in International Investment Law: More Balanced, Less Isolated, Increasingly Diversified*. Oxford: Oxford University Press.

[163] European Union, Canada, and Mauritius are the key supporters of this. See A. Roberts. A. 2018. 'Incremental, Systemic and Paradigmatic Reform of Investor-State Arbitration', *American Journal of International Law* 112 (forthcoming).

[164] S. Puig and G. Shaffer. 2018. 'Imperfect Alternatives: Institutional Choice and the Reform of Investment Law', *Amercian Journal of International Law* 112 (forthcoming) (hereinafter Puig and Shaffer, 'Imperfect Alternatives').

[165] Puig and Shaffer, 'Imperfect Alternatives'.

Another way to conceptualize BITs is as instruments that promote the formal version of international rule of law.[166] For instance, one of the elements considered an integral part of international rule of law is that there should be a process of independent adjudication in order to ensure accountability of exercise of public power.[167] In view of this, it is argued that arbitrators in ISDS foster international rule of law by the independent and impartial application of the governing law.[168] Likewise, BITs also foster international rule of law by imposing restraints on the host state's exercise of public power (for example, by obligating states to treat foreign investors fairly and equitably).[169] Looked this way, BITs and ISDS are an important part of the legal infrastructure imperative for the working of the global economy under the framework of rule of law.[170]

1.3 The Purpose of This Book

Against this global backdrop of the proliferation of BITs, rising ISDS claims, and the global debate on BITs and ISDS, the purpose of this

[166] On international rule of law see S. Chesterman. 2008. 'An International Rule of Law?', *American Journal of Comparative Law* 56: 331 (hereinafter Chesterman, 'An International Rule of Law?').

[167] Chesterman, 'An International Rule of Law?', p. 342; André Nollkaemper. 2011. *National Courts and the International Rule of Law*. Oxford, New York: Oxford University Press, p. 5.

[168] C. Browerand S. Schill. 2009. 'Is Arbitration a Threat or a Boon to the Legitimacy of International Investment Law', *Chicago Journal of International Law* 9:471. See also E. Petersmann. 2009. 'International Rule of Law and Constitutional Justice in International Investment Law and Arbitration', *Indiana Journal of Global Legal Studies,* 16(2):518. Also see P. Ranjan. 2016. 'National Contestation of International Investment Law and International Rule of Law', in *Rule of Law at National and International Levels: Contestations and Deference* M. Kanetake and A. Nollkaemper (eds), pp. 115–42.Oxford: Hart Publishing (hereinafter Ranjan, 'National Contestation of International Investment Law and International Rule of Law').

[169] Ranjan, 'National Contestation of International Investment Law and International Rule of Law', pp. 115–42.

[170] S. Schill and V. Djanic. 2018. 'Wherefore Art Thou? Towards a Public Interest-Based Justification of International Investment Law', *ICSID Review – Foreign Investment Law Journal* 33: 29 (hereinafter Schill and Djanic, 'Wherefore Art Thou?').

book is to study closely India's approach towards investment treaties by tracing the origin, evolution, and the current state of play. Given the global attention that BITs have drawn, several country-specific case studies have emerged.[171] There are several interrelated reasons to study India's BITs as a case study. First, India is one of the fastest-growing economies in the world,[172] and the third most attractive destination for FDI, after China and the US.[173] The total FDI flows to India have increased from $4,029 million in 2000–1 to $546,452 million as of March 2018.[174] This not only shows deep economic integration of India with the world economy but also the presence of large numbers of foreign investors in India. Second, India, starting from 1994 to date, has signed more than 80 investment treaties (see Annex of the book). These BITs have been signed with many developed countries such as the UK, Germany, France, Australia, and key emerging markets like China and Russia.[175] India is currently

[171] For example see W. Shan and N. Gallagher. 2009. *Chinese Investment Treaties: Policies and Practice*. Oxford: Oxford University Press.

[172] According to the International Monetary Fund (IMF), India's Gross Domestic Product (GDP) at market prices grew by 6.6 per cent in 2016 only next to China where this number stands at 6.7 per cent. Further, according to the IMF, India's GDP in 2017 and 2018 is estimated to grow at 7.2 and 7.7 per cent, respectively, which is higher than China's projected growth where these numbers stand at 6.5 and 6 per cent, respectively—See International Monetary Fund (IMF). 2017. 'A Shifting Global Economic Landscape', *World Economic Outlook Update* (January), https://www.imf.org/external/pubs/ft/weo/2017/update/01/pdf/0117.pdf, accessed 12 March 2018.

[173] UNCTAD. 2016. 'Global Investment Trends Monitor, No. 24', available at https://unctad.org/en/PublicationsLibrary/webdiaeia2016d3_en.pdf, 6 October.

[174] Department of Industrial Policy and Promotion, Ministry of Commerce and Industry, Government of India. 2018. 'Quarterly Fact Sheet, Fact Sheet on Foreign Direct Investment from April 2000 to March 2018', http://dipp.nic.in/sites/default/files/FDI_FactSheet_29June2018.pdf, March, accessed 12 July 2018. According to the Indian government, FDI inflows include equity inflows plus reinvested earnings plus other capital.

[175] UNCTAD. n.d. 'International Investment Agreements Navigator: India', http://investmentpolicyhub.unctad.org/IIA/CountryBits/96, accessed 12 March 2018.

negotiating a BIT with Canada[176] and the US.[177] From around 2005 onwards, India has signed Comprehensive Economic Cooperation Agreements (CECAs or FTAs) covering trade and investment liberalization, competition policy, trade facilitation, rules of origin, and intellectual property rights. India has signed such FTAs containing investment agreements with countries, namely, Singapore,[178] Japan,[179] Malaysia,[180] and Korea.[181] India has signed an investment

[176] Government of Canada. 2016. 'Canada-India Foreign Investment Promotion and Protection Agreement Negotiations', http://international.gc.ca/trade-commerce/trade-agreements-accords-commerciaux/agr-acc/india-inde/fipa-apie/background-contexte.aspx?lang=eng, 14 December, accessed 12 March 2018.

[177] The US and India have been negotiating a BIT since 2009. During President Barack Obama's visit to India in 2015 with Prime Minister Narendra Modi, and building further on past US–India discussions, both presidents issued a Joint Statement 'instruct[ing] their officials to assess the prospects for moving forward with high-standard bilateral investment treaty discussions given their respective approaches'—see The White House, Office of the Press Secretary. 2015. 'U.S.-India Joint Statement I "Shared Effort; Progress for All"', 25 January, https://obamawhitehouse.archives.gov/the-press-office/2015/01/25/us-india-joint-statement-shared-effort-progress-all, accessed 12 March 2018 (hereinafter India–US Joint Statement 2015). On difficulties between US and India BIT negotiations, see 'BIT of a Bumpy Ride'. 2016. *The Hindu*, 2 June, http://www.thehindu.com/opinion/op-ed/Bit-of-a-bumpy-ride/article14378406.ece, accessed 12 March 2018.

[178] 'Comprehensive Economic Cooperation Agreement Between the Republic of India and the Republic of Singapore', (29 June 2005, entered into force 1 August 2005), http://dot.gov.in/sites/default/files/India%20Singapore%20CECA%2001.08.2005.pdf. (hereinafter India–Singapore CECA).

[179] 'Comprehensive Economic Partnership Agreement between Japan and the Republic of India' (16 February 2011, entered into force 1 August 2011), https://www.mofa.go.jp/region/asia-paci/india/epa201102/pdfs/ijcepa_ba_e.pdf. (hereinafter India–Japan CEPA).

[180] 'Comprehensive Economic Cooperation Agreement between the Government of Malaysia and The Government of The Republic of India', (18 February 2011, entered into force 1 July 2011), http://fta.miti.gov.my/miti-fta/resources/Malaysia-India/MICECA.pdf. (hereinafter India–Malaysia CECA).

[181] 'Comprehensive Economic Partnership Agreement between the Republic of Korea and the Republic of India' (7 August 2009, entered into force

agreement with Association of Southeast Asian Nations (ASEAN).[182] These FTA investment chapters along with provisions on investment protection also contain market access provisions, which do not exist in any of the existing Indian BITs which deal only with post-establishment, that is, protecting foreign investment after it has entered the territory. India started signing BITs in early 1990s as a part of its overall strategy of economic liberalization adopted in 1991 and had the clear objective of attracting foreign investments.[183]

Third, this deepening integration of India with the global economy through BITs and high foreign investment inflows have made India vulnerable to BIT claims from foreign investors of more than 80 different countries. Indeed, in last few years, close to 20 foreign corporations have either commenced BIT arbitrations against India or have made their intentions known to do so.[184] This includes leading corporations like Vodafone, Cairn Energy, Telenor, Nokia, and Nissan.[185] These corporations have used BITs to challenge a wide

---

1 January 2010), http://commerce.nic.in/trade/india%20korea%20cepa%202009.pdf. (hereinafter India–Korea CECA).

[182] 'Agreement on Investment under the Framework Agreement on Comprehensive Economic Cooperation between the Association of Southeast Asian Nations and the Republic of India', (12 November 2014, yet to come into force), https://www.asean.org/storage/2016/04/ASEAN-India-Investment-Agreement-ASEAN-version.pdf. (hereinafter ASEAN–India FTA). Also see Chapters 3–5.

[183] See Prabhash Ranjan. 2014. 'India and Bilateral Investment Treaties – A Changing Landscape', *ICSID Review of Foreign Investment Law Journal* 29:419 (hereinafter Ranjan, 'India and Bilateral Investment Treaties – A Changing Landscape'); Prabhash Ranjan. 2012. *India's International Investment Agreements and India's Regulatory Power as a Host Nation*, PhD thesis, King's College London, https://kclpure.kcl.ac.uk/portal/files/13524464/Studentthesis-_2013.pdf, accessed 12 March 2018 (hereinafter Ranjan, *India's International Investment Agreements and India's Regulatory Power as a Host Nation*).

[184] See Chapter 6. Also see UNCTAD. n.d. 'India – as Respondent State, Investment Policy Hub', http://investmentpolicyhub.unctad.org/ISDS/CountryCases/96?partyRole=2, accessed 12 March 2018 (hereinafter UNCTAD, 'India – as Respondent State').

[185] See Chapter 6. Also see UNCTAD, 'India – as Respondent State'.

range of India's sovereign regulatory measures such as actions of the Indian judiciary, retrospective amendments in tax laws by the Indian parliament, and cancellation of telecom and spectrum licenses by the executive.[186] In addition to these BIT notices, there have been three instances where foreign investors have successfully proved that India violated her BIT obligations; first in *White Industries* v. *India* in 2011, where a BIT tribunal held that India violated her obligations under the India–Australia BIT; second, in *Devas* v. *India* in 2016, an ISDS tribunal held that India violated her obligations under the India–Mauritius BIT;[187] third, in *Deutsche Telekom* v. *India* in December 2017, an ISDS tribunal held that India violated her obligations under the India–Germany BIT.[188] These decided cases and the ongoing disputes, when they get decided, would contribute to the emergence of the case law on Indian BITs.

Despite India's mammoth BIT programme, BITs in India didn't attract much critical attention from 1994 to the end of 2011. This was mainly because of India's marginal involvement with ISDS.[189] However, things started to change post-2011 when India was swamped by numerous ISDS claims brought by foreign investors under different Indian BITs as mentioned before.[190] As a reaction to these ISDS claims, India reviewed its BITs and adopted a new Model BIT in 2016,[191] with the claimed objective of providing 'appropriate

[186] See Chapter 6. Also see UNCTAD, 'India – as Respondent State'.

[187] See Chapters 4, 5, and 6.

[188] *Deutsche Telekom AG* v. *Republic of India*, PCA Case No 2014-10, 13 December 2017.

[189] See Chapter 3.

[190] See Chapters 6 and 7.

[191] Government of India. 2016. 'Model Text for the Indian Bilateral Investment Treaty 2016', http://mof.gov.in/reports/ModelTextIndia_BIT.pdf, 14 January, accessed 12 March 2018 [hereinafter 2016 Indian Model BIT]. Important to keep in mind that the Indian Model BIT contains two dates—28 December 2015 given in the letter accompanying the text; and 14 January 2016 on the website of the Ministry of Finance, Government of India as the date of publication of the BIT— https://www.finmin.nic.in/office-memorandum, accessed 12 March 2018. In this book, we use the 14 January 2016 date, and thus call the Model BIT as 2016 Indian Model BIT and *not* 2015 Indian Model BIT.

protection to foreign investors in India' 'while maintaining a balance between investor's rights and the government's obligations'.[192]

India has also terminated BITs with many countries.[193] India now wishes to renegotiate investment treaties with all these countries based on its new Model BIT.[194] However, despite this termination, all the provisions of the terminated BITs shall continue to remain effective for investments made before the date of termination for a further period of 15 years.[195] Another outcome of the review of BITs has been that India has asked some of its treaty partner countries to consider issuing joint interpretive statements (JIS) to clarify ambiguities in treaty texts so as to avoid expansive interpretations by arbitration tribunals.[196] This new approach towards BITs will not just impact all the existing treaty partner countries but also all those countries with whom India wishes to negotiate or renegotiate investment treaties.

[192] Saurabh Garg, Ishita G. Tripathy, and Sudhanshu Roy. 2016. 'The Indian Model Bilateral Investment Treaty: Continuity and Change' in *Rethinking Bilateral Investment Treaties – Critical Issues and Policy Choices* Kavaljit Singh and BurghardIgle (eds), pp. 69–80. New Delhi: Both Ends, Madhyam and SOMO; Department of Economic Affairs, Ministry of Finance, Government of India. 2016. *Transforming the International Investment Agreement Regime: The Indian Experience*, http://unctad-worldinvestmentforum.org/wp-content/uploads/2015/03/India_side-event-Wednesday_Model-agreements.pdf, 20 July, accessed 12 March 2018. (India's presentation in a Side Event at World Investment Forum 2016).

[193] See, Government of India, Ministry of Commerce and Industry, Department of Industrial Policy and Promotion, 'Lok Sabha Unstarred Question No. 1290' (25 July 2016), http://164.100.47.190/loksabhaquestions/annex/9/AU1290.pdf, accessed 12 March 2018. See Annex of the book.

[194] Press Information Bureau, Government of India, Ministry of Finance. 2015. 'Model Text of the Bilateral Investment Treaty', http://pib.nic.in/newsite/PrintRelease.aspx?relid=133412, accessed 12 March 2018.

[195] For example see Article 16(1) of the India–Netherlands BIT. Also see Chapter 7.

[196] Government of India, Ministry of Finance, Department of Economic Affairs. 2016. 'Office Memorandum - Regarding Issuing Joint Interpretative Statements for Indian Bilateral Investment Treaties', http://indiainbusiness.nic.in/newdesign/upload/Consolidated_Interpretive-Statement.pdf, 8 February, accessed 12 March 2018 (hereinafter, Consolidated Interpretative Statement). Also see Chapter 7.

These developments necessitate a comprehensive documentation of India's approach towards BITs examining critically the various developments. While some work has been done on the Indian BITs,[197] a detailed and comprehensive account of Indian BITs right from tracing their evolution to the current state of play in the form of a book is yet to be offered. Although a recent book discusses Indian BITs, it offers a descriptive and uncritical account of the Indian BIT programme.[198] This book adds value to the existing literature on Indian BITs by undertaking not merely a descriptive but also a critical examination of India's approach towards BITs by locating it in India's economic policy in general and foreign investment policy in particular.

1.4 Structure of the Book

In order to study India's approach to BITs, the book divides India's approach to BITs into three different phases. These phases are from 1947 (that is, when India gained political independence from British rule) to 1990 (Phase I); from 1991 to 2010 (Phase II); and from 2011 to present (Phase III). These phases are described as phases

[197] S. Rao. 2000. 'Bilateral Investment Promotion Agreements: A Legal Framework for the Protection of Foreign Investments', *Commonwealth Law Bulletin* 26:623–4; D. Krishan. 2008. 'India and International Investment Law', in *India and International Law* B.N. Patel (ed.), p. 277 (Vol. 2). Martinus Nijhoff: Leiden/Boston; Prabhash Ranjan. 2015. 'Comparing Investment Provisions in India's FTAs with India's Standalone BITs: Contributing to the Evolution of New Indian BIT Practice', *Journal of World Investment Treaties* 16:899–930; Grant Hanessian and Kabir Duggal. 2017. 'The Final 2015 Indian Model BIT: Is This the Change the World Wishes to See', *ICSID Review of Foreign Investment Law Journal*, <doi:10.1093/icsidreview/siw020>, accessed 12 March 2018. Also see Amokura Kawharu and Luke R. Nottage. 2017. 'Models for Investment Treaties in the Asian Region: An Underview', *Arizona Journal of International & Comparative Law* (forthcoming); Ajay K. Sharma. 2015. 'A Good Offence Is Not Always the Best Defence: Critiquing the Standards of Protection under the 2015 Indian Model BIT', *Business Law Reveiw* 36:203–07.

[198] Aniruddha Rajput. 2017. *Protection of Foreign Investment in India and Investment Treaty Arbitration*. Hague: Kluwer International (hereinafter Rajput, *Protection of Foreign Investment in India and Investment Treaty Arbitration*).

of refusal, acceptance, and backlash, respectively, as regards India's approach to BITs is concerned.

Phase I, discussed in Chapter 2, is called the phase of 'refusal' to sign BITs because India did not sign any BIT in this period. Phase II (Chapters 3–5) is called the phase of 'acceptance' of BITs because India enthusiastically started signing BITs during this phase. Phase III (Chapters 6–8) is called the phase of 'backlash' against BITs because India, as mentioned earlier, due to large number of claims brought against it launched a review of Indian BITs. India also started contesting BITs and ISDS post 2010. Important to note that, this author in a paper written in 2014 on Indian BITs in *ICSID Review*,[199] and in a paper written in 2015 that was made publicly available in early 2016[200] has already talked about studying India's approach towards BITs by dividing them into these three phases. Rajput has later followed the same chronological division.[201]

Vandevelde has argued that a state's foreign investment policy is generally an element of its larger economic policy.[202] Thus, an integral part to study India's approach towards BITs, in each of these phases, is to first document and discuss critically the overall nature of the Indian economy, that is, whether India followed a closed or a liberalized economic model and how this impacted India's overall policy towards foreign investment promotion and protection domestically. Subsequently, in each of these phases, the book discusses how the overall policy towards foreign investment domestically played or didn't play a role in India's approach towards foreign investment in international law including BITs.

This method to study the evolution of India's approach to BITs by first understanding India's economic policy to foreign investment followed by examining India's approach to protection of foreign

[199] Ranjan, 'India and Bilateral Investment Treaties—A Changing Landscape', pp. 419–50.

[200] Prabhash Ranjan. 2018. 'India and Bilateral Investment Treaties: From Rejection to Embracement to Hesitance?'. In '*Locating India' in the Contemporary International Legal Order*, R. Babu and S. Burra (eds). Springer, https://papers.ssrn.com/sol3/papers.cfm?abstract_id=2728840, accessed 12 March 2018.

[201] See Rajput, *Protection of Foreign Investment in India and Investment Treaty Arbitration*, Chapter 2.

[202] Vandevelde, *Bilateral Investment Treaties*, p. 75.

investment under international law was employed by this author in 2012 as part of doctoral research work at King's College London.[203] Rajput has later followed it.[204] In a loose way this method is inspired from the policy-oriented approach of the New Haven School of international law.[205] According to the New Haven School of international law, the notion international lawmaking comprises a 'process of communication' that comprises three different streams: 'policy content', 'authority signal', and 'control intention'.[206] Elaborating on these three coaxial messages, Riesman argued that first, there must be a policy about the production and distribution of some value; second this policy which must be recognized by the audience as being communicated by lawmakers who have the authority to do so; and third, 'there must be capacity and willingness to make a preferential expression effective'.[207] This policy-oriented method is handy to understand the developments in India's phase of 'acceptance'.

In Chapter 2, the book discusses India's approach towards foreign investment in general, by subdividing it into two time periods—1947 till 1965 followed by 1965 to 1990. The chapter also discusses India's approach towards international investment law by dividing it between multilateral and bilateral level. Chapter 3 discusses how India started moving towards embracing BITs by locating its origin in the massive economic liberalization programme India launched in

[203] Ranjan, *India's International Investment Agreements and India's Regulatory Power*.

[204] See Rajput, *Protection of Foreign Investment in India and Investment Treaty Arbitration*, Chapter 2.

[205] For an introduction on the New Haven School of International Law see W.M. Reisman, S. Wiessner, and A.R. Willard. 2007. 'The New Haven School: A Brief Introduction', *Yale Journal of International Law* 32: 575.

[206] M.W. Reisman. 1981. 'International Law Making: A Process of Communication', *American Society of International Law Proceedings* 75(101): 113. Also see R. Higgins. 1972. 'Diverging Anglo-American Attitudes to International Law', *Georgia Journal of International and Comparative Law* 2: 1; H.H. Koh. 2007. 'Is There a "New" New Haven School of International Law?', *Yale Journal of International Law* 32:559.

[207] Riesman, 'International Law Making', p. 113. Also see A. Bianchi. 2016. 'International Legal Theories: An Inquiry Into Different Ways of Thinking'. Oxford: Oxford University Press, pp. 91–108.

1991 that marked the adoption of a liberal foreign investment policy. The chapter also discusses some of the salient features of India's BIT programme during this phase. Chapters 4 and 5, using a positivist approach to law, map and discuss the international investment law that binds India in light of the ISDS arbitral jurisprudence. The two chapters discuss some key jurisdictional, substantive, and procedural provisions such as definition of investment, Most Favoured Nation (MFN), FET, monetary transfer provisions, expropriation, general exception provisions, and ISDS in India's BITs. Chapter 6 discusses the ISDS claims that have been brought against post 2010 that triggered the backlash against BITs, by carefully examining the reasons behind these claims. Chapter 7 maps the backlash by discussing the various developments that took place in India post the ISDS claims. In order to assess the developments pertaining to backlash, the chapter has used the Right to Information Act to collect information from the Indian government on some of the issues. Chapter 8 critically discusses the 2016 Indian Model BIT—the most significant outcome of India's decision to review its BITs post 2010. Chapter 9 offers the conclusion and argues for an investment treaty practice that is influenced by the combined normativity of embedded liberalism and the formal version of international rule of law.

PHASE I

REFUSAL

2

Economic Nationalism

Refusal to Bilateral Investment Treaties

We start our discussion by focusing on the first phase from 1947 till 1990 when India didn't undertake international treaty law obligations regarding promotion and protection of foreign investment. As discussed in Chapter 1, we first begin by discussing India's general approach towards foreign investment from 1947 till 1990. This period is further divided into two broad phases: 1947 till 1965 and 1966 till 1990[1] (Section 2.1). This period can be described as the phase of economic nationalism where the aim was that India's economic policy should serve its political policy of self-reliance and sovereignty.[2] Economic nationalists in many Third World States of Asia and Africa prescribed economic policies such as import substitution industrialization (ISI—a strategy that aims at eliminating importation of a commodity and allows for the production locally);[3]

[1] Also see Chapter 1.

[2] For more on economic nationalism as a theoretical construct see Darel E. Paul and Abla Amawi (eds). 2013. *The Theoretical Evolution of International Political Economy*. Oxford University Press, pp. 80–2.

[3] For more on this see Jagdish Bhagwati and Padma Desai. 1975. *India: Planning for Industrialization.* Oxford: Oxford University Press (hereinafter Bhagwati and Desai, *India*).

protective tariffs, and investment regulations.[4] In these phases, we see how India approached foreign investment domestically focusing on key economic and legal developments. Against this backdrop, the chapter then studies India's approach towards promotion and protection of foreign investment under international law (Section 2.2).

2.1 India's Foreign Investment Policy from 1947 till 1990

In order to study this period, as mentioned, we divide it into two phases—1947 till 1965 and 1966 till 1990.

2.1.1 1947 till 1965: Nehru's Vision, Statesmanship, and Pragmatism

India's economic vision, after independence from the British in 1947, was deeply inspired from the economic vision of India's first Prime Minister Jawaharlal Nehru. Nehru was inspired from the Soviet Union economic model with focus on heavy industry and five-year plans.[5] Nehru, in his autobiography wrote: 'I had long been drawn to socialism and communism, and Russia had appealed to me ... with all her blunders, Soviet Russia had triumphed over enormous difficulties and taken great strides towards this new order.'[6] Under Nehru's leadership, India began its economic journey by creating the Planning Commission of India in March 1950 whose job inter alia

[4] K. Vandevelde. 1998. 'The Political Economy of a Bilateral Investment Treaty', *American Journal of International Law*, 92(4): 621–41 at 622.

[5] For a discussion on Indian economy during Nehru's years, see Bhagwati and Desai, *India*; Padma Desai and JagdishBhagwati. 1975. 'Socialism and Indian Economic Policy', *World Development* 3(4):213–21 (hereinafter Desai and Bhagwati, 'Socialism and Indian Economic Policy'); Bhagwati, Jagdish and T.N. Srinivasan. 1975. *Foreign Trade Regimes and Economic Development: India*. New York: National Burea of Economic Research; Baldev Raj Nayar. 1972. *The Modernization Imperative and Indian Planning*. Delhi: Vikas Publications; Vijay Joshi and I.M.D. Little. 1994. *India: Macroeconomics and Political Economy 1961-91*. Washington DC: World Bank.

[6] Jawaharlal Nehru. 1936 (first published in 1936, republished in 2004). *An Autobiography: Toward Freedom,* New Delhi: Penguin, pp. 377–8 (hereinafter Nehru, *An Autobiography*).

was to formulate five-year plans for the most effective and balanced utilization of India's resources.[7] The first five-year plan launched in April 1951 laid down the foundations 'for achieving the socialist pattern of society'.[8] The second five-year plan took the vision of establishing a 'socialist pattern of society'.[9] The plan document clarified that the 'socialist pattern of society' meant that the basic criterion for determining the lines of advance must not be private profit but social gain.[10] The plan document also clarified that the socialist pattern of society is not to be regarded as a rigid pattern and that it is not rooted in any doctrine or dogma.[11] These five-year plans, like Soviet Russia, focused on rapid industrialization with focus on heavy or capital-intensive industry.[12] The other pivot of the industrialization strategy was on the small-scale cottage industry.[13]

An integral part of the Indian industrialization strategy during this period was planned development and ISI.[14] Of course, India was not the only country to follow planning and ISI. As Rodrik has pointed

[7] See Planning Commission. 1952. 'Introduction', *1st Five Year Plan (1951–56)*, http://planningcommission.gov.in/plans/planrel/fiveyr/index2.html, 7 December, accessed 10 March 2018.

[8] See Planning Commission.1956. 'Introduction' para 3, *2nd Five Year Plan (1956–61)*, http://planningcommission.gov.in/plans/planrel/fiveyr/index2.html, 14 May, accessed 10 March 2018 (hereinafter Planning Commission. 'Introduction', *2nd Five Year Plan (1956-61)*).

[9] See Planning Commission. 'Introduction', *2nd Five Year Plan (1956-61)*; Chapter 2.

[10] See Planning Commission. 'Introduction', *2nd Five Year Plan (1956-61)*; Chapter 2.

[11] See Planning Commission. 'Introduction', *2nd Five Year Plan (1956-61)*; Chapter 2.

[12] See Planning Commission. 'Introduction', *2nd Five Year Plan (1956-61)*; Chapter 2; Arvind Panagariya, 2008. *India: The Emerging Giant*. Oxford: Oxford University Press, p. 24 (hereinafter Panagariya, *India*).

[13] See Planning Commission. 'Introduction', *2nd Five Year Plan (1956-61)*; Chapter 2; Panagariya, *India*, p. 24.

[14] Nagesh Kumar. 1995. 'Industrialization, Liberalisation and Two Way Flows of Foreign Direct Investment: Case of India', *Economic and Political Weekly* 30(5):3228 (hereinafter Kumar, 'Industrialization, Liberalisation and Two Way Flows of Foreign Direct Investment').

out that during 1950s and 1960s planning and ISI 'were the rallying cries of economic reformers in poor nations'.[15] During this period, Indian government's policy towards industry was restrictive.[16] The three key elements of the industrial policy were—first, dominant role of the public sector in the development of heavy industry; second, private sector regulation through licensing; third, distribution and price controls.[17] The dominant role of the public sector in the Indian economy was clearly articulated by Nehru who said:

> we welcome private capital and private enterprise, but, the responsibility for development, as I said, falls on Government. In a highly developed country like America, conditions are different. But in India it has become inevitable that if we have to build on solid foundations and go up, Government must be a party to it. The public sector thus becomes very important.[18]

In short, India adopted a mixed economy focussing on self-reliance, where state ownership of vital industries was the dominant part. Thus, the public sector had a cardinal role to play. This economic philosophy was consistent with India's political goals of self-sufficiency, political independence, and national sovereignty.

A critical difference between the Indian and the Soviet economic model was that India's five-year plans were imposed on a mixed economy and not on a completely state owned economic system.[19] Moreover, as Desai and Bhagwati observe, Nehruvian socialism was guided more by a

> Fabian-type gradualism [and not on Soviet style communism relying on violent means to achieve a socialistic society] which characterized the transition to public ownership, in toto and of the key sectors … the government, through successive five-year plans, sought to increase the share of the public sector in total investment, expecting at the end

[15] Dani Rodrik. 2004. 'Growth Strategies', *NBER Working Paper Series (Working Paper 10050)*, https://drodrik.scholar.harvard.edu/files/dani-rodrik/files/growth-strategies.pdf, accessed 10 March 2018.

[16] Panagariya, *India*, p. 31.

[17] Panagariya, *India*, p. 31.

[18] Nehru, *Jawaharlal Nehru's Speeches*, Vol. 3, p. 62.

[19] Desai and Bhagwati, 'Socialism and Indian Economic Policy'.

> of such a sustained effort to raise the government's share of the capital stock to a dominant level: the approach to the Marxist goal of public ownership was thus to be asymptotic.[20]

From 1951 to 1965, the Indian economy as a whole and the Indian industry in particular grew at a healthy rate of 4.1 per cent[21] and 7.1 per cent per annum,[22] respectively, and attracted praise.[23] However, Nehru's economic model based on five-year plans also attracted criticism.[24] T.N. Srinivasan, a leading economist, critiqued the excessive focus on capital and heavy industry by arguing that 'had a greater share of investment been devoted to labour-intensive light manufacturing industries producing consumer goods to supply domestic and foreign markets, growth would have accelerated and reduced poverty much more than what was achieved during 1950-80'.[25] Similarly, Milton Friedman critiqued the Indian investment strategy that focused on two extremes, that is, capital and heavy industry,

[20] Desai and Bhagwati, 'Socialism and Indian Economic Policy', p. 213. Also important to note, as Desai and Bhagwati observe that it was the second five year plan (1956–61) that had a far great imprint of the Soviet-style planning framework than the first five year plan—see Desai and Bhagwati, 'Socialism and Indian Economic Policy', p. 214.

[21] Desai and Bhagwati, 'Socialism and Indian Economic Policy', p. 5.

[22] Bipin Chandra Pal, Aditya Mukherjee, and Mridula Mukherjee. 2008. *India Since Independence*. Delhi: Penguin, p. 450.

[23] See K.N. Raj. 1965. *Indian Economic Growth: Performance and Prospects*. New Delhi: Allied Publishers,p. 2. Also see Bhagwati and Desai, 'Socialism and Indian Economic Policy', p. 64.

[24] T.N. Srinivasan. 2011. *Growth Sustainability and India's Economic Reforms*. New Delhi: Oxford University Press (hereinafter Srinivasan, *Growth Sustainability and India's Economic Reforms*); Milton Friedman. 1955. 'A Memorandum to the Government of India', http://www.indiapolicy.org/debate/Notes/friedman.htm, accessed 10 March 2018 (hereinafter Friedman, 'A Memorandum to the Government of India'). Also see Tirthankar Roy. 2015. 'Another Look: The Economic Legacies of Colonial Rule in India', *Economic and Political Weekly* 50(15), http://www.epw.in/journal/2015/15/special-articles/economic-legacies-colonial-rule-india.html, accessed 10 March 2018.

[25] Srinivasan, *Growth Sustainability and India's Economic Reforms*. Also see Pulapre Balakrishnan. 2007. 'The Recovery of India: Economic Growth in the Nehru Era', *Economic and Political Weekly* 42(45/46):52–66.

on one hand and handicrafts on the other hand at the cost of small and moderate size industry.[26] C. Rajagopalachari and M.R. Masan who founded the Swatantra Party (the only intellectually rigorous experiment in centre-right politics in India, which sadly failed) also critiqued Nehru's economic model for imposing too many controls and quotas on businesses and free enterprises.[27]

Interestingly, notwithstanding India's restrictive policies towards the private sector, in this phase, Nehru's government had a relatively liberal and open foreign investment regime.[28] In order to understand the approach of the Nehru government on foreign investment we divide the discussion in two parts: first, general approach towards foreign investment; second, a conscious decision not to nationalize private investment including foreign investment.

2.1.1.1 General Policy on Foreign Investment

In early 1947, foreign investors, especially American investors, were concerned about the fate of their investment in newly independent India.[29] They feared nationalization of their investments.[30] On 15 December 1947, Nehru told a chamber of commerce in Calcutta

[26] Friedman, 'A Memorandum to the Government of India'. Also see B.R. Shenoy. 1955. 'A Note of Dissent on the Memorandum of the Panel of Economists', https://indiapolicy.org/debate/Notes/shenoy.PDF, accessed 10 March 2018.

[27] See the essays of C. Rajagopalachari and M.R. Masani. 1959. 'For Freedom, Farm and Family', http://indianliberals.in/uploads/periodicals/PDF_218_0mlnfkFor%20Freedom,%20Farm%20and%20Family.pdf, accessed 10 March 2018.

[28] Panagariya, *India*; Nagesh Kumar.1994. *Multinational Enterprises and Industrial Organisation: The Case of India*. New Delhi: Sage Publications; Michael Kidron. 1965. *Foreign Investment in India*. London: Oxford University Press (hereinafter Kidron, *Foreign Investment in India*); N. Kumar. 1998. 'Liberalisation and Changing Patterns of Foreign Direct Investments', *Economic and Political Weekly* 33(22):1321 (hereinafter Kumar, 'Liberalisation and Changing Patterns of Foreign Direct Investments').

[29] M. Srinivas Chary. 1995. *The Eagle and the Peacock: U.S. Foreign Policy Toward India Since Independence*. Connecticut and London: Greenwood Press, p. 46 (hereinafter Chary, *The Eagle and the Peacock*).

[30] Chary, *The Eagle and the Peacock*, p. 46.

that his government would welcome foreign capital and technical assistance.[31] Later, on 6 April 1949, Nehru himself laid down the foreign investment policy statement in the constituent assembly.[32] In this statement, Nehru noted that his government would encourage new foreign capital on mutually advantageous terms.[33] He promised 'national treatment' to foreign investors (that is, no discrimination between domestic and foreign companies) and assured foreign investors that no restrictions would be imposed on remitting profits and dividends.[34] Further, the statement noted that though majority ownership by Indians was preferred, foreign capital having control over a company for a limited period would not be objected if in national interest.[35]

Nehru's vision on foreign investment was re-articulated by his finance minister, John Mathai, who in his 1950–1 budget speech said that that 'foreign capital is necessary in this country, not merely for the purpose of supplementing our own resources, but for the purpose of instilling a spirit of confidence among our own investors'.[36] Finance minister Mathai then went on to state that it is necessary India should consider providing reasonable conditions of security

[31] Chary, *The Eagle and the Peacock*, p. 46.

[32] See Kumar, 'Industrialization, Liberalisation and Two Way Flows of Foreign Direct Investment', p. 3225; Panagariya, *India*, p. 30; A. Palit. 2009. 'India's Foreign Investment Policy: Achievements and Inadequacies', https://www.ifri.org/sites/default/files/atoms/files/av18palitfinal.pdf, accessed 10 March 2018 (hereinafter Palit, 'India's Foreign Investment Policy').

[33] Panagariya, *India*, p. 30. Also see R. Nagaraj. 2003. 'Foreign Direct Investment in India in 1990s', *Economic and Political Weekly* 38(17):1701; Kumar, 'Liberalisation and Changing Patterns of Foreign Direct Investments', p. 1321.

[34] Panagariya, *India*, p. 30; Kumar, 'Industrialization, Liberalisation and Two Way Flows of Foreign Direct Investment, p. 3229; Chary, *The Eagle and the Peacock*, p. 47. Also see Kidron, *Foreign Investment in India*.

[35] Panagariya, *India*, p. 30; Yvonne Miller. 1981. 'India's Regulation of Direct Foreign Investment: Article 29 of the 1973 Foreign Exchange Regulation Act', *Boston College Third World Law Journal* 2(1):65.

[36] John Mathai. 1950. 'Budget Speech 1950-51', http://www.indiabudget.gov.in/bspeech/bs195051.pdf, 28 February, accessed 10 March 2018, p. 8 (hereinafter Mathai, 'Budget Speech 1950-51').

and fair treatment to foreign investors who are willing to take the risk of investing their money in India.[37] Mathai, referring to Nehru's 6 April 1949 statement, said that it represents the government's policy on foreign investment.[38] Mathai, implementing Nehru's vision on foreign investment, reduced business profit-tax, personal income tax, and the rate of super-tax as applied to foreign companies and their employees.[39]

This not just showed a receptive attitude towards foreign investment but also underlined the importance of providing security and protection to foreign investment in India. The credit for this liberal stand on foreign investment goes entirely to Nehru because the 1948 Industrial Policy Resolution (IPR) had adopted a hostile tone to foreign investment.[40] The resolution said that a law be enacted to scrutinize every single foreign investment project before giving approval and that, as a rule, the major interest in ownership and effective control should always be with Indians.[41] This hostility towards foreign investment was broadly shared by Nehru's own party, that is, the Indian National Congress[42] and by the left-wing political parties.[43] Even, the Indian private sector and the capitalist class were not keen on foreign investment.[44] The *Plan of Economic Development for India*, also famously known as the 'Bombay Plan', prepared by

[37] Mathai, 'Budget Speech 1950-51'.

[38] Mathai, 'Budget Speech 1950-51'.

[39] Mathai, 'Budget Speech 1950-51'; Panagariya, *India*, p. 30.

[40] See paragraph 10 of the 1948 IPR cited in Panagariya, *India*, p. 29. Also see Sarvepalli Gopal. 1984. *Jawaharlal Nehru: A Biography*. Cambridge: Harvard University Press, pp. 96–9.

[41] Panagariya, *India*, p. 29.

[42] For example, the Economic Reform Committee of the All India Congress Committee in its 1948 report had called for a careful examination of foreign capital should so as to ensure that the economic controls remain with the nationals of India.

[43] Panagariya, *India*, p. 29.

[44] See Sanjaya Baru. 2015. 'The Economic Imperatives Shaping Indian Foreign Policy', in *The Oxford Handbook of Indian Foreign Policy*, David M. Malone, C. Raja Mohan, and Srinath Raghavan (eds), p. 328. Oxford: Oxford University Press (hereinafter Baru, 'The Economic Imperatives Shaping Indian Foreign Policy').

leading Indian industrialists like J.R.D. Tata and G.D. Birla in 1945 asked the government to step in and fill the investment gap rather than allow foreign direct investment and gave preference to external loans and foreign aid instead of foreign investment.[45] But Nehru, the statesman, while announcing the foreign investment policy statement on 6 April 1949 significantly diluted the 1948 IPR. Nehru was pragmatic enough to understand that foreign investment was critical for India to plug the savings gap and to bring in valuable foreign exchange.

In the second five-year plan, in 1957, foreign investment was further liberalized by the government giving a host of concessions and incentives to foreign investors in order to attract foreign exchange.[46] In 1961, the Indian Investment Centre (IIC) was set up with offices in major investor countries to promote foreign investments in India. At the beginning of the third five-year plan in 1961, the Indian government issued a list of industries where foreign investment was welcome.[47] This included some industries that were reserved for the public sector like drugs, fertilizer, synthetic rubber, and aluminum.[48] In 1961, according to Kidron's estimates, at least two-fifths of the organized large-scale sector and one-fourth of the entire modern sector in India was under foreign investment.[49] This claim is corroborated by the fact that the FDI stock in India, from 1948 to 1964, more than doubled from Rs 2560 million to Rs 5665

[45] Baru, 'The Economic Imperatives Shaping Indian Foreign Policy'. On the 'Bombay Plan' also see Vivek Chibber. 2011. *Locked in Place: State-Building and Late Industrialization in India*. New Jersey, Princeton University Press, p. 235 (hereinafter Chibber, *Locked in Place*).

[46] Kumar, 'Industrialization, Liberalisation and Two Way Flows of Foreign Direct Investment', p. 3225; Kumar, 'Liberalisation and Changing Patterns of Foreign Direct Investments', p. 1321.

[47] Kumar, 'Industrialization, Liberalisation and Two Way Flows of Foreign Direct Investment', p. 3225; Kumar, 'Liberalisation and Changing Patterns of Foreign Direct Investments', p. 1321.

[48] Kumar, 'Industrialization, Liberalisation and Two Way Flows of Foreign Direct Investment', p. 3225; Kumar, 'Liberalisation and Changing Patterns of Foreign Direct Investments', p. 1321

[49] John Adams. 1967. 'Review of *Foreign Investments in India* by Michael Kidron', *The Journal of Asian Studies* 26(3): 509 at 510.

million.[50] The protection that India accorded to local manufacture played an important role in giving India a locational advantage that encouraged market-seeking FDI.[51]

Thus, Nehru's India was not opposed to foreign investment despite coming out of colonial rule of 200 years. Foreign capital was welcome if it could assist in India's development and help the Indian private sector. This approach of Nehru was consistent with the approach of an economic nationalist that foreign investment is welcome if it promotes the political goals of national independence and economic development.[52] Nehru's approach to foreign investment was guided by economic pragmatism and not by some doctrinaire belief. In pure economic terms, once development of heavy industries was considered absolutely necessary for a country's development and since the country was running short on capital, allowing foreign investment became imperative.[53] But, this does not mean that India embraced foreign investment during this period, in the same way, India did post 1991.[54] Nehru was also aware of the complications that foreign capital could give rise to in a newly independent country.[55]

2.1.1.2 Nehru's Views on Nationalization

An integral aspect of Nehru's economic vision was the absence of large scale, ideology-driven nationalization of private, domestic, and foreign investment. It is interesting to note that in 1947, the Economic Programme Committee of the All India Congress Committee had

[50] Kumar, 'Industrialization, Liberalisation and Two Way Flows of Foreign Direct Investment', p. 3225.

[51] Kumar, 'Industrialization, Liberalisation and Two Way Flows of Foreign Direct Investment', p. 3225. Also see Panagariya, *India*, p. 31. Also see Chibber, *Locked in Place*, p. 235.

[52] See Vandevelde. *Bilateral Investment Treaties*, p. 77.

[53] I am grateful to my colleague, Debdtata Saha, from faculty of economics at the South Asian University for bringing this point to my attention.

[54] See Chapter 3 for discussion on role of foreign investment in India post 1991.

[55] Jawaharlal Nehru. 1958. *Jawaharlal Nehru's Speeches, 1953-57*. New Delhi: Publications Division, Government of India, p. 82 (hereinafter Nehru, *Jawaharlal Nehru's Speeches, 1953-57*).

decided that for exisiting undertakings in India the process of transfer from private to public ownership would commence after five years.[56] This position met with stiff resistance from the Indian capitalist class.[57] Due to these concerns, the 1948 Industrial Policy Resolution made some changes on the policy on nationalization.[58] The policy said that the issue of nationalization would be dealt after 10 years on the basis of circumstances existing at that time.[59]

On 17 February 1948, Nehru in a speech to the Constituent Assembly made a case against nationalization by saying that 'if we squander our resources in merely acquiring for the state existing industries … for the moment we may have no other resources left, and we would have spoiled the field for private enterprise too. So, it is far better for the state to concentrate on certain specific, vital, new industries, than go about nationalizing many of the old ones'.[60]

Nehru expessed his disliking for nationalization on many occasions. For example, in a letter Nehru wrote to the chief ministers on 3 March 1953, he said:

> [A]s for nationalization, the real test is how far this adds to our productive capacity as well as to the smoother working of our Plan. Mere nationalization does not add to that productive capacity much, if it all. It might indeed mean a lessening of it. At the most it means a transfer of ownership with the same production and the available resources being utilized for compensation. It is far better to use our resources for new State enterprises, leaving the old ones to carry on as they are, subject to some kind of control by the State. Thus production grows and the public sector grows till it becomes the dominant sector.[61]

[56] Bipin Chandra, Mridula Mukherjee, and Aditya Mukherjee. 2008. *India Since Independence*. Penguin, p. 446 (hereinafter Chandra, Mukherjee, and Mukherjee, *India since Independence*).

[57] Chandra, Mukherjee, and Mukherjee, *India since Independence*, p. 446.

[58] Chandra, Mukherjee, and Mukherjee, *India since Independence*, p. 446.

[59] Chandra, Mukherjee, and Mukherjee, *India since Independence*, p. 446.

[60] Cited in Jagdish Bhagwati and Arvind Panagariya. 2012. *India's Tryst with Destiny*. London: Harper Collins, p. 3. Also see the Report of the Economic Affairs Committee of the All Indian Congress Committee.1948. https://www.scribd.com/document/89345357/Economic-Programme-Committee-Report-1948.

[61] Nehru's letter dated 3 March 1953 cited in Ramachandra Guha. 2012. *Makers of Modern India*. Penguin: New Delhi, pp. 337–8.

Nehru also expressed his anguish at how some political leaders in India loosely used words like confiscation and expropriation of private proprety utterly disregarding the constitutional provisions. During the discussions on the fourth amendment, on right to property, to the Indian Constitution (discussed later in the chapter), Nehru speaking in the Parliament, reminded his fellow parliamentarians that 'it is odd that words like confiscation of property and expropriation are thrown about when actually what the Constitution—or the amended Constitution, if you amend it—says is that there will be no such thing except by law and except on payment of compensation'.[62]

Nehru's views against nationalization was not just limited to domestic investment but also extended to foreign capital. During the discussions on the fourth amendment of the Constitution on right to property (discussed later in the chapter), Nehru made it very clear that his government was against nationalization of foreign investment. Nehru said in the parliament:

> I am surprised to hear the proposal being put forward repeatedly that we must confiscate or expropriate foreign capital. I cannot imagine anything more thoughtless and unrealistic; it has no relation to reality ... Let us not ... pursue this talk of expropriating foreign capital; it is not worth it. We are not such a poor country as to go about indulging in tactics which will lose us the goodwill and the credit of the world, and which will, perhaps, leave a feeling of wrong-doing in our minds and hearts.[63]

Desai and Bhagwati argue that since Nehru's approach towards socialism was Fabian-type gradualism, 'nationalizations of existing capital stock were de facto ruled out'.[64]

Earlier, Nehru had also assured foreign investors that if and when foreign enterprises are compulsorily acquired, compensation would be paid on a fair and equitable basis.[65] Furthermore, Nehru said that in case of such expropriation, necessary facilities would be

[62] Nehru, *Jawaharlal Nehru's Speeches (1953-57)*, p. 125.

[63] Nehru, *Jawaharlal Nehru's Speeches (1953-57)*, p. 131.

[64] Desai and Bhagwati, 'Socialism and Indian Economic Policy', p. 213.

[65] Granville Austin. 2001. *The Indian Constitution: Cornerstone of a Nation.* New Delhi: Oxford University Press, p. 95.

made available to foreign investors for remitting their money back home.[66]

Consequently, barring some instances, foreign investment was not nationalized in India during this phase.[67] The few instances of nationalization of foreign investment involved were as follows. First, the Imperial Bank of India, which had 10 per cent British shareholders, was nationalized in 1955 in order to spread banking services.[68] The compensation that was awarded to these shareholders in this case was three-times the original capital[69] paid fully in cash.[70] To the Indian shareholders the compensation was paid partly in cash and partly in government-owned bonds.[71] Second, India nationalized life insurance business in 1956 to spread insurance services to the entire population[72] that affected foreign insurers who were doing business in India.[73] Like in the case of imperial bank nationalization, a robust method for paying compensation was designed and implemented 'so as to dispel fears of confiscatory tendencies'.[74] Third, the decision of the Mysore government (a state within India from 1948 to 1956 that later became part of the state of Karnataka), to nationalize Kolar Gold mines, which were under the management of a British Company,

[66] See Constituent Assembly Debates, 10 September 1949, https://indiankanoon.org/doc/1127370/, accessed 10 March 2018.

[67] See S.C. Jain. 1983. *Nationalisation of Foreign Property, A Study in North-South Dialogue*. New Delhi: Deep and Deep Publications, pp. 236–41 (hereinafter Jain, *Nationalisation of Foreign Property*); S. Rao. 2000. 'Bilateral Investment Promotion Agreements: A Legal Framework for the Protection of Foreign Investments', *Commonwealth Law Bulletin* 26:623–4 (hereinafter Rao, 'Bilateral Investment Promotion Agreements').

[68] Jain, *Nationalisation of Foreign Property*, p. 236.

[69] M.J. Kust 1964. *Foreign Enterprise in India: Law and Polices*. Bombay: Chapel Hill, p. 102 (hereinafter Kust, *Foreign Enterprise in India*).

[70] Jain, *Nationalisation of Foreign Property*, p. 236.

[71] Jain, *Nationalisation of Foreign Property*, p. 236.

[72] Life Insurance (Emergency Provisions) Act, 1956.

[73] See K.N. Kabra. 1986. 'Nationalisation of Life Insurance in India', *Economic and Political Weekly*, 21(47):2045–53 (hereinafter Kabra. 'Nationalisation of Life Insurance in India').

[74] Kabra. 'Nationalisation of Life Insurance in India', p. 2051.

John Taylor and Sons Ltd.[75] The compensation was based on the market value of the company's shares though on the intervention of the central government, the Mysore government paid a higher compensation.[76]

In sum, Nehru's speeches and statements show that India consciously decided not to expropriate foreign investment. Even if it did, in some cases, it was based on public interest, following a legal process and after payment of compensation. India's approach towards nationalization of foreign investment was very different from the approach countries like Soviet Russia[77] and China[78] followed where foreign investment was expropriated by the state without compensation or restitution in violation of international law.[79] The Chinese approach to nationalization of foreign investment, as part of the 1949 Communist revolution, was that the right to nationalize foreign property was an inherent attribute of national territorial sovereignty, and

[75] *Economic and Political Weekly*. 1995. 'Weekly Notes', *Economic and Political Weekly* 7(29, 16 July): 840.

[76] Jain, *Nationalisation of Foreign Property*, p. 236. Also see Kust, *Foreign Enterprise in India*, p. 102; Kidron, *Foreign Investment in India*, p. 135.

[77] The Second All-Russian Congress of Soviets abolished private property in land without compensation through a decree issued on 26 October 2017—see B.A. Wortely. 1959. *Expropriation in Public International Law*. Cambridge: Cambridge University Press, p. 61 (hereinafter Wortley, *Expropriation in Public International Law*). See generally, J.W. Salacuse. 2015. *The Law of Investment Treaties*. Oxford: Oxford University Press, pp. 72–5.

[78] Qingjiang Kong. 1998. 'Bilateral Investment Treaties: The Chinese Approach and Practice', *Asian Yearbook of International Law* 8:105 (hereinafter Kong, 'Bilateral Investment Treaties'); See L.A. Pinard. 1984. 'United States Policy Regarding the Nationalization of American Investments: The People's Republic of China's Nationalization Decree of 1950', *California Western International Law Journal* 14:148. Stephan W. Schill. 2007. 'Tearing down the Great Wall: The New Generation Investment Treaties of the People's Republic of China', *Cardozo J. Int'l & Comp. L.* 15:73 (hereinafter Schill, 'Tearing down the Great Wall').

[79] The Second All-Russian Congress of Soviets abolished private property in land without compensation through a decree issued on 26 October 2017—see Wortely, *Expropriation in Public International Law*. See generally Salacuse, *The Law of Investment Treaties*.

that the exercise of this fundamental right was not subject to any pre-condition such as public purpose, due process, and compensation.[80]

Thus, while Nehru was inspired by the Soviet Union economic model and was sympathetic to China,[81] he was also fully aware of the excesses of communist regimes.[82] The fact that the Indian approach to foreign investment differed from China is even more remarkable in view of the fact both India and China, as Sornarajah argues, 'shared [a] colonial experience in which foreign investment and international trade were the basis of subsequent political domination'.[83] Yet, Nehru's economic pragmatism and visionary leadership, rather than belief in a dogma or an ideology, ensured that Indian approach to foreign investment promotion and protection differed from China.[84]

India's commitment towards protecting private property was evident from the fact that the right to property was given the status of a

[80] Kong, 'Bilateral Investment Treaties'. Also see Schill, 'Tearing down the Great Wall', pp. 77–8. For a detailed comparative perspective on India and China's approach towards international law see Prabhakar Singh. 2015. 'Sino–Indian Attitudes to International Law: Of Nations, States and Colonial Hangovers', *The Chinese Journal of Comparative Law* 3(2):348–74.

[81] Guy Arnold. 2016. *The Third World Handbook*. London: Bloomsbury, p. 81. Nehru even supported the admission of China to the UN Security Council. For an insightful analysis see Nabarun Roy. 2017. 'In the Shadow of Great Power Politics: Why Nehru Supported PRC's Admission to the Security Council', *The International History Review* 40(2):376–96.

[82] Nehru in his autobiography writes,'I dislike also much that has happened in Russia, and especially the excessive use of violence in normal times'—Nehru, *An Autobiography*, p. 610.

[83] M. Sornarajah. 2010. 'India, China and Foreign Investment', in *China, India and the International Economic Order*M. Sornarajah and Jiangyu Wang (eds), p. 135. Cambridge: Cambridge University Press (hereinafter Sornarajah, 'India, China and Foreign Investment').

[84] For a general comparison between India and China on the issue of foreign investment see Sornarajah, 'India, China and Foreign Investment'; Prabhash Ranjan. 2015. 'Bilateral Investment Treaties and Right to Health: Comparing Chinese and Indian BITs', in *Socio Economic Rights In Emerging Free Markets—Comparative Perspectives From India And China*,S. Deva (ed.), pp. 236–61. London: Routledge.

fundamental right under the Indian Constitution in 1950.[85] Article 19(1) (f) of the Indian Constitution as originally enacted in 1950 guaranteed the fundamental right to every citizen to acquire, hold, and dispose property.[86] Additionally, the Constitution contained Articles 31(1) and 31(2) (which provided protection to property from unlawful deprivation and extended to both citizens and non-citizens)[87] as originally enacted were in the following terms:

(1) No Person shall be deprived of his property save by authority of law.
(2) No property, movable or immovable, including any interest in, or in any company owning any commercial or industrial undertaking, shall be taken possession of or acquired for public purposes under any law authorising the taking of such possession or such acquisition, unless the law provides for compensation for the property taken possession of or acquired and either fixes the amount of the compensation, or specifies the principles on which, and the manner in which, the compensation is to be determined and given.[88]

Right to property and protection from unlawful deprivation of property were fundamental rights till 1978. The period from 1950 till

[85] For a discussion on right to property under Indian Constitution, see Pradyumna K. Tripathi. 1972. *Some Insights into Fundamental Rights*. Bombay: University of Bombay, pp. 211–306; Mahendra Pal Singh. 2008. *V.N. Shukla's Constitution of India*, 11 edition. New Delhi: Eastern Book Co New Delhi, pp. 273–301 (hereinafter Singh, *V.N. Shukla's Constitution of India*); Tom Allen. 2007. 'Property as a Fundamental Right in India, Europe and South Africa', *Asia-Pacific Law Review* 15(2): 193–218; Granville Austin. 1999. *The Indian Constitution: Cornerstone of a Nation*. Oxford: Oxford University Press, pp. 87–99. NamitaWahi. 2015. 'The Fundamental Right to Property in the Indian Constitution', 10 August, http://dx.doi.org/10.2139/ssrn.2661212, accessed 10 March 2018 (hereinafter Wahi, 'The Fundamental Right to Property in the Indian Constitution').

[86] See Singh, *V.N. Shukla's Constitution of India*, pp. 155–7.

[87] See Chief Justice of India Patanjali Sastry in *State of West Bengal* v. *Subodh Gopal Bose*, AIR 1954 SC 92.

[88] The Article also had sub-clauses (3), (4), (5), and (6), which are not mentioned here—See Singh (2008), 274–5.

1978 saw six amendments to right to property.[89] Post 1978, right to property is recognized in the Indian Constitution as a constitutional right in Article 300A.[90]

The requirement to pay compensation, if the state takes property, was part of the fundamental right to property as mentioned in Article 31(2), as originally enacted. The provision mentioned that compensation has to be paid if the state acquired the property. However, the word 'compensation' was not qualified by any adjective like 'just or equivalent'. Notwithstanding this, the Supreme Court of India in cases before 1955 held that the word 'compensation' meant just and equivalent compensation.[91] These rulings triggered the fourth amendment in 1955 which made adequacy of compensation non-justiciable.[92]

Notwithstanding this, the Supreme Court of India continued to exercise the power of judicial review on the issue of compensation although in a different form. In cases after the fourth amendment, the Supreme Court held that although the quantum of compensation was not justiciable, the principles on which compensation was based were.[93] However, there was a difference. Some cases like *Vajravelu* v. *Special Deputy Collector* and *Union of India* v. *Metal Corporation of India* held that the principles on which compensation was based should provide for 'just equivalent' and only if the principles provide for such compensation they will be outside the pale of judicial

[89] For detailed discussion on this see Singh, *V.N. Shukla's Constitution of India*, pp. 283–8.

[90] The Forty Fourth Constitutional Amendment, 1978, deleted Articles 19(1)(f) and 31 from Part III, the chapter on Fundamental Rights in the Constitution.

[91] *State of West Bengal* v. *Bella Banerjee,* AIR 1954 SC 170; *State of Madras* v. *D Namasivaya Mudaliar,* AIR 1965 SC 190. This is despite the fact that the Constitutional Assembly debates made it clear that the legislature was the final authority on adequacy of compensation—S.P. Sathe. 1970. 'Right to Private Property', *Economic and Political Weekly* 5(18): 743 (hereinafter Sathe, 'Right to Private Property').

[92] Sathe, 'Right to Private Property', p. 743.

[93] See *Vajravelu* v. *Special Deputy Collector,* AIR 1965 SC 1017; *Union of India v Metal Corporation of India,* AIR 1967 SC 637; *State of Gujrat* v. *Shantilal Mangaldas and others,* AIR 1969 SC 634.

scrutiny. This was not followed in *State of Gujrat* v. *Shantilal*, where it was held that as long as principles provided for compensation and the compensation was not illusory, the court could not intervene. However, the earlier line was resurrected in *RC Cooper* v. *Union of India* by the Supreme Court.[94] Although these cases did not involve foreign investment per se, yet useful to throw light on issues pertaining to compensation for expropriation.

2.1.2 1966 to 1990: Indira Gandhi's Protectionism and Left-wing Populism

Nehru, after serving as India's prime minister for 17 years died on 27 May 1964. After Nehru's death, for a very short period of 13 days, Gulzarilal Nanda became India's prime minister. He was succeeded by Lal Bahadur Shastri who became the prime minister on 9 June 1964. Sadly, Shastri passed away on 11 January 1966. After Shastri's sudden death, Indira Gandhi, Nehru's daughter, became the prime minister on 24 January 1966 and remained in office till 24 March 1977. She became the prime minister again in 1980 and remained in office till 1984 when she was assassinated. Her politics and economics were to shape India's trajectory for the next two decades including India's foreign investment policy. In order to study the period, we divide this discussion into two phases: 1966 to 1980 and 1981 to 1990.

2.1.2.1 1966 to 1980

In order to understand Indira Gandhi's economics, it is critical to understand her politics briefly. In the 1967 general elections, the Congress party received a major setback. Although it managed a majority on its own, the total number of seats it won in the Lok

[94] On these cases also see H.M. Seervai. 1967. *Constitutional Law of India: A Critical Commentary*. New Delhi: Universal Law Publishing Co. Ltd., pp. 359–60; Singh (2008), 284–6; M.P. Jain. 2003. *Indian Constitutional Law*. Nagpur: Wadhwa, pp. 1483–8; Sathe, 'Right to Private Property'; S.P. Sathe. 1971. 'Supreme Court, Parliament and Constitution-II', *Economic and Political Weekly* 6(35): 1873.

Sabha (the lower house of the Indian Parliament) came down to 283 from 361 in the 1962 general elections. Due to this electoral setback and other reasons, Indira Gandhi altered her economic approach to win back support.[95] She consciously adopted the 'language of socialism' (or more appropriately the language of populism), which she believed was the only language the general masses wanted to hear.[96] This radical leftward shift led to differences between the members of the Congress party leading to a split in the party in 1969.[97] Post 1969, Indira Gandhi could remain in power only with the help of communist parties and some other regional parties, which, in turn, heightened her radical leftward shift in her policies.[98]

Like a true populist she didn't have much faith in institutions (judiciary, free press, etc.) that, in any liberal democracy, perform the critical role of imposing checks on abuse of public power by the executive. She believed in speaking directly to the electorate. She coined populist slogans like '*garibi hatao*' (remove poverty) to capture the imagination of the general population. In order to strengthen her populist appeal, Indira Gandhi even went to the extent of amending the Consutution. The 26th Constitutional amendment to abolish privy purses—constitutionally guaranteed stipends to the rulers of India's former princely states—is a case in point. True to her populist instincts she justified reneging on this important constitutional promise[99] in the name of creating equal rights for all citizens. The fact that this constitutional amendment was brought about after the Supreme Court had declared the de-recognition of all princely state rulers, attempted through a Presidential order, by Indira Gandhi's government in 1970 illegal,[100] speaks volumes about her respect for institutions.

[95] Sunil Khilnani. 2016. *Incarnations: A Hisotry of India in 50 Lives*. India: BBC and Penguin, pp. 385–6 (hereinafter Khilnani, *Incarnations*).

[96] Khilnani, *Incarnations*.

[97] Chandra, Mukherjee, and Mukherjee, *India since Independence*, p. 459.

[98] Chandra, Mukherjee, and Mukherjee, *India since Independence*, p. 459.

[99] See Arvind P. Datar. 2013. 'Who Betrayed Sardar Patel?', *The Hindu*, 19 November.

[100] H. H. Maharajadhiraja Madhav Rao v. Union of India on 15 December, 1971 AIR 530.

The populist and socialist rhetoric she adopted paid her rich electoral dividends as she handsomely won the 1971 general elections.[101] Unlike Nehru, who believed in decentralization and evolving consensus through democratic means, his daughter was a polarizing and an authoritarian figure. She believed in centralizing power. This tendency to centralize power reached its pinnacle when Indira Gandhi imposed national emergency in the country in 1975 supsending civil and political liberties—the same liberties that people of India had obtained after a long freedom struggle against the British.

During this entire period, India took a more conscious shift towards protectionism based on inward-looking economic policies.[102] Unlike Nehru's pragmatism, Indira Gandhi made a decisive shift towards adopting socialist economic policies guided by a heavy dose of populism. This included going on a nationalizing spree. Her nationalization campaign started with the managerial takeover of a private company called Jayanti Shipping Company in 1966[103] followed by complete acquisition in 1971.[104] For political reasons, she nationalized banks in 1969.[105] In fact, nationalization of banks was part of her socialist agenda laid down in the ten-point programme in 1967, aiming at redistribution of income. It also included nationalization of insurance, curbing monopolies, and imposing urban land ceiling.[106] True to this programme, as Shubhankar Dam so lucidly writes,[107]

[101] Chandra, Muherjee and Mukherjee 459, Khilnani, 386–7.

[102] Kumar, 'Liberalisation and Changing Patterns of Foreign Direct Investments', p. 1322. Also see Palit,'India's Foreign Investment Policy', pp. 6–7.

[103] The Jayanti Shipping Company (Taking Over of Management) Act 1966.

[104] Jayanti Shipping Company (Acquisition of Shares) Act, 1971

[105] I.G. Patel. 2002. *Glimpses of Indian Economic Policy: An Insider's View*. New Delhi: Oxford University Press, p. 135. See Banking Companies (Acquisition and Transfer of Undertakings) Act, 1970. Also see *Rustom Cavasjee Cooper* v. *Union of India*, AIR 1970 SC 564 (hereinafter *Cooper* v. *Union of India*) popularly known as the Bank Nationalization case.

[106] Shruti Rajagopalan. 2016. 'Constitutional Change: A Public Choice Analysis', in *The Oxford Handbook of the Indian Constitution*, Madhav Khosla, Sujit Choudhry, Pratap Bhanu Mehta (eds), p. 136. Oxford: Oxford University Press.

[107] Shubhankar Dam. 2015. *Presidential Legislation in India*. Cambridge: Cambridge University Press, pp. 76–8 (hereinafter Dam, *Presidential Legislation in India*).

from 1966 till 1976, Indira Gandhi's government passed as many as 20 ordinances,[108] later enacted as legislations, nationalizing a host of private sectors such as coal mines,[109] copper,[110] textiles,[111] wagons,[112] iron,[113] and cotton.[114] Arvind Panagariya rightly describes this period as a phase where socialism struck with vengeance.[115]

As part of this socialist plan of redistribution of income, another development in this period was the enactment of the 25th constitutional amendment Act to keep adequacy of compensation outside the jurisdiction of courts. Thus, there was clearly an attempt not just to nationalize private business like banks but also to ensure that adequacy of compensation was outside the judicial scrutiny of courts. Finally, in 1978, the 44th constitutional amendment Act robbed 'right to property' of its fundamental right status and made it a constitutional right as part of Article 300A of the Indian Constitution.

While the Nehru government had nationalized only life insurance and left out general insurance, Indira Gandhi nationalized general insurance in 1972, purportedly to serve the needs of the economy better and to prohibit concentration of economic wealth in the hands of a few.[116] Under the General Insurance Nationalisation Act, 52 foreign insurer companies were nationalized.[117] Also, just before

[108] Dam, *Presidential Legislation in India*, p. 77.

[109] Coking Coal Mines (Nationalisation) Act 1972; Coal Mines (Taking Over of Management) Act, 1973; Coal.

Mines (Nationalisation) Act, 1973. Also see *Sanjeev Coke Manufacturing* v. *Bharat Coking Coal Ltd,* 1983 AIR 239.

[110] Indian Copper Corporation (Acquisition of Undertaking) Act 1972.

[111] Sick Textile Undertakings (Nationalisation) Act 1974. Also see *Minerva Mills Ltd. & others* v. *Union Of India & others,* 1980 AIR 1789.

[112] The Burn Company and Indian Standard Wagon Company (Nationalisation) Act, 1976.

[113] The Indian Iron And Steel Company (Acquisition Of Shares) Act, 1976.

[114] The Laxmirattan and Atherton West Cotton Mills (taking over of management) Act, 1976. Also see *National Textiles Corporation (South Maharashtra) Limited* v. *Tamil Nadu Co-operative Marketing Federation Ltd.*, AIR 1998 SC 2658.

[115] Panagariya, *India*, pp. 47–67.

[116] General Insurance Business (Nationalisation) Act 1972. See Section 2 of the Act.

[117] Jain, *Nationalisation of Foreign Property*, p. 237.

this nationalization, the 25th Constitutional Amendment Act was enacted that substituted the word 'compensation' in Article 31(2) with the word 'amount' and it expressly ousted judicial review of the adequacy of compensation. This amendment was enacted specifically to overturn the Supreme Court ruling in the bank nationalization case[118] that held that the court has the power of judicial review in cases where compensation offered for expropriation was illusory.[119] As Jain writes, subsequent to these amendments, some foreign investors were not happy with the compensation given by the Indian government.[120] Another major sector that was nationalized during this phase was oil.[121] This impacted three foreign oil companies—Burmah-Shell, ESSO, and Caltex.[122] According to Jain, compensation given to these companies was based on mutual negotiations.[123]

As part of this broader economic strategy based on socialistic, populist, and nationalistic criteria, the receptive attitude towards foreign investment, that India exhibited during Nehru's time, also started to change in the late 1960s. Under Indira Gandhi's leadership, India started adopting a hostile policy towards foreign investment. This was evident in the fourth five-year plan document that said:

> [I]t is necessary to subject every proposal for foreign collaboration to fairly rigid tests. Import of foreign know-how particularly in sophisticated industrial fields would continue to be required. Even here, it would be essential to make simultaneous efforts for the adaptation of

[118] Wahi, 'The Fundamental Right to Property in the Indian Constitution'.

[119] Wahi, 'The Fundamental Right to Property in the Indian Constitution'. See *Cooper* v. *Union of India*.

[120] Jain, *Nationalisation of Foreign Property*, p. 237.

[121] The Esso (Acquisition Of Undertakings In India) Act, 1974; The Burmah Shell (Acquisition Of Undertakings In India) Act, 1976; The Caltex (acquisition of shares of Caltex oil refining (India) limited Act, 1977.

[122] The Esso (Acquisition Of Undertakings In India) Act, 1974; The Burmah Shell (Acquisition Of Undertakings In India) Act, 1976; The Caltex (acquisition of shares of Caltex oil refining (India) limited Act, 1977. Saumitra Chaudhury. 1977. 'Nationalisation of Oil Companies in India', *Economic and Political Weekly* 12(10): 437–44.

[123] Jain, *Nationalisation of Foreign Property*, p. 239.

> such know-how through indigenous effort and to improve on it to avoid the need for future purchases.[124]

For these purposes, a new agency called the Foreign Investment Board (FIB) was set up to deal with all foreign investment or collaboration cases with up to 40 per cent equity.[125] Proposals with more than 40 per cent equity were to be screened by a cabinet committee.[126] To assist the FIB, a list was drawn up of industries and products where foreign investment may be allowed or not permitted.[127] Restrictions were imposed on FDI proposals that didn't involve transfer of technology.[128] The government also imposed restrictions on renewals of foreign collaboration agreements.[129]

Some new laws that imposed controls on private businesses was also enacted. For example, in 1969, India enacted a Monopolies and Restrictive Trade Practices Act, which gave the government sweeping powers to regulate big businesses.[130] It had an adverse impact on the growth of industry since it defined monopoly in terms of

[124] Government of India. 1970. *Fourth Five-Year Plan 1969*, Chapter 14, http://planningcommission.nic.in/plans/planrel/fiveyr/index4.html, 18 July.

[125] Kumar, 'Industrialization, Liberalisation and Two Way Flows of Foreign Direct Investment', p. 3225; Panagariya, *India*, p. 60; A.V. Desai. 1993. 'Output and Employment Effects of Recent Policy Changes', in *Recent Developments in Indian Economy* Uma Kapila (ed), p. 124. Delhi: Academic Foundation.

[126] Kumar, 'Industrialization, Liberalisation and Two Way Flows of Foreign Direct Investment', p. 3225.

[127] Desai, 'Output and Employment Effects of Recent Policy Changes', p. 124. Kumar, 'Industrialization, Liberalisation and Two Way Flows of Foreign Direct Investment', pp. 3229–30; Panagariya, *India*, p. 60.

[128] Kumar, 'Industrialization, Liberalisation and Two Way Flows of Foreign Direct Investment', p. 3230.

[129] Kumar, 'Industrialization, Liberalisation and Two Way Flows of Foreign Direct Investment', p. 3230.

[130] Panagariya, *India*, p. 60; N. Nanda. 2009. 'The Indian Growth Story: Myths and Realities', *Journal of Asian and African Studies* 44(6):750 (hereinafter Nanda, 'The Indian Growth Story'). *Tata Engineering and Locomotive Co. Ltd.* v. *The Registrar of the Restrictive Trade Agreement* (1977) 2 SCC 55; *Mahindra and Mahindra Ltd.* v. *Union of India (UOI) and another* (1979) 2 SCC 529.

size[131] irrespective of the effect on the market and even if the size and market share of the firm concerned were small by world standards.[132] Similarly, India enacted a new Patents Act in 1970 which abolished 'product' patent in foods, chemicals and drugs; thus, only patents relating to the methods or processes of manufacture of such substances could be obtained.[133]

As Panagariya argues, these restrictions begun to choke off the inflow of foreign investment and technology to India.[134] Further damage to foreign investment came with enactment of the Foreign Exchange Regulation Act (FERA) in 1973.[135] Foreign Exchange Regulation Act greatly tightened the regulatory regime on foreign capital in India.[136] The law required all non-bank foreign branches and companies incorporated in India that had foreign equity share in excess of 40 per cent could do business in India only if they obtained permission from the RBI.[137] This permission was granted by the RBI only if foreign branches and companies diluted their foreign equity share to 40 per cent or less than that.[138] However,

[131] Section 2(d) of the MRTP Act defined a 'dominant undertaking' as an undertaking which, by itself or along with inter-connected undertakings produces, supplies, distributes or otherwise controls not less than one-fourth of the total goods that are produced, supplied or distributed in India or any substantial part thereof.

[132] Nanda., 'The Indian Growth Story', p. 740. Also see Aditya Bhattacharjea. 2002. 'Trade, Investment and Competition Policy: An Indian Perspective', in *India and the WTO* Aaditya Matto et al. (eds), pp. 203–04. Washington DC: World Bank and Oxford University Press.

[133] See Section 5 of the Indian Patent Act 1970 now omitted by the 2005 amendment. For more on this see Shamnad Basheer. 2005. 'India's Tryst with TRIPS: The Patents (Amendment) Act, 2005', *Indian Journal of Law and Technology* 1:15.

[134] Panagariya, *India*, p. 61.

[135] On FERA 1973, see S. Chaudhary. 1979. 'FERA: Appearance and Reality', *Economic and Political Weekly* 14(16):734 (hereinafter Chaudhary, 'FERA: Appearance and Reality'); Panagariya, *India*, p. 61.

[136] P. Agrawal. 2002. 'Economic Impact of Foreign Direct Investment in South Asia', in *A Handbook*, NernardHoekman, Aaditya Mattoo, and Philip English (eds), pp. 119–120. Washington, DC: World Bank.

[137] Panagariya, *India*, p. 61.

[138] Panagariya, *India*, p. 61; Kumar, 'Liberalisation and Changing Patterns of Foreign Direct Investments', p. 1322.

some foreign investments, such as companies operating in high-technology sectors or companies engaged in manufacturing and exporting 60 per cent or more of its output, were not subject to the 40 per cent rule.[139] As a result of this law, a large number of foreign companies such as British Paints (India), Reckitt and Colman, Godfrey Philips, Cadbury India, Otis Elevator, etc., diluted their stake.[140] Companies that didn't dilute their stake to 40 per cent or less or didn't fall in one of the exceptions to the 40 per cent rule were not given 'national treatment', that is, treatment equal to domestic investment.[141] Two leading American corporations, IBM and Coca Cola, were asked by the RBI to stop their operations in India for failing to comply with FERA.[142] Foreign Exchange Regulation Act also led to 52 other firms winding up their operations in India.[143] As a result, of these regulatory measures strangulating foreign investment, the FDI stock in India increased marginally from Rs 9,160 million in March 1974 to Rs 9,332 million in March 1980.[144] The Gross Domestic Product growth rate of India fell to

[139] Kumar, 'Liberalisation and Changing Patterns of Foreign Direct Investments', p. 1322; Panagariya, *India*, p. 61.

[140] See Chaudhary, 'FERA: Appearance and Reality', p. 737, which gives the list of companies that diluted their stake.

[141] Industrial Policy 23 December 1977, Department of Industrial Development, Ministry of Industry. Also see Section 29 of FERA.

[142] Chaudhary, 'FERA: Appearance and Reality', p. 734. Also see Kumar, 'Liberalisation and Changing Patterns of Foreign Direct Investments', p. 1322; R. Nagraj. 2003. 'Foreign Direct Investment in India in 1990s', *Economic and Political* Weekly 38(17): 1701. Also see I.J. Ahluwalia. 1991. *Productivity and Growth in Indian Manufacturing.* New York & Oxford: Oxford University Press; Arvind Virmani. 2005. 'Policy Regimes, Growth and Poverty in India: Lessons of Government Failure and Entrepreneurial Success!', ICRIER Working Paper No 170 (hereinafter Virmani, 'Policy Regimes, Growth and Poverty in India').

[143] Chaudhary, 'FERA: Appearance and Reality', p. 734.

[144] Kumar, 'Industrialization, Liberalisation and Two Way Flows of Foreign Direct Investment', p. 3230. Some commentators have argued that during the time of national emergency imposed in 1975 by Indira Gandhi, there was a slight change towards encouraging foreign capital to participate in Indian industry. See V. Hewitt. 2008. *Political Mobilisation and Democracy in India: States of Emergency.* New York: Routledge. Also see S. Shin. 2014. 'FDI in India: Ideas, Interests and Institutional Changes', *Economic and Political Weekly* XLIX: 66 (hereinafter Shin, 'FDI in India').

a miserable 2.9 per cent in 1965–79[145] as against a respectable 4.1 per cent from 1950–65.[146]

2.1.2.2 1981 to 1990[147]

Indira Gandhi, after losing office in 1977, returned to power in 1980. However, this time she realigned herself with the organized private sector and gave up her socialist rhetoric of 1960s and 1970s.[148] Indira Gandhi, who was hostile to businesses earlier, turned friendly and adopted policies that Rodrik and Subramniam describe as pro-business policies.[149]

Due to low economic growth, lower international competitiveness of Indian goods and low export potential of Indian manufactured goods in the 1970s, her government adopted limited liberalization and de-regulation in 1980s.[150] The 1980s saw a shift from import substitution strategy to an export neutral promotion strategy and witnessed a higher rate of GDP growth to 5.7 per cent annually in the 1980s.[151] This period saw a return or re-emergence of a receptive

[145] National Accounts Statistics of India, Central Statistical Organization.

[146] National Accounts Statistics of India, Central Statistical Organization.

[147] Panagariya describes the period from 1981 to 1988 as 'liberalization by stealth' – See Panagariya, *India*, pp. 78–94.

[148] Dani Rodrik and Arvind Subramanian. 2004. 'From "Hindu Growth" to Productivity Surge: The Mystery of the Indian Growth Transition', IMF Working Paper, https://www.imf.org/external/pubs/ft/wp/2004/wp0477.pdf, accessed 10 March 2018.

[149] Compare this with their description of the 1991 economic reform policies as pro-market policies discussed in Chapter 3.

[150] Virmani, 'Policy Regimes, Growth and Poverty in India'; Kumar, 'Liberalisation and Changing Patterns of Foreign Direct Investments', p. 1322. Also see B.R. Nayar. 2007. 'Globalization and India's National Autonomy' in *Globalization and Politics in India* B.R. Nayar (eds), pp. 346–7. New Delhi: Oxford University Press (hereinafter Nayar, 'Globalization and India's National Autonomy').

[151] Virmani, 'Policy Regimes, Growth and Poverty in India'. Also see M.S. Ahluwalia. 2002. 'Economic Reforms in India Since 1991: Has Gradualism Worked?', *Journal of Economic Perspectives* 16 (7):67; Ministry of Finance, Government of India. 2001. *Economic Survey* (2001–02). New Delhi: Ministry of Finance.

attitude towards FDI signalled in some key changes, such as limited flexibility being introduced in foreign ownership and exceptions introduced to the 40 per cent ceiling rule on the merits of individual investment proposals.[152] Despite this friendly approach to businesses that economists have talked about to distinguish Indira Gandhi of the 1980s from her previous avatar, Indira Gandhi passed another 11 ordinances, later passed as laws by the parliament, nationalizing a host of private industries.[153] As Dam observes, she nationalized another set of banks[154] and other economic activities like manufacturing cars,[155] cement,[156] flour mills,[157] rubber,[158] dockyard business,[159] and more textile mills.[160]

The other sign of a receptive attitude towards foreign investment was evident in the late 1980s, when Rajiv Gandhi was India's prime minister. Rajiv Gandhi in 1988 had said that India's policy towards foreign investment was not an open-door policy and that foreign investment was permitted as per India's terms.[161] Yet, he recognized the importance of foreign investment over loans that had to be repaid whereas investment led to outflows only after production and payment of taxes over profits.[162] Rajiv Gandhi also emphasized on the need to absorb more foreign investment that would be to the

[152] Kumar, 'Liberalisation and Changing Patterns of Foreign Direct Investments', p. 1322. For a detailed discussion see Panagariya, India, pp. 78–94.

[153] Dam, *Presidential Legislation in India*, p. 78.

[154] The Banking Companies (Acquisition and Transfer of Undertakings) Act, 1980.

[155] The Maruti Limited (Acquisition and Transfer of Ownership) Act, 1980.

[156] The Dalmia Dadri Cement Limited (Acquisition and Transfer of Undertakings) Act, 1981.

[157] The Ganesh Flour Mills Company Limited (Acquisition and Transfer of Undertakings) Act, 1984. Also see *Hindustan Vegetable Oils* v. *Progressive Industries and Ors.*, 1995 SCC (6) 174.

[158] The Incheck Types Limited and National Rubber Manufactures Nationalization Act, 1984.

[159] The Hooghly Docking & Engineering Company Limited (Acquisition and Transfer of Undertaking) Act, 1984.

[160] The British India Corporation (Acquisition of Shares) Act, 1981.

[161] Shin, 'FDI in India', p. 68.

[162] Shin, 'FDI in India', p. 68.

advantage of the Indian economy.[163] There was an increase in inflows between 1985 to 1991, although the annual average for all foreign investment from 1970 to 1991 was only about US$99 million.[164]

In sum, India's policy towards foreign investment was receptive in initial years (1950 to end of the 1960s). However, even this attitude was cautious and never meant embracing foreign investment wholly but only as per need such as helping in bringing in foreign exchange or plugging the domestic savings gap.[165] This cautious receptive attitude changed in the late 1960s and in the 1970s with a tremendous and open shift towards indigenous industries, to the extent of discriminating against foreign companies. Post the 1980s there was some liberalization towards foreign investment though the nationalization spree of Indira Gandhi continued from 1980 to 1984. On the whole, foreign investment didn't figure very prominently in India's economic policy in this phase. Broadly speaking, the Indian economic model was based on indigenization, economic nationalism and self-reliance, developing heavy capital industries, and inward-looking economic policies. This changed dramatically in the 1990s.[166]

2.2 India's Approach towards International Investment Law

India's overall policy towards foreign investment from 1947 till 1990 provides a useful background to understand India's stand on international investment law during this period. In order to discuss India's approach towards international investment law, we divide the discussion into three parts. First, we discuss India's approach to international law generally especially after India's political independence. Second, we look at India's approach towards international investment law at the multilateral level, that is, how India dealt with these issues at forums such as the United Nations or at other forums such as the Asian-African Legal Consultative Organization (AALCO). Third, we

[163] Shin, 'FDI in India', p. 68.

[164] Nayar, 'Globalization and India's National Autonomy', pp. 379–80.

[165] Arvind Virmani. 2003. 'India's External Reforms: Modest Globalisation Significant Gains', *Economic and Political Weekly* XXXVII (32, 9–15 August): 3377–90; Nayar, 'Globalization and India's National Autonomy'.

[166] See Chapter 3.

discuss India's approach towards international investment law at the bilateral level, that is, how it dealt with international law on foreign investment with a single country at a bilateral level.

2.2.1 India's Approach towards International Law

India was keen to build a new international legal order based on equality and sovereignty of nations founded on the spirit of nationalism and economic self-reliance followed domestically. This was reflected in Nehru's speech in the Asian Relations Conference held in March 1947, even before India was formally independent.[167] Nehru said:

> For too long have we of Asia been petitioners in Western courts and chancelleries. The story must now belong to the past. We propose to stand on our own legs and to co-operate with all others who are prepared to co-operate with us. We do not intend to be the playthings of the others ... The countries of Asia can no longer be used as pawns by others; they are bound to have their own policies in world affairs.[168]

In his address to the United Nations General Assembly on 3 November 1948, Nehru said:

> May I say, as a representative from Asia, that we honour Europe for its culture and for the great advance in human civilization which it represents? May I say that we are equally interested in the solution of European problems; but may I also say that the world is something bigger than Europe, and you will not solve your problems by thinking that the problems of world are mainly European problems. There are vast tracts of the world, which may not in the past, for a few generations, have taken much part in world affairs. But they are awake, their people are moving and they have no intention whatever of being ignored or being passed by.[169]

[167] On Nehru and International law see R.P. Anand. 2002. 'Jawaharlal Nehru and International Law', *Indian Journal of International Law* 42(1):5–29.

[168] Jawahar Lal Nehru. 1947. 'Asia Finds Herself Again', Inaugural speech at Asian Relations Conference.New Delhi, 23 March1947, vol. I, n. 9, p. 301.

[169] Jawahar Lal Nehru. 1948. 'Our Objectives', *Nehru's Speeches*, Vol I. New Delhi: Publications Division, Government of India, p. 257.

This is not to suggest that India did not accept international law rules, despite having played no role in developing many of these international law standards.[170] Nehru was all in favour of accepting the tenets of international law.[171] In fact, as R.P. Anand, one of the foremost Indian international lawyers, has written, not just India, but all newly independent developing countries 'mostly accepted the treaties concluded by the European countries on their behalf and before their independence'.[172] However, India wanted to emphasize, as Radhabinod Pal India's member at the International Law Commission (ILC) said that after the creation of newly independent countries, creation of international law was not 'the prerogative of countries bearing the cultural heritage of the west but the common task of all members of the international community'.[173]

Nehru articulated India's vision of international law based on five principles (also called Panchsheel):

1. Mutual respect for each other's territorial integrity and sovereignty;
2. Mutual non-aggression;
3. Mutual non-interference in each other's internal affairs;

[170] See R.P. Anand. 2004. *Studies in International Law and History: An Asian Perspective*. Lieden/Boston: Martinus Nijhoff, p. 9.

[171] Anand, *Studies in International Law and History*, n 148, pp. 8–9. Also see generally C.H. Alexandrowicz. 1954. 'Grotius and India', *Indian Yearbook of International Affairs* 4:357.

[172] Anand, 'Jawaharlal Nehru and International Law', n 148, pp. 9–10. However, Nehru, in 1955, in context of the liberation of Goa from Portugal, did mention that 'independent India' was 'in no way bound by any old or modern treaty between other countries to which [India has] not subscribed'—see J. Nehru. 1983. 'Reply to Debate on Goa in Lok Sabha, July 26, 1955', in *India's Foreign Policy: Selected Speeches, September 1946 – 2 April 1961*, p. 113. New Delhi: The Publications Division, Ministry of Information and Broadcasting, Government of India.

[173] R.B. Pal. 1962. 'Future Role of the International Law Commission in the Changing World', *United Nations Review* 9:31. Also see R.B. Pal. 1957. 'Yearbook of the International Law Commission', *United Nations Summary Records* 1:158.

4. Equality and mutual benefit; and
5. Peaceful coexistence.[174]

In other words, India and other developing countries stressed on building a new international legal order emphasizing their sovereign status.[175] India and other developing countries did not reject international law's basic character and nature but questioned its colonial content and wanted to shape it in a way that it fully reflected the changed realities of the new emerging global order.[176] Respect for international law is recognized in the Indian Constitution. Article 51 (c) of the Indian Constitution states that the Indian State shall endeavour to foster respect for international law and treaty obligations in the dealings of organized peoples with one another.[177]

Chimni has described the approach that most Indian scholars adopted post India's independence towards international law as

[174] See Jawahar Lal Nehru. 1983. 'From Speech in Lok Sabha, September 17, 1955', in *Speeches*, vol. IV, Jawahar Lal Nehru, p. 99. Delhi: Publications Division. For a detailed discussion on this see Prabhakar Singh. 2015. 'India Before and After the Right of Passage Case', *Asian Journal of International Law* 5:176–208.

[175] See R.P. Anand. 1962. 'The Role of New Asian-African Countries in the Present International Legal Order', *American Journal of International Law* 56:383 (hereinafter Anand, 'The Role of New Asian-African Countries in the Present International Legal Order'); S.N. Guha Roy. 1961. 'Is the Law of Responsibility of States for Injuries to Aliens a Part of Universal International Law?', *American Journal of International Law* 55:863 (hereinafter Guha, 'Is the Law of Responsibility of States for Injuries to Aliens a Part of Universal International Law?').

[176] See Anand, 'The Role of New Asian-African Countries in the Present International Legal Order', p. 383; Guha, 'Is the Law of Responsibility of States for Injuries to Aliens a Part of Universal International Law?', p. 863; P.S. Rao. 2005. 'The Indian Position on Some General Principles of International Law', in *India and International Law*Bimal Patel (ed.), pp. 33–66. Leiden: Martinus Nijhoff.

[177] See generally V.S. Mani. 1995. 'Effectuation of International Law in the Municipal Legal Order: The Law and Practice of India', *Asian Yearbook of International Law* 5:145; V.G. Hegde. 2010. 'Indian Courts and International Law', *Leiden Journal of International Law* 23(1):53. *D K Basu* v. *State of West Bengal*, 1997 1 SCC 416.

formalist dualism—rejection of colonial content of international law and, at the same time, acceptance of its emancipatory potential.[178] Chimni writes that a theory of formalist dualism saw Indian scholarship advance a critique of colonial international law but embrace a narrative of progress in the present. Chimni problematizes this formalist dualism approach by arguing that given the positivist orientation of most Indian scholars, they failed to understand the nature and character of the international system and the role of international law.[179] This failure arose, according to Chimni, because the Indian scholars or TWAIL I did not understand the economic and political structures of global capitalism and the neocolonial character of international law.[180] Chimni blames this on the 'methodological weaknesses of the formalist and statist orientation'.[181] The statist orientation of TWAIL I is blamed on their failure to combine the critique of the international order along with the critique of the internal order from the standpoint of subaltern groups and classes.[182] Chimni, therefore, calls for adopting a critical dualist approach 'that problematizes the structure, ideology, and practices of global capitalism'.[183]

[178] B.S. Chimni. 2010. 'International Law Scholarship in Post-colonial India: Coping with Dualism', *Leiden Journal of International Law* 23:23–51 (hereinafter Chimni, 'International Law Scholarship in Post-colonial India'. This approach to international law that scholars like Anand demonstrate towards international law has also been described as the Third World Approaches to International Law (TWAIL – I)—see A. Anghie and B.S. Chimni. 2003. 'Third World Approaches to International Law and Individual Responsibility in Internal Conflicts', *Chinese Journal of International Law* 2(1):77 (hereinafter Anghie and Chimni, 'Third World Approaches to International Law and Individual Responsibility in Internal Conflicts'). Also see Prabhakar Singh. 2010. 'Indian International Law: From a Colonized Apologist to a Subaltern Protagonist', *Leiden Journal of International Law* 23: 79–103.

[179] Chimni, 'International Law Scholarship in Post-colonial India', p. 40.

[180] Chimni, 'International Law Scholarship in Post-colonial India', p. 40.

[181] Chimni, 'International Law Scholarship in Post-colonial India', p. 24.

[182] Chimni, 'International Law Scholarship in Post-colonial India', p. 41.

[183] Chimni, 'International Law Scholarship in Post-colonial India', p. 41. Also see Balakrishnan Rajagopal. 2004. *International Law from Below: Development, Social Movements and Third World Resistance*. New York: Cambridge

Chimni's criticism of TWAIL I (or formalist dualism as he calls it) has certain contradictions. First, at one level Chimni accepts that TWAIL I challenged the colonial underpinnings of international law, yet he claims that these scholars failed to understand the real character of international law. In other words, it seems that Chimni equates critique of international law with critique of global capitalism and argues that former cannot be effectively critiqued till the latter is critiqued. This may be true for Marxist international lawyers but not for everyone else. Second, Chimni also gives an impression that the the internal order that persisted in India at that time was capitalistic in nature. As has been discussed in the chapter, this is not accurate. The internal order in India was surely not Marxist or communist in nature, but it was deeply influenced by socialistic principles emphasizing on public ownership of means of production, redistribution of income (especially during Indira Gandhi's time), and limited role for the private and especially the foreign sector. Indira Gandhi's entire radical leftist approach towards economic policy—ranging from bank nationalization to abolition of privy purses—was often justified in the name of subaltern classes. However, this changed post the 1990s as has been explained.

In any case, the internal order in countries that were officially against global capitalism, that is, in communist countries such as USSR, China, Cambodia, was far more authoriatiran and repressive, politically and economically, than in constitutional democracies like India. India consciously decided not to follow the route of communism.[184] In other words, blaming the lack of critique of the internal

---

University Press. This critical dualist approach is also called as TWAIL – II – for more on this Chimni and Angie, 'Third World Approaches to International Law and Individual Responsibility in Internal Conflicts'; Chimni, 'The Past, Present and Future of International Law', p. 499; B.S. Chimni. 2017. *International Law and the World Order*. Cambridge: Cambridge University Press, pp. 15–17.

[184] Dr B.R. Ambedkar, the chief architect of the Indian Constitution, in his last speech to the Constituent Assembly on 25 November 1949 had said the following: 'The condemnation of the Constitution largely comes from two quarters, the Communist Party and the Socialist Party. Why do they condemn the Constitution? Is it because it is really a bad Constitution? I venture to say no'. The Communist Party want a Constitution based upon the principle of

order for the so-called statist orientation of TWAIL I Indian scholars does not do justice to their scholarship.

2.2.2 At the Multilateral Level

Although, as discussed before, India did not shut its door to foreign investment, its development strategy focussed on industrialization dominated by the public sector and state control. This policy rooted in economic nationalism and self-reliance explains India's approach to international law on foreign investment during this period. Also, India's approach to international investment law mirrors India's approach to international law in general, that is, of formalist dualism. Although India did not enter into any investment treaty during this phase, and questioned the content of international investment law, it did not completely reject all the basic principles of international law for the protection of foreign investment. India, in fact, tried to shape its content in a manner that reflected the new realities of the world and in manner that was by and large consistent with its domestic approach towards foreign investment. For this purpose, it used multilateral forums such as the United Nations and also the ILC. The core issues pertaining to foreign investment at that time were expropriation of foreign investment,[185] compensation for expropriation, and minimum standard of treatment for aliens.[186] In a way, all these

---

the Dictatorship of the Proletariat. They condemn the Constitution because it is based upon parliamentary democracy. The Socialists want two things. The first thing they want is that if they come in power, the Constitution must give them the freedom to nationalize or socialize all private property without payment of compensation. The second thing that the Socialists want is that the Fundamental Rights mentioned in the Constitution must be absolute and without any limitations so that if their Party fails to come into power, they would have the unfettered freedom not merely to criticize, but also to overthrow the State'—The Wire Staff. 2017. 'Lessons for Today in Ambedkar's Last Address to the Constituent Assembly', https://thewire.in/government/ambedkar-constitution-assembly-democracy, 14 April.

[185] See the discussion in Chapter 5 on expropriation.

[186] See Chapter 4 for a discussion on this minimum standard of treatment of aliens.

are interrelated and thus, a strict segregation may not be possible. We now discuss the issues India raised and supported along with other developing countries at different multilateral forums.

ALCC/AALCO

A key development in the 1950s was the setting up of Asian Legal Consultative Committee (ALCC) on 15 November 1956 with India, and six other Asian countries, being the founding member.[187] The formation of this organization was an outcome of the historic Bandung conference in Indonesia in 1955.[188] On the recommendation of Nehru, in 1958, African countries also became members of this group and later this group came to be known as AALCO with its primary objective being to act as an advisory body to member states on international law matters.

At the fourth session of this committee, member countries adopted a document called 'Principles Concerning Admission and Treatment of Aliens'.[189] This document is critical as it gives us a glimpse of understanding of India on protection of foreign investors and their investment though the term 'alien' here is not restricted to just foreign investors. Article 11 of this document states: 'Subject to local laws, regulations, and orders and subject also to the condition, imposed for his admission into the State, an alien shall have the right to acquire, hold and dispose of property.' Further Article 12 (1) states: 'The State shall, however, have the right to acquire, expropriate or nationalize the property of an alien. Compensation shall be paid for such acquisition, expropriation or nationalisation in accordance with local laws,regulations and orders.' This language showed that while these countries were willing to accord certain rights to aliens

[187] For more on ALCC (now called AALCO) see—http://www.aalco.int/, accessed 10 March 2018.

[188] For more on ALCC (now called AALCO) see— http://www.aalco.int/, accessed 10 March 2018.

[189] Asian Legal Consultative Committee (ALCC), 1961. 'Principles Concerning Admission and Treatment of Aliens', (Adopted in the fourth session), http://www.aalco.int/PRINCIPLES%20CONCERNING%20ADMISSION%20AND%20TREATMENT%20OF%20ALIENS.pdf, accessed 10 March 2018.

under international law, they also wanted to expressly retain their right to expropriate and pay compensation as per the national laws of the host country. This language clearly signalled that while the alien will be lawfully treated without arbitrariness, this treatment will be as per the national laws of the host country and, thus, will be in accordance with the principle of national treatment. In other words, this stand of India and other Asian and African countries rejected a minimum standard of treatment of aliens independent of national treatment as many developed countries have historically argued.

ILC

Likewise, in 1957, the Indian member of the ILC, Radhabinod Pal, challenged the draft report of the Special *Rapporteur* Garcia Amador who linked the issue of content of the international minimum standard with fundamental human rights concept.[190] Pal challenged the European hegemony of international law arguing that the geography of international law has changed in the post-war period with the rise of a large number of newly independent nation states in Asia like India and hence these countries should be involved in developing international law.[191] Pal said,

> now that international law must be regarded as embracing other peoples, it clearly required their consent no less; and that fact must be steadily borne in mind in attempting to determine to what extent alien property or alien interests in the newly freed countries merited the protection that international law could afford.[192]

[190] F.V. Garcia Amador. 1957. 'State Responsibility', Document A/CN.4/106, International Law Commission Yearbook, p. 104.

[191] Pal, 'Yearbook of the International Law Commission', n 151, p. 158. Garcia Amador's position has also been criticised by Sir Ian Brownlie – See Ian Brownlie. 2008. *Principles of Public International Law*. Oxford: Oxford University Press, p. 527.

[192] Pal, 'Yearbook of the International Law Commission', n 151, p. 158. Garcia Amador's position has also been criticised by Sir Ian Brownlie—See Ian Brownlie. 2008. *Principles of Public International Law*. Oxford: Oxford University Press, p. 527 (hereinafter Brownlie, *Principles of Public International Law*).

Thus, Pal challenged the content of the proposed international minimum standard in economic relations and argued that it was nothing but an attempt to thrust on the rest of the world the European notion of the international minimum standard without understanding the social and economic difficulties of countries like India.[193]

United Nations

In 1962, the UN General Assembly adopted a resolution declaring permanent sovereignty over natural wealth and resources (PSNR).[194] Paragraph 4 of the PSNR resolution said,

> Nationalization, expropriation or requisitioning shall be based on grounds or reasons of public utility, security or the national interest which are recognized as overriding purely individual or private interests, both domestic and foreign. In such cases the owner shall be paid appropriate compensation, in accordance with the rules in force in the State taking such measures in the exercise of its sovereignty and in accordance with international law. In any case where the question of compensation gives rise to a controversy, the national jurisdiction of the State taking such measures shall be exhausted. However, upon agreement by sovereign States and other parties concerned, settlement of the dispute should be made through arbitration or international adjudication. [195]

Arguably, the adoption of the PSNR indicates the rejection of the law relating to responsibility of states espoused by developed countries.[196]

[193] Pal, 'Yearbook of the International Law Commission', n 151, p. 158. Garcia Amador's position has also been criticised by Sir Ian Brownlie – See Brownlie, *Principles of Public International Law*, p. 527.

[194] General Assembly Resolution 1803 (XVII).1962. 'Permanent Sovereignty Over Natural Resources', https://www.ohchr.org/Documents/ProfessionalInterest/resources.pdf, 14 December, accessed 10 March 2018.

[195] General Assembly Resolution 1803 (XVII), 'Permanent Sovereignty OverNatural Resources', art. 4.

[196] See R.P. Anand. 1966. 'Attitude of the Asian-African States towards Certain Problems of International Law', *International and Comparative Law Quarterly* 15(I, January): pp. 55–75. This effort of developing countries like India to challenge existing customary law was challenged by many capital-exporting countries—A. Anghie. 2004. *Imperialism, Sovereignty, and the Making*

Three points can be made about this paragraph. First, it recognized the right of States to nationalize/expropriate provided it was in accordance with public interest and payment of adequate compensation. Second, the compensation to be paid was to be determined in accordance with the domestic laws and its sovereignty exercised in accordance with international law. Third, for any dispute on the question of compensation, domestic remedies should be exhausted subject to any agreement providing for dispute resolution through arbitration. India attested to these principles, as the Indian representative said in the UNGA in 1962, that countries had the right to nationalize or expropriate foreign investment in national interest, but this should be accompanied by adequate compensation.[197]

Another major quest of India and other developing countries was to use the UN to build a New International Economic Order (NIEO).[198] India was one of the active supporters of this

---

of International Law. Cambridge: Cambridge University Press, pp. 226–44. A number of theories, aimed to support the interests of foreign investments, like doctrine of state succession and doctrine of acquired rights were used by western scholars to repudiate the position of developing countries like India in support of customary law that had developed when India and many other developing countries were colonies of Europe—H. Waldock. 1962. 'General Course on Public International Law', *Rec. de Cours* 106:49–53. This rule is also reflected in Restatement (Third) of Foreign Relations Law of the United States § 102 (c) Comment d. Also see J.T. Gathii. 2009. 'War and International Investment Law', *International Community Law Review* 11:363–4.

[197] As cited in Jain, *Nationalisation of Foreign Property*, p. 248.

[198] For discussion on NIEO and related developments see Bhagwati and Desai, *India*, n 2; Upendra Baxi. 1984. 'The New International Economic Order, Basic Needs and Rights: Notes Towards Development of the Right to Development', in *Role of Law and Judiciary in Transformation of Society*, D.A. Desai (ed.). New Delhi: Kamlakar Prakashan; K. Hossain and S.R. Chowdhury (eds). 1984. *Permanent Sovereignty over Natural Resources in International Law.* London: Palgrave Macmillan; M. Bedjaouti. 1979. *Towards a New International Economic Order.* Holmes and Meier: Holmes and Meier Publishing London, New York; A. Rozental. 1976. 'The Charter of Economic Rights and Duties of States and the New International Economic Order', *Virginia Journal of International Law* 16:309; Sornarajah, 'India, China and Foreign Investment', pp. 122–4; T. Weiler. 2011. 'An Historical Analysis of the Function of the

initiative.[199] The enthusiasm and the active support for the NIEO in India in the 1960s and 1970s can be gauged from the articles written by Indian government officials and Indian international law academics in India's leading international law journal—*The Indian Journal of International Law*.[200] India and other developing countries made an effort to evolve a NIEO in 1970s, in the words of an Indian diplomat, as 'a response to a position of political and economic dominance exercised by the metropolitan powers and their nationals over the natural resources, raw materials and labour in developing countries during the colonial era'.[201] This vision of the NIEO was formulated in the UNCTAD resolution passed in 1972, which 'stressed the urgency to establish generally accepted norms to govern

---

Minimum Standard of Treatment in International Investment Law', in *New Directions in International Economic Law*, T. Weiler andF. Baetens (eds), pp. 330–7. Leiden: Martinus Nijhoff.

199 K.B. Lall. 1978. 'India and the New International Economic Order', *International Studies* 17:435. Legal validity of the Declaration by the UN General Assembly in 1974 adopted on NIEO—for a different framework of enquiry to ascertain the legal status see—R. Khan. 1978. 'The Normative Character of the New International Economic Order—A Framework of Enquiry', *Indian Journal of International Law* 18:294 (hereinafter Khan, 'The Normative Character of the New International Economic Order). For a critical assessment of all the UN General Assembly resolutions adopted as an effort to build the NIEO see—A. Akinsanya. 1978. 'Permanent Sovereignty Over Natural Resources and the Future of Private Foreign Investment in the Third World', *Indian Journal of International Law* 18:175.

200 N.P. Jain. 1979. 'An Approach to the New International Economic Order', *Indian Journal of International Law* 19: 544;P.C. Rao. 1975. 'Charter of Economic Duties and Rights', *Indian Journal of International Law* 15:351 (hereinafter Rao, 'Charter of Economic Duties and Rights'); Khan, 'The Normative Character of the New International Economic Order', p. 294; S.K. Agarwala. 1977. 'The Emerging International Economic Order', *Indian Journal of International Law* 17:261 (hereinafter Agarwala, 'The Emerging International Economic Order'); S.P. Shukla. 1978. 'New International Economic Order', *Indian Journal of International Law* 18:290.

201 Rao,'Bilateral Investment Promotion Agreements', p. 623. Also see Anghie and Chimni, 'Third World Approaches to International Law and Individual Responsibility in Internal Conflicts', p. 82.

international economic relations systematically and recognized that it is not feasible to establish a joint order and a stable order as long as a charter to protect the rights of all countries, and in particular the developing States, is not formulated'.[202] This period also witnessed a perpetual effort made by developing countries to influence norms in international law in many fields, such as pertaining to monetary law;[203] environment;[204] and multinational corporations.[205]

This effort to build a NIEO was further bolstered by the adoption of the Charter of Economic Rights and Duties of States (CERDS) by the United Nations General Assembly, on 12 December 1974, with 120 countries voting in favour with six against[206] and 10 abstentions.[207] India supported CERDS.[208] The aim of this Charter was to formulate norms related to economic matters having international dimensions benefitting developing countries.[209] India supported CERDS and took active part at every stage in its drafting.[210]

Article 2(2) (a) of the Charter gives every state the right to regulate foreign investment in accordance with its domestic laws and national priorities. Ten developed countries (mainly capital exporting countries) opposed this provision because they wanted host countries to treat foreign investments as per what they thought to be their

[202] See proceedings of the UN Conference on Trade and Development, Third Session, Vol.1, UN Sales No.E.73.II/D.4.

[203] Resolution on Monetary Reform, U.N.G.A. Res. A/Res/2565(XXIV) of 13 December 1969.

[204] Resolution on Development and Environment, A/Res/2849(XXVI) of 20 December 1971.

[205] See S.K. Chatterjee. 1991. 'The Charter of Economic Rights and Duties of States: An Evaluation After 15 Years', *International and Comparative Law Quarterly* 40(3):669–72 (hereinafter Chatterjee,'The Charter of Economic Rights and Duties of States').

[206] These six countries were Belgium, Denmark, The Federal Republic of Germany, Lexembourg, United Kingdom, and United States of America.

[207] The relevant provisions of the Charter are discussed in the chapters on Expropriation and FET.

[208] Rao,'Charter of Economic Duties and Rights', p. 369.

[209] Chatterjee, 'The Charter of Economic Rights and Duties of States', p. 669.

[210] Rao, 'Charter of Economic Duties and Rights', p. 369. Also see Chatterjee, 'The Charter of Economic Rights and Duties of States', p. 669.

international obligations.[211] However, India and other developing countries maintained foreign investors should be subject to national laws of the country.[212]

Similarly, Article 2(2) (b) of CERDS on transnational corporations (TNCs) gives every state the right to regulate and supervise the activities of the TNCs within its national jurisdiction in accordance with her laws and national priorities. An Indian scholar commenting on this in 1977 wrote that 'developed countries recognized that a state may control their entry and activities within its territory, they wanted the corporations to retain the protection of the international standards applicable to foreigners',[213] which was not acceptable to India and other developing countries.

Article 2(2)(c) of CERDS gives every state the right to nationalize and expropriate foreign investment and decide the question of compensation as per its national laws and priorities. It further states that any dispute on the question of compensation shall be determined by the domestic courts applying the national law. On the demand of developed countries that the question of compensation should be decided as per the principles of international law, India and other developing countries denied the existence of any such principle in international law.[214]

ICSID

The Convention on the Settlement of Investment Disputes between States and Individuals of Other States of 1965[215] (ICSID Convention) was formulated by the Executive Directors of the

[211] See Rao,'Charter of Economic Duties and Rights', p. 360. Also see S. Pahuja. 2011. *Decolonising International Law: Development, Economic Growth and the Politics of Universality*. Cambridge: Cambridge University Press: 148–55.

[212] Rao,'Charter of Economic Duties and Rights', p. 351.

[213] See Agarwala, 'The Emerging International Economic Order'.

[214] See Rao, 'Charter of Economic Duties and Rights', p. 351; See Agarwala,'The Emerging International Economic Order'.

[215] Convention on the Settlement of Investment Disputes between States and Nationals of Other States (opened for signature 18 March 1965, entered into force 14 October 1966) ('ICSID Convention'). 1965. http://icsid.worldbank.org/ICSID/StaticFiles/basicdoc/CRR_English-final.pdf, 18 March, accessed 10 March 2018.

International Bank for Reconstruction and Development (the World Bank). The executive directors, on 18 March 1965, submitted the Convention, with an accompanying Report, to the World Bank member governments for their consideration with a view to its signature and ratification.[216] The Convention entered into force on 14 October 1966, when it had been ratified by 20 countries.[217] This convention gives direct individual rights to investors to bring disputes against states.

India did not accept the convention.[218] However, most Indian commentators have not offered cogent reasons. One commentator offers two explanations for India not joining the ICSID Convention.[219] First, India, during this phase, built a socialist pattern of economy and thus was wary of foreign investment.[220] Second, India's endeavour to build a NIEO where primacy should be given to national law in deciding questions related to regulation of foreign investment especially issues related to compensation.[221] In other words, it has been argued that India did not join the ICSID Convention because it

[216] Convention on the Settlement of Investment Disputes between States and Nationals of Other States (opened for signature 18 March 1965, entered into force 14 October 1966) ('ICSID Convention'). 1965. http://icsid.worldbank.org/ICSID/StaticFiles/basicdoc/CRR_English-final.pdf, 18 March, accessed 10 March 2018.

[217] Convention on the Settlement of Investment Disputes between States and Nationals of Other States (opened for signature 18 March 1965, entered into force 14 October 1966) ('ICSID Convention'). 1965. http://icsid.worldbank.org/ICSID/StaticFiles/basicdoc/CRR_English-final.pdf, 18 March, accessed 10 March 2018.

[218] See D. Krishan. 2008. 'India and International Investment Law', in *India and International Law* (Vol. 2), B.N. Patel (ed.), p. 277. Martinus Nijhoff: Leiden/Boston. Also see Guha, 'Is the Law of Responsibility of States for Injuries to Aliens a Part of Universal International Law?'; Anand, *Studies in International Law and History*.

[219] Rajput, *Protection of Foreign Investment in India and Investment Treaty Arbitration*, pp. 180–2.

[220] Rajput, *Protection of Foreign Investment in India and Investment Treaty Arbitration*, pp. 180–2.

[221] Rajput, *Protection of Foreign Investment in India and Investment Treaty Arbitration*, pp. 180–2.

resisted the 'the idea of invocation of international law for protection of foreign investment.'[222]

While this is broadly true these are oversimplified explanations. The reality is more nuanced. The fact of the matter is that India actively and intricately participated in the ICSID Convention negotiations and made many useful interventions as the negotiating history of the convention clearly shows.[223]

B.N. Adarkar, the Additional Secretary to ministry of finance, representing India in the consultative meeting of legal experts on settlement of investment disputes in 1964 clearly articulated India's stand on foreign investment. He said:

> in India there were no foreign exchange restrictions as regards remittance of profits or dividends, and in cases of approved investments, investors were free to repatriate their capital, including capital appreciation. If foreign property was acquired by the government, just compensation was provided. Agreements were entered into with foreign investors, and many of them included clauses for arbitration. India ordinarily would therefore not object in principle to a Convention of the type proposed.[224]

Likewise, on 30 September 1963, K.S. Rajan, another Indian expert said, 'India had entered into many agreements with foreign investors—many of them containing clauses providing for reference, in the event of a dispute, to the President of the International Chamber of Commerce, or similar body—no dispute had so far arisen'.[225] In other words, India was keen to attract private capital, maintain a favourable investment claimate and give foreign investors necessary safeguards including additional rights.[226]

[222] Rajput, *Protection of Foreign Investment in India and Investment Treaty Arbitration*, pp. 180–2.

[223] World Bank. 1970. *History of the ICSID Convention* (Volumes I and II). Washington DC: World Bank.

[224] ICSID. 1970. *Convention on the Settlement of Investment Disputes between States and Nationals of Other States*, Vol. II.1. Washington DC: World Bank Group, p. 469 (hereinafter ICSID, *Convention on the Settlement of Investment Disputes between States and Nationals of Other States*).

[225] Negotiating History of the ICSID Convention, Volume II.1, p. 182.

[226] ICSID, *Convention on the Settlement of Investment Disputes between States and Nationals of Other States*, p. 476.

However, India had some reservations about the ICSID Convention.[227] First, India believed that the [ICSID] Convention, by setting up a forum where individuals and States were placed on par, marked an important departure from international law.[228] Second, India also argued that the Convention gave foreign investors additional rights of unspecified scope without imposing any countervailing obligations on them.[229] Third, India also had certain public-policy-related reservations to the Convention especially pertaining to the jurisdiction. For instance, India argued that refusing jurisdiction of ICSID might be bona fide where 'the matter concerned national policy', or 'did not involve discrimination between foreign and national investors or conflict with any contractual obligation of the State'.[230] India argued that 'in such cases no purpose would be served by submitting it to an international tribunal because an award involving a change in the national law would be unenforceable'.[231] Specifically on the question of jurisdiction of the ICSID Convention, B.N. Lokur, India's Law Secretary, who also participated in the negotiations proposed the following draft:

> The jurisdiction of the Center shall extend to investment disputes between a Contracting State and a national of another Contracting State. Each Contracting State shall notify to the Center the class or classes of investment disputes which it would in principle consider submitting to the jurisdiction of the Center. The Center shall exercise

[227] ICSID, *Convention on the Settlement of Investment Disputes between States and Nationals of Other States*, p. 476. Also see intervention of B.N. Adarkar, ICSID 1970, 469–70.

[228] ICSID, *Convention on the Settlement of Investment Disputes between States and Nationals of Other States*, Vol. II.1.

[229] ICSID, *Convention on the Settlement of Investment Disputes between States and Nationals of Other States*, Vol. II.1, p. 476.

[230] ICSID, *Convention on the Settlement of Investment Disputes between States and Nationals of Other States*, p. 470.

[231] ICSID, *Convention on the Settlement of Investment Disputes between States and Nationals of Other States*, p. 470. For an excellent analysis of the concerns of many capital importing countries on ICSID Convention see J. Taylor. 2018. *The Rise of Investor-State Arbitration: Politics, Law and Unintended Consequences*. Oxford. Oxford University Press, pp. 146–80.

> jurisdiction only over such dispute of the class or classes so notified only if the parties thereto have in writing consented to submit the dispute to the Center either before or after it has arisen.[232]

Thus, India proposed two caveats to the jurisdiction of the centre. First, a dispute should be submitted to the centre only if express consent was given by the state. Second, each country should have the right to notify to ICSID, the class or classes of investment disputes that it would like to consider submitting to ICSID's jurisdiction.[233] The final version of Article 25(1) of the ICSID Convention although provides for consent of the parties does not provide for the right of countries to notify the classes or investment disputes that it would like to consider to ICSID.

Another major reservation India had was with regard to the finality of the arbitral award, that is, to give effect to the awards as if they were a final judgement of the court of that state.[234] India argued that under general principles of municipal law 'execution of international arbitral awards was subject to certain exceptions, viz. (i) where the dispute was not of a kind arbitrable under the law of the state concerned, and (ii) where enforcement of the award would be contrary to its public policy'.[235] To build its case against automatic enforcement of ICSID awards, India gave the example of the New York Convention on the recognition and enforcement of foreign arbitral awards that contained such exceptions.[236]

From India's interventions made in the negotiations of the ICSID Convention, it is quite evident that not just India was welcoming of foreign investment but also that in principle India was not against

[232] Negotiating History of ICSID Convention, Volume I, p. 831.

[233] Legal Committee on Settlement of Disputes, Working Group IV (30 November 1964).

[234] ICSID, *Convention on the Settlement of Investment Disputes between States and Nationals of Other States*, pp. 520–1.

[235] ICSID, *Convention on the Settlement of Investment Disputes between States and Nationals of Other States*, pp. 520–1.

[236] ICSID, *Convention on the Settlement of Investment Disputes between States and Nationals of Other States*, pp. 520–1. Also see S. Jayasimha, R. Raghavan, and S. Tigadi. 2018. 'ICSID and India: Should India Ratify the ICSID Convention', *Transnational Dipsute Management Journal* 15: 1.

foreign investors using international arbitration to settle disputes with the states—a fact that most Indian international lawyers have not adequately highlighted. However, India had certain reservations, as discussed earlier and thus decided not to join the ICSID Convention.

2.2.3 At the Bilateral Level

India's approach to international investment law at the bilateral level was different from the multilateral level. Most international lawyers who have written on India's approach towards international law have not emphasized much on this part. Although, India did not sign a BIT in this phase, it did express its willingness to enter into investment agreements to reassure foreign investors about the safety of their investment in India. The Indian finance minister, in 1959, had said that the Indian government was keen to consider entering into suitable agreements with those countries which had programmes for insuring investments of their nationals in foreign countries.[237] The minister went on to specifically express the concern of foreign investors saying that, subject to approval by the Indian and the home state of the investor, India could enter into an investment agreement to ensure that foreign investment is not expropriated without payment of full compensation.[238]

The statement of the finance minister and Nehru's pragmatic approach towards foreign investment as discussed earlier explains why the Nehru government, despite following a socialistic pattern of society, entered into investment guarantee agreements (IGA) with United States of America and West Germany through exchange of letters in 1957[239] and 1964, respectively.[240] Under the IGA with the

[237] As cited in Jain, *Nationalisation of Foreign Property*, p. 232.

[238] Jain, *Nationalisation of Foreign Property*, p. 232.

[239] India, Guaranty of Private Investment, Agreement Effected by Exchange of Notes, Signed at Washington 19 September 1957; Entered into force 19 September 1957 (India–US IGA).

[240] India, Guaranty of Private Investment, Agreement Effected by Exchange of Notes, Signed at Washington 19 September 1957; Entered into force 19 September 1957 (India–US IGA); Rao, 'Bilateral Investment Promotion Agreements'.

US, the US government issued a guaranty to a US project in India if it was approved by the Indian government.[241] No such guaranty was issued for US projects in India that were not approved by the Indian government. Furthermore, the IGA also provided that if the US government made payments in US dollars to any person under any such guaranty, the Indian government will recognize the transfer to the US of any right, title or interest of such person in assets, currency, credits or other property on account of which such payment was made.[242] In other words, this was an agreement to allow for repatriation of profits or other interests. Likewise, the two countries agreed that if the US government acquired Indian rupee accounts pursuant to such guaranties, they shall be accorded treatment no less favourable than that accorded to private funds arising from transactions of US nationals comparable to the transactions covered by such guaranties.[243] Also, such rupee amounts will be freely available to the US government for administrative expenditures.[244] Thus, the IGA covered risks pertaining to currency inconvertibility in respect of profits.

According to Jain, India's IGA with West Germany signed in 1964 covered risks against nationalization, expropriation, and impossibility of conversion of rupees in West German currency.[245] The agreement with West Germany also provided national treatment to German investors and no less favourable treatment than other foreign investors in similar circumstances.[246] The agreement also envisaged payments of 'fair and equitable compensation' to a German investor if the investor was 'directly or indirectly deprived of his investment by nationalization or expropriation'.[247] This provision was prefaced by the following statement: The Government of India do not intend, as a rule, to nationalize or expropriate approved foreign investments. Any decision to nationalize or expropriate a German investment or

[241] See India–US IGA.
[242] See India–US IGA.
[243] See India–US IGA.
[244] See India–US IGA.
[245] Jain, *Nationalisation of Foreign Property*, p. 233.
[246] Jain, *Nationalisation of Foreign Property*, p. 233.
[247] Jain, *Nationalisation of Foreign Property*, p. 233.

part of it taken by the Government of India shall be based on practical considerations and be taken in national interest.[248]

In other words, India's investment agreement with West Germany of 1964 provided more substantive protections to foreign investment. Interestingly, this agreement even talked of protection from unlawful indirect expropriation. Although, indirect expropriation is a feature of most BITs, the fact that India had accepted this in an agreement in 1964 reveals that there was some divergence between what India was espousing multilaterally and bilaterally.[249] All the multilateral declarations discussed earlier to which India was a party, made references to only expropriation. It can be argued that these references were to direct and not to indirect expropriation.

Another fact that's not adequately highlighted is that during this phase India also signed many bilateral double taxation avoidance agreements (DTAAs), which also had a bearing on foreign investment. First such DTAA was signed in 1958 with Switzerland[250] followed by another agreement with West Germany in 1960.[251] Till the end of 1990, India signed DTAAs with more than 40 countries including countries like US, Netherlands, Canada, and Australia.[252]

2.3 Summing up

The chapter has looked at the evolution of India's approach towards international investment law, against the backdrop of India's overall

[248] Jain, *Nationalisation of Foreign Property*, p. 233.

[249] See generally Andrew Guzman. 1997. 'Why LDCs Sign Treaties That Hurt Them: Explaining the Popularity of Bilateral Investment Treaties', *Vanderbilt Journal of International Law* 38: 639.

[250] Agreement between the Government of India and the Swiss Federal Council concerning the taxation of enterprises operate aircraft (Notification No. GSR 761(E), dated 29 August 1958).

[251] Agreement between the Government of India and the Government of the Federal Republic of Germany for Avoidance of Double Taxation on Income (Notifications No. GSR 1090, dated 13 September 1960, GSR 282(E), dated 27 April 1979 and GSR 107(E), dated 2 March1990).

[252] Income Tax Department, Government of India, https://www.incometaxindia.gov.in/pages/international-taxation/dtaa.aspx.

and economic approach towards foreign investment. After independence, from the period 1947–65, India followed a relatively open and liberal foreign investment regime. Nehru's economic pragmatism ensured that India kept its doors open to foreign investment though the economic model was led by the public sector. Nehru also consciously opposed nationalization of foreign investment in total contradiction to what countries like Soviet Russia and China did. However, India turned towards the Left during Indira Gandhi's time imposing restrictions on foreign investment. India's approach towards international investment law, at least at the multilateral level, reflected the domestic approach towards foreign investment. While India contested some aspects like the minimum standard of treatment of aliens, it also accepted that if foreign investment is expropriated adequate compensation should be paid. India wanted to have more control on questions like adequacy of compensation and thus espoused that these issues be governed by domestic law. The history of ICSID negotiations also shows that India as such was not opposed to the idea of foreign investors using international arbitration to settle disputes with India though it was against putting foreign investors and host states at the same pedestal as far as international law is concerned. This 'formal dualism', that is, questioning the colonial content and at the same time trying to shape international law in a manner that suited the interests of India was not so visible at the bilateral level. At the bilateral level, India appeared more open to international law on protection of foreign investment although India did not sign a BIT during this phase. As Guzman has argued that many developing countries at multilateral forums opposed the existence of principles like payment of 'prompt, adequate and effective' compensation for expropriating foreign investment, but at the same time signed investment treaties bilaterally with developed countries recognizing the same principles.[253] To a very limited extent, this was true for India as well.

[253] A. Guzman. 1997. 'Why LDCs Sign Treaties That Hurt Them: Explaining the Popularity of Bilateral Investment Treaties', *Virginia Journal of International Law* 38: 639.

PHASE II

ACCEPTANCE

3

Economic Liberalism

Embracing Bilateral Investment Treaties

The limited liberalization and deregulation of the Indian economy in the 1980s pursued by the Congress-led Government of Indira Gandhi and Rajiv Gandhi, as mentioned in the last chapter, resulted in the GDP growing at an average rate of 5.6 per cent in the 1980s, as opposed to 2.9 per cent in the 1970s.[1] However, this growth rate was fuelled by the build-up of severe external debt culminating in severe Balance of Payment (BoP) crisis. The crisis, that arose in 1990–1, resulted in Indian foreign exchange reserves worth only two weeks of imports.[2] India's foreign exchange reserves were US$3.11 billion at

[1] M.S. Ahluwalia. 2017. 'India's 1991 Reforms: A Retrospective Overview', in *India Transformed: 25 Years of Economic Reforms* Rakesh Mohan (ed), p. 47. New Delhi: Penguin (hereinafter Ahluwalia, 'India's 1991 Reforms').

[2] See M.S. Ahluwalia. 2002. 'Economic Reforms in India Since 1991: Has Gradualism Worked?', *Journal of Economic Perspectives* 16(7): 67; Arvind Virmani. 2003. 'Modest Globalisation, Significant Gains: India's External Reforms', *Economic and Political Weekly* 38(32): 3373–4 (hereinafter Virmani, 'Modest Globalisation, Significant Gains'); Thirukodikaval Srinivasan and Suresh Tendulkar. 2003. *Reintegrating India with the World Economy.* Washington DC: Institute of International Economics, p. 9.

the end of August 1990, which fell sharply to just US$ 896 million by mid-January 1991.[3]

In this chapter, we briefly discuss the 1991 economic crisis and the economic reforms that this crisis triggered including some global developments that impacted the thinking of the Indian policymakers (Section 3.1). The chapter shows that due to the economic reforms of 1991 India embraced foreign investment, which, in turn, sowed the seeds of the phase of acceptance of BITs from 1991 till 2010. The chapter then discusses the growth of the Indian BIT programme by looking at its geographical spread and other related patterns (Section 3.2). The chapter then discusses the key distinguishing features of the acceptance phase: BITs as instruments to promote and protect foreign investment (Section 3.3); marginal involvement of India with ISDS (Section 3.4); and negligible discussion on the interface between BITs and exercise of regulatory power by India during the acceptance phase (Section 3.5).

The other key distinguishing feature of the acceptance phase is that the BITs India signed in this phase contained 'capital-exporting' country features or a 'capital-exporting' country model.[4] This 'capital-exporting' country BIT model contained elaborate and broadly worded substantive and procedural assurances for protection of foreign investment, except for right to establishment, with scant exceptions, reservations, and carve-out provisions.[5] By adopting these BITs that represented laissez-faire liberalism, India significantly departed

[3] Ramesh Jairam. 2015. *To the Brink and Back: India's 1991 Story*. Delhi: Rupa, p. 11 (hereinafter Jairam, *To the Brink and Back*).

[4] Compare this with China's experience, which, in its first phase, entered into BITs which had limited substantive and procedural protection for foreign investment—See Nils Eliason. 2011. 'Chinese Investment Treaties: A Procedural Perspective', in *Foreign Investment and Dispute Resolution Law and Practice in Asia* Luke Nottage and Vivienne Bath (eds), p. 90. New York/London: Routledge.

[5] Jurgen Kurtz describes this phase as the 'growth' phase of the investment treaty norms where the 'classic' model BIT developed by the western states, aimed at protecting foreign investment, during the 'inception' phase of investment treaty norms was '*simply rolled out and replicated in large numbers*'—See Jurgen Kurtz. 2012. 'The Shifting Landscape of International Investment Law and its Commentary', *American Journal of International Law* 106: 686.

from its earlier stand on protection of foreign investment under international law. The broadly worded provisions, depending on the exercise of arbitral discretion, can be interpreted to give precedence to investment protection over India's exercise of regulatory power. This particular feature of the acceptance phase will be discussed in Chapters 4 and 5.

3.1 Setting the Scene: The 1991 BoP Crisis and Spurring of Economic Reforms

Vijay Joshi and I.M.D. Little, two distinguished commentators on the Indian economy, have documented the roots of the 1990–1 BoP crisis in the policy stance taken by the Indian government post the second oil shock (1979–80).[6] Joshi and Little argue that post the oil-shock, in the 1980s, India's fiscal debt deteriorated and, both, domestic and foreign debt increased rapidly.[7] Furthermore, Rajiv Gandhi's government neglected the ominous signs on the fiscal front evident in 1985/6 and allowed fiscal worsening to continue apace.[8] I.G. Patel, a former governor of the Reserve Bank of India (RBI) and a distinguished economist, commenting on the reasons behind the 1991 crisis wrote:

> [I]f the present [1991] crisis is the greatest we have faced since independence, it is for no underlying economic factor which is more adverse now than what we have had to contend with in the past several decades. It is because successive governments in the 1980s chose to abdicate their responsibility to the nation for the sake of short-term partisan political gains and indeed out of sheer political cynicism.[9]

[6] Vijay Joshi and I.M.D. Little. 1994. *India: Macroeconomics and Political Economy*. New Delhi: Oxford University Press, p. 190 (hereinafter Joshi and Little, *India*).

[7] Joshi and Little, *India*, p. 190.

[8] Joshi and Little, *India*, p. 190. Also see Yashwant Sinhaand Vinay K. Srivastava. 2017. 'The Economic Reforms in India: A Historical Review' in *The Future of Indian Economy* Yashwant Sinha and Vinay K. Srivastava (eds), pp. 3–4. New Delhi: Rupa.

[9] Indraprasad Gordhanbhai Patel. 1992. 'New Economic Policies: A Historical Perspective', *Economic and Political Weekly* 27 (1/2): 43. Also see

The fact that the roots of the 1991 crisis lay in the fiscal profligacy of the 1980s was observed by none other than Manmohan Singh, who on 5 March 1991,[10] said, 'since the mid-eighties we have borrowed excessively and the fiscal deficit has gone out of control. We could have avoided this situation if we had attended to the balance of payments problem much earlier.'[11] Manmohan Singh, while making the above comment, would have had no foreboding that a few months later he would be the finance minister dealing with the crisis.

The reckless fiscal profligacy of the 1980s led to a deep macroeconomic crisis, and in 1990–1, the Indian economy was in shreds. The deteriorating economic indicators were proof enough of the gravity of the crisis that stared India. Government's internal debt had increased from 35 per cent of GDP in 1980–1 to 53 per cent in 1990–1.[12] The wholesale or producer price inflation in 1991 stood at 10.3 per cent, and with no check on expenditure the combined fiscal deficit of the central state governments was more than 9 per cent of the GDP.[13] The current account deficit of India's BoP, at almost 3 per cent of the GDP, was highest in decades.[14] In order to fight the crisis, India even mortgaged gold—twice—in May 1991 to the Union Bank

Arvind Virmani. 2001. 'India's BoP Crisis and External Reform: Myths and Paradoxes', http://www.icrier.org/pdf/AV-%20on%20BoP%20crisis.pdf, accessed 24 February 2018.

[10] Sanjaya Baru, Interview with Manmohan Singh, Economic Advisor to Prime Minister Chandra Shekhar (5 March 1991) cited in Ramesh, *To the Brink and Back*, p. 17.

[11] Sanjaya Baru, Interview with Manmohan Singh, Economic Advisor to Prime Minister Chandra Shekhar (5 March 1991) cited in Ramesh, *To the Brink and Back*, p. 17. Also see *Frontline*, Interview with K.N. Raj, Economist (mid-July 1991) echoing the same view cited in Ramesh, *To the Brink and Back*, Annexure 10.

[12] Government of India. 1993. *Economic Survey* (1991-92) Part II. New Delhi: Ministry of Finance, Government of India, p. 13.

[13] Omkar Goswami. 2017. 'Remembering 1991 … and Before', in *India Transformed: 25 Years of Economic Reforms* Rakesh Mohan (ed.). p. 73. New Delhi: Penguin (hereinafter Goswami, 'Remembering 1991 … and Before').

[14] Goswami, 'Remembering 1991 … and Before', p. 73.

of Switzerland to raise US$ 200 million[15] and then again in July 1991 to the Bank of England to raise US$ 400 million.[16] This crisis was accompanied by a period of political instability as the nation saw three prime ministers changing from December 1989 till June 1991.[17] India had to engage with international financial institutions like the IMF and the World Bank for financial assistance to overcome the BoP crisis.[18]

Finally, it was left to Prime Minister P.V. Narasimha Rao's minority government that assumed charge on 21 June 1991 to sort out the crisis. About a month later, on 24 July 1991, Manmohan Singh, Finance Minister in government, presented India's general budget in the Indian Parliament.[19] The Narasimha Rao government utilized the BoP crisis to usher in a new economic era departing from the old economic policy followed by India since independence. The budget outlined the broad contours of a new economic era (now famous as 1991 economic reforms) by focussing on two aspects—first, a macroeconomic consolidation package aimed at reducing the fiscal

[15] Sinha and Srivastava,'The Economic Reforms in India: A Historical Review', p. 12; Ramesh, *To the Brink and Back*, p. 44.

[16] Specifically, on the transport of gold in July 1991, see Statement of Finance Minister Manmohan Singh on gold transactions, Lok Sabha, 18 July 1991. See Shaji Vikraman. 2017. 'In fact: How Govts Pledged Gold to Pull Economy Back from the Brink', The Indian Express, 5 April, https://indianexpress.com/article/explained/in-fact-how-govts-pledged-gold-to-pull-economy-back-from-the-brink/ Also see Rakesh Mohanand Vandana Aggarwal. 1995. 'Commands and Control: Planning for Industrial Development, 1951–90', *Journal of Comparative Economics* 14(4): 681–713.

[17] V.P. Singh became India's seventh Prime Minister on 2 December 1989, followed by Chandra Shekhar on 10 November 1990. The Chandra Shekhar government fell after a few months paving way for general elections that led to P.V. Narasimha Rao becoming India's Prime Minister on 21 June 1991.

[18] Panagariya, *India*, p. 103.; Vijay Joshi. 2016. *India's Long Road Ahead: The Search for Prosperity*. Gurgaon: Penguin, pp. 25–6 (hereinafter Joshi, *India's Long Road Ahead*).

[19] Manmohan Singh, Minister of Finance. 1991. 'Budget 1991–92 Speech', http://www.indiabudget.gov.in/bspeech/bs199192.pdf, 24 July, accessed 24 February 2018.

deficit and attending the immediate BoP crisis;[20] second, proposing and implementing a range of structural reforms intended to boost economic efficiency and stimulate India's economic growth.[21] As part of these structural reforms India started taking steps towards gradually dismantling quantitative restrictions on imports, bringing down tariff rates from a peak of 300 per cent to 35 per cent; and comprehensive reform of the exchange control regime.[22]

Measures aimed at liberalizing FDI and Foreign Institutional Investment (FII) inflows to overcome the problem of over-dependence on debt were also introduced.[23] Bold measures aimed at liberalizing

[20] Manmohan Singh, Minister of Finance, 'Budget 1991-92 Speech'. 1991. http://www.indiabudget.gov.in/bspeech/bs199192.pdf, 24 July, accessed 24 February 2018. M.S. Ahluwalia. 2016. 'The 1991 Reforms: How Home-grown Were They?', *Economic and Political Weekly* 29:39 (hereinafter Ahluwalia, 'The 1991 Reforms').

[21] Ahluwalia, 'The 1991 Reforms', pp. 44–5. It is important to keep in mind that the process for the economic reforms that were officially kick-started on 24 July 1991 had begun in May 1990 much before the Narasimha Rao government took charge. Prime Minister V.P. Singh, impressed by the performance of the Southeast Asian nations, had asked his special secretary, Montek Singh Ahluwalia, in May 1990, to prepare a paper on what India could do to emulate the performance of the Southeast Asian countries. Ahluwalia prepared a note titled,'Restructuring India's Industrial and Trade Policies,' which popularly came to be known as the M-document in India's policy circles at that time. Among other things the M-document talked about liberalization of the Indian foreign direct investment regime. Yashwant Sinha, finance minister in the Chandra Shekhar government, also did very critical ground work to counter the 1991 crisis, though he could not present the budget outlining the economic reforms that he intended to because the Chandra Shekhar government fell on 6 March 1991—see Yashwant Sinha. 2007. *Confessions of a Swadeshi Reformer*, pp. 7–8. New Delhi: Penguin.

[22] For a detailed discussion on these economic reforms, see Ahluwalia, 'The 1991 Reforms'; Chakravarthi Rangarajan. 2010. 'Two Episodes in the Reform Process', in *India's Economy: Performance and Challenges* Shankar Acharya and Rakesh Mohan (eds), p. 100. New Delhi: Oxford University Press (hereinafter Rangarajan,'Two Episodes in the Reform Process'); Arvind Panagariya. 2003. 'Growth and Reforms during 1980s and 1990s', *Economic and Political Weekly* 39(25):2581; Thirukodikaval Srinivasan. 2011. *Growth, Sustainability and India's Economic Reforms*. New Delhi: Oxford University Press.

[23] See Rangarajan, 'Two Episodes in the Reform Process', p. 100.

FDI included automatic approval of FDI up to 51 per cent in high-priority industries; 100 per cent foreign equity in the energy sector; setting up of a Foreign Investment Promotion Board (FIPB) to act as a single window clearance for foreign investment proposals; opening up new sectors such as mining and telecommunications for foreign investment; amendment of the foreign exchange regulation act to treat foreign companies with more than 40 per cent ownership at par with fully owned Indian companies.[24] The new industrial policy of 1991 recognized that 'foreign investment would bring attendant advantages of technology transfer, marketing expertise, introduction of modern managerial techniques and new possibilities for promotion of exports'.[25] Thus, reforming India's FDI policy became an integral part of the 1991 industrial policy.[26] The 1991 industrial policy allowed investment through two routes—the automatic route (where no permission is needed from the government) and the approved route (requiring prior government permission). The reopening of the country to foreign investment in the 1991 industrial policy also meant that the ghost of the East India Company was finally laid to rest.[27]

These structural reforms and the reforms of the external sector signalled a major change in India's perception towards foreign investment and marked a paradigm shift in India's economic thinking.[28]

[24] For more details, see N. Kumar. 1998. 'Liberalisation and Changing Patterns of Foreign Direct Investments', *Economic and Political Weekly* 33(22):1323–4; Nirupam Bajpai and Jeffery Sachs. 2001. 'Foreign Direct Investment in India: Issues and Problems', *HIID Development Discussion Paper No. 759/2001*; R. Nagaraj. 2003. 'Foreign Direct Investment in India in 1990s', *Economic and Political Weekly* 38(17):1701.

[25] Government of India. 1991. 'India's New Industrial Policy of 1991', http://dipp.nic.in/sites/default/files/chap001_0_0.pdf, accessed 28 February 2018.

[26] Arvind Virmani. 2005. 'Policy Regimes, Growth and Poverty in India: Lessons of Government Failure and Entrepreneurial Success!', ICRIER Working Paper No. 170.

[27] See Ahluwalia, 'India's 1991 Reforms', p. 48.

[28] In India, there has been a general attitude of suspicion towards business and this suspicion could be traced back to India's experience with the East India company—see Kaushik Basu. 2003. 'The Indian Economy: Up to 1991 and Since', BREAD Working Paper No 052, http://ibread.org/bread/system/files/bread_wpapers/052.pdf, accessed 28 February 2018.

In many ways, this marked a major shift from economic nationalism India practised thus far towards economic liberalism[29] that understood the value of freeing the markets from state control. India, slowly but surely, started to lift its self-imposed economic exile, and began to move from a close, inward-looking economic model based on import-substitution to a liberalized and outward-looking economic model.[30] The new economic paradigm, inspired from economic liberalism, showed greater trust in markets, valued freer trade, and took steps towards freer movement of capital across borders. This is not suggest that since 1991 India embraced classical economic liberalism of the kind John Locke[31] or Adam Smith[32] had propagated, but the paradigm shift from economic nationalism towards liberalism was obvious.

It is important to bear in mind that these reforms were not undertaken simply in return for the financial assistance that international bodies like the IMF and the World Bank extended to India,[33] as left-leaning academics opposed to economic liberalization claim.[34] Interestingly, the Left in India criticized these reforms despite China accelerating in the same direction since 1978 and despite the collapse of communism and socialistic-model of economic growth world over in late 1980s and early 1990s. Chimni, for example, mentions that the liberalization of the Indian economy in 1991 could not be rolled back because of the fact 'that India had to meet the conditions of the IMF, and subsequently abide by the obligations undertaken in the Final Act of the Uruguay Round' (that led to the creation of the WTO).[35]

[29] For a discussion on economic liberalism, see Darel E. Paul and Abla Amawi. 2013. *The Theoretical Evolution of International Political Economy*. New York: Oxford University Press, pp. 48–79; Vandevelde, *Bilateral Investment Treaties*, pp. 75–80.

[30] These economic reforms had their critiques as well—see the Statement issued by 35 'left oriented' economists on 8 July 1991 cited in Jairam Ramesh, *To the Brink and Back*, Annexure 6.

[31] See generally Donald Winch. 1985. 'Economic Liberalism as Ideology: The Appleby Version', *The Economic History Review* 38: 287–97.

[32] See generally Vandevlde, *Bilateral Investment Treaties*, pp. 75–6.

[33] Ahluwalia,'The 1991 Reforms', p. 39.

[34] Ahluwalia, 'India's 1991 Reforms', p. 51.

[35] Chimni, 'International Law Scholarship in Post-colonial India, p. 44

However, this oversimplified claim ignores the nuance, as Ahluwalia has argued, that there was a 'home grown process of rethinking on economic policy', independent of pressure from international institutions that played an important role in undertaking these reforms.[36] Ahluwalia gives several reasons for this.[37] First, as pointed out in Chapter 2, the seeds of change were sown in the 1980s itself with talk about moving towards a more flexible and liberalized trade regime.[38] Second, Ahluwalia also argues that in areas such as 'trade liberalization and shift to a market-determined exchange rate, the reform package went beyond what the IMF and World Bank were advocating'.[39] Third, due to political unacceptability, India's economic reforms consciously decided not to include privatization of public sector units, despite it being part of the Washington consensus propagated by institutions like the IMF.[40] Fourth, the fact that these reforms continued even after the end of the BoP crisis by the end of 1993, as discussed later in the chapter, and by all political parties who ruled India despite having different ideological preferences, shows that there was an internal commitment to undertake these reforms that went beyond the conditionalities imposed by bodies like the IMF.

The third world approaches to international law scholars in India have not been able to fully appreciate the strong economic rationale that triggered a conscious shift in the Indian economic thinking. TWAIL-ers continue to look at just one side of the picture and thus believe that these reforms were an outcome of the imperial global order and were not an outcome of internal conviction,[41] which is not true. The tendency to continuously keep imagining the presence of imperial ghosts in whatever one sees often blurs the vision making it difficult to see things objectively.

[36] Ahluwalia, 'The 1991 Reforms'.

[37] Ahluwalia,'The 1991 Reforms'.

[38] Ahluwalia, 'The 1991 Reforms'.

[39] Ahluwalia,'The 1991 Reforms', p. 42, Ahluwalia,'India's 1991 Reforms', pp. 51–2.

[40] Ahluwalia,'India's 1991 Reforms', pp. 51–2.

[41] See Chimni, 'International Law Scholarship in Post-colonial India'.

Rodrik and Subramanian have argued that these changes in India's economic policy signalled a pro-market[42] orientation of the Indian State with the focus 'on removing impediments to markets and aims to achieve this through economic liberalization', as against the pro-business[43] orientation of the 1980s.[44] These reforms by ending the license raj that benefitted existing big businesses were a break from the past. These economic policies put the Indian economy on a much faster economic growth track. India's GDP numbers clearly prove this. According to the World Bank data, in 1960, India's GDP was US$ 36 billion, which increased to US$ 266 billion by the end of 1991.[45] This shows an increase of about US$ 230 billion in 31 years or an increase of around US$ 7 billion per year. From US$ 266 billion in 1991, India's GDP, by the end of 2017, jumped to US$ 2.601 trillion[46] or US$ 2601 billion. This shows an increase of US$ 2335 billion in a period of 26 years or an increase of around US$ 89 billion per annum.

Thus, after India adopted a relatively liberal economic order, the Indian GDP grew at an impressive rate of US$ 89 billion per year (from 1992–2017) as against a paltry rate of US$ 7 billion per year (from 1960–1991). This faster economic growth also led to a rapid reduction in poverty in India. For example, in 1993–4, 45.7 per cent Indians were below the poverty line.[47] This number, in 2011–12, just in 18 years, fell to 22 per cent[48] (a very significant decline—almost

[42] Pro-market orientation means adopting policies that foster truly and freely competitive markets with a level playing field for everyone.

[43] Pro-business orientation means promoting and protecting the fortunes of existing businesses at the cost of new entrants.

[44] Dani Rodrik and Arvind Subramanian. 2004. 'From "Hindu Growth" to Productivity Surge: The Mystery of the Indian Growth Transition', IMF Working Paper, https://www.imf.org/external/pubs/ft/wp/2004/wp0477.pdf, accessed 28 February 2018.

[45] World Bank. n.d. https://data.worldbank.org/country/india.

[46] World Bank. n.d. https://data.worldbank.org/country/india.

[47] Dev, S. Mahendra. 2016. 'Economic Reforms, Poverty and Inequality', http://www.igidr.ac.in/pdf/publication/WP-2016-009.pdf, p. 24 (hereinafter Dev, 'Economic Reforms, Poverty and Inequality', p. 24) .

[48] Dev, 'Economic Reforms, Poverty and Inequality', p. 24. Also see Angus Deaton. 2013. *The Great Escape: Health, Wealth, and the Origins of Equality*. Princeton and Oxford: Princeton University Press, p. 250.

half—especially when compared to what happened from 1947 to 1991). The rate of poverty reduction was fastest from 2004–5 to 2011–12, for all social groups, when the Indian economy grew at an average rate of 8 per cent per annum,[49] thus establishing a direct link between economic growth and poverty reduction. As Rangarajan and Dev argue, after the adoption of economic reforms in 1991, poverty in India declined by 1.36 percentage points per annum, almost three times more than 0.44 percentage points per annum prior to 1991.[50] As of June 2018, the number of people living in extreme poverty in India has fallen to around 5 per cent of the total population;[51] thus, India is on the verge of eliminating extreme poverty.[52] The fact that this high reduction in poverty has coincided with more than 25 years of high economic growth rates since 1991 is not a mere coincidence. Globally, India has been the biggest contributor to poverty reduction between 2008–11 (the years when the Indian economy grew at more than 8 per cent per annum) by lifting around 140 million people out of poverty.[53]

The 1991 economic reforms and reforms taken thereafter have dented poverty rates India—an important fact that cannot be ignored. Indian TWAIL scholars like Chimni who critique India's adoption of economic reforms in 1991, do so by evoking emotive terms like 'two Indias and two worlds'[54] without offering any hard economic data or statistics to make a convincing case that the 1991 economic reforms have not worked for the poor. For instance, Chimni writing in 2007, argued that 'the government contends, and not entirely without

[49] 'Economic Reforms, Poverty and Inequality', p. 24. Also see Angus Deaton. 2013. *The Great Escape: Health, Wealth, and the Origins of Equality*. Princeton and Oxford: Princeton University Press, p. 250.

[50] Rangarajan C. and M. Dev. 2018. 'How the Data Sets Stack Up', http://www.thehindu.com/todays-paper/tp-opinion/how-the-data-sets-stack-up/article23428911.ece.

[51] World Data Lab, http://www.worldpoverty.io/.

[52] UNDP. 2015. 'Eradicating Poverty is One of the Sustainable Development Goals (SDGs) Identified by the UN', http://www.undp.org/content/undp/en/home/sustainable-development-goals/goal-1-no-poverty.html.

[53] World Bank. 2014–15. *Global Monitoring Report: Ending Poverty and Sharing Prosperity*. Washington DC, p. 20.

[54] Chimni,'The Past, Present and Future of International Law'.

merit, that economic growth will lead to the reduction of poverty and inequality. The problem is that it has not yet happened'.[55] To substantiate this claim he cites a 2005 UNDP report that talks about human development index (HDI).[56] The conceptual flaw here is that elimination of poverty is being confused with India's rank in the HDI, which is much more comprehensive concept that includes other things apart from poverty reduction. Further, even this claim is made without talking about the poverty figures and HDI rank of India before India embarked on the road of economic reforms in 1991. The fact is that, according to the World Bank, the number of Indians living below poverty line in 1993 was 45.7 per cent, as mentioned earlier. This number fell to 37.2 per cent in 2004[57]—more than 7 percentage points in just about a decade, something that Chimni does not report while writing in 2007. Writing in 2011, Chimni repeats the same claim in the context of India—that there is a realization that increased economic growth rates do not translate into development as freedom.[58] Again no evidence is provided to back this claim. In place of empirical evidence, Chimni adopts the Marxist 'class' vocabulary to make his case. This includes attempts to show how the transnational capitalist class (TCC) is exploiting the transnational oppressed class (TOC).[59] The problem is not that these arguments are completely without merit. The problem is that they are based on selective examination or, at times, no examination of evidence, and thus results into overstating the case. The fact is that

[55] Chimni, 'The Past, Present and Future of International Law', p. 211.

[56] Chimni, 'The Past, Present and Future of International Law', p. 211.

[57] 'Poverty Head Count Ratio at National Poverty Lines', https://data.worldbank.org/indicator/SI.POV.NAHC?locations=IN.

[58] Chimni, B.S. 2011. 'The World of TWAIL: Introduction To The Special Issue', Trade Law & Development 3(1): 14, 20 (hereinafter Chimni, 'The World of TWAIL').

[59] Chimni, B.S. 2013. 'Critical Theory and International Economic Law: A Third World Approach to International Law (TWAIL) Perspective'. In *Research Handbook on Global Justice and International Economic Law*, John Linarelli (ed.), pp. 251–73. Cheltenham/ Northampton: Edward Elgar Publishing (hereinafter Chimni, 'Critical Theory and International Economic Law'). See Chapter 1.

in 2011, as already noted earlier, poverty rate in India, due to faster economic growth, had fallen to 22 per cent (refer to the poverty numbers given earlier).

One concedes that the 1991 economic reforms haven posed new challenges such as widening income inequality in India.[60] But one has to look at all sides to comprehensively understand the full picture and not indulge in ideological cherry-picking. Moreover, as Simon Kuznets showed that as economies developed, income inequality first increased, and only after a level of economic development is reached, income inequality starts to decrease.[61] In any case, the high income inequality in India underlines the importance of making the economic growth process inclusive.

Another major challenge 1991 economic reforms have posed is the rapid spread of crony capitalism—a perverse manifestation of capitalism where private entities and the government collude to rig the competitive rules or laws of market economy to favour the colluding private entities, often in exchange for money or other such considerations.[62] Arguably, the current economic environment in India resembles that of America's gilded age of the nineteenth century.[63] However, this challenge requires bringing about large-scale governance and institutional reforms and cannot be an argument to question India's post-1991 movement towards greater economic liberalism premised on free markets.

[60] See L. Chancel and P. Pikkety. 2017. 'Indian Income Inequality, 1922-2015: From British Raj to Billionarie Raj?', http://wid.world/wp-content/uploads/2017/12/ChancelPiketty2017WIDworld.pdf.

[61] S. Kuzents. 1955. 'Economic Growth and Income Inequality', *American Economic Review* 45:1. This finding of Kuznets while true for Western European countries is not consistent across other countries—see D. Acemoglu and J. Robinson. 2002. 'The Political Economy of Kuznets Curve', *Review of Development Economics* 6(2): 183.

[62] See Chiranjib Sen. 2017. 'Curbing Crony Capitalism in India', Working Paper No 5, Azim Premji University; James Crabtree. 2018. *The Billionaire Raj*. New York: Harper Collins (hereinafter Crabtree, *The Billionaire Raj*).

[63] Crabtree, *The Billionaire Raj*; Jayant Sinha and AshutoshVarshney. 2011. 'It is Time for India to Rein in its Robber Barons', *Financial Times*, 7 January.

3.1.1 Global Developments

It is also interesting to observe that globally, the period of the late 1980s and early 1990s, witnessed some major economic developments.[64] The success story of the East Asian economies (Japan, Hong Kong, Republic of Korea, and Singapore) and of the Southeast Asian economies (Indonesia, Malaysia, and Thailand) had shown that high rates of private investment combined with policies focussing on export promotion can lead to high economic growth.[65] The success of these developing economies underlined the need for a policy shift in India towards a more open and market-based economic model.[66]

T.N. Srinivasan has argued that there were two other international developments that had an impact on the 1991 reforms. First was the collapse of the Soviet Union.[67] The Soviet-styled planned economy model, the ideological alternative to free market capitalism, had inspired Indian policymakers for most of its post-independence history, as mentioned in Chapter 2. However, the collapse of the Soviet Union in 1990–1 'knocked the bottom out of Soviet style planning'.[68] The Soviet model was abandoned by the entire communist world,[69] which, in turn, massively dented the credibility and acceptability of the economic strategy and model India followed since independence.[70] During this time, there was also a realization among developing countries that import-substitution industrialization had not worked as well as had been expected.[71] Among the

[64] Also see Chapter 1.

[65] World Bank. 1993. *The East Asian Miracle: Economic Growth and Public Policy*. Oxford Univeristy Press: New York, pp. 40–2.

[66] Montek Singh Ahluwalia. 2002. 'Economic Reforms in India since 1991: Has Gradualism Worked?', *Planning Commission,* planningcommission.nic.in/aboutus/speech/spemsa/msa008.doc, accessed 28 February 2018.

[67] Srinivasan, *Growth Sustainability and India's Economic Reforms*.

[68] Srinivasan, *Growth Sustainability and India's Economic Reforms*.

[69] John Rapley. 1996. *Understanding Development: Theory and Practice in the Third World* (3rd Edition). Boulder: Lynne Rienner, p. 70; Mark Kramer. 1992. 'Eastern Europe Goes to Market', *Foreign Policy* 86:134.

[70] Joshi, *India's Long Road Ahead*, p. 26.

[71] Jeffery Frieden. 2006. *Global Capitalism*. London and New York: W. W. Norton & Company, pp. 351–6.

developing countries there was a growing consensus about the desirability of attracting foreign investment through free market policies and by creating a favourable environment.[72] The growth and spread of neo-liberalism from the late 1970s and early 1980s, as discussed in Chapter 1, was a very important factor shaping the global environment from which India could not remain immune for long.

The second pertinent international development according to Srinivasan was the rapid growth of China, since Deng Xiaoping opened the state to world economy in 1978 and let the market forces play a greater role in the Chinese economy.[73] As a result of these economic reforms, per capita income of China galloped by 6.6 per cent a year from 1978 to 2003.[74] The success of Chinese economic reforms created an impetus in India to move away from a model based on economic insularity and bureaucratic controls to an open-economy model that recognized the significance of the private sector and market forces.[75]

3.1.2 Post 1991

Post 1991, India's FDI policy has only experienced further liberalization. For instance, in 1992–3, India allowed direct portfolio investment by foreign institutional investors in the Indian equity market.[76] Similarly, in 1996–7, the number of industries part of the automatic approval list for FDI increased to 48.[77] This was further liberalized in 1999–2000 when India moved towards a negative list approach

[72] Richard Caves. 1996. *Multinational Enterprise and Economic Analysis* (2nd edition). Cambridge: Cambridge University Press, p. 249; Dean Hanink. 1994. *The International Economy: A Geographic Perspective*. United States: Wiley, p. 234; Kenneth Vandevelde. 1998. 'Investment Liberalisation and Economic Development: The Role of Bilateral Investment Treaties', *Columbia Journal of Transnational Law* 36:501 (hereinafter Vandevelde, 'Investment Liberalisation and Economic Development').

[73] Srinivasan, *Growth Sustainability and India's Economic Reforms*.

[74] Angus Maddison. 2007. *Chinese Economic Performance in the Long Run* (2nd edition). Paris: OECD, p. 20.

[75] Srinivasan, *Growth Sustainability and India's Economic Reforms*, n 22.

[76] Virmani, 'Modest Globalisation, Significant Gains', p. 3378.

[77] Virmani, 'Modest Globalisation, Significant Gains', p. 3377.

where all sectors were opened for FDI under the automatic approval route barring a few sectors.[78] In the late 1990s and early 2000s, foreign investors were assured that there would be a further reduction in red tape and bureaucratic controls making it easier for them to invest in India.[79]

Another major development was India's acceptance of Articles VIII (2), (3), and (4) obligations of the IMF Fund articles.[80] Article VIII of IMF Articles provides general obligations of member countries of the IMF including the obligation not to impose restrictions on the current account transactions.[81] Thus, the Indian rupee became officially convertible on the current account.[82] In fact, India even started debating full capital account convertibility (CAC, that is, moving towards liberalizing country's capital account) for which, in 1997, a committee was constituted by the Reserve Bank of India (RBI).[83] The committee was mandated to look into the possibility of fuller CAC in India.[84] This committee recommended movement towards CAC in a phased manner provided there was fiscal consolidation, a mandated inflation target and strengthening of the financial system.[85] However, this report was followed by the East Asian currency crisis and as a result movement towards full CAC was put on the back

[78] Virmani, 'Modest Globalisation, Significant Gains', p. 3377.

[79] See Yashwant Sinha. 1998. 'Budget Speech 1998-99', http://www.indiabudget.gov.in/ub1998-99/bs/bs6.htm, accessed 28 February 2018.

[80] International Monetary Fund. 2011. 'IMF Country Report No. 11/50', http://www.imf.org/external/pubs/ft/scr/2011/cr1150.pdf, p. 7, accessed 28 February 2018.

[81] International Monetary Fund Articles of Agreement (2016), Article VIII (2). Also see the chapter on monetary transfer provisions.

[82] Also see Virmani, 'Modest Globalisation, Significant Gains', p. 3380.

[83] Reserve Bank of India. 1997. 'Report of the Committee on Capital Account Convertibility', http://rbidocs.rbi.org.in/rdocs/PublicationReport/Pdfs/14029.pdf, accessed 28 February 2018 (hereinafter Reserve Bank of India. 'Report of the Committee on Capital Account Convertibility'). This committee was headed by SS Tarapore and hence is known the Tarapore committee report.

[84] Reserve Bank of India. 'Report of the Committee on Capital Account Convertibility'.

[85] Reserve Bank of India, 'Report of the Committee on Capital Account Convertibility'.

burner.[86] Nonetheless, a few years later, measures were taken towards liberalizing the capital account.[87]

Since 1991, India's economic policy has not just continued to recognize the importance of foreign investment but also taken numerous steps to promote it.[88] The 2017 FDI policy states that 'it is the intent and objective of the Government of India to attract and promote foreign direct investment in order to supplement domestic capital, technology and skills, for accelerated economic growth'.[89]

[86] In 2006, another committee was constituted to study CAC, under the leadership of S.S. Tarapore (same person who headed the first committee also called Tarapore committee—hereinafter Tarapore II). This committee also recommended that movement towards fuller CAC will require a better management of the liquidity risk, strengthening of the banking system and also fiscal consolidation—Reserve Bank of India. 2007. 'Report of the Committee on Fuller Capital Account Convertibility', http://rbidocs.rbi.org.in/rdocs/PublicationReport/Pdfs/72250.pdf, accessed 28 February 2018. Also see Ramachandra Patil. 2010. 'Financial Sector Reforms: Realities and Myths', *Economic and Political Weekly* 45 (19): 48.

[87] See the budget proposals of 2001–02—Yashwant Sinha. 2001. 'Budget Speech 2001-02: Capital Account Liberalisation', http://www.indiabudget.gov.in/ub2001-02/bs/capital.htm, accessed 28 February 2018.

[88] See P. Chidambaram, 'Budget Speech 2006-07' [43]. 2006, http://www.indiabudget.gov.in/ub2006-07/bs/speecha.htm, accessed 28 February 2018.See Department of Industrial Policy and Promotion, Ministry of Commerce and Industry, Government of India. 2010. 'Consolidated FDI Policy' [1.1.9], http://dipp.nic.in/sites/default/files/fdi_circular_1_2010%20%207_1.pdf, accessed 28 February 2018; Department of Industrial Policy and Promotion, Ministry of Commerce and Industry, Government of India. 2013. 'Consolidated FDI Policy' [1.1.1], http://dipp.nic.in/sites/default/files/FDI_Circular_01_2013%20%202%281%29.pdf, accessed 28 February 2018. Also see WTO Report by the Secretariat. 2011. 'Trade Policy Review Report India' WT/TPR/G/249, https://docsonline.wto.org/dol2fe/Pages/FE_Search/FE_S_S009-DP.aspx?language=E&CatalogueIdList=134359,131826,92476,107561,81496,25701,42365,75303&CurrentCatalogueIdIndex=2&FullTextHash=&HasEnglishRecord=True&HasFrenchRecord=True&HasSpanishRecord=True, accessed 28 February 2018. Also see David Collins. 2013. *The BRIC States and Outward FDI*. Oxford: Oxford University Press, pp. 96–8.

[89] Government of India, Department of Industrial Policy and Promotion. 2017. 'Consolidated FDI Policy' (Effective from 28 August 2017), http://

Since 1990s, India has also progressively liberalized the sectors in which FDI is allowed. Thus, barring certain sectors and activities such as gambling, lottery business, chit funds, real estate, manufacturing tobacco, FDI is allowed in all sectors subject to sector-specific conditions.[90] Now, India has even opened sectors like defence production and manufacturing for FDI.[91] Today, as shall be discussed in Chapter 6, foreign investment occupies a conspicuous place in India's international economic policy for which India is willing to provide protection as per international treaty law.[92]

Further proof of India's move towards openly embracing foreign investment, post 1991, comes from the introduction of new economic legislations that have a bearing on foreign investment. For example, in 1999, India enacted the Foreign Exchange Management Act (FEMA), which replaced the protectionist and anti-foreign investment FERA Act,[93] in order to consolidate and amend the law relating to foreign exchange and with the objective of facilitating external trade and payment.[94] It is interesting to note that the intention to replace FERA with legislation was declared by Manmohan Singh in his 1994–5 budget speech.[95] Other key economic legislations introduced or amended post 1990s having direct or indirect

---

dipp.nic.in/sites/default/files/CFPC_2017_FINAL_RELEASED_28.8.17.pdf, accessed 28 February 2018.

[90] Government of India, Department of Industrial Policy and Promotion, 'Consolidated FDI Policy'

[91] Press Information Bureau. 2017. 'FDI in Defence Sector', http://pib.nic.in/newsite/PrintRelease.aspx?relid=160287, 31 March, accessed 28 February 2018.

[92] For a critical discussion on India's changed Foreign Economic Policy, See Bhupinder Chimni. 2010. 'Mapping Indian Foreign Economic Policy', *International Studies* 47(2–4):163–85.

[93] See Chapter 2 for discussion on the FERA Act.

[94] The need to have the new legislation was also because of India's acceptance of International Monetary Fund Articles of Agreement (2016), Article VIII, on 20 August 1994.

[95] Manmohan Singh. 1994. 'Budget Speech 1994-95', http://www.indiabudget.gov.in/bspeech/bs199495.pdf, p.3, accessed 28 February 2018 (hereinafter Singh, 'Budget 1993-94 Speech').

bearing on foreign investment are—the amendment of the Indian Patent Act, 1970, introducing a product patent regime for pharmaceuticals in compliance with WTO obligations; amendment of the Customs Tariff Act 1975 in order to introduce WTO-consistent provisions on anti-dumping; enactment of a Competition Act in 2002 replacing the anti-market MRTP Act; the enactment of the Special Economic Zone (SEZ) Act in 2005 aimed at establishment of special economic zones in order to boost exports; the enactment of a new Arbitration and Conciliation Act in 1996 (amended in 2015) aimed at consolidating and amending the law relating to domestic arbitration, international commercial arbitration, and enforcement of foreign arbitral awards.

Thus, 1991 onwards, India's policy to foreign investment underwent a paradigm shift from what it was in 1947 till 1990. Attracting more foreign investment became an integral part of India's economic policy. This change in India's economic policy towards foreign investment triggered the change in India's approach to foreign investment under international law that we discuss now.

3.2 Signing of BITs

Towards the end of 1992, when Finance Minister Manmohan Singh, having announced the 1991 economic reforms and allowing portfolio investment by foreign institutional investors, was in the UK, he was asked about the protection for foreign investments in India.[96] India's treatment of foreign investors under Section 29 of the FERA Act before the dawn of the 1991 reforms gave rise to these genuine concerns. On his return to India, Singh asked his officials at the department of economic affairs of the ministry of finance to start working on an international foreign investment treaty that would provide confidence to foreign investors willing to invest in India.[97] This became critical for India to demonstrate to the world its seriousness about the economic

[96] ShajiVikraman. 2017. 'In fact: When India Arrived at a Foreign Investment Protection Plan', 5 April, http://indianexpress.com/article/explained/in-fact-when-india-arrived-at-a-foreign-investment-protection-plan/, accessed 28 February 2018 (hereinafter Vikraman. 'In fact').

[97] Vikraman. 'In fact'.

reforms process that started in 1991. In his 1993 budget speech to the Indian Parliament, Finance Minister Manmohan Singh signalled the role of BITs as an important means of attracting foreign investment in India.[98] Singh said that many countries, including the UK, Germany, and the United States, had expressed interest in signing BITs with India and that the Indian government indicated a willingness to enter into bilateral negotiations on this issue.[99] In his next budget speech in 1994, Singh, while talking about liberalization of foreign investment, informed the Indian parliament that India is negotiating BITs with major capital-exporting countries.[100]

India soon developed a model BIT in 1993, modelled on the Organisation for Economic Co-operation and Development's (OECD) Draft Convention for Protection of Foreign Property of 1967.[101] The 1967 OECD Draft Convention provided foreign investors fair and equitable protection; just compensation, that is, compensation representing the genuine value of the property affected to be paid without undue delay, for expropriation; and recourse to international arbitration for settlement of disputes between foreign investors and host states.[102] Adopting a Model BIT based on the OECD Model showed India's willingness to accept those very

[98] Manmohan Singh. 1993. 'Budget 1993-94 Speech', http://www.indiabudget.gov.in/bspeech/bs199394.pdf, p.7, accessed 28 February 2018.

[99] Singh, 'Budget 1993-94 Speech'.

[100] Singh, 'Budget 1993-94 Speech'.

[101] Saurabh Garg, Ishita G. Tripathi, and Sudhanshu Roy. 2016. 'The Indian Model Bilateral Investment Treaty: Continuity and Change', in *Rethinking Bilateral Investment Treaties: Critical Issues and Policy Challenges* Kavaljit Singh and BurghardIlge (eds), p. 69. New Delhi: Both Ends, Madhyam and Somo (hereinafter Grag, Tripathi, and Roy, 'The Indian Model Bilateral Investment Treaty'). For details on the OECD draft convention see—OECD Council. 1967. 'OECD Draft Convention on the Protection of Foreign Property', *The International Lawyer* 2(2): 331–53 (hereinafter OECD, 'OECD Draft Convention on the Protection of Foreign Property'). Press Information Bureau, Model Text for the Bilateral Investment Treaty. 2015. 16 December, http://pib.nic.in/newsite/PrintRelease.aspx?relid=133411, accessed 28 February 2018. However, the text of the 1993 Model BIT is not available in public domain.

[102] OECD, 'OECD Draft Convention on the Protection of Foreign Property'.

international legal principles for protection of foreign investment that it had opposed in the 1960s and 1970s.[103] It showed a voluntary transition from the formalist-dualism of the previous phase as Chimni calls it.[104] A massive change of heart took place because India was now willing to subject her regulation of foreign investment to the scrutiny of international legal principles that it had opposed all along at various multilateral forums.[105]

The third world approaches to international law scholars in India who critique India embracing the neoliberal economic order do not account for the massive economic changes that took place in India during this period, which made India shift and adopt those international legal principles that it had not fully embraced in the 1960s and 1970s.[106] There was a strong economic rationale for India to move towards adoption of BITs (which in TWAIL terminology would be a tool to pursue the neocolonial and imperial project).

India adopted a model BIT in an eagerness and enthusiasm to signal readiness to the outside world to offer extensive treaty-based protection, both substantially and procedurally, to foreign investment, to attract more capital.[107] India, at that point of time, was

[103] Also see Chapters 4 and 5.

[104] See Chapter 2. It may be argued that the TWAIL-II scholarship that started emerging post 1990s in India and at other places, focusing on 'critical-dualism', was to counter the fact that many 'third world' countries (on whose behalf many of the developing country scholars spoke) gave up their opposition to certain principles of the international legal order and willingly embraced the liberal economic order. These countries gave up their opposition in view of the empirical evidence that the inward-looking economic model that they had followed thus far had not brought the economic benefits that were anticipated. Also see, Antonius R. Hippolyte. 2016. 'Correcting TWAIL's Blind Spots A Plea for a Pragmatic Approach to International Economic Governance', *International Community Law Review* 18: 34–52. Also see, P.S. Rao. 2015. 'The Nature and Function of International Law: An Evolving International Rule of Law', *Indian Journal of International Law* 55: 459.

[105] See Chapter 2.

[106] See also the discussion in Chapters 4 and 5.

[107] Interview with former Indian Official who was associated with Indian BITs (name withheld) (November 2011). This 'grand bargain' has been the basis of BITs between developed and developing countries—see J.W. Salacuse

quite concerned about high foreign investment flows into China and thus wanted to attract more foreign investment.[108] This concern over high foreign investment inflows to China over India is corroborated by the statement of Prime Minister Rajiv Gandhi in 1988, even before the 1991 economic reforms took place. Rajiv Gandhi, on foreign investment inflows to China and India, had said: 'foreign investment in socialist China is about Rs 2000 crore per year. Foreign investment in India is only Rs 100 crore per year'.[109] Rajiv Gandhi then went on to emphasize that India could absorb a larger flow of foreign investment, which would be to India's advantage.[110]

On 14 March 1994 India signed its first BIT (an agreement to promote and protect foreign investment) with its erstwhile colonial ruler, the UK.[111] In order to signal its commitment to attract and protect foreign investment, on 6 January 1994, couple of months before signing the BIT with the UK, India formally joined the convention establishing the Multilateral Investment Guarantee Assurance (MIGA),[112] after signing it in April 1992.[113] Multilateral

---

and N.P. Sullivan. 2005. 'Do BITs Really Work? An Evaluation of Bilateral Investment Treaties on Foreign Investment: The Search for a Grand Bargain', *Harvard International Law Journal* 46:67.

[108] Interview with former Indian Official who was associated with Indian BITs (name withheld) (November 2011).

[109] Rajiv Gandhi's speech to the Confederation of Indian Industry in 1988 cited in Shin, 'FDI in India', p. 68.

[110] Rajiv Gandhi's speech to the Confederation of Indian Industry in 1988 cited in Shin, 'FDI in India', p. 68.

[111] Agreement between the Government of the United Kingdom of Great Britain and Northern Ireland and the Government of the Republic of India for the promotion and the protection of investments, 14 March 1994, http://investmentpolicyhub.unctad.org/Download/TreatyFile/1613, accessed 28 February 2018.

[112] World Bank. n.d. 'Member Countries', http://www.worldbank.org/en/about/leadership/members#4, accessed 28 February 2018, last updated July 2018.

[113] D. Krishan. 2008. 'India and International Investment Law', in *India and International Law* (Vol. 2)B.N. Patel (ed.), p. 277. Leiden/Boston: Martinus Nijhoff (hereinafter Krishan, 'India and International Investment Law').

Investment Guarantee Assurance is a member of the World Bank Group and the objective of MIGA is to boost foreign investment flows for productive purposes especially to developing countries.[114]

After signing the BIT with the UK, from 1994 till the end of 2000, India went on a BIT-signing spree. India signed as many as 40 BITs in six years, an average of 6–7 BITs each year.[115] India's treaty partners included developed countries like Germany, Italy, Denmark, Netherlands, France, Switzerland, Australia, Austria, Spain, and Sweden.[116] During this phase, India also signed BITs with many developing countries from Asia, Africa, and Latin America such as Malaysia, Turkmenistan, Tajikistan, Korea, Israel, Sri Lanka, Thailand, Oman, Indonesia, Egypt, Zimbabwe, and Argentina.[117]

From 2001 onwards till the end of 2010, India signed BITs with another 39 countries.[118] Thus, although the pace with which India signed BITs from 2001 to 2010 slowed down in comparison to the immediately preceding period of 1994 to 2000, India still signed an average of four BITs per year during this 10-year period. The Bilateral Investment Treaties signed in this phase largely included developing countries. Some of the countries with whom India signed a BIT in this phase are Ukraine, Ghana, Finland, China, Saudi Arabia, Mexico, Bangladesh, Colombia, Iceland, Uruguay, and Latvia.[119]

India also revised its Model BIT in 2003.[120] Recently, it was claimed that the 2003 Model BIT was revised by adding an

[114] World Bank Convention establishing the Multilateral Investment Guarantee Agency (1988), Article 2.

[115] UNCTAD. n.d. 'India: Bilateral Investment Treaties (BITs)', http://investmentpolicyhub.unctad.org/IIA/CountryBits/96#iiaInnerMenu, accessed 28 February 2018 (hereinafter UNCTAD. 'India').

[116] UNCTAD. 'India'.

[117] UNCTAD. 'India'.

[118] UNCTAD. 'India'.

[119] UNCTAD. 'India'.

[120] Important to bear in mind that the actual text that is available in public domain does not carry the date. However, UNCTAD calls it the 2003 Indian Model BIT—Indian Model Text of BIPA—Agreement between the Government of the Republic of India and the Government of the Republic of

Annexure to clarify the meaning of indirect expropriation.[121] It was also claimed that India's treaty with China signed on 1 August 2007 was the first agreement to incorporate this change.[122] However, no evidence has been presented to substantiate this claim. The text of the 2003 Model BIT that is available on the UNCTAD website contains no such Annexure.[123] The website of the Finance Ministry does not contain the text of the 2003 Model BIT. Also, while the India–China BIT does contain a Protocol with regard to interpretation of expropriation,[124] in view of the fact that the publicly available version of the 2003 Model BIT does not contain any such Annex, one is unsure if the Protocol was based on the 2003 Model BIT. The 2003 Model BIT contained the same broadly formulated provisions contained in the 1967 OECD draft convention for the protection of foreign investment. Thus, the BIT template continued to be guided by laissz-faire liberalism.

In 2005, India launched the second strand of binding itself to international investment law—it started entering into FTAs (or comprehensive economic partnership agreements—CEPA as they are called in India) with a chapter on foreign investment. The first such FTA with investment chapter was signed with Singapore in 2005 followed by one with South Korea in 2009.[125]

We now turn to discussing the key characteristics of the first phase of the Indian BIT programme.

---------------- for the Promotion and Protection of Investments. http://investmentpolicyhub.unctad.org/Download/TreatyFile/2871, accessed 28 February 2018. The same text as 2003 Model BIT is also available at https://www.italaw.com/sites/default/files/archive/ita1026.pdf, accessed 28 February 2018.

[121] Garg, Tripathi, and Roy, 'The Indian Model Bilateral Investment Treaty'.

[122] Garg, Tripathi, and Roy,'The Indian Model Bilateral Investment Treaty'.

[123] See the budget proposals of 2001–02—Yashwant Sinha. 2001. 'Budget Speech 2001-02: Capital Account Liberalisation', http://www.indiabudget.gov.in/ub2001-02/bs/capital.htm, accessed 28 February 2018.

[124] See Chapter 5 for a discussion on the meaning of such protocols on expropriation in India's BITs.

[125] UNCTAD. n.d. 'India: Treaties with Investment Provisions (TIPs)', http://investmentpolicyhub.unctad.org/IIA/CountryBits/96#iiaInnerMenu, accessed 28 February 2018.

3.3 BITs As Instruments to Promote and Protect Foreign Investment

As evident from the discussion, the Indian policy on foreign investment involved two important parts: investment promotion and investment protection. Thus, the core reason behind signing the BITs was to promote and protect foreign investment as evident from the statements of different Indian Finance Ministers, from 1994 to 2011, in 'compendiums' of Indian BITs. In the first volume (published in 1996–7) Finance minister P. Chidambaram wrote that after the adoption of liberal economic policies in 1991, India initiated the process of entering into BITs with a view to boost investor confidence[126] to attract foreign investment. A similar view has been repeated in all subsequent volumes, by different finance ministers belonging to different governments.[127] This reason was also reflected in India's statement at the WTO in 1999, where India stated that BITs 'promote' foreign investment through 'protection', that is, by providing foreign investment various substantive protection combined with an international investor–state dispute settlement.[128] Therefore, India started entering into BITs in order to provide a predictable investment climate to foreign investors in India.[129]

The press releases issued by India after entering into BITs with different countries also reveal that BITs are primarily about providing protection to foreign investment with the hope that they will increase

[126] P. Chidambaram. 1997. 'Foreword', in *India's Bilateral Investment Promotion and Protection Agreements*, Volume I, pp. 1–2. New Delhi: Ministry of Finance.

[127] See Sinha, 'Foreword', in *India's Bilateral Investment Promotion and Protection Agreements*, pp. 3–4; P. Mukherjee. 2009. 'Foreword', in *India's Bilateral Investment Promotion and Protection Agreements*, Volume VII, pp. 3–4. New Delhi: Ministry of Finance, India.

[128] WTO. 1999. 'Communication from India: Working Group on the Relationship between Trade and Investment of the WTO', WT/WGTI/W/71, 13 April, https://docs.wto.org/dol2fe/Pages/FE_Search/FE_S_S009-DP.aspx?language=E&CatalogueIdList=31254,68269,49199,29278,29429,29240,18128,46302,17620,75255&CurrentCatalogueIdIndex=2&FullTextHash=, accessed 28 February 2018 (hereinafter WTO, 'Communication from India').

[129] WTO, 'Communication from India'.

foreign investment. For example, the press release on India–China BIT states that 'the agreement will increase investment between India and China'.[130] The same view is echoed in the press release issued on the occasion of signing of the India–Brunei BIT. The press release provides 'the Agreement, which seeks to promote and protect investments from either country in the territory of the other country with the ultimate objective of increasing bilateral investment flow…'.[131]

That the reason behind India signing BITs was the promotion and protection of investments is also evident upon a study of the title of the BITs.[132] For instance, the title of the India–UK BIT emphasizes two core values—investment promotion and investment protection. The same is true for the 2003 Model BIT, in addition to numerous BITs. India's BITs with Kuwait and Saudi Arabia use positive

[130] Press Information Bureau. 2006. 'Bilateral Investment Promotion Agreement with China',16 November, http://pib.nic.in/newsite/erelease.aspx?relid=22062, accessed 28 February 2018.

[131] Ministry of Finance Press Release. 2008. 'A Bilateral Investment Promotion and Protection Agreement between the Government of the Republic of India and the Government of His Majesty The Sultan and Yang Di-Pertuan of Brunei Darussalam', May, http://finmin.nic.in/press_room/2008/may_details.asp?pageid=2, accessed 28 February 2018. Also see Press Information Bureau. 2008. 'India Exchanges Instruments of Ratification on BIPA with Iceland',16 December, http://pib.nic.in/newsite/erelease.aspx?relid=45695, accessed 28 February 2018; Press Information Bureau Press Release. 2009. 'BIPA with Jordan comes into Force', 22 January, http://pib.nic.in/newsite/erelease.aspx?relid=46919, accessed 28 February 2018; Press Information Bureau Press Release. 2009. 'Bipa Between India And Serbia Comes Into Force', 24 February, http://pib.nic.in/release/rel_print_page1.asp?relid=47891, accessed 28 February 2018.

[132] Title of a treaty can be an important indicator of the object and purpose of the treaty—see R.K. Gardiner. 2008. *Treaty Interpretation*. Oxford: Oxford University Press, pp. 180–1. The tribunal in *Plama* v. *Bulgaria* deduced the object and purpose of the BIT by referring to the preamble and also the title of the BIT, which referred to 'mutual encouragement and protection of investments'—*Plama Consortium Limited* v. *Republic of Bulgaria*, ICSID Case No. ARB/03/24 [193], Award, 27 August 2008 (hereinafter *Plama* v. *Bulgaria*). Also see *SGS Société Générale de Surveillance SA* v. *Republic of the Philippines*, ICSID Case No. ARB/02/6, 29 January 2004 (hereinafter *SGS* v. *Philippines*).

connotations such as 'encouragement' of investments instead of 'promotion', thereby implying the same meaning.

Further, the preamble of a BIT may also provide a glimpse of the overall object and the purpose of the BIT.[133] The preamble of the India–UK BIT states the following objectives:

1. Desiring to create conditions favourable for fostering greater investment by investors of one state in the territory of the other state;
2. Recognizing that the encouragement and reciprocal protection under international agreement of such investment will be conducive to the stimulation of individual business initiative and will increase prosperity in both states.

Several Indian BITs as well as the 2003 Indian Model BIT share a similar preamble. These preambles focus on creating conditions favourable for encouraging investment flows; and recognizing that encouragement and protection of investment will stimulate business activity and increase prosperity. Although, the Preamble talks about 'stimulating business initiative' and 'increase in prosperity' in both the countries, these objectives are not self-standing but are linked to encouragement and protection of investment. Thus, it is an underlying presumption that the encouragement and protection of investment will result in increased prosperity in states and will stimulate individual business initiative.[134]

[133] Many ISDS tribunals have looked at the preamble of the BIT to determine the BIT's object and purpose, see *Siemens A.G.* v. *Argentina*, ICSID Case No. ARB/02/8 [80-81], Decision on Jurisdiction, 3 August 2004; Award, 6 February 2007; *Azurix Corp* v. *Argentina*, ICSID Case No. ARB/01/12 [307], Award, 14 July 2006. For a different view on this see C. McLachlan. 2008. 'Investment Treaties and General International Law', *International and Comparative Law Quarterly* 57: 371; J. Kurtz. 2010. 'Adjudging the Exceptional at International Law: Security, Public Order and Financial Crisis', *International and Comparative Law Quarterly* 59: 351 (hereinafter Kurtz, 'Adjudging the Exceptional at International Law').

[134] In this context, see also Alvarez and Khamsi, 'The Argentine Crisis and Foreign Investors', where, in the context of the argument on the preamble in the US-Argentina BIT, it has been argued that 'greater economic cooperation' and

Few Indian BITs contain more values in the Preamble apart from investment promotion and protection. For example, the Preamble in the India–Australia BIT provides that 'investment relations should be promoted and economic relations strengthened in accordance with the internationally accepted principles of mutual respect for sovereignty, equality, mutual benefit, non-discrimination and mutual confidence'. In contrast, the Preambles of India's FTAs with Singapore and Korea refer to multiple values such as 'rights to pursue economic philosophies suited to their development goals'; 'rights to realise their national policy objectives'; and 'optimal use of natural resources in accordance with the objective of sustainable development, seeking both to protect and preserve the environment'.[135]

3.3.1 BITs and FDI Inflows to India

While the total FDI flowing into India increased from US$ 4,029 million in 2000–1 to US$ 43,478 million in 2016–17,[136] the role BITs played in such development needs to be analysed. Many studies have been undertaken to examine the link between BITs and FDI inflows. According to UNCTAD, majority of studies find a positive relationship between investment treaties and FDI inflows.[137] For

'economic development' are not self-standing goals in the preamble but possible outcomes of protecting foreign investment, which is the object and purpose—Alvarez and Khamsi, 'The Argentine Crisis and Foreign Investors'.

[135] The preamble in these two agreements is for the entire treaty and not just the investment chapter. For more discussion on this see Prabhash Ranjan. 2011. '"Object and Purpose" of Indian International Investment Agreements: Failing to Balance Investment Protection and Regulatory Power' in *Foreign Investment and Dispute Resolution: Law and Practice in Asia*, V. Bath and L. Nottage (eds), pp. 192–211. London: Routledge.

[136] Department of Industrial Policy and Promotion, Ministry of Commerce and Industry, Government of India. n.d. 'Quarterly Fact Sheet, Fact Sheet on Foreign Direct Investment from April 2000 to March 2017', http://dipp.nic.in/sites/default/files/FDI_FactSheet_January_March2017.pdf, accessed 28 February 2018, updated March 2017. According to the Indian government, FDI inflows include equity inflows plus reinvested earnings plus other capital.

[137] UNCTAD. 2014. 'The Impact of International Investment Agreements on Foreign Direct Investment: An Overview of Empirical Studies 1998-2014', http://investmentpolicyhub.unctad.org/Upload/Documents/unctad-web-diae-pcb-

example, a 2005 study done by Neumayer and Spess using panel data for 119 countries over the period 1970 to 2001 shows a positive effect of BITs on FDI inflows.[138] Another study that took asample of 28 home and 83 host countries found a significant positive impact between BITs and FDI inflows.[139] In another study Tobin and Rose-Ackerman conclude that 'BITs do attract FDI to developing countries, but … cannot entirely substitute for an otherwise weak investment environment'.[140] Some studies also find that the content of the BIT, that is, if the treaty includes certain substantive protection guarantees, it positively influences FDI flows.[141] For example, ISDS provisions encourage FDI inflow.[142] Some studies, however, also find little or no impact of BITs on FDI inflows.[143]

2014-Sep%2016.pdf, accessed 28 February 2018 (hereinafter UNCTAD, 'The Impact of International Investment Agreements on Foreign Direct Investment').

138 E. Neumayer and L. Spess. 2005. 'Do Bilateral Investment Treaties Increase Foreign Direct Investment to Developing Countries?', *World Development* 33(10):1567–85.

139 A. Berger, M. Busse, P. Nunnenkamp, and M. Roy. 2013. 'Do Trade and Investment Agreements Lead to More FDI? Accounting for Key Provisions Inside the Black Box', *International Economics and Economic Policy* 10(2):247–75. Also see J. Tobin and S. Rose-Ackerman. 2006. 'Bilateral Investment Treaties: Do They Stimulate Foreign Direct Investment?', Yale University (mimeo); R. Banga. 2008. 'Government Policies and FDI Inflows of Asian Developing Countries: Empirical Evidence', in *Economic Reform in Developing Countries: Reach, Range, Reason* J.M. Fanelli and L. Squire (eds), pp. 117–46. Cheltenham and Northampton: Edward Elgar.

140 J. Tobin and S. Rose-Ackerman. 2011. 'When BITs Have Some Bite: The Political-Economic Environment for Bilateral Investment Treaties?', *The Review of International Organizations* 6(1):1–32.

141 UNCTAD, 'The Impact of International Investment Agreements on Foreign Direct Investment'.

142 A. Berger, M. Busse, P. Nunnenkamp, and M. Roy. 2011. 'More Stringent BITs, Less Ambiguous Effects on FDI? Not a BIT!', *Economics Letter* 112(3):270–2 (hereinafter Berger, Busse, Nunnenkamp, and Roy, 'More Stringent BITs, Less Ambiguous Effects on FDI'). Also see Shiro Armstrong. 2018. 'The Impact of Investment Treaties and ISDS Provisions on FDI in Asia and Globally', in *International Investment Treaties and Arbitration Across Asia*, Julien Chaisse and Luke Nottage (eds), pp. 57–82. Leiden: Brill Nijhoff.

143 M. Hallward-Driemeier. 2003. 'Do Bilateral Investment Treaties Attract FDI? Only a Bit and They Could Bite', *World Bank Policy Research Paper*, Vol. 1,

While there may exist a correlation between BITs and increase in foreign investment, inflows from foreign investors are more related to macroeconomic factors such as the host country's overall economic stability, advantages as a location, level of infrastructure, and other related factors.[144] Nevertheless, as majority of studies show, BITs could have a positive impact on FDI flows because by signing a BIT the host country signals congenial investment environment, offers treaty-based protection, and thus enhanced security for investment.[145] Thus, it is argued that from the perspective of investors, BITs and other IIAs provide stability, protect investors and, more generally, contribute to a better investment climate.[146]

In the case of India, it is not known whether the Indian government ever conducted a study investigating the impact of BITs on FDI inflows. It appears that India primarily signed BITs in the acceptance phase, on the presumption that BITs promote investment.

Few studies undertaken to examine the relationship of BITs and FDI in the context of India show BITs have had a positive impact on FDI inflows.[147] One study examines the impact of BITs on

---

WPS 3121. C. Peinhardt and T. Allee. 2012. 'Failure to Deliver: The Investment Effects of US Preferential Economic Agreements', *The World Economy* 35: 757.

[144] J. Salacuse. 1990. 'BIT by BIT: The Growth of Bilateral Investment Treaties and Their Impact on Foreign Investment in Developing Countries', *International Lawyer* 24:673 (hereinafter Salacuse, 'BIT by BIT); Also see, Vandevelde, 'Investment Liberalisation and Economic Development', p. 524.

[145] Vandevelde, 'Investment Liberalisation and Economic Development', pp. 522–5; UNCTC. 1988. 'Bilateral Investment Treaties' (Doc. No. ST/CTC/65) (hereinafter UNCTC, 'Bilateral Investment Treaties'); R. Kotera. 2008. 'Regulatory Transparency' in *The Oxford Handbook of International Investment Law*, P. Muchlinski, Federico Ortino, and Christoph Schreur (eds), p. 624. Oxford: Oxford University Press (hereinafter Kotera, 'Regulatory Transparency').

[146] Vandevelde, 'Investment Liberalisation and Economic Development', pp. 522–5; UNCTC, 'Bilateral Investment Treaties'; Kotera, 'Regulatory Transparency'. Also see other studies that show a positive relationship between BITs and FDI inflows—Berger, Busse, Nunnenkamp, and Roy, 'More Stringent BITs, Less Ambiguous Effects on FDI?'.

[147] Rashmi Banga. 2003. 'Impact of Government Policies and Investment Agreements on FDI Inflows', *ICRIER Working Paper No 116*, http://www.icrier.

FDI inflows in 15 Asian developing countries including India from 1980–1 to 1999–2000. The study shows that BITs signed by these 15 countries with developed countries had a strong and significant impact on FDI inflows.[148] However, BITs signed by these 15 countries with developing countries did not have positive impact on foreign investment inflows.[149] As regards India, this study included only 14 Indian BITs from 1994 till 2000,[150] although, as noted before, India had signed 40 BITs during this period.[151] According to this study, till the year 2000, out of the 14 Indian BITs, 9 were with developed countries. On the basis of this study, it can be argued that BITs have had a positive impact on the rise in FDI inflows from US$ 393 million in 1992–3 to US$ 4,029 million in 2000–1.

Recent studies also manifest the positive impact of BITs signed by India during the acceptance phase. A study by Bhasin and Manocha considers the impact of BITs on FDI inflows in India from 2001–12.[152] Bhasin and Manocha conclude that 'BITs have contributed to rising FDI inflows by providing protection and commitment to foreign investors contemplating investment in India'.[153] Similarly, the preliminary results of another study on India

> finds that although the signing of individual BITs had an insignificant impact on FDI inflows into India, the *cumulative* effect of signing

---

org/pdf/WP116.pdf, accessed 28 February 2018 (hereinafter Banga, 'Impact of Government Policies and Investment Agreements on FDI Inflows').

[148] Banga, 'Impact of Government Policies and Investment Agreements on FDI Inflows'.

[149] Banga, 'Impact of Government Policies and Investment Agreements on FDI Inflows'.

[150] Banga, 'Impact of Government Policies and Investment Agreements on FDI Inflows', p. 23

[151] It is possible that information about many of these BITs signed by India was not available in public domain when the study was carried out in 2003.

[152] Niti Bhasin and Rinku Manocha. 2016. 'Do Bilateral Investment Treaties Promote FDI Inflows? Evidence from India', *Vikalpa: The Journal for Decision Makers* 14:275 (hereinafter Bhasin and Manocha, 'Do Bilateral Investment Treaties Promote FDI Inflows?').

[153] Bhasin and Manocha, 'Do Bilateral Investment Treaties Promote FDI Inflows?', p. 285.

> BITs is significant and so is the coefficient associated with the signing of FTAs. Since almost all of India's investment treaties provide for full ISDS protections, these preliminary results suggest that ISDS could have a positive influence on overall foreign investment, albeit in a non-obvious compound manner.[154]

Although, in this phase, India primarily looked at BITs as a tool to attract and protect foreign investment in India, towards the end of this phase, India started to emerge as a capital exporter, which brought about a change in India's perception towards BITs. India's total FDI outflows (loans and equity) increased from US$ 7,856.49 million in 2005–6 to US$ 18,506 million in 2008–9.[155] This increase did not change India's character, overall, as a net capital-importing country. Nevertheless, such an increase in foreign investment outflows, towards the end of the first phase, initiated the re-characterization of BITs from key instruments of attracting and protecting foreign investment in India to instrument ensuring protection of Indian investment abroad.[156] This explains India's BITs with African countries like Mozambique, Senegal, and Sudan post 2005 and also with other developing and least developed countries like Bahrain, Trinidad and Tobago, Saudi Arabia, Myanmar and Bangladesh—countries where India has capital-exporting interest.

3.4 Marginal Involvement of India with ISDS

Despite signing close to 80 BITs, in this phase, foreign investors didn't challenge India's measures under BITs unlike the 'backlash' phase from 2011 onwards.[157] Although, according to UNCTAD,

[154] Luke Nottage and Jaivir Singh. 2016. 'Does ISDS Promote FDI? Asia-Pacific Insights from and for Australia and India', *Asian Pacific Arbitration Forum*, http://afia.asia/2016/11/does-isds-promote-fdi-asia-pacific-insights-from-and-for-australia-and-india/, accessed 28 February 2018.

[155] H.R. Khan. 2012. 'Outward Indian FDI – Recent Trends and Emerging Issues', *Reserve Bank of India Speeches*, http://rbi.org.in/scripts/BS_SpeechesView.aspx?Id=674, 3 March, accessed 28 February 2018.

[156] Interview with an official of the Ministry of Finance (name withheld), August 2010.

[157] See Chapter 6.

in the acceptance phase, nine ISDS claims were brought against India,[158] all these cases were brought in 2003–4 and pertained to one particular investment project—the Dabhol energy project in the state of Maharashtra in India.[159]

This case involved an FDI project related to the building of an electrical power plant in India in the early 1990s, soon after the adoption of the 1991 Indian liberalization programme. Enron Corporation, along with General Electric (GE) Corporation and Bechtel Enterprises, formed a company called Dabhol Power Company (DPC) in Maharashtra, a western Indian state, to generate electrical power.[160] This formed the biggest FDI investment in India at that time.[161] Dabhol Power Company entered into an agreement with the Maharashtra State Electricity Board (MSEB), a public sector enterprise, as the sole purchaser of the power generated by DPC.[162] Subsequently, due to political opposition to the project on grounds of alleged irregularities and the high cost of power charged by DPC, MSEB cancelled the contract to purchase power, leaving DPC without a consumer to sell electrical power.[163] Further, the Central Government of India, which acted as a counter guarantor, after making some payments, also declined to pay DPC for various reasons.[164] Dabhol Power Company was restrained from starting an international arbitration by anti-arbitration injunctions issued by Indian courts.[165]

158 UNCTAD, 'India—as Respondent State'.

159 UNCTAD, 'India—as Respondent State'.

160 UNCTAD, 'India—as Respondent State'.

161 UNCTAD, 'India—as Respondent State'.

162 UNCTAD, 'India—as Respondent State'.

163 For detailed facts of the case, *see* P. Kundra. 2008. 'Looking Beyond the Dabhol Debacle: Examining Its Causes and Understanding Its Lessons', *Vanderbilt Journal of Transnational Law* 41:908 (hereinafter Kundra, 'Looking Beyond the Dabhol Debacle'); *see also* G.V. Harten. 2011. 'TWAIL and the Dabhol Arbitration', *Trade, Law and Development* 3(1):136 (hereinafter Harten, 'TWAIL and the Dabhol Arbitration').

164 For detailed facts of the case, *see* Kundra, 'Looking Beyond the Dabhol Debacle', p. 908; *see also* Harten, 'TWAIL and the Dabhol Arbitration', p. 136.

165 For detailed facts of the case, *see* Kundra, 'Looking Beyond the Dabhol Debacle', p. 908; *see also* Harten, 'TWAIL and the Dabhol Arbitration', p. 136.

The Mauritius-based subsidiaries of GE and Bechtel, relying on the India–Mauritius BIT, challenged India's measures, including the judicial action of issuing anti-arbitration injunctions by courts, as violations of the India–Mauritius BIT.[166] Before an ISDS award could be issued a mutual settlement was reached[167] whereby India awarded a mammoth compensation (one-billion dollars, according to some estimates)[168] to foreign investors.

Notwithstanding the settlement on this issue, the Dabhol episode resulted in two uncontested arbitral awards—an ICC determination[169] and an Overseas Private Investment Corporation (OPIC) determination.[170] Both tribunals found India guilty of breaching its obligations.[171] Among other conclusions, the OPIC found that the 'active litigation strategy of the State Electricity Board to prevent effective arbitration despite having agreed to honour arbitration in the Contractual Agreement—thereby blocking DPC's arbitration rights against the State Electricity Board (MSEB), the State government (GOM) and the Central Government (GOI)' constituted a violation of its obligations. It also found the 'actions of the government,

[166] In fact, this dispute resulted in two BIT claims by the project companies, as well as seven BIT claims by the project lenders. All of these claims against India, however, have since been settled. See Manu Sanan. 2012. 'The White Industries Award: Shades of Grey', *Journal of World Investment and Trade* 13(4):661.

[167] *The Tribune*. 2005. 'GE Settles Dabhol Dispute', https://www.tribuneindia.com/2005/20050703/biz.htm, 3 July.

[168] J. Ghosh. 2010. 'Treacherous Treaties', *Frontline*, 3 December, http://www.frontlineonnet.com/fl2724/stories/20101203272409200.htmonline, accessed 28 February 2018.

[169] *Capital India Power Mauritius I and Energy Enterprises (Mauritius) Company* v. *India* (ICC Case No. 12913/MS, IIC 43 [80], 2005). This arbitration was based on a contract—the Dabhol Power Corporation Shareholders Agreement.

[170] Bank of America NA, *Memorandum of determinations*, IIC 25 (30 September 2003), India (OPIC), United States; Overseas Private Investment Corporation.

[171] *Capital India* v. *India*, supra n 139; Bank of America NA, *Memorandum of determinations*, IIC 25 (30 September 2003), India (OPIC), United States; Overseas Private Investment Corporation.

supported by the judiciary, by effectively blocking revenue collection, escrow account arrangements and a letter of credit, constituted a 'deprivation of the fundamental rights of the insured as a creditor, including the rights against security'—thereby violating international law.'[172]

The Dabhol cases did not quite trigger a change in India's BIT practice. Nonetheless, in the immediate aftermath of *Dabhol*, there were some indications that India realized that its BITs offer wide protection to investments and some of these provisions required dilution.[173] For example, the investment chapter in India–Singapore FTA signed in 2005, just after the *Dabhol case*, depicted some change in India's approach to BITs.[174] The provisions in the investment chapter of the India–Singapore FTA balance investment protection with regulatory power of the host state by providing national treatment protection to investments, covering wide assets under the definition of investment providing a wider treaty coverage to investors, on the one hand; and by not having provisions such as MFN and fair and equitable treatment, having a general exceptions clause designed to give leeway to countries to adopt measures for the protection of public health, environment, and other regulatory objectives, on the other.[175] This is a marked departure from India's 2003 model BIT. However, this change was unique and was not continued in subsequent BITs that India entered after 2005 with countries like China, Iceland, and Syria, which continued to have same broad and ambiguous BIT provisions as found in India's earlier BITs. The only exception to this is the investment chapters in India's FTAs with Korea, Japan, and Malaysia.[176] Thus, the change after the *Dabhol* debacle was reflected only in investment provisions that were part of

[172] *Capital India* v. *India*, para 83.

[173] Indian Official quoted in L.E. Peterson. 2003. 'Bechtel and GE Mount Billion Dollar Investment Treaty Claim against India', *INVEST-SD News Bulletin*, 23 September (hereinafter Peterson, 'Bechtel and GE Mount Billion Dollar Investment Treaty Claim against India').

[174] Peterson, 'Bechtel and GE Mount Billion Dollar Investment Treaty Claim against India'.

[175] See Chapters 4 and 5.

[176] Chimni, 'The World of TWAIL'.

FTAs and not in standalone investment treaties. One key reason for this difference is that FTAs with investment chapters are negotiated by Ministry of Commerce, which has better capacity in negotiating economic treaties (because of its experience with WTO negotiations) than Ministry of Finance, which deals with standalone investment treaties.

India's marginal involvement with ISDS was, thus, a defining characteristic of the acceptance phase. Lack of BIT claims against India does not mean that foreign investors never faced regulatory troubles in India during this period. Indeed, there are many examples of disputes between foreign companies and the Indian State on various regulatory issues such as taxation during the acceptance period.[177] However, barring the DPC's case, no BIT claim was brought against India. One probable explanation for this could be that BITs were not so popular amongst foreign investors. Indeed, as the UNCTAD statistics show, the use of ISDS by foreign investors picked up pace only after 2003–4.[178]

One commentator has argued that one of the reasons BIT claims were not brought against India during this phase was because the Indian judicial system is efficient and independent.[179] As part of the Indian constitutional order, under the 'separation of powers' doctrine, the Indian judiciary is independent from the executive and the legislature.[180] Not just this, 'independence of judiciary' is part of the

[177] *E-Funds IT Solutions* v. *DIT*, Civil Appeal 6082 of 2015, 24 October 2017 (SC); *Vodafone International Holdings BV* v. *Union of India*, (2012) 6 SCC 613; *Commissioner Of Income Tax, New Delhi* v. *M/S Eli Lilly & Company (India) Pvt. Ltd.*, (2009) 3 TMI 33 (SC); *DIT (International Taxation)* v. *Morgan Stanley & Co Inc.*, (2007) 292 ITR 416 (SC); *Formula One World Championship Ltd.* v. *CIT*, (2017) SCC Online SC 474; *ITO* v. *Right Florists Limited*, ITA No. 1336/Kol/2011; [2013] 143 ITD 445 (Kol).

[178] UNCTAD. 2015. 'Recent Trends in IIAs and ISDS', http://unctad.org/en/PublicationsLibrary/webdiaepcb2015d1_en.pdf, accessed 28 February 2018.

[179] Aniruddha, *Protection of Foreign Investment in India and Investment Treaty Arbitration*, p. 29.

[180] For a detailed and insightful discussion on this see M.P. Singh. 2000. 'Securing the Independence of the Judiciary: The Indian Experience', *Indiana International and Comparative Law Review* 10(2): 245.

basic structure doctrine of the Indian Constitution.[181] However, it is difficult to accept that the Indian judicial system is efficient especially given the huge backlog of cases that various law commissions of India report[182] and even the recent Economic Survey of the Indian government has pointed out.[183] Moreover, India has an abysmal rank of 164 when it comes to 'enforcing contracts' under the World Bank's ease of doing business,[184] which also points to the extremely slow nature of the Indian judicial system. The fact that the first ISDS award issued against India in *White Industries* v. *India*[185] was filed in light of judicial delays, also points to the tardy pace at which the Indian judiciary disposes cases. Moreover, if efficiency and independence of the Indian judiciary was one of the reasons for BIT claims not being brought against India from 1994–2010, then the trend ought to have continued post 2010.[186] In other words, efficiency and independence of the Indian judicial system surely couldn't have been the reason for negligible BIT claims against India during the acceptance phase.

3.5 Negligible Discussion on the Interface between Indian BITs and Regulatory Power

In this phase, there was hardly any discussion in India, on the interface between BITs and host country's right to regulate. This was

[181] See *Union of India* v. *Sankal Chand, HimmatlalSheth*, AIR 1977 SC 2328: (1977) 4 SCC 193; *S.P. Gupta* v. *President Of India And Others* AIR 1982 SC 149 at 197, 198; *Supreme Court Advocates-records- Association* v. *Union of India*, (1993) 4 SCC 441; *Supreme Court Advocates-on-Record Association and Anr.* v. *Union Of India* on 16 October, Writ Petition (Civil) No. 13 OF 2015, https://indiankanoon.org/doc/66970168/.

[182] Law Commission of India, 'Arrears and Backlog: Creating Additional Judicial (wo)manpower' (Report No. 224, July 2014); Law Commission of India, 'Reforms in the Judiciary – Some Suggestions' (Report No. 230, August 2009); Law Commission of India, 'Report on Insolvency Laws' (Report No. 26, 1964).

[183] Arvind Subramanian. 2018. '"Ease of Doing Business" Next Frontier: Timely Justice', *Economic Survey 2017-18*, 1: pp. 131–44.

[184] The World Bank. n.d. 'Doing Business Rankings: Enforcing Contracts', http://www.doingbusiness.org/data/exploretopics/enforcing-contracts, accessed 28 February 2018, last updated in March 2018.

[185] See Chapter 6.

[186] See Chapter 6.

despite growing global evidence about the conflict between investment protection and the host country's regulatory power such as the cases involving Argentina coming to the fore as discussed in Chapter 1. These cases demonstrate the tension in BITs between investment protection and host country's right to regulate. Many countries, developed and developing, have responded to this interface differently. However, none of these developments triggered any debate within India to reassess or revisit Indian BITs.

On the contrary, the little evidence availaible suggests that India looked at BITs favourably because India believed that these treaties gave countries enough policy flexibility to pursue their developmental objectives while giving a certain degree of comfort and safety to foreign investments.[187] India also believed that BITs do not impose many restrictions on host states in following their domestic investment policies because the BITs that India signed provide for investment protection post establishment.[188] Thus, all international legal obligations such as granting MFN treatment and national treatment kick in only after the investment has been established. In other words, the belief was that since India had the right to screen foreign investment at the border and admit it only if it was in accordance with India's laws and domestic policies, BITs would not curtail India's regulatory freedom.[189] While this is true at one level, right to regulate

[187] WTO. 2000. 'Communication from India: Working Group on the Relationship between Trade and Investment of the WTO', WT/WGTI/W/86, 22 June, https://docs.wto.org/dol2fe/Pages/FE_Search/FE_S_S009-DP.aspx?language=E&CatalogueIdList=65619,104843,29951,48241,31254,68269,27696,29222,53230,29240&CurrentCatalogueIdIndex=7&FullTextHash=&HasEnglishRecord=True&HasFrenchRecord=True&HasSpanishRecord=True, accessed 28 February 2018.

[188] WTO. 1999. 'Communication from India: Working Group on the Relationship between Trade and Investment of the WTO', WT/WGTI/W/71, 13 April, https://docs.wto.org/dol2fe/Pages/FE_Search/FE_S_S009-DP.aspx?language=E&CatalogueIdList=31254,68269,49199,29278,29429,29240,18128,46302,17620,75255&CurrentCatalogueIdIndex=2&FullTextHash=, accessed 28 February 2018. Also see Nagesh Kumar. 2003. 'Investment on WTO Agenda: A Developing Country Perspective and Way Forward for Cancun Ministerial Conference', *Economic and Political Weekly* 38(30): 3177–88.

[189] WTO. 1999. 'Communication from India: Working Group on the Relationship between Trade and Investment of the WTO', WT/WGTI/W/71,

is not restricted merely to deciding which foreign investment shall be allowed or not allowed to enter. Regulatory conduct of the state can also impact existing foreign investment, that is, foreign investment that has been allowed to enter post screening. India did not carefully examine the import of the broadly worded provisions in the BIT such as FET, etc., when applied to existing foreign investment.

There are several reasons for lack of focus on the impact of BITs on India's regulatory power in this phase. First, the presence of the all-pervasive one-dimensional approach towards BITs—that these treaties are instruments aimed at attracting and protecting foreign investment alone—as discussed earlier. Thus, the Indian government hardly considered that BITs could impact exercise of India's regulatory power.[190]

India's stand on BITs and its impact on regulatory power was in sharp contrast to the stand that India took on the multilateral agreement on investment (MAI) negotiations in the WTO during this phase. The various submissions made by India in the late 1990s and early 2000s to the WTO show that the core reason behind India opposing an investment agreement at the WTO was because it believed that it would curtail India's right to regulate especially because of the apprehension that such an agreement would provide pre-entry protection to foreign investment.[191]

Second, and equally important, the lack of ISDS claims against India, in this phase, created an impression in the minds of policymakers that there was no need to study the interface between BITs and host state's right to regulate.[192] In fact, policymakers cited absence

---

13 April. Also see Nagesh Kumar. 2003. 'Investment on WTO Agenda: A Developing Country Perspective and Way Forward for Cancun Ministerial Conference', *Economic and Political Weekly* 38(30): 3177–88 (hereinafter Kumar, 'Investment on WTO Agenda').

[190] Most officials of the ministry of finance, interviewed by the author before the surge in ISDS notices against India, were not willing to accept that there could be an interface between investment protection under BITs and India's exercise of regulatory power despite the global evidence (August 2010).

[191] See India's submissions to the WTO in late 1990s and early 2000s available at the Centre for WTO Studies website, http://wtocentre.iift.ac.in/SG1/, accessed 28 February 2018.

[192] Interview with two officials of the ministry of finance (names withheld), September 2010.

of BIT claims as proof of lack of interface between Indian BITs and India's right to regulate.[193]

Third, the Indian Parliament rarely debated about BITs during this phase. Very few occasions arose where questions regarding the signing of a new BIT or the advantage of having investment provisions in FTAs were raised.[194] This is in stark contrast to the attention that BITs have drawn in the Indian Parliament post 2010.[195] An important reason for the lack of debate in Parliament was the lack of legislative changes required due to BITs. In India, treaties are ratified by the Executive and not by the Parliament of India and hence, generally speaking, discussion on a treaty takes place when a legislative change is introduced by the Executive in Parliament in order to meet the obligation imposed by the international treaty.[196] This is not to suggest that the Parliament cannot discuss the significance of BITs if it so desires; however, it has not done so far mainly because it is oblivious of the significance of BITs. This is in contrast to the WTO agreements, which have been discussed in the Indian Parliament especially due to the legislative changes required to fulfill ensuing obligations.[197]

[193] Interview with two officials of the ministry of finance (names withheld), September 2010. Poulsen's study corroborates this point for many developing countries. See L. Poulsen. 2011. 'Sacrificing Sovereignty by Chance: Investment Treaties, Developing Countries and Bounded Rationality', *London School of Economics*, PhD Thesis, pp. 216–56.

[194] One such occasion was when a question was asked by P.K. Javedkar in 2010—see P.K. Javdekar, Member of Parliament in Rajya Sabha, on Bilateral Investment Treaties (BITs), 'Unstarred Question No. 2615' (20 April 2010), http://164.100.47.5:8080/members/website/quest.asp?qref=153265, accessed 28 February 2018.

[195] See Chapter 7.

[196] *Union of India* v. *Azadi Bachao Andolan*, (2003) 263 ITR 706 (SC); *M.I. Patel* v. *Union of India*, (1970) 3 SCC 400; *Rosiline George* v. *Union of India*, (1994) 2 SCC 80.

[197] For example, the provisions of the TRIPS agreement got attention of the Parliament when India was debating amendments to its Patent Act of 1970 due to the WTO obligations. Even in the context of these obligations it has been argued that there is a need to expand the role of Parliament from not just debating how the treaty provisions already accepted and ratified by

Fourth, there was a lack of legal expertise in the field of international investment law in India within the government, in academia,[198] and in civil society.[199] Most leading think tanks in India, working on international trade and foreign investment were dominated by economists or public policy professionals,[200] and focussed on trade and investment issues largely from an economic perspective. This was a direct outcome of India's active involvement in the WTO negotiations during this phase. As a result, a rigorous academic analysis and continuous commentary focussing on full implications of BITs on India was not carried out. Barring some literature,[201] the dearth of

---

the Executive should be transformed into domestic laws, but also to decide whether India should accept the international treaty obligations in the first place at all—R. Saxena. 2007. 'Treaty Making Powers: A Case for Federalisation and Parliamentarisation', *Economic and Political Weekly* 42(1):24; National Commission to Review the Working of the Constitution. 2002. 'Treaty Making Power under Our Constitution', http://lawmin.nic.in/ncrwc/ncrwcreport.htm, accessed 28 February 2018; V.R. Krishna Iyer. 2003. *Constitutional Miscellany.* Lucknow: Eastern Book Company.

198 This is not true for international law in general. However, few international lawyers wrote on international investment law during this period.

199 On the issue of constraints in legal capacity to deal with investment arbitration amongst Emerging Powers including India also see Mihaela Papa. 2013. 'Emerging Powers in International Dispute Settlement: From Legal Capacity Building to a Level Playing Field', *Journal of International Dispute Settlement* 4(1):103.

200 Some of the leading think tanks that worked on WTO and foreign investment issues during this phase were—Research and Information System for Developing Countries (RIS); Indian Council for Research on International Economic Relations (ICRIER); Centre for WTO Studies; UNCTAD India; and CUTS International. Another think tank that did commendable work on WTO issues during this phase was the Centre for Trade and Development (CENTAD).

201 S. Rao. 2000. 'Bilateral Investment Promotion Agreements: A Legal Framework for the Protection of Foreign Investments', *Commonwealth Law Bulletin* 26:623; Krishan, 'India and International Investment Law'; Prabhash Ranjan. 2008. 'International Investment Agreements and Regulatory Discretion: Case Study of India', *Journal of World Investment and Trade* 9(2):209. Some literature also appeared looking at an investment agreement in the WTO—see Kumar, 'Investment on WTO Agenda', n 156.

academic literature on Indian BITs proves this point. This again is in sharp contrast to the post-2010 period where large amount of good-quality academic literature on Indian BITs is being generated.[202]

Fifth, BITs and issues related to BITs didn't attract much media attention during this phase largely due to the bilateral nature of the treaties and most importantly due to the lack of ISDS claims against India. This lack of media attention also contributed to the overall atmosphere of the government, policymakers, and academics (both international lawyers and economists) not taking BITs too seriously. This lack of media attention is again in sharp contrast to what has happened post 2010 mainly because of an explosion of ISDS claims against India.[203]

3.6 Summing up

The Balance of Payment crisis of 1991 led to the advent of economic reforms in 1991 that changed the course of economic trajectory for ever. As a conscious break from the past, India undertook many bold structural economic reforms. Liberalization of foreign investment was one of them. This embracement of foreign investment led India to discard its old protectionist approach to the protection of foreign investment under international law followed in 1960s and 1970s and ushered in an age of acceptance of BITs.[204] India started negotiating and signing BITs from 1992 with the clear objective of promoting and protecting foreign investment in India. Studies have shown that BITs signed by India did have a positive effect on foreign investment in India.

If one were to describe the developments during the acceptance phase using the language of the policy-oriented approach of the New Haven School of international law, as discussed in Chapter 1, it will mean three things. First, India adopted a policy on foreign investment aimed at producing and distributing the value of investment

[202] See Chapters 7 and 8.

[203] See the footnotes in Chapters 6, 7, and 8 that show the continuous media commentary on Indian BITs post the White Industries case.

[204] See Chapters 4 and 5 also.

promotion and protection. Second, by entering into BITs with broad investment protection standards India made use of international law as a process to communicate to the audience (especially foreign investors in the developed world) that the policy enjoyed authority. Third, by agreeing to broad ISDS provisions in the BITs, India showed the 'capacity and willingness to make the preferential expression effective'. In other words, India's approach to international investment law through BITs fitted the broad pattern of 'policy content', 'authority signal', and 'control intention' of the policy-oriented approach outlined by Reisman.[205]

The BIT template that India followed during this phase was based on laissez-faire liberalism. Foreign investors rarely used BITs to sue India at international tribunals. As a result, the broad and vague nature of BITs signed by India (discussed in the next two chapters) and the implications of BITs on India's right to regulate did not attract much attention. Absence of BIT claims meant that no critical review of investment treaties was undertaken during this phase.

205 See Chapter 1.

4

India's BITs

Mapping the Acceptance—I

In this and the following chapter we will scrutinize the key jurisdictional, substantive, and dispute resolution provisions in India's standalone BITs and FTA investment chapters. These BITs and FTA investment chapters together form the core of international investment law binding India to protect foreign investments. As mentioned in Chapter 1, and as will be further discussed in Chapter 7, while India has terminated some of its BITs, the survival clauses present in those BITs shall continue to bind India internationally for coming 10 to 15 years. This chapter will study the following provisions contained in India's BITs and FTA investment chapters: definition of investment (Section 4.1); fair and equitable treatment (Section 4.2); MFN treatment (Section 4.3); and full protection and security (Section 4.4) across all the BITs and FTA investment chapters signed by India. The aforesaid provisions are common to all Indian BITs and FTA investment chapters. However, the language of these provisions undergoes minor variations from one treaty to the other. In order to better understand the import of the language of these provisions, they will be situated within the broader jurisprudence of the ISDS. For each of these provisions, the discussion will first focus on the meaning of the provision along with a brief note pertaining to the interpretation of the provision in

ISDS jurisprudence. Subsequently, the language imported in each of these provisions in India's standalone BITs and FTA investment chapters will be examined.

4.1 Definition of Investment

The definition of investment in a BIT plays a crucial role in determining the scope of application of rights and obligations under the treaty and the eventual establishment of jurisdiction of an ISDS tribunal.[1] Most BITs define investment 'as every type of asset' followed by several illustrative categories.[2] In addition, many of these BITs also allow foreign investors and respective host states to submit disputes to the ICSID.[3] An International Centre for the Settlement of Investment Disputes tribunal may exercise jurisdiction over a dispute only upon the fulfillment of certain conditions imposed by the ICSID convention.[4] One such condition imposed under Article 25(1) of the ICSID Convention is that 'the jurisdiction of the Centre shall extend to any legal dispute arising directly out of an investment'.[5] The term 'investment' itself remains undefined in

[1] See generally Dolzer and Schreuer, *Principles of International Investment Law*, 2nd edition, pp.60–78 (hereinafter Dolzer and Schreur, *Principles of International Investment Law*); Salacuse, *The Law of Investment Treaties*; Vandevelde, *Bilateral Investment Treaties*, pp. 166–86; M. Sattorova. 2012. 'Defining Investment under the ICSID Convention and BITs: Of Ordinary Meaning, Telos, and Beyond', *Asian Journal of International Law* 2(1): 267–90.

[2] Dolzer and Schreuer, *Principles of International Investment* Law, p. 63; K. Yannaca-Small. 2010. 'Definition of Investment: An Open-ended Search for a Balanced Approach', in *Arbitration Under International Investment Agreements*, K. Yannaca-Small (ed.), p. 243 at 245. Oxford: Oxford University Press. (hereinafter Yannaca-Small, *Definition of Investment*).

[3] Convention on the Settlement of Investment Disputes between States and Nationals of Other States (opened for signature 18 March 1965, entered into force 14 October 1966) 575 U.N.T.S. 159 ('ICSID Convention').

[4] Yannaca-Small, *Definition of Investment*, p. 248.

[5] See ICSID Convention, art 25(1). For a detailed commentary on Article 25 of ICSID Convention see C. Schreuer. 2001. *The ICSID Convention: A Commentary*. Cambridge: Cambridge University Press, pp. 82–344 (hereinafter Schreuer, *The ICSID Convention*).

the ICSID Convention.[6] Therefore, a central issue for many ICSID tribunals dealing with BIT disputes has been what constitutes investment?[7] Is the meaning of 'investment' restricted to the definition provided for in the BIT or should the asset in question also qualify as an 'investment' under Article 25(1) of the ICSID Convention?[8] Tribunals have sought to answer this question by adopting a two-tier test or the 'double-keyhole approach'.[9] Accordingly, the requirement of 'investment' has to be satisfied under the relevant BIT as well as under Article 25(1) of the ICSID Convention.[10] ICSID tribunals like *Salini* v. *Morocco* have held that an asset shall be an 'investment', under Article 25(1) of the ICSID Convention if it satisfies certain economic characteristics such as, certain duration of investment, assumption of risk, a substantial commitment, and significance for the host state's development (this is also known as the Salini test).[11]

[6] Schreuer, *The ICSID Convention*, pp. 82–344; Dolzerand Schreur, *Principles of International Investment Law*, n 1, p. 65. Also see A. Broches. 1966. 'The Convention on the Settlement of Investment Disputes: Some Observations on Jurisdiction', *Columbia Journal of Transnational Law* 5: 261 at 268.

[7] See *Salini Costruttori SpA and Italstrade SpA* v. *Kingdom of Morocco*, ICSID Case No. ARB/00/4, Decision on Jurisdiction, 23 July 2001 (hereinafter *Salini v* Morocco); *SGS Société Générale de Surveillance SA* v. *Islamic Republic of Pakistan*, ICSID Case No.ARB/01/13, Decision on Jurisdiction, 6 August 2003; *Saipem Spa* v. *People's Republic of Bangladesh*, ICSID Case No ARB/05/07, Decision on Jurisdiction, 21 March 2007.

[8] See *Salini* v. Morocco, paras 37–40.

[9] Dolzerand Schreuer, *Principles of International Investment Law*.

[10] *CSOB* v. *Slovakia*, ICSID Case No ARB/97/4, Decision on Jurisdiction (24 May 1999) para 68; *Malaysian Historical Slavors, SDN, BHD* v. *Malaysia*, ICSID Case No ARB/05/10, Award (17 May 2007) para 55.

[11] *Salini* v. Morocco para 56; *AES Corporation* v. *Argentina*, ICSID Case No. ARB/02/17, Decision on Jurisdiction (26 April 2005) para 88; *Jan de Nul* v. *Egypt*, ICSID Case No. ARB/04/13, Decision on Jurisdiction (16 June 2006) paras 90–96. A fifth dimension of 'a certain regularity of profit and return' was laid down in *Fedax* v. *Venezuela*, ICSID Case No. ARB/96/3, Decision on Jurisdiction (11 July 1997) para 43. Some tribunals have attacked the so-called Salini criteria – *BiwaterGauff* v. *Tanzania*, Award (24 July 2008) para 323; *Malaysian Historical Salvors* v. *Malaysia*, Decision on Annulment (16 April 2009).

Despite the above standard, ICSID tribunals have not always maintained consistency in determining the economic characteristics essential for an asset to satisfy the definition of investment under Article 25(1).[12] The number of requisite economic criteria has consequently fluctuated from three to six.[13] In this regard, the requirement that an investment should contribute to the host state's economic development has proved to be the most controversial due to the inherent subjectivity involved in making such determinations.[14] Some ICSID tribunals have sought refuge in the principle of party autonomy while defining investment, thus highlighting the preference accorded to the definition of 'investment' within the BIT to determine jurisdiction as against the economic characteristics that find no mention in the ICSID convention.[15]

A related question arises with respect to determining how a non-ICSID tribunal would interpret the term investment in a BIT. This issue assumes great relevance particularly for India, which is not a member of the ICSID, and thus only a non-ICSID tribunal can adjudicate disputes involving India. Non-ICSID tribunals have not been consistent in dealing with the issue of meaning of investment. On the one end of the spectrum is the case of *Romak* v. *Uzbekistan,* wherein the tribunal observed that the term 'investments' under the BIT had an 'inherent meaning', irrespective of whether the dispute arose under the ICSID or United Nations Commission on International Trade and Law (UNCITRAL) rules.[16] According to the tribunal, this 'inherent meaning' of investment entails 'a

[12] Dolzer and Schreur, *Principles of International Investment Law*, p. 75.

[13] Dolzer and Schreur, *Principles of International Investment Law*, p. 75.

[14] See *Phoenix Action Ltd.* v. *Czech Republic*, ICSID Case No. ARB/06/5, Award, 15 April 2009, para 85. More recently see *Philip Morris* v. *Uruguay*, available at www.italaw.com/sites/default/files/case-documents/italaw7417.pdf, accessed on 15 March 2018.

[15] *Malaysian Histrocial Salvors SDN BHD* v. *Malaysia*, ICSID Case No. ARB/05/10, Award on Jurisdiction, 17 May 2007, Decision on Application for Annulment, 16 April 2009.

[16] *Romak SA (Switzerland)* v. *Uzbekistan,* Permanent Court of Arbitration, Case No. AA280, Award, 26 November 2009, paras 115–120, 207 (hereinafter *Romnak* v. *Uzbekistan*).

contribution that extends over a certain period of time and that involves some risk'.[17]

On the other hand, some non-ICSID tribunals like in *Flemingo* v. *Poland*,[18] while interpreting definition of 'investment' in the India–Poland BIT, held that 'jurisdictional restrictions deriving from the notion of "investment" in Article 25 of the ICSID Convention, as emphasised by various ICSID tribunals such as the Salini panel, do not apply to the present arbitration'.[19] The claimant in this case was the Flamingo Duty Free Shop Pvt. Ltd. (FDF), a company incorporated under the laws of India, and a part of the Flamingo Group, which was the owner of its polish subsidiary involved in the duty-free operations at the Chopin airport in Warsaw, Poland, through indirect shareholding. The issue involved in this case was whether the claimant's indirect shareholding in the Polish entity constituted investment or not under the India–Poland BIT. The tribunal held that Article 1(1) of the India–Poland BIT contains a very broad definition of the term 'investment', namely: 'the term investment means every kind of asset established or acquired, in accordance with the national laws of the Contracting Party in whose territory the investment is made [...]'.[20] It further held that 'Article 1(1) of the BIT provides that "in particular, though not exclusively", investments include: "c) rights to any performance under contract having a financial value"'.[21] On the basis of this broad definition of investment in the BIT, the tribunal concluded that FDF had made an investment under the treaty, clearly rejecting the need for an asset to satisfy the different economic characteristics, which were declared to be part of investment in *Romak* v. *Uzbekistan*.

[17] *Romnak* v. *Uzbekistan*. Also see *Alps Finance and Trade AG* v. *The Slovak Republic*, UNCITRAL, Adhoc Arbitration, Award, 5 March 2011, paras 230–247.

[18] *Flemingo Duty Free Shop Private Limited* v. *Republic of Poland*, Permanent Court of Arbitration, Award, 12 August 2016 (hereinafter *Flemingo* v. *Poland*). This was the first instance of an Indian investor successfully suing a host state for BIT violation.

[19] *Flemingo* v. *Poland*, para 298.

[20] *Flemingo* v. *Poland*, para 296.

[21] *Flemingo* v. *Poland*, para 300.

Another case pertaining to India in this matter is *White Industries* v. *India*, where a non-ICSID arbitral tribunal was mandated to interpret the India–Australia BIT where investment means 'every kind of asset'.[22] The submissions made by India before the Tribunal argued for the presence of certain economic characteristics (such as commitment of resources, assumption of risk, etc.) in an activity for its categorization as 'investment'. The tribunal, however, held that the correct approach to assess 'whether an "investment" has been made is to consider the plain and ordinary meaning of the words used in the BIT in their context and in the light of its object and purpose and to determine whether the matters relied on by White satisfy the definition employed in the BIT'.[23] In response to India's argument, the tribunal held that the India–Australia BIT does not support India's position.[24] The tribunal held that the test developed by ICSID tribunals, where an asset has to satisfy economic characteristics to qualify as an investment, (or the so-called Salini test) was not applicable in the current case since the dispute was not under an ICSID tribunal.[25] Thus, on the basis of the definition of investment in the BIT, the tribunal held that the investor's contractual rights amounted to an investment under the India–Australia BIT.[26] Curiously, the tribunal then went on to examine whether the four characteristics given by the Salini tribunal were satisfied or not.[27] In light of this discussion, let us see how investment is defined in India's standalone BITs and FTA investment chapters.

4.1.1 India's Standalone BITs

Article 1 (b) of the 2003 Indian Model BIT states:

[22] Agreement between the Government of the Australia and the Government of the Republic of India on the Promotion and Protection of Investments, (signed 26 February 1999, entered into force 4 May 2000) ('India–Australia BIT') art. 1.

[23] *White Industries Australia Limited* v. *Republic of India*, UNCITRAL, Final Award, 30 November 2011, para 7.3.2 (hereinafter *White Industries* v. *India*).

[24] *White Industries* v. *India*, para 7.3.8.

[25] *White Industries* v. *India*, paras 7.4.8 and 7.4.9.

[26] *White Industries* v. *India*, para 7.4.7.

[27] *White Industries* v. *India*, paras 7.4.10 to 7.4.19.

> 'investment' means every kind of asset established or acquired including changes in the form of such investment, in accordance with the national laws of the Contracting Party in whose territory the investment is made and in particular, though not exclusively, includes:
>
> (i) movable and immovable property as well as other rights such as mortgages, liens or pledges;
> (ii) shares in and stock and debentures of a company and any other similar forms of participation in a company;
> (iii) rights to money or to any performance under contract having a financial value;
> (iv) intellectual property rights, in accordance with the relevant laws of the respective Contracting Party;
> (v) business concessions conferred by law or under contract, including concessions to search for and extract oil and other minerals'

Essentially, all standalone Indian BITs contain the aforesaid definition of investment. Standalone Indian BITs provide a broad-asset-based definition of investment where every kind of asset including direct investment, portfolio investment, intellectual property rights, and rights to money or to any performance under contract having a financial value, business concessions conferred under law or contract are identified as investment. Does such a broad definition of investment mean that an ISDS tribunal against India will have jurisdiction over disputes involving foreign assets irrespective of whether these assets satisfy the economic characteristics of investment? The answer to this question depends on the discretion exercised by the non-ICSID arbitral tribunal. One approach on the lines of *Flemingo* would mean that a large number of assets, even if they do not meet the inherent economic characteristics of investment, would qualify as investment under the BIT. As a result, a wide range of regulatory measures introduced by the state affecting the assets of foreign investors could be challenged as potential breaches of the BIT.

Few standalone Indian BITs specifically state that for an asset to qualify as investment, certain economic characteristics must be satisfied. For instance, while Article 2.1 of the India–Colombia BIT states that 'investments shall mean every type of assets that have been established or acquired by investors', Article 2.3 states that minimum characteristics of investment shall be—'the commitment of capital or other resources', 'the expectation of gain or profit', and 'the assumption of risk for the investor'. This approach institutionalizes the *Salini* criteria minus the condition requiring significant contribution to the host state's development. India–Mexico BIT is another standalone BIT, which states that investment means those assets that involve commitment of capital, expectation of gain or profit or an assumption of risk.[28] The India–Mexico BIT also lists an exhaustive definition of investment restricted to assets specifically provided for in the treaty.[29] In sum, barring few Indian BITs, most contain a broad asset-based definition of investment without much textual guidance regarding the minimum characteristics that need to be satisfied by the assets.

4.1.2 Investment Chapters in India's FTA

India's FTA investment chapters also define investment as every kind of asset owned or controlled by the investor.[30] However, the FTA investment chapters, unlike standalone BITs, provide additional factors requisite for an asset to classify as an investment.[31] These FTAs,

[28] Agreement Between The Government of the Republic of India and The Government of the United Mexican States on the Promotion and Protection of Investments (signed 21 May 2007, entered into force 23 February 2008) ('India–Mexico BIT'), art. 1(7).

[29] Agreement Between The Government of the Republic of India and The Government of the United Mexican States on the Promotion and Protection of Investments (signed 21 May 2007, entered into force 23 February 2008) ('India–Mexico BIT'), art. 1(7).

[30] See Comprehensive Economic Partnership Agreement between Republic of India and Japan (signed 16 February 2011, entered into force 1 October 2011) ('India–Japan FTA') art. 3(i); Comprehensive Economic Cooperation Agreement between the Government of Malaysia and the Government of Republic of India (24 September 2010) ('India–Malaysia FTA') art. 10.2(d); India–Korea Comprehensive Economic Partnership Agreement (7 August 2009) ('India–Korea FTA') art. 10.1; Comprehensive Economic Cooperation Agreement between the Republic of India and the Republic of Singapore (29 June 2005) ('India–Singapore FTA') art. 6.1 (1).

[31] The only exception to this is the India Singapore FTA investment chapter, which, like most standalone BITs, provides for a broad asset-based definition of investment without providing for specific economic characteristics. See India–Singapore FTA, art. 6.1.

like the India–Colombia and the India–Mexico BIT, state that an investment must possess certain characteristics like commitment of capital or other resources, the expectation of gains or profits or the assumption of risk.[32] Interestingly, the definition of investment in none of these FTA investment chapters includes contribution to the host state's development as a criterion for an asset to qualify as investment. The specific mentioning of these criteria will ensure that even a non-ICSID tribunal must satisfy itself of the fulfillment of these economic characteristics to establish its jurisdiction.

4.2 Fair and Equitable Treatment

Fair and Equitable Treatment (FET) has emerged as the most important standard of treatment in BITs,[33] attracting considerable scholarly attention.[34] Numerous ISDS claims employ violation of FET as a catch-all provision to seek sanctioning of several legislative, regulatory, and administrative actions of the host state.[35] One major reason for

[32] See India–Malaysia FTA, art 10.2 (d); India-Korea FTA, art. 10.1; Agreement on Investment under the Framework Agreement on Comprehensive Economic Cooperation between the Association of Southeast Asian Nations and the Republic of India (12 November 2014)(India–ASEAN Investment Agreement') art. 2(e); India–Japan FTA, art. 3(i) Note 2.

[33] Andrew and Paradell, *Law and Practice of Investment Treaties*, p. 254; Salacuse, *The Law of Investment Treaties*, p. 219. (describing FET as the *grundnorm* or basic norm of the investment treaty system).

[34] Salacuse, *The Law of Investment Treaties*; Vandevelde, *Bilateral Investment Treaties*, p. 43.

[35] Surya Prasad Subedi. 2008. *International Investment Law*. Oxford: Hart Publishing, p. 172; See *Pope and Talbot Inc.* v. *The Government of Canada*, UNCITRAL, Award on the Merits of Phase 2, 10 April 2001, at para 110 (hereinafter *Pope and Talbot* v. *Canada*); *Mondev International Ltd.* v. *United States*, ICSID Case No. ARB (AF)/99/2, Award, 11 October 2002; *Merrill and Ring Forestry L.P.* v. *Canada*, ICSID Case No. UNCT/07/1, Award, 31 March, 2010 (hereinafter *Merril* v. *Canada*); *TECO Guatemala Holdings LLC* v. *Republic of Guatemala*, ICSID Case No. ARB/10/23, Award, 19 December 2013, para 454 (hereinafter *Teco* v. *Guatemala*); *Bilcon of Delaware, William Ralph Clayton, William Richard Clayton, Douglas Clayton and Daniel Clayton* v. *Government of Canada*, PCA Case No. 2009–04, Award on Jurisdiction and Liability, 17 March 2015, paras 442–44. See also, Gus Van Haretn. 2007. *Investment Treaty Arbitration and Public Law*. Oxford: Oxford University Press, p. 89.

over-utilization of FET is the lack of normative content[36] of FET in most BITs.[37] The lack of normative content has consequently given rise to a debate regarding the meaning of FET provisions.[38]

According to one view, FET merely refers to the customary international law minimum standard of treatment of aliens (hereinafter IMS).[39] The basic premise of IMS is that 'an alien is protected against unacceptable measures of the host state by rules of international law which are independent of those of the host State'.[40] Reliance upon IMS to interpret FET is compelling especially in BITs that link FET to customary international law.[41] A good example of a treaty provision linking FET with IMS is Article 1105(1) of NAFTA, which

[36] Scholars have described FET as wide, tenuous and imprecise—See M. Sornarajah. 2004. *The International Law on Foreign Investment.* Cambridge: Cambridge University Press, p. 332; V. Lowe. 2002. 'Regulation or Expropriation', *Current Legal Problems* 55: 447; C. Schreuer. 2005. 'Fair and Equitable Treatment in Arbitral Practice', *Journal of World Investment and* Trade 6: 364; Salacuse, *The Law of Investment Treaties*, p. 241; Vandevelde, *Bilateral Investment Treaties*, p. 69.

[37] Newcombe and Paradell, *Law and Practice of Investment* Treaties, p. 254. See also, M.C. Porterfield. 2014. 'An International Common Law of Investors Rights', *University of Pennsylvania Journal of International Law* 27(1): 99.

[38] Salacuse, *The Law of Investment Treaties*, p. 245.

[39] Salacuse, *The Law of Investment Treaties*, p. 245.

[40] Dolzer and Schreuer, *Principles of International Investment Law*, p. 3; See E. Root. 1910. 'The Basis of Protection to Citizens Residing Abroad', *American Journal of International Law* 4: 521. On FET and international minimum standard, see generally Martins Paparinskis. 2013. *The International Minimum Standard and Fair and Equitable Treatment.* Oxford: Oxford Univeristy Press.

[41] See *Alex Genin, Eastern Credit Limited, Inc and A.S. Baltoil (US)* v. *The Republic of Estonia*, ICSID Case No. ARB/99/2, Award, 25 June 2011; *Occidental Exploration* v. *Ecuador*; Interpretative Note to the Art. 1105 NAFTA—Minimum Standard of Treatment in Accordance with International Law (1) Article 1105(1) prescribes the customary international law minimum standard of treatment of aliens as the minimum standard of treatment to be afforded to investments of investors of another Party. (2) The concepts of 'fair and equitable treatment' and 'full protection and security' do not require treatment in addition to or beyond that which is required by the customary international law minimum standard of treatment of aliens. (3) A determination that there has been a breach of another provision of the NAFTA, or of a separate international agreement, does not establish that there has been a breach of Art. 1105(1).

states that 'each party shall accord to investments of investors of another party treatment in accordance with international law, including fair and equitable treatment and full protection and security.' This provision is subject to an official interpretation by the NAFTA free trade commission (FTC), which states that Article 1105(1) represents IMS and does not require treatment in addition to or beyond what is required under customary international law.[42]

However, even in such BITs, the debate regarding the content of IMS persists. On the one hand, scholars and Tribunals argue that the content of the FET should be determined as per the 1926 case, *Neer* v. *Mexico*[43]. This case did not concern investment but the murder of a US citizen in Mexico—where US–Mexico General Claims Commission said that for treatment of an alien to constitute an international delinquency it 'should amount to an outrage, to bad faith, to wilful neglect of duty or to an insufficiency of action so far short of international standards that every reasonable and impartial man would readily recognize its insufficiency' (hereinafter the Neer standard).[44] The investor–state dispute settlement tribunals, like the tribunal in *Glamis Gold* v. *United States,*[45] held that the Neer standard of 1926 reflects IMS.[46]

On the other hand, tribunals have held that the IMS is not frozen in time and is 'constantly in a process of development'[47] and, thus, barring for cases pertaining to safety and due process, 'today's minimum standard is broader than that defined in the Neer case

[42] NAFTA FTC Note of Interpretation, 31 July 2001.

[43] *LFH Neer and PE Neer* v. *United Mexican States* (Docket No 136), General Claims Commission – United States and Mexico, 4 UNRIAA 60 (15 October 1926) (hereinafter *Neer* v. *Mexican States*).

[44] *Neer* v. *Mexican States*; See also, *Elettronica Sicula SpA* (ELSI) (*U.S.* v. *Italy*), 1989 ICJ Rep. 15.

[45] *Glamis Gold* v. *The United States of America*, UNCITRAL, Award (8 June, 2009) para 614 (hereinafter *Glamis Gold* v. *USA*).

[46] *Glamis Gold* v. *USA*, paras 598–627.

[47] *ADF Group Inc.* v. *United States of America*, ICSID Case No. ARB (AF)/00/1, Award, 9 January, 2003, para 179 (hereinafter *ADF* v. *USA*); See also *Merril* v. *Canada,* paras 205–11; See also *Gold Reserve Inc.* v. *Bolivarian Republic of Venezuela*, ICSID Case No. ARB(AF)/09/1, Award, 22 September, 2014, para 567.

and its progeny.'[48] The tribunal in *Devas* v. *India*[49] said that the content of the IMS is not frozen as defined in Neer v. Mexico.[50] As an example of this evolution—the tribunal in *Glamis Gold* v. *USA* stated that legitimate expectations[51] is part of Article 1105(1) of NAFTA (where FET is linked to IMS) in such situations where a host state's conduct 'creates reasonable and justifiable expectations on the part of an investor (or investment) to act in reliance on said conduct'.[52]

Thus, even in BITs where FET is linked to the customary international law standard, there exists no consensus regarding the meaning of this standard especially in the context of judging a host state's regulatory behaviour.[53] As a consequence, the determination of the actual content of the standard depends on arbitral discretion.

[48] See *ADF* v. *USA*, para 113; *Merril* v. *Canada*, para 213; See also *International Thunderbird Gaming Corp.* v. *United Mexican States*, UNCITEAL, Arbitral Award, 26 January 2006, para 193 (hereinafter *Thunderbird* v. *Mexico*); Roland Klager. 2011. *Fair and Equitable Treatment in International Investment Law*. Cambridge: Cambridge University Press, 48–61.

[49] Also see Chapter 6.

[50] Devas v. India, para 457.

[51] The concept of legitimate expectations has become central to the FET standard in most BITs – Técnicas Medioambientales Tecmed, *S.A* v. *The United Mexican States*, ICSID Case No. ARB (AF)/00/2, Award, 29 May2003 (hereinafter *S.A* v. *USA*); *Occidental Exploration* v. *Ecuador*, para 183, 190; *Enron Award*, para 260; *PSEG Global Inc., The North American Coal Corporation, and Konya Ingin Electrik Üretimve Ticaret Limited Sirketiv Republic of Turkey*, ICSID Case No. ARB/02/5, Award, at para 252–253, 19 January 2007 (hereinafter *PSEG Global* v. *Turkey*); *Duke Energy* v. *Republic of Ecuador*, ICSID Case No.ARB/04/19, Award, at para 340, 18 August 2008 (hereinafter *Duke Energy* v. *Ecuador*).

[52] *Glamis Gold* v. *USA*, para 621; Thunderbird, note 159, at para 147. Also see Mesa Power Group LLC v. Government of Canada (PCA Case No. 2012–17), Award, 24 March 2016, paras 502–505.

[53] Henckels, 'Protecting Regulatory Autonomy through Greater Precision in Investment Treaties'; Reisman, W. Michael. 2015. 'Canute Confronts the Tide: States versus Tribunals and the Evolution of the Minimum Standard in Customary International Law', *ICSID Review—Foreign Investment Law Journal*. 30: 616.

The alternate view on FET is that its meaning is not restricted to IMS, but is broader and autonomous.[54] This view is particularly strong in those BITs where the FET provision appears as an autonomous standard, that is, without being linked to the customary international law standard.[55] Article 4(1) of the India–Mauritius BIT, which was the subject matter of dispute in the *Devas* v. *India* case, is a good example of this.[56] It reads as follows: 'Investments and returns of investors of either Contracting Parties shall at all times be accorded fair and equitable treatment in the territory of the other Contracting Party.' This provision does not link FET with IMS. India, in this case, argued that FET provision was no more than what is envisaged in the IMS as articulated in *Neer* v. *Mexico*.[57] The tribunal, however, didn't agree with India. On the issue of link between FET and IMS, the tribunal said it subscribes to the following view articulated in *El Paso* v. *Argentina*:

[54] Dolzer and Schreuer, *Principles of International Investment Law*, p. 134.

[55] For example, Indian Model Text of Bilateral Investment Promotion and Protection Agreement 2003 (http://www.italaw.com/sites/default/files/archive/ita1026.pdf.), art. 3 (2) provides the FET provision as: 'Investments and returns of investors of each Contracting Party shall at all times be accorded fair and equitable treatment in the territory of the other Contracting Party.' There is no reference to customary international law (accessed on 15 March 2018). See generally, the discussion on this in Salacuse, The Law of *Investment Treaties*, pp. 249–51; F.A. Mann. 1981. 'British Treaties for the Promotion and Protection of Investments', *British Yearbook of International Law*, 52: 241, 244.

[56] The *Devas* v. *India* dispute arose under the India–Mauritius BIT, when the government cancelled an agreement signed in 2005 between Antirx, the marketing arm of the Indian Space Research Organisation (ISRO), a government entity, with Devas Multimedia, a multimedia services provider. As per this agreement, Antrix was supposed to provide 70 MHz of S-band satellite spectrum to Devas for providing multimedia services to mobile users across India. However, on 2 July 2010, the Indian Space Commission decided to annul the agreement in view of the alleged increasing need of the military for the S Band spectrum. This decision to annul the contract was announced by ISRO on 8 February 2011. Finally, on 17 February 2011, the cabinet committee on security (CCS) annulled the Antrix-Devas contract – see Chapter 6 for more details.

[57] *Devas* v. *India*, paras 452–453.

> The Tribunal considers this discussion to be somewhat futile, as the scope and content of the minimum standard of international law is as little defined as the BIT's FET standard, and as the true question is to decide what substantive protection is granted to foreign investors through the FET. The issue is not one of comparing two undefined or weakly defined standards; it is to ascertain the content and define the BIT standard of fair and equitable treatment.[58]

The tribunal also held that since the content of the FET provision in the India–Mauritius BIT is not defined, in other words, it is autonomous, and thus it needs to be determined by using rules of the VCLT.[59] However, the autonomous standard provides no guidance as to the content of the FET provision, which, in turn, provides unfettered adjudicative discretion to ISDS tribunals.[60]

An outcome of this unfettered discretion is that the tribunals have held that protecting an investor's 'legitimate expectations' is also part of the FET.[61] For example, the *Devas* v. *India* tribunal also held that the legitimate expectations of the investors have generally been considered central to its definition.[62] Likewise in *Deutshe Telekom* v. *India*, the tribunal held that FET includes not just the protection of legitimate expectations, but also the protection from conduct that is arbitrary, unreasonable, disproportionate, and lacking in good faith.[63] The tribunal also held that FET includes principles of due process and transparency.[64]

58 *El Paso Energy International Co.* v. *The Argentine Republic*, ICSID Case No. ARB/03/15, Award, 2011, para 335 (hereinafter *El Paso* v. *Argentine Republic*).

59 *Devas* v. *India*, para 457.

60 Salacuse, *The Law of Investment Treaties*, p. 251.

61 Salacuse, *The Law of Investment Treaties*, pp. 253–9. Also see *S.A* v. *USA*; *Occidental Exploration* v. *Ecuador*, para 183, 190; Enron Award, note 8, at para 260; *PSEG Global* v. *Turkey*; *Duke Energy* v. *Ecuador*, para 340; *Hassan Awdi, Enterprise Business Consultants, Inc. and Alfa El Corporation v Romania*, ICSID Case No. ARB/10/13, Award, 2 March 2015, paras 312–333.

62 *Devas* v. *India*, para 463.

63 *Deutsche Telekom* v. *India*, para 336.

64 *Deutsche Telekom* v. *India*, para 336.

Most ISDS tribunals invoke the notion of 'legitimate expectations' as part of the FET provision by merely relying on arbitral precedent.[65] Some have contested the notion of legitimate expectation being part of the FET provision because 'it does not correspond, in any language, to the ordinary meaning to be given to the terms fair and equitable'.[66] Even if legitimate expectations form a part of the FET provision, the unaddressed issue is the scope and extent of its meaning. Some cases, such as *Tecmed* v. *Mexico* have imputed a broad meaning to legitimate expectations, holding that 'the foreign investor expects the host state to act in a consistent manner, free from ambiguity and totally transparently in its relations with the foreign investor, so that it may know beforehand any and all rules and regulations that will govern its investments … to be able to plan its investment and comply with such regulations.'[67] This makes legitimate expectation an overly expansive catch-all phrase capable of impugning all regulatory measures of the host state.[68] In *Devas* v. *India*, the tribunal held that investors were entitled to legitimate expectations that, in accordance with the BIT and as part of general obligation under international law, the host state would deal with them in good faith.[69]

On the other hand, some ISDS tribunals have narrowed down the meaning of legitimate expectations. For example, in *Glamis* v. *Mexico*, the tribunal narrowed it down to situations where a host state induces an investor to make an investment by making specific representations to the investor, which investor relies upon to make the investment, and then the host state frustrates the representation made.[70] Likewise, in *Urbaser* v. *Argentina*, the tribunal held that an

[65] Michele Potesta, Legitimate Expectations in Investment Treaty Law: Understanding the Roots and the Limits of a Controversial Concept 28 *ICSID Review* 88, 89 (2013).

[66] Separate Opinion of Arbitrator Pedro Nikken in *AWG* v. *Argentina*, para 3

[67] *Tecmed*, para 154.

[68] *MTD Equity* v. *Chile* (Annulment Proceeding), para 67; Christopher F. Dugan, Don Wallace, Noah Rubins, and Borzu Sabahi. 2008. *Investor State Arbitration*. Oxford/ NewYork: Oxford University Press, p. 513.

[69] *Devas* v. *India*, para 465.

[70] See *Glamis* v. *Mexico*, para 620. Also see *Blusun S.A., Jean-Pierre Lecorcier and Michael Stein* v. *Italian Republic*, ICSID Case No. ARB/14/3, Award,

investor's expectations should be placed in a legal framework that embraces the rights and obligations of the host state, subject to the BIT protections.[71]

4.2.1 India's Standalone BITs

All standalone Indian BITs, except for the India–Turkey BIT,[72] contain a FET provision. Article 3(2) of the 2003 Indian Model BIT gives the FET provision stating—'Investments and returns of investors of each Contracting Party shall at all times be accorded fair and equitable treatment in the territory of the other Contracting Party.' The meaning of FET is not given in the model BIT. It only states that foreign investment has to be accorded FET 'at all times'. The FET provision is part of Article 3, which is titled as 'Promotion and Protection of Investment'. Paragraph 1 of Article 3 states—'Each Contracting Party shall encourage and create favourable conditions for investors of the other Contracting Party to make investments in its territory, and admit such investments in accordance with its laws and policy'. Thus, the sub-article of the provision containing FET emphasizes on encouraging and creating favourable conditions for foreign investment.

The fair and equitable treatment provision in the Model BIT, despite its titular wording 'promotion and protection of investments' exists as a standalone provision and is not combined with protection

---

27 December 2016, paras 372, 374; *CervinInvestissements S.A. and Rhone Investissements S.A.* v. *Republic of Costa Rica, I*CSID Case No. ARB/13/2, Award, 7 March 2017, para 509. *See also* Article 8.10 (4) of the CETA; Michele Potesta, Legitimate Expectations in Investment Treaty Law: Understanding the Roots and the Limits of a Controversial Concept 28 *ICSID Review* 88, 105–10 (2013).

[71] *Urbaser S.A. and Consorcio de Aguas Bilbao Biskaia, Bilbao Biskaia Ur Partzuergoa* v. *Argentine Republic,* ICSID Case No. ARB/07/26, Award, 8 December 2016, para 619. Also see para 622.

[72] Agreement Between the Republic of India and the Republic of Turkey Concerning the Reciprocal Promotion and Protection of Investments (signed 17 September 1998, entered into force 18 October 2007) ('India–Turkey BIT'). This BIT makes a reference to fair and equitable treatment in the preamble of the treaty.

and security of investments or with national treatment and MFN clause. The same formulation of FET exists in several Indian BITs.[73] A few other Indian BITs contain a slightly different formulation of the FET provision and do not exist in a standalone form, but in combination with either full protection or security,[74] or in combination

[73] See 'India–Australia BIT' art. 3(2), Agreement between the Government of the Republic of India and The Government of the State of Israel (signed 29 January 1996, entered into force 18 February 1997) ('India–Israel BIT') art. 3(2), Agreement between The Government of The Republic of India and The Government of the Republic of Poland for the Promotion And Protection of Investments (signed 7 October 1996, entered into force 31 December 1997) ('India–Poland BIT') art. 3(2), Agreement Between The Government of The Republic of India And The Government of The Democratic Socialist Republic of Sri Lanka for the Promotion And Protection of Investments (signed 22 January 1997, entered into force 13 February 1998) ('India–Sri Lanka BIT') art. 3(2), Agreement Between The Government of The Republic of India and The Government of The Arab Republic of Egypt For The Promotion And Reciprocal Protection of Investments (signed 9 April 1997, entered into force 22 November 2000) ('India–Egypt BIT') art. 2(2), Agreement between The Government of The Republic of India and The Government of The Socialist Republic of Vietnam for The Promotion and Protection of Investments (signed 8 March 1997, entered into force 1 December 1999) ('India–Vietnam BIT') art. 3(2), Agreement between The Government of The Republic of India and The Government of Romania for The Promotion And Reciprocal Protection of Investments (signed 17 November 1997, entered into force 9 December 1999) ('India–Romania BIT') art. 3(2), Agreement between The Government of The Republic of India and The Government of The People's Republic of China for The Promotion and Protection of Investments (signed 21 November 2006, entered into force 1 August 2007 ('India–China BIT') art. 3(2).

[74] See Agreement Between The Government of The Republic of India and The Government of The United Kingdom of Great Britain and Northern Ireland for The Promotion And Protection of Investments (signed 14 March 1994, entered into force 6 January 1995) ('India–UK BIT') art. 3(2), The Agreement between The Republic of India and the Federal Republic of Germany for the Promotion and Protection of Investments (signed 10 July 1995, entered into force 13 July 1998) ('India–Germany BIT') art. 3(2), Agreement between The Government of the Republic of India and The Government of the Italian Republic for the Promotion and Protection of Investment (signed 23 November 1995, entered into force 26 March 1998) ('India–Italy BIT') art. 3(2), Agreement between The

Republic of India And The Czech Republic for The Promotion And Protection of Investments (signed 11 October 1996, entered into force 6 February 1998 ('India–Czech Republic BIT'), art. 2(2), Agreement on The Promotion And The Reciprocal Protection of Investments Between The Republic of India and The Kingdom of Spain (signed 30 September 1997, entered into force 16 October 1998) ('India–Spain BIT') art. 4(1), Agreement between The Government of The Republic of India and The Swiss Confederation for The Promotion And Protection of Investments (signed 4 April 1997 entered into force 16 February 2000) ('India–Switzerland BIT') art. 3(2), Agreement on Reciprocal Protection and Promotion of Investments between The Government of The Republic of India and The Government of The Republic of Uzbekistan (signed 18 May 1999, entered into force 28 July 2000) ('India–Uzbekistan BIT') art. 2(2), Agreement between The Government of The Republic of India And The Government of The Kingdom of Morocco for The Promotion and Protection of Investments (signed 13 February 1999, entered into force 22 February 2001 ('India–Morocco BIT') art. 2(2), Agreement between The Government of The Republic of India and The Government of The Kingdom of Sweden for The Promotion And Reciprocal Protection of Investments (signed 4 July 2000, entered into force 1 April 2001) ('India–Sweden BIT') art. 3(2), Agreement between Government of The Republic of India and The Government of The Kingdom of Thailand for the Promotion and Protection of Investments (signed 10 July 2000, entered into force 13 July 2001) ('India–Thailand BIT') art. 3(2), Agreement between The Government of The Republic of India and The Government of Republic of Trinidad and Tobago for The Promotion and Protection of Investments (signed 12 March 2007, entered into force 7 September 2007) ('India–Trinidad and Tobago BIT') art. 3(2), Agreement between The Government of The Republic of India and The Government of The Hellenic Republic on The Promotion and Reciprocal Protection of Investments (signed 26 April 2007, entered into force 12 April 2008) ('India–Hellenic Republic BIT') art. 3(2), Agreement between The Government of The Republic of India and The Government of The Republic of Iceland for The Promotion and Protection of Investments (signed 29 June 2007, entered into force 16 December 2008) ('India–Iceland BIT') art. 3(2), India–Mexico BIT, art. 5(1), Agreement between The Government of The Republic of India and The Federal Government of The Federal Republic of Yugoslavia for The Reciprocal Promotion and Protection of Investments (signed 31 January 2003, entered into force 24 February 2009) ('India–Serbia BIT') art. 3(2), Agreement between The Government of The Republic of India and The Government of The Republic of Senegal for The Promotion and Protection of Investments (signed 3 July 2008, entered into force 17 October 2009) ('India–Senegal BIT') art. 3(2).

with national treatment and MFN.[75] All these BITs contain an unqualified FET provision with no guidance as to the normative content of the FET standard. Consequently, the FET formulation in large number of India's standalone BITs strengthens the argument of the FET being an autonomous provision. This, as discussed earlier, including in Devas v. India, provides unfettered adjudicative discretion to ISDS tribunals to supply content to these broad and vague FET provisions.

A few BITs provide for a qualified FET by linking it to the IMS. For example, Article 5(3)(a) of the India–Mexico BIT provides that the obligation to accord FET treatment to investments does not require treatment in addition to or beyond that which is required by the customary international law minimum standard of treatment of aliens.[76] The fair and equitable treatment formulation in the India–Colombia BIT is important in this regard. While, Article 3(3) of the BIT obligates the state to accord FET treatment to foreign investment, Article 3(4)(a) clarifies that FET includes the prohibition against denial of justice in criminal, civil, or administrative proceedings in accordance with the principle of due process.[77]

4.2.2 Investment Chapters in India's FTAs

Unlike India's BITs the FET provision in India's FTAs are linked to IMS. For example, Article 10.4 (1) of the investment chapter of India–Korea FTA states,

> Each Party shall accord to an investment of an investor of the other Party in its territory 'fair and equitable treatment' and 'full protection and security.' The concepts of 'fair and equitable treatment' and 'full protection and security' do not require treatment in addition to or

[75] Agreement between The Government of The Republic of India and The Government of The Kingdom of Denmark Concerning The Promotion and Reciprocal Protection of Investments (signed 6 September 1995, entered into force 28 August 1996) ('India–Denmark BIT') art. 3(2).

[76] India–Mexico BIT, art. 5(3)(a).

[77] Agreement for the Promotion and Protection of Investments between the Republic of Colombia and the Republic of India (signed on 10 November 2009, entered into force 2 July 2012) ('India–Colombia BIT') art. 3(4).

> beyond that which is required by the customary international law minimum standard of treatment of aliens.

Likewise, Article 87 of India–Japan FTA states, 'Each Party shall accord to investments of investors of the other Party treatment in accordance with international law, including fair and equitable treatment and full protection and security'. It further provides:

> This paragraph prescribes the customary international law minimum standard of treatment of aliens as the minimum standard of treatment to be afforded to investments of investors of the other Party. The concepts of 'fair and equitable treatment' and 'full protection and security' do not require treatment in addition to or beyond that which is required by the customary international law minimum standard of treatment of aliens. A determination that there has been a breach of another provision of this Agreement, or of a separate international agreement, does not establish that there has been a breach of this paragraph.

A similar provision linking FET with IMS also exists in Article 10.5 of the investment chapter of India–Malaysia FTA. In contrast, the investment chapter of India's FTA with Singapore does not contain the FET provision.

As discussed earlier, the interpretation of the FET provision in these FTA investment chapters would also depend on arbitral discretion because of lack of consensus on the content of the FET provision despite linking it with IMS.

The discussion on FET provision in Indian BITs shows that India in the 'acceptance' phase had no hesitance to embrace the IMS in its BITs. This is important given the opposition India had demonstrated in past to the existence of such a standard in international law.[78]

4.3 Full Protection and Security

Another major treaty provision common to most BITs is 'full protection and security' (FPS). Host states undertake an obligation to provide FPS to foreign investment. Like the provision on FET, BITs often do

[78] See Chapter 2.

not define the meaning of FPS. This has given rise to debate whether FPS is confined to physical safety and protection of investments or does it also include other kinds of protection.[79] Several tribunals have interpreted FPS to mean that it puts the host state under an obligation to merely ensure physical safety and protection of foreign investment.[80] Some arbitral tribunals have, however, expanded the meaning of FPS to also include regulatory and legal security.[81] For instance, in *CME* v. *Czech Republic*, the tribunal, while analysing the obligation of 'full security and protection', held that 'the host state is obligated to ensure that neither by amendment of its laws nor by actions of its administrative bodies is the agreed and approved security and protection of the foreign investor's investment withdrawn or devalued'.[82]

4.3.1 India's Standalone BITs

The clause promising FPS is present in only a few standalone Indian BITs. The 2003 Model BIT does not contain the provision. The full protection and security provision generally states that countries shall accord to investments as well as to investors in respect of such

[79] Dolzer and Schreuer, *Principles of International Investment Law*, pp. 160–1.

[80] See *Asian Agricultural Products* v. *Sri Lanka*, ICSID Case No. ARB/87/3, Final Award, 27 June 1990, para 54 at 130 (hereinafter *Asian Agricultural* v. *Sri Lanka*); *American Manufacturing & Trading, Inc.* v. *Republic of Zaire*, ICSID Case No. ARB/93/1, Award, 21 February 1997; *Copper Mesa Mining Corporation* v. *Republic of Ecuador*, PCA No. 2012-2, Award, 15 March 2016, paras 6.78 to 6.85; *Ampal-American Israel Corp., EGI-Fund (08-10) Investors LLC, EGI-Series Investments LLC, BSS-EMG Investors LLC and David Fischer* v. *Arab Republic of Egypt*, ICSID Case No. ARB/12/11, Decision on Liability and Heads of Loss, 21 February 2017, paras 285–290.

[81] Newcombe and Paradell, *Law and Practice of Investment Treaties*, p. 310.

[82] *CME Czech Republic* v. *The Czech Republic*, UNCITRAL, Partial Award, 13 September 2001, para 613; See also *Azurix Corp.* v. *Arg.*, ICSID Case No. ARB/01/12, Award, 14 July 2006, paras 406–408; *Siemens* v. *Argentina*, ICSID Case No. ARB/02/8, Award, 6 February 2007, para 303; *National Grid* v. *Argentina*, UNCITRAL, Award, 3 November 2008, paras 187–90; *Total S.A.* v. *Argentine Republic*, ICSID Case No. ARB/04/1, Decision on Liability, 27 December 2010, para 343.

investments, at all times, full protection and security in their territory.[83] Some indication regarding the meaning or scope of FPS is provided in certain BITs. For instance, Article 3(4)(b) of the India–Colombia BIT provides that the FPS standard does not imply, in any case, a better treatment to that accorded to nationals of the host state. Likewise, the India–Mexico BIT that also contains FPS provision states that this obligation does not require treatment in addition to or beyond that which is required by the customary international law minimum standard of treatment of aliens.[84] Some Indian BITs provide for protection and security of investments by linking it to domestic law. For instance, Article 3(3) of the India–Slovenia BIT provides that the host state shall accord protection and security to investments subject to its laws.[85] Since most of the standalone BITs that contain the FPS provision do not specifically limit it to physical protection and security, a broader approach adopted by tribunals like *CME* v. *Czech Republic*, as mentioned before, cannot be ruled out.

4.3.2 Investment Chapters in India's FTAs

All Indian FTA investment chapters (with Korea, Malaysia, and Japan), barring the India–Singapore FTA, contain FPS provision. These free trade agreement investment chapters link FPS with customary international law. For example, Article 87.1 of the India–Japan FTA investment chapter states—The concepts of 'fair and equitable treatment' and 'full protection and security' do not require treatment in addition to or beyond that which is required by the customary international law minimum standard of treatment of aliens.[86] The

[83] India–Germany BIT, art. 3 (2). Also see India–Austria BIT art. 2(2); India–Bahrain BIT; India–Brunei BIT; India–Czech Republic BIT; India–Denmark BIT; India–Finland BIT; India–France BIT; India–Greece BIT; India–Hungary BIT; India–Iceland BIT; India–Italy BIT; India–Kuwait BIT; India–Latvia BIT; India–Lithuania BIT; India–Macedonia BIT; India–Morocco BIT; India–Netherlands BIT; India–Saudi Arabia BIT; India–Switzerland BIT; India–Thailand BIT; India–Uzbekistan BIT.

[84] India–Mexico BIT, art. 5(3)(a).

[85] Also see India–Senegal BIT art. 3(2); India–Australia BIT art. 3(3).

[86] Similar provision occurs in Article 10.5(2) of the India–Malaysia FTA and Article 10.4(1) of the India–Korea FTA.

India–ASEAN investment agreement also imposes an obligation on host states to provide full protection and security to foreign investments.[87] However, it also offers two important clarifications: first, as given in Article 87.1 of the India–Japan FTA investment chapter, that FPS does not require treatment in addition to what is required under CIL;[88] second, FPS requires each party to take such measures as may be reasonably necessary to ensure the protection and security of investments.[89] The second clarification might be useful to counter broad interpretations of the FPS provision beyond physical protection and security.

4.4 Most Favoured Nation Treatment

The most favoured nation provision in BITs aims to create a level-playing field for all foreign investors by prohibiting the host state from discriminating against investors from different countries.[90] The actual working of an MFN clause in a BIT can be understood with this simple illustration as discussed by Schill.[91] Let us assume three states: A (the granting state), B (the beneficiary state), and C (the third state). Further, assume that states A and B have entered into a treaty containing an MFN clause (primary treaty). Now, If state A extends certain benefits to state C, state B can invoke the MFN clause in the primary treaty to ensure that state A extends the same benefits to it provided the granted benefits to state C fall within the

[87] India–ASEAN Investment Agreement, art. 7(1).

[88] India–ASEAN Investment Agreement, art. 7(2)(c).

[89] India–ASEAN Investment Agreement, art. 7(2)(b).

[90] OECD. 2004. 'Most-Favoured-Nation Treatment in International Investment Law', OECD Working Papers on International Investment, 2004/02, OCED Publishing, http://www.oecd.org/daf/inv/investment-policy/WP-2004_2.pdf,accessed on 15.3.2018; Okezic Chukwumerije. 2007. 'Interpreting Most-Favoured-Nation Clauses in Investment Treaty Arbitrations', *Journal of World Investment and Trade* 8: 597, 608; Jürgen Kurtz. 2004. 'The MFN Standard and Foreign Investment: An Uneasy Fit', *Journal of World Investment and Trade* 5: 861, 873 (hereinafter Kurtz, *MFN Standard and Foreign Investment*).

[91] Schill, *Multilateralization of International Investment Law*, p. 140.

scope of application of the MFN clause contained in the primary treaty between A and B.[92] In ISDS claims, foreign investors have often used the MFN provision of the primary BIT (under which the dispute between investor and state arises) to successfully borrow a favourable substantive provision granted by the host state under another BIT (secondary BIT).[93] Foreign investors have also relied upon the MFN provision in the primary BIT to borrow beneficial ISDS provisions from secondary BITs[94] with varying degrees of

[92] Schill, *Multilateralization of International Investment Law*, p.126; Endre Ustor. 1997. 'Most Favoured Nation Clause', in *Encyclopedia of Public International Law* Volume III, R. Bernhardt and P. Macalister-Smith (eds), p. 468, Amsterdam: North-Holland Publishing. Also see United Nations. 1978 [reprinted 1978]. 'Report of the International Law Commission on the Work of its Thirtieth Session 8 May-28', U.N. Doc. A/33/10, 2 Yearbook of International Law Commission.

[93] *See, Vladimir Berschader and Moïse Berschader* v. *The Russian Federation*, SCC Case No. 080/2004, Award, 21 April 2006, para 179; *Asian Agricultural Products* v. *Sri Lanka*, para 54. Although in this case, the investor could not succeed because of being unable to show that Sri Lanka's BIT with Switzerland contained a more beneficial provision. See para 54; *MTD Equity* v. *Republic of Chile*, ICSID Case No. ARB/01/7, Award, 25 May 2004; *Bayindir Insaat Turizm Ticaret Ve Sanayi A.Ş* v. *Islamic Republic of Pakistan*, ICSID Case No. ARB/03/29, Decision on Jurisdiction, 14 November 2005; Also see *Rumeli Telekom* v. *Republic of Kazakhstan*, ICSID Case No. ARB/05/16, Award, 29 July 2008, paras 572, 575; *Pope and Talbot* v. *Canada*; *IçkaleInsaat Limited Sirketi* v. *Turkmenistan*, ICSID Case No. ARB/10/24, Award, 8 March 2016, paras 328–329. Also see Schill, *Multilateralization of International Investment Law.*

[94] See Rudolf Dolzer and Terry Myers. 2004. 'After Tecmed: Most Favoured Nation Clauses in International Investment Protection Agreements', *ICSID Review – Foreign Investment Law Journal* 19: 49; Stephen Fietta. 2005. 'Most Favoured Nation Treatment and Dispute Resolution under Bilateral Investment Treaties: A Turning Point?' *International Arbitration Law Review* 8:131; Dana H. Freyer and David Herlihy. 2005. 'Most Favoured Nation Treatment and Dispute Settlement in Investment Arbitration', *ICSID Review – Foreign Investment Law Journal* 20: 58; Locknie Hsu. 2006. 'MFN and Dispute Settlement', *Journal of World Investment and Trade* 7: 25; Kurtz, *MFN Standard and Foreign Investment*; Schill, *Multilateralization of International Investment Law* pp. 151–72; Abby Cohen Smutny and Lee A. Steven. 2010. 'The MFN Clause: What are its Limits?', in *Arbitration Under International Investment Agreements*, K. Yannaca-Small ed.,

success.[95] Foreign investors have also relied upon the MFN provision to try to broaden the ISDS tribunal's jurisdiction.[96]

In *White Industries* v. *India*[97] the MFN provision of the India–Australia BIT (the primary treaty) was relied upon by an Australian investor to import favorable substantive provisions related to 'effective means of asserting claims and enforcing rights' from the India–Kuwait BIT (secondary treaty) into the India–Australia BIT.[98] The most favoured nation provision in the India–Australia BIT is as follows:

> A Contracting Party shall at all times treat investments in its own territory on a basis no less favourable than that accorded to investments or investors of any third country.[99]

---

p. 351, Oxford: Oxford University Press; Martins Paparinskis. 2011. 'MFN Clauses and International Dispute Settlement: Moving beyond Mafezzini and Plama?', *ICSID Review – Foreign Investment Law Journal* 26: 14.

[95] See *Emilio Augustine Mafezzini* v. *Spain*, ICSID Case No. ARB/97/7, Award, 13 November 2000; *Siemens A.G.* v. *The Argentine Republic*, ICSID Case No. ARB/02/8, Decision on Jurisdiction, 3 August 2004, para 108; *Gas Natural* v. *Argentina*, ICSID Case No. ARB/03/10, Decision of the Tribunal on Preliminary Questions on Jurisdiction, 17 June 2005, para 49; *Suez, Sociedad General de Aguas de Barcelona, S.A. & Vivendi Universal, S.A. v Argentine Republic*, ICSID Case No. ARB/03/19, Decision on Jurisdiction, 3 August 2006, para 59; Also see, *Wintershall Aktiengesellschaft* v. *The Argentine Republic*, ICSID Case No. ARB/04/14, Award, 8 December 2008, paras 159–60.

[96] See *Mesa Power Group LLC* v. *Government of Canada*, PCA Case No. 2012–17, Award, 24 March 2016, para 401–402; *Beijing Urban Construction Group Co. Ltd.* v. *Republic of Yemen*, ICSID Case No. ARB/14/30, Decision on Jurisdiction, 31 May 2017, para 116; *Anglia Auto Accessories Ltd* v. *The Czech Republic*, SCC Case No. 2014/181, Final Award, 10 March 2017, para 166.

[97] *White Industries* v. *India*. See *Investment Treaty News*. 2012. 'The White Industries Arbitration: Implications for India's Investment Treaty Programme', 13 April, https://www.iisd.org/itn/2012/04/13/the-white-industries-arbitration-implications-for-indias-investment-treaty-program/, accessed 15 March 2018. (hereinafter, *The White Industries Arbitration*); Manu Sanan. 2012. 'The White Industries Award: Shades of Grey', *Journal of World Investment & Trade* 13: 661 (hereinafter Sanan, *The White Industries Award*).

[98] *White Industries* v. *India*, paras 11.1.1–11.1.5. For more details on this case, see *The White Industries Arbitration*; Sanan, *The White Industries Award*.

[99] India–Australia BIT, art. 4.2.

India argued such importation would 'fundamentally subvert the carefully negotiated balance of the BIT.'[100] The tribunal, dismissing India's arguments, allowed for the importation of the substantive provision from the secondary BIT into the primary BIT.[101] The tribunal held that an importation of the substantive provision into the primary BIT served the purpose for which countries have incorporated the MFN provision in the BIT.[102] Post this setback, India took the stand that use of the MFN provision by foreign investors to borrow beneficial substantive and procedural provisions from third country BITs, in order to replace or supplement the provisions of the primary BIT, disturbs the various strategic, diplomatic, and political reasons behind negotiating bilateral treaties.[103] The subsequent Indian Model BIT, therefore, does not include MFN provision.[104]

4.4.1 India's Standalone BITs

The most favoured nation provision in Article 4(1) of India's 2003 Model BIT is as follows—Each Contracting Party shall accord to investments of investors of the other Contracting Party, treatment which shall not be less favourable than that accorded either to investments of its own or investments of investors of any third state. This provision exists in combination with the provision on national treatment and is not subject to any exceptions. The only exceptions, as provided under Article 4(3), are that MFN provision does obligate the extension of 'benefit of any treatment, preference or privilege resulting from:

[100] *White Industries* v. *India*, para 11.2.1.

[101] *White Industries* v. *India*, paras 11.2.2—11.2.8; See also *Bayindir Insaat Turizm Ticaret Ve Sanayi A.Ş* (n 73); *MTD Equity* (n 73).

[102] *White Industries* v. *India*, para 11.2.4; See also U.N. Commission. 1979. 'Draft Articles on Most Favoured Nation Clauses with commentaries', U.N. Doc. A/CN.4/SER.A/1978/Add.1.

[103] Statement by India at the World Investment Forum 2014, UNCTAD, http://unctad-worldinvestmentforum.org/wp-content/uploads/2014/10/Mayaram.pdf, last accessed on 15 March 2018; Garg, Tripathi, and Roy, 'The Indian Model Bilateral Investment Treaty.

[104] Garg, Tripathi, and Roy,'The Indian Model Bilateral Investment Treaty', p. 76.

(a) any existing or future customs unions or similar international agreement to which it is or may become a party, or
(b) any matter pertaining wholly or mainly to taxation'.

This language of the provision of MFN is followed in almost all Indian BITs with the only difference that some Indian BITs further obligate providing treatment 'not less favourable' for various activities related to the investment.[105] For example, Article 4(1) of the India–UK BIT provides that 'each Contracting Party shall accord to investments of investors of the other Contracting Party, including their operation, management, maintenance, use, enjoyment, or disposal by such investors, treatment which shall not be less favourable than that accorded ... to investments of investors of any third state'. Similar language exists in many Indian BITs.[106]

[105] For detailed discussion on MFN provision in Indian BITs see Prabhash Ranjan. 2015. 'MFN Provision in Indian Bilateral Investment Treaties – A Case for Reform', *Indian Journal of International Law* 55: 39–64.

[106] See India–Germany BIT, art. 4(1); Agreement between the Republic of India and the Kingdom of Netherlands for the Promotion and Protection of Investments (signed 6 November 1995, entered into force 1 December 1996) ('India–Netherlands BIT') art. 4(2); India–Italy BIT, art. 4(1); India–Israel BIT, art. 4(1); India–Czech Republic BIT, art. 3 (1); India–Switzerland BIT, art. 4(1); Agreement between The Government of The Republic of India And The Government of The Kingdom of Morocco for The Promotion And Protection of Investments (signed 13 February 1999, entered into force 22 February 2001) ('India–Morocco BIT') arts 3(1), 3(2); India–Australia BIT arts 4(1), 4(3); India–Argentina BIT, arts 4(1), 4(2); India–Argentina BIT arts 3(1) and 3(2); Agreement between The Government of The Republic of India and The Government of The Lao People's Democratic Republic for The Promotion And Protection of Investments (signed 9 November 2000, entered into force on 5 January 2003) ('India–Lao PDR BIT') arts 4(1), 4(2); Agreement between The State of Kuwait and The Republic of India for The Encouragement and Reciprocal Protection of Investment (signed 27 November 2001, entered into force 28 June 2003) ('India–Kuwait BIT') arts 5(1), 5(2); Agreement between The Government of The Republic of India And The Government of Republic of Cyprus for The Mutual Promotion And Protection Of Investments (signed 9 April 2002, entered into force 12 January 2004) ('India–Cyprus BIT') arts 4 (1), 4 (2); India–Finland BIT, arts 4(1), 4(2); Agreement between The Government of The Republic of India and The Government of The Kingdom of Bahrain for

Further, the provision of MFN in most Indian BITs does not contain the 'like circumstances' clause. This potentially broadens the application of the MFN provision to cover investments, which may be in different sectors, regions, etc. However, a contrary stand was taken by a tribunal in the case of *Parkerings* v. *Lithunaia*,[107] wherein the tribunal held that 'the essential condition of the violation of a MFN clause is the existence of a different treatment accorded to another foreign investor in a similar situation'.[108]

Another key feature of the MFN provision in Indian BITs is that the MFN provision in all Indian BITs is subject to two standard exceptions. Host state is not obliged to extend to foreign investors benefit of any treatment or preference that results from—first, any existing or future Customs Union or similar international agreement; and second, any matter pertaining wholly or mainly to taxation. Certain Indian BITs contain narrower or broader exceptions than these two. For instance, India–Russia BIT does not contain the exception relating to taxation and is therefore a narrower exception. Broader exceptions are also found in some other BITs like India–Colombia BIT. Article 4(3) of India–Colombia BIT states 'the most favoured nation treatment to be granted in like circumstances referred to in this Agreement does not encompass mechanisms for the settlement of investment disputes …'[109] This covers both investor–state dispute settlement mechanism and state–state dispute settlement mechanism. Similarly, Article 5(3) of India UAE BIT provides that the MFN provision shall not apply to procedural or jurisdictional matters.[110]

The Promotion and Protection of Investments (signed 13 January 2004, entered into force 5 December 2007) ('India–Bahrain BIT') arts 4(1), 4(2).

[107] *Parkerings Compagniet* v. *Republic of Lithuania*, ICSID Case No. ARB/05/8, Award (11 September 2007).

[108] *Parkerings Compagniet* v. *Republic of Lithuania*, ICSID Case No. ARB/05/8, Award (11 September 2007) para 369. Also see *Goetz and others* v. *Burundi*, ICSID Case No. ARB/95/3, Award (10 February 1999) para 121.

[109] India–Colombia BIT, art. 4(3).

[110] Agreement between the Government of Republic of India and the Government of the United Arab Emirates on the Promotion and Protection of Investments (signed 12 December 2013), art. 5.3.

A very important aspect of the MFN provision in Indian BITs is its application to the post-establishment phases. This is evident from the fact that granting of MFN treatment is not linked to 'establishment', but only to those stages of investment, which follow after investment has been made. In other words, at the stage of entry or admission, India has the policy-space of treating different foreign investments in a different manner without being accused of violating the MFN provision.

4.4.2 Investment Chapters in India's FTAs

Barring India's investment chapter in FTA with Japan, none of the FTA investment chapters contain MFN provision. The implication of this is that no foreign investor from these three countries could borrow beneficial provisions from other investment treaties signed by India. Further, if India provides favourable treatment to other foreign investors in terms of application of measures at the domestic level, investors from these three countries will not be able bring claims against India for violation of MFN treatment.

The most favoured nation provision in Article 87 of the India Japan FTA provides as follows:

> Each Party shall accord to investors of the other Party and to their investments treatment no less favourable than that it accords, in like circumstances, to investors of any non-Party and to their investments with respect to the management, conduct, operation, maintenance, use, enjoyment and sale or other disposition of investments in its Area.

The most favoured nation provision is further subject to the following restrictions, which are not present in the standalone Indian BITs—first, any existing non-conforming measure as set out in the Schedules of the treaty.[111] Second, the MFN provision is subject to sector-specific restrictions as contained in the Annex of the treaty.[112]

[111] Comprehensive Economic Partnership Agreement between Republic of India and Japan (signed 16 February 2011, entered into force 1 October 2011) ('India–Japan FTA'), art. 90.1.

[112] Comprehensive Economic Partnership Agreement between Republic of India and Japan (signed 16 February 2011, entered into force 1 October 2011) ('India–Japan FTA'), art. 90.2.

Third, MFN provision 'shall not apply to any measure covered by the exceptions to, or derogations from, obligations under Articles 3 and 4 of the TRIPS Agreement, as specifically provided in Articles 3 through 5 of the TRIPS Agreement'.[113] Fourth, MFN provision shall not apply to Government Procurement.[114] Subjecting the MFN provision to these exceptions provides more regulatory space to the host state.

4.5 Summing up

The provisions discussed in this chapter reflect a broad, vague, and indeterminate normative content. India, in this phase, was essentially a 'rule-taker' in international investment law by adopting the 'exporting-country' model BIT provisions. There is very little textual clarity regarding the scope and extent of these provisions, thereby providing unfettered arbitral discretion. Such discretion is further exasperated in India's standalone BITs than her FTA investment chapters. In view of the ISDS jurisprudence, the legal import of these provisions may vary from case to case creating uncertainty for both foreign investors and host states. Moreover, depending on arbitral discretion, these broad and vaguely worded provisions are capable of interpretation that gives precedence to investment protection over the host state's sovereign regulatory power, instead of striking a balance between the two. The discussion also shows how India embraced certain concepts like IMS that it was wary of in the 'refusal' phase. This reveals a departure from some of the principles contained in the CERDS that India advocated as part of the NIEO in the 1970s, as discussed in Chapter 2.

[113] Comprehensive Economic Partnership Agreement between Republic of India and Japan (signed 16 February 2011, entered into force 1 October 2011) ('India–Japan FTA'), art. 90.6.

[114] Comprehensive Economic Partnership Agreement between Republic of India and Japan (signed 16 February 2011, entered into force 1 October 2011) ('India–Japan FTA'), art. 90.7.

5

India's BITs

Mapping the Acceptance—II

Continuing our discussion on the key features of Indian BITs, in this chapter we study the following provisions: expropriation (Section 5.1); monetary transfer provisions (Section 5.2); general exception clauses (Section 5.3); and the ISDS provisions (Section 5.4). Like Chapter 4, this chapter also discusses these provisions against the background of ISDS jurisprudence that has emerged on these four issues. The discussion on these provisions, like Chapter 4, is divided between standalone BITs and FTA investment chapters.

5.1 Expropriation

As is well known, a very important substantive provision in most BITs is the rule against expropriation whereby a state is prohibited from—'taking' privately owned property, directly or indirectly, except for public purpose, in accordance with due process and with compensation.[1] Where expropriation takes place fulfilling all the

[1] See generally Salacuse, *The Law of Investment Treaties*, pp. 313–57; Dolzer and Schreuer, *Principles of International Investment Law*, pp. 98–129; Newcombe and Paradell, *Law and Practice of Investment* Treaties, pp. 341–69.

conditions as aforementioned, it is lawful; non-fulfilment of any of these conditions renders it unlawful.[2] Direct expropriations—'taking' coming through the State actions thereby depriving investors of legal title[3]—have become rare.[4] As modern states adopt a number of regulations to regulate various spheres of life, instances of indirect interference with investor's property rights have become more prominent. However, the difficulty is in determining when such indirect interference constitutes expropriation.[5] Indirect expropriation refers to the deprivation of the substantial benefits flowing from the investment without any formal 'taking' of the property.[6] Whether the host country's regulatory measures result in indirect expropriation is a question that has acquired prominence due to a range of sovereign regulatory functions being challenged as acts of expropriation by different foreign investors under BITs in the last decade or so. This includes expropriation cases against Argentina for adopting regulatory measures to save itself from an extremely severe economic

[2] Prabhash Ranjan and Pushkar Anand. 2016. 'Determination of Indirect Expropriation and Doctrine of Police Power in International Investment Law', in *Judging the State in International Trade and Investment Law*, Leila Choukroune (ed.), pp. 127–51 (hereinafter Ranjan and Anand, 'Determination of Indirect Expropriation and Doctrine of Police Power in International Investment Law').

[3] Salacuse, *The Law of Investment Treaties*, p. 322.

[4] Dolzer and Schreuer, *Principles of International Investment Law*, p. 101.

[5] See generally *Feldman* v. *Mexico*, ICSID Case No. ARB(AF)/99/1, Award, 16 December 2002. Feldman, supra note 9, at para100 (The Feldman tribunal recognised the difficulty by saying that direct expropriation was relatively easy whereas 'it is much less clear when the governmental action that interferes with broadly-defined property rights … crosses the line from valid regulation to compensable taking'); Org. for Econ. Co-Operation & Dev., Principles of Corporate Governance (2004); Spears, 'The Quest for Policy Space in a New Generation of International Investment Agreements', pp. 1049–52; Ursula Kriebaum. 2007. 'Regulatory Takings: Balancing the Interests of the Investor and the State', *Journal of World Inv. & Trade* 8: 717.

[6] Dolzer and Schreuer, *Principles of International Investment Law*, p. 92; Salacuse, *The Law of Investment* Treaties, p. 297; *Starrett Housing Corporation* v. *Islamic Republic of Iran*, 4 Iran-US CTR 122, 154 (1983). See also *Tippetts, Abbett, McCarthy, Stratton and TAMS-AFFA Consulting Engineers of Iran* v. *Islamic Republic of Iran*, 6 Iran-US CTR 219, 225 (1984).

and financial crisis; claims of expropriation for environment-related regulatory measures;[7] regulatory measures aimed at addressing the supply of drinking water;[8] regulatory measures involving sovereign functions like taxation.[9]

However, most BITs do not provide much guidance on how to determine whether a host state's regulatory measure amounts to indirect expropriation or not. Over a period, ISDS tribunals have developed different tests for ascertaining whether indirect expropriation has taken place or not. First, *sole effects test* where the focus is only on the severity of the effect of the regulatory measure on foreign investment.[10] According to this test, measures that do not constitute direct expropriation may nevertheless constitute indirect expropriation if the effect of the regulatory measure causes a substantial deprivation of foreign investment.[11]

Second, police powers doctrine according to which state measures that are prima facie a lawful exercise of powers of the government (such as adopting a measure pursuing legitimate public welfare objective) may affect foreign interests considerably without amounting to expropriation.[12] Apart from these two tests, there is a third

[7] See *Metalclad Corporation* v. *United Mexican States*, ICSID Case No. ARB(AF)/97/1, Award, 30 August 2000; *Methanex Corp.* v. *U.S., NAFTA-UNCITRAL*, Award, 3 August 2005 (hereinafter *Methanex Corp.* v. *U.S).*

[8] See *Biwater Gauff Ltd* v. *United Republic of Tanzania,* ICSID Case No. ARB/05/22, Award, (24 July 2008).

[9] See *Occidental Exploration* v. *Ecuador*; *EnCana Corporation* v. *Republic of Ecuador*, LCIA Case No. UN3481, Award, 3 February 2006.

[10] See Ben Mostafa. 2008. 'The Sole Effects Doctrine, Police Powers and Indirect Expropriation under International Law', *Australian Journal of International Law* 15: 267–96 (hereinafter Mostafa, 'The Sole Effects Doctrine').

[11] See *Pope and Talbot* v. *Canada*; *PSEG Global* v. *Turkey*, paras 278–80; *CMS Gas Transmission Co* v. *Argentina*, ICISD Case No. ARB/01/8, Award, para 262, 12 May 2005; *Mamidoil Jetoil Greek Petroleum Products Societe Anonyme S.A.* v. *Republic of Albania*, ICSID Case No. ARB/11/24, Award, 30 March 2015, paras 566, 570.

[12] See Brownlie, *Principles of Public International Law*, p. 532; G.C. Christie. 1962. 'What Constitutes a Taking of Property under International Law?', *British Yearbook of International Law* 38: 307, 335–8; J. Wagner. 1999. 'International Investment, Expropriation and Environmental Protection',

test for determining indirect expropriation, *proportionality test,* which requires balancing the public purpose behind the regulatory measure with the effect that measure has on foreign investment.[13] The proportionality test will have three steps[14] which must be assessed

---

Golden Gate U. L. Rev., 29: 465, 517–19; George H Aldrich. 1994. 'What Constitutes a Compensable Taking of Property? The Decisions of the Iran United States Claims Tribunal', *American Journal of International Law,* 88: 585, 609; Alain Pellet. 2015. 'Police Powers or the State's Right to Regulate', in *Building International Investment Law: The First 50 Years of ICSID,* Meg Kinnear, Geraldine Fischer, Jara Minguez Almeida, Luisa Fernanda Torres, and Mairée Uran Bidegain (eds), 447–62 South Holland: Wolters Kluwer; *Methanex,* p. 4, para 7; *Saluka Investments BV* v. *The Czech Republic,* UNCITRAL, Partial Award, para 284, 17 March 2006; *El Paso* v. *Argentina,* ICSID Case No. ARB/03/15, Award, 31 October 2011; *Philip Morris Brand Sàrl (Switzerland), Philip Morris Products S.A. (Switzerland) and Abal Hermanos S.A. (Uruguay)* v. *Oriental Republic of Uruguay,* ICSID Case No. ARB/10/7, Award, 8 July 2016, para 307. *WNC Factoring Ltd (WNC)* v. *The Czech Republic* (PCA Case No. 2014-34), Award, 22 February 2017, paras 294–395.

13 See Alec Stone Sweet. 2010. 'Investor-State Arbitration: Proportionality's New Frontier', *Law & Ethics of Human Rights* 4(1):48-76; Henckels. 'Indirect Expropriation and the Right to Regulate'; Prabhash Ranjan. 2014. 'Using Public Law Concept of Proportionality to Balance Investment Protection with Regulation in International Investment Law: A Critical Appraisal', *Cambridge J. Int'l & Comp. L.*3: 853, 883; *S.A* v. *USA,*; *LG&E Energy Corporation* v. *The Argentine Republic,* ICISD Case No. ARB/02/1, Award, para 195; (Jul. 25, 2007); *El Paso,* para 241; *Lemire* v. *Ukr.*, ICSID Case No. ARB/06/18, Decision on Jurisdiction and Liability, para 285 (Jan. 14, 2010); PL Holdings S.a.r.l. v. Poland (SCC Case No. 2014/163), Partial Award, 28 June 2017, paras 373–391.

14 Kingsbury and Schill. 2010. 'Public Law Concepts to Balance Investors' Rights with State Regulatory Actions in the Public Interest – The Concept of Proportionality', in *International Investment Law and Comparative Public Law,* S. Schill (ed.) pp. 75, 85–8. Oxford: Oxford University Press (hereinafter Kingsbury and Schill, 'Public Law Concepts to Balance Investors' Rights with State Regulatory Actions in the Public Interest'); A.S. Sweet. 2010. 'Investor-State Arbitration: Proportionality's New Frontier', *Law and Ethics of Human Rights* 4: 47; U. Kriebaum. 2007. 'Regulatory Takings: Balancing the Interests of the Investor and the State', *Journal of World Investment and Trade* 8: 717; A. Kulick. 2012. *Global Public Interest in International Investment Law,* pp. 186–9. Cambridge: Cambridge University Press; C. Henckels. 2012. 'Indirect

cumulatively.[15] First, whether the measure is suitable for legitimate public purpose—this will require a causal link between the measure and its object.[16] If the measure satisfies the first step, then the second step will be to find out whether the measure is necessary, that is, whether there is a less restrictive alternative measure that will achieve the same objective.[17] If indeed the measure is 'necessary', the third step (also known as proportionality *stricto sensu*) will involve balancing the effects of the measure on the right that has been affected with public benefit sought to be achieved by the measure.[18] One of the critiques of the proportionality test is that it vests much discretion in the hands of arbitral tribunals to weigh and balance complex value-laden regulatory measures that host states wish to pursue against the effect of these measures on foreign investment.[19] Such weighing and balancing by the arbitral tribunal runs the risk of very important public policy objectives being trumped by interests of investors in

---

Expropriation and the Right to Regulate: Revisiting Proportionality Analysis and the Standard of Review in Investor-State Arbitration', *Journal of International Economic Law* 15: 223 (hereinafter Henckels, Indirect Expropriation and the Right to Regulate'); E. Leonhardsen. 2011. 'Looking for Legitimacy: Exploring Proportionality Analysis in Investment Treaty Arbitration', *Journal of International Dispute Settlement* 1 (hereinafter Leonhardsen, 'Looking for Legitimacy').

[15] Leonhardsen, 'Looking for Legitimacy'; Jan H. Jans. 2000. 'Proportionality Revisited', *Legal Issues of Economic Integration* 27: 240–1 (hereinafter Jans, 'Proportionality Revisited').

[16] Leonhardsen, 'Looking for Legitimacy'; See also Jans, 'Proportionality Revisited', p. 240

[17] Jans, 'Proportionality Revisited', p. 240; Kingsbury and Schill, 'Public Law Concepts to Balance Investors' Rights with State Regulatory Actions in the Public Interest', pp. 86–7.

[18] Jans, 'Proportionality Revisited', p. 241; Kingsbury and Schill, 'Public Law Concepts to Balance Investors' Rights with State Regulatory Actions in the Public Interest', pp. 87–8.

[19] W.W. Burke-White and A.V. Staden. 2010. 'Private Litigation in a Public Law Sphere: Standard of Review in Investor-State Arbitrations', *Yale Journal of International Law* 35:283, 323 (hereinafter Burke-White and A.V. Staden, 'Private Litigation in a Public Law Sphere').

situations where the arbitral tribunal is of the view that costs of the effect outweigh the benefit.[20]

The problem is that often BITs do not offer much guidance on how to determine indirect expropriation, and therefore which test to apply in any given case depends primarily on the discretion of the ISDS tribunal.

5.1.1 India's Standalone BITs

Article 5(1) of the 2003 Model BIT states that 'investments of investors of either Contracting Party shall not be nationalised, expropriated *or subjected to measures having effect equivalent to nationalisation or expropriation* (hereinafter referred to as 'expropriation') in the territory of the other Contracting Party except for a public purpose in accordance with law on a non-discriminatory basis and against fair and equitable compensation'. In other words, the Indian Model BIT recognizes that the State can expropriate foreign investment for public purpose, following the due process of law, on a non-discriminatory basis and against due compensation. If foreign investment is expropriated following all these conditions, the expropriation is lawful, else it is unlawful.

That these conditions need to be satisfied for the lawfulness of expropriation was confirmed by the tribunal in *Devas Mauritius* v. *India*[21] while interpreting Article 6(1) of the India–Mauritius BIT, which contains language similar to the 2003 Model BIT—'Investments of investors of either Contracting Party in the territory of the other Contracting Party shall not be nationalised, expropriated or subjected to measures having effects equivalent to nationalisation or expropriation except for public purposes under due process of law, on a non-discriminatory basis and against fair and equitable compensation'. The tribunal, in this case, discussed all the four elements and concluded that India had unlawfully expropriated investor's investment because it did not pay compensation to the investor.[22] India's

[20] See, Burke-White and A.V. Staden, 'Private Litigation in a Public Law Sphere'.

[21] *Devas* v. *India*, paras 412–425.

[22] *Devas* v. *India*, paras 420–422, 425.

liability for expropriating foreign investment was fixed with respect to that investment that was taken by the State for reasons other than 'essential security interest'.[23]

While all Indian BITs provide a clear distinction between lawful and unlawful expropriation, none of them explain how to determine expropriation. The language given in the 2003 Model BIT and large number of other BITs that 'investments shall not be nationalised, expropriated or subject to measures having effect equivalent to nationalisation or expropriation'[24] is not very helpful in defining what constitutes expropriation. More or less same formulation exists in two more Indian BITs; India–Morocco BIT—'any other measure having equivalent effect'; and India–France BIT—'any other measure having the effect of dispossession'. A somewhat related formulation is given in India–Qatar BIT that states 'the investment shall not be subject, either directly or indirectly, to any act of expropriation or nationalisation or to any other procedure of similar effect …'.[25] The above-mentioned language points to just one factor to determine indirect expropriation, that is, 'effect'. This gives credence to the 'sole effects test' to determine indirect expropriation in these BITs, that is, whether an indirect expropriation has occurred depends solely on the effect of the governmental measure on property. The investor–state dispute settlement tribunals interpreting other BITs containing language similar to the ones found in majority of Indian BITs have confirmed this. For example, in *AWG* v. *Argentina,*[26] where

[23] *Devas* v. *India*, para 422. Also see Chapters 4 and 6.

[24] See India–Netherlands BIT; India–Germany BIT; India–Denmark BIT; India–UK BIT; India–Sri Lanka BIT; India–Vietnam BIT; India–Myanmar BIT; India–Indonesia BIT; India–Israel BIT; India–Russia BIT; India–Denmark BIT; India–Poland BIT; India–Czech Republic BIT; India–Spain BIT; India–Oman BIT; India–Kyrgyz Republic BIT; India–Romania BIT; India–Bulgaria BIT; India–Philippines BIT; India–Morocco BIT; India–Sweden BIT; India–Thailand BIT; India–Croatia BIT; India–Argentina BIT; India–Cyprus BIT; India–Finland BIT; India–Mauritius BIT; India–Mongolia BIT; India–Portugal BIT; India–Tajikistan BIT; India–Ukraine BIT; India–Yemen BIT.

[25] Also see India–Kuwait BIT; India–Uzbekistan BIT; India–Mexico BIT and India–Turkey BIT.

[26] *AWG* v. *Argentina*, ICSID Case No. ARB/03/19, 30 July 2010 (hereinafter *AWG* v. *Argentina*).

the expropriation provision in the UK–Argentina BIT contains the phrase 'subjected to measures having effect equivalent to nationalisation or expropriation', the tribunal held that specific reference to 'effects' in the BIT 'affirms the importance of evaluating "effects" of the measure on the investment in determining whether an expropriation has taken place'.[27] Similarly, in *Encana* v. *Ecuador*, the Canada–Ecuador BIT, which was under consideration, had almost similar formulation of the expropriation provision as found in majority of Indian BITs—'subjected to measures having an effect equivalent to expropriation'. In this case, the tribunal focused on the 'effect' of the measure on foreign investment to determine whether indirect expropriation had occurred or not.[28]

However, the focus on 'effect' of the regulatory measure on foreign investment to determine indirect expropriation in the text of majority of Indian BITs does not answer the key question, that is, how severe the effect should be. The tribunal in *Philip Morris* v. *Uruguay*, while interpreting the expropriation provision in the Switzerland–Uruguay BIT (that has language almost similar to many Indian BITs)[29] stated that 'in order to be considered an indirect expropriation, the government's measures interference with the investor's rights must have a major adverse impact on the claimant's investments'.[30] The tribunal further clarified that for regulatory measures to have a major adverse

[27] *AWG* v. *Argentina*, para 133.

[28] *Encana* v. *Ecuador*, paras 173–78. Also see *Tippets, Abbett, McCarthy Stratton* v. *TAMS AFFA Consulting Engineers of Iran*, (1984), 6 Iran-US CTR 219 at 225-26; *Starrett Housing Corp* v. *Iran*, 4 Iran-US CTR 122, *Enron* v. *Argentina*, para 244 and *Patrick Mitchell* v. *The Democratic Republic of Congo* (Annulment Proceedings) ICSID Case No. ARB/99/7, para 53; *Telenor Mobile Communications A.S.* v. *Republic of Hungary*, ICSID Case No. ARB/04/15, Award, 13 September, 2006, paras 64–65; *Spyridon Roussalis* v. *Romania*, ICSID Case No. ARB/06/1, Award, 7 December 2011, para 328; *Philip Morris Brands Sàrl, Philip Morris Products S.A. and Abal Hermanos S.A.* v. *Oriental Republic of Uruguay*, ICSID Case No. ARB/10/7 (8 July 2016), para 192.

[29] Article 5(1) of the Switzerland–Uruguay BIT provides that '*Neither of the Contracting Parties shall take, either directly or indirectly, measures of expropriation, nationalization or any other measure having the same nature or the same effect against investments belonging to investors of the other Contracting Party*'.

[30] *Philip Morris* v. *Uruguay*, para 192.

impact, the regulatory measures should lead to 'substantial deprivation' of investment's value, use, or enjoyment.[31] The effect can certainly be more than substantial deprivation such as cases where the deprivation is complete or total. For example, the tribunal in *Total SA* v. *Argentina*[32] held that under international law those measures that do not constitute direct expropriation may nevertheless result in indirect expropriation 'if an effective deprivation of the investment is thereby caused'.[33]

In other words, the language 'measures having effect equivalent to nationalisation or expropriation' in a large number of Indian BITs provides a textual basis to the 'substantial deprivation' test. An important offshoot of this is that an adverse effect on foreign investment that results in economic hardship will not qualify as indirect expropriation.[34] This allows enough space for India to adopt regulatory measures for its various regulatory needs even if they result in adverse economic effect on foreign investment till this effect does not reach the high threshold of substantial deprivation.[35]

[31] *Philip Morris* v. *Uruguay*, para 192. Indeed the tribunal in *Pope and Talbot* v. *Canada*, held that '*under international law, expropriation requires a 'substantial deprivation*'. See *Pope and Talbot* v. *Canada*, *supra* note 37 at para. 96. Also see *PSEG Global* v. *Turkey* paras 278–80; *CMS* (n 10) Decision on Liability, para 262. *LG&E* v. *Argentina*, para 194; *Sempra* v. *Argentina* paras 284–85; *BG Group* v. *Argentina*, UNCITRAL, 24 December 2007, at paras. 258–66; *Enron* v. *Argentina supra* note 6 para 245. *AWG Group Ltd.* v. *The Argentine Republic*, UNCITRAL, Decision on Liability, 30 July 2010, at para. 134; *Corn Products International* v. *Mexico,* ICSID Case No. ARB (AF)/04/01, (NAFTA), Decision on Responsibility, 15 January 2008, at para 91.

[32] *Total SA* v. *Argentina,* ICSID Case No ARB/04/01, Decision on Liability, 27 December 2010 (hereinafter *Total SA* v. *Argentina*).

[33] *Total SA* v. *Argentina,* para 195.

[34] For example, the tribunal in *Impregilo* v. *Argentina* held that '*Expropriation is to be distinguished from less far-reaching measures which regulate or restrict the right to use property. Such measures may also have serious economic effects for the investor but do not constitute expropriation*'—*Impregilo* v. *Argentina*, para 270. Also see Mostafa, 'The Sole Effects Doctrine', pp. 282–4.

[35] Rahim Moloo and Justin Jacinto. 2011. 'Environmental and Health Regulation: Assessing Liability under Investment Treaties', *Berkley Journal of International Law* 29: 1, 24.

To sum up, the language of large number of India's BITs supports the use of the sole effect test to determine indirect expropriation. Nonetheless, as mentioned before, which test will be used to determine indirect expropriation would ultimately depend on the discretion of the arbitral tribunal.[36]

A small minority of India's standalone BITs, apart from stating that investments shall not be nationalized, expropriated, or subjected to 'measures having effect equivalent to nationalisation or expropriation', also provide specific factors that should be taken into account in determining 'measures having effect equivalent to expropriation'.[37] For example, the protocol to the India–China BIT gives the shared understanding of India and China regarding the interpretation of the expropriation provision given in Article 5 of the BIT. The protocol states that

> With regard to the interpretation of expropriation under Article 5, the Contracting Parties confirm their shared understanding that:

[36] There are some instances where ISDS tribunals look at factors other than adverse effect on foreign investment such as proportionality of the host state's measures – see *El Paso Energy International Company* v. *The Argentine Republic*, ICSID Case No. ARB/03/15, Award, 31 October 2011, para 241.

[37] See Annex on Clarification on Indirect Expropriation in Agreement between The Republic of India and The Slovak Republic for The Promotion and Reciprocal Protection of Investments (signed 25 September 2006, entered into force 16 June 2007) (India–Slovakia BIT); Annex on Interpretation of 'Expropriation' in India–Trinidad and Tobago BIT; Ad Article 5 of the Protocol to the Agreement between the Republic of India and the People's Republic of China on Promotion and Protection of Investments (India–China BIT); Side letter on Interpretation of Expropriation in Article 5 to India–Iceland BIT; Agreement between The Government of The Republic of India and Government of The Kingdom of Saudi Arabia Concerning The Encouragement and Reciprocal Protection of Investments (signed 25 January 2006, entered into force 20 May 2008) (India–Saudi Arabia BIT) art. 4(2); Porotocol on Article 5 of India–Brunei Darussalam BIT; Annex on Interpretation of Expropriation in Article 5 of India–Syria BIT; Annex on Interpretation of Expropriation in Article 5 of India–Jordan BIT; Annex on Interpretation of Expropriation in Article 5 of India–Mozambique BIT; Annexure 5.1 for interpreting with greater certainty Article 5 of India–Senegal BIT; Protocol to India–Lithuania BIT Ad art 5; Annex on Interpretation of Expropriation in Article 5 of India–Latvia BIT.

1) A measure of expropriation includes, apart from direct expropriation or nationalization through formal transfer of title or outright seizure, a measure or series of measures taken intentionally by a Party to create a situation whereby the investment of an investor may be rendered substantially unproductive and incapable of yielding a return without a formal transfer of title or outright seizure.
2) The determination of whether a measure or a series of measures of a Party in a specific situation, constitute measures as outlined in paragraph 1 above requires a case by case, fact based inquiry that considers, among other factors:
   i) the economic impact of the measure or a series of measures, although the fact that a measure or series of measures by a Party has an adverse effect on the economic value of an investment, standing alone, does not establish that expropriation or nationalization, has occurred;
   ii) the extent to which the measures are discriminatory either in scope or in application with respect to a Party or an investor or an enterprise;
   iii) the extent to which the measures or series of measures interfere with distinct, reasonable, investment-backed expectations;
   iv) the character and intent of the measures or series of measures, whether they are for bona fide public interest purposes or not and whether there is a reasonable nexus between them and the intention to expropriate.
3) Except in rare circumstances, non-discriminatory regulatory measures adopted by a Contracting Party in pursuit of public interest, including measures pursuant to awards of general application rendered by judicial bodies do not constitute indirect expropriation or nationalization.[38]

The above language rules out the use of the 'substantial deprivation' test to determine indirect expropriation. Instead, by requiring an ISDS tribunal to focus on both, the effect of the measure and the character of the measure, the treaty gives textual basis towards using the proportionality test to determine indirect expropriation. However, as mentioned earlier, the proportionality test vests much discretion in the hands of arbitral tribunals. For instance, the text quoted earlier is

[38] Protocol to India–China BIT.

silent on whether an ISDS tribunal, while determining indirect expropriation, should attach more weight to the effect of the regulatory measure on foreign investment or to the character of the measure or to the distinct, reasonable, and investment-backed expectations.

Another interesting aspect of the India–China BIT protocol quoted earlier is the 'except in rare circumstances' clause. This clause makes it clear that India can adopt genuine regulatory measures to pursue legitimate public welfare objectives such as public health and environment.[39] However, the India–China BIT does not define 'except in rare circumstances'. In fact, barring few Indian BITs,[40] most Indian BITs that contain this clause do not explain the meaning of 'except in rare circumstances' and thus its actual import is subject to arbitral discretion. The India–Brunei Darussalam BIT—a BIT that defines this phrase—states that 'except in rare circumstances' implies that 'measures are so severe in light of their purpose that they cannot be reasonably viewed as having been adopted and applied in good faith'.[41] This formulation states that the measure adopted by the host state will have to be assessed against the purpose for which it has been adopted and if the adverse effect of the measure (on foreign investment) outweighs the purpose (benefits of the measure), then the measure will be viewed as not adopted in good faith and thus, unreasonable. This again directs an ISDS tribunal to indulge in a proportionality test to determine whether indirect expropriation has taken place though the threshold is higher since the measures have to be 'severe in light of their purpose'. In other words, for an indirect expropriation to occur, the adverse effect of the measure should be 'severe' enough to outweigh the benefits of the measure.

Some Indian BITs simply state that 'non-discriminatory regulatory actions by a Party that are designed and applied to protect legitimate public welfare objectives including health, safety and environmental concerns, do not constitute expropriation or nationalization'.[42] In contrast to the language of the India–China BIT and other Indian

[39] This clause is present in Indian BITs given in n 35. See Moloo and Jacinto, Environmental and Health Regulation, p. 37.

[40] India–Brunei Darussalam BIT.

[41] India–Brunei Darussalam BIT, Ad Article 5 (d).

[42] India–Trinidad Tobago (Ad Article 5(3); India–Saudi Arabia (Article 5(3).

BITs mentioned earlier, this clause is not prefaced by the phrase 'except in rare circumstances'. The significance behind not having this phrase as the preface is that it means in no situation a legitimate measure adopted by the host state for a public welfare objective shall amount to expropriation. This formulation endorses the 'police powers' test. However, this formulation is problematic for two reasons. First, it will be difficult to reconcile this provision, signifying the 'police powers' test, with those provisions in the expropriation provision that provide for a proportionality test. For example, in India–Trinidad and Tobago BIT, Paragraph 2 of the Annex on Expropriation provides for the proportionality test in determining whether a measure or a series of measures constitutes indirect expropriation;[43] and at the same time Paragraph 3 states that nondiscriminatory regulatory actions to protect legitimate public welfare objectives do not constitute expropriation. In other words, if a foreign investor challenges a regulatory measure, purporting to promote a public welfare objective, as expropriation, the outcome might vary depending on whether the criteria given in paragraph 2 or 3 are used. Second, such a broad provision is subject to misuse by the state.

5.1.2 Investment Chapters in India's FTAs

Investment chapters in India's FTAs also cover both direct and indirect expropriation. The language of expropriation provision in India's FTA investment chapters is completely different from the majority of Indian BITs. In fact, it resembles the language of a small minority of Indian BITs discussed earlier such as the India–China BIT. Thus, like the India–China BIT, India's FTA investment chapters also provide detailed criterion to determine indirect expropriation such as the effect of the measure on foreign investment, purpose behind the measure, and so on.[44]

Also, India's FTA investment chapters, like few Indian BITs, provide that 'except in rare circumstances, non-discriminatory regulatory

[43] Paragraph 2 of the Annex of India–Trinidad and Tobago BIT is same as paragraph 2 of the Protocol of the India–China BIT discussed in the text.

[44] See [India–Singapore (Expropriation Annex 3 (1) (c)); India–Malaysia FTA (Annex 10-1); India–Korea FTA (Annex 10-A)]; India–ASEAN Investment agreement art. 8(3).

actions by a Party that are designed and applied for legitimate public welfare objectives such as health, safety and the environment, do not constitute measures having effect equivalent to nationalization or expropriation'.[45] Barring, the India–Korea FTA, other FTAs do not define the meaning of 'except in rare circumstances'. Annex 10 A 3 (b) of the India–Korea FTA states that 'except in rare circumstances' implies 'when measures are extremely severe or disproportionate in light of its purpose and effect'. This language, as discussed in the case of India–Brunei BIT, points to a proportionality test with a very high threshold for determining indirect expropriation. In other words, for an indirect expropriation to occur, the regulatory measures have to be 'extremely severe'.[46]

Another distinguishing feature of the expropriation provision in India's FTA investment chapters is that, unlike India's BITs, they do not apply to issuance of compulsory licenses (CLs). For instance, Article 92.5 of the India–Japan FTA states that the expropriation provision shall not apply with respect to the grant of CLs concerning intellectual property in accordance with the TRIPS Agreement[47] Similarly, Article 8(7) of the India–ASEAN investment agreement provides that 'this article does not apply to the issuance of compulsory licenses granted in relation to intellectual property rights, in accordance with the TRIPS agreement'.[48] While the India–Malaysia and India–Japan FTAs only talk about the non-applicability of

[45] India–Singapore Annex on Exprorpriation; Annex 10 on Expropriation of the India Japan FTA; Annex 10-1 on Indirect Expropriation in India Malaysia FTA; Annex 10-A on Expropriation in India Korea FTA.

[46] On this point also see Henckel, 'Indirect Expropriation and the Right to Regulate'.

[47] Article 92.5 of India–Japan EPA states – '*This Article shall not apply with respect to the grant of compulsory licenses concerning intellectual property in accordance with the TRIPS Agreement.*' Also see Article 10.7 (6) of India–Malaysia FTA; Article 10.12 (6) of the India–Korea EPA; Article 6.5 (6) of The India–Singapore EPA.

[48] Also see Article 10.7(6) of the India–Malaysia FTA which provides – '*This Article does not apply to the issuance of compulsory licenses granted in relation to intellectual property rights in accordance with the WTO Agreement on Trade Related Aspects of Intellectual Property Rights.*' Also see Article 6.5(6) of the India–Singapore FTA.

the expropriation provision in the situations of issuance of CLs, the India–Korea and India–Malaysia BITs go beyond this and also exempt the application of expropriation provision to revocation, limitation or creation of intellectual property provided such revocation, limitation and creation is consistent with the TRIPS agreement.

Since Indian standalone BITs are silent on this issue, foreign investors can bring ISDS claims against issuance of CLs that impact their patent rights.[49] Let us understand this with the help of the following example. India issued its first CL in March 2012 in favour of a domestic generic pharmaceutical company called Natco Pharma for a patent granted on a drug to treat kidney and liver cancer to Bayer.[50] This compulsory licence was issued under Section 84 of the Indian Patent Act on the following grounds—unreasonable prices, reasonable requirements of public not being met and lack of local manufacturing.[51] The issuance of CL was upheld by the Supreme Court of India.[52] Bayer can

[49] For a detailed discussion on this see Prabhash Ranjan. 2008. 'Medical Patents and Expropriation in International Investment Law—With Special Reference to India', *Manchester Journal of International Economic Law* 5(3): 72–104; Prabhash Ranjan. 2019. 'Pharmaceutical Patents and Expropriation in Indian Bilateral Investment Treaties', in *Regulation and Investment Disputes: Asian Perspectives*, Mahdev Mohan and Chester Brown (eds). Cambridge University Press, forthcoming (hereinafter Ranjan, 'Pharmaceutical Patents and Expropriation in Indian Bilateral Investment Treaties').

[50] *Bayer Corp.* v. *Natco Pharma.Ltd.*, Order No. 45/2013 (Intellectual Property Appellate Board, Chennai, 2013); Shamnad Basheer. 2012. 'Breaking News: India's first Compulsory License Granted', available at https://spicyip.com/2012/03/breaking-news-indias-first-compulsory.html, 12 March, accessed on 17 March 2018; Unni. 2015. 'Compulsory Licensing of Pharmaceutical Patents in India: Whether the Natco Decision Will Meet the Global Benchmarks?', *European Intellectual Property Review* 37: 296.

[51] For more details on this case see Unni (2015) above at n 17; Yogesh Pai. 2015. 'Promoting Diversity in Pharmaceutical Innovation and Access: India's Experience in the Post-TRIPS World', in *Diversity in Intellectual Property: Identities, Interests and Intersections*, Irene Calboli and Srividhya Ragavan (eds), p. 76. Cambridge: Cambridge University Press; Enrico Bonadio. 2012. 'India Grants a Compulsory License of Bayer's Patented Cancer Drug: The Issue of Local Working Requirement', *European Journal of Risk Regulation* 3(2): 247–50.

[52] *Bayer Corporation* v. *Union of India*, Petition for Special Leave to Appeal (C) NO (S). 30145/2014, 12 December 2014.

challenge this regulatory measure under the India Germany BIT as an expropriation of its patent right because intellectual property right is included in the definition of investment and there is no specific immunity created for issuance of CL from claims on expropriation. As a result, an ISDS tribunal will have jurisdiction to decide whether the issuance of compulsory license by India is legal or not.[53] Of course, a foreign investor bringing an ISDS claim for issuance of a CL does not mean that the investor shall necessarily prevail over the State. Nonetheless, in light of the fact that CL is a crucial tool to meet public health objectives like increasing the accessibility to cheaper medicines,[54] this is a significant issue for India under those BITs that do not specifically exclude issuance of CLs from the ambit of expropriation. India's FTA investment chapters by excluding issuance of CLs from the ambit of the expropriation provision, provided they have been issued in a manner that's consistent with the TRIPS agreement, are more supportive of India's right to regulate.

5.1.3 Compensation

On the issue of compensation for expropriation, most Indian BITs provide for fair and equitable compensation. Additionally, Indian BITs contain requirements of prompt and expeditious compensation making the compensation provision stringent. Indian BITs also contain principles on the basis of which the compensation that is to be paid to the investor will be calculated. A very large number of BITs state that the value of the compensation should be either the genuine value of the investment or the genuine market value of the

[53] For more on this see Ranjan, 'Pharmaceutical Patents and Expropriation in Indian Bilateral Investment Treaties'.

[54] See generally Carlos M. Correa. 2007. *Trade Related Aspects of Intellectual Property Rights: A Commentary on the TRIPS Agreement*. New York: Oxford University Press, p. 313; Sisule F. Musungu. 2008. 'The TRIPS Agreement and Public Health', in *Intellectual Property and International Trade The TRIPS Agreement*, Carlos Correa and Abdulqawi A. Yusuf (eds). Netherlands: Wolters Kluwer, pp. 421–69. Also see Shamnad Basheer and Mrinalini Kochupillai. 2005. 'The Compulsory License in India: Past, Present and Future', http://papers.ssrn.com/sol3/papers.cfm?abstract_id=1685129&download=yes, accessed 7 March 2015.

investment or the fair market value of the investment. Further, all Indian BITs require that interest should be paid to the investor on a fair and equitable rate or at a commercial rate; thus they do not seem to adopt a uniform or consistent standard.

5.2 Monetary Transfer Provision (MTP)

Monetary Transfer Provisions (MTPs) in BITs regulate the transfer of funds related to investment in and out of the country.[55] Monetary Transfer Provisions in BITs should not be confused with admission requirement clauses under which a host state is obligated to admit new investments.[56] Monetary Transfer Provisions in BITs cover transfers related to investments that have been made (such as allowing entry of new capital to augment existing investment or to allow outflow of incomes derived from the investment made). A typical MTP in a BIT identifies the 'transfer' or 'payment' to which the provision applies and also provides the conditions governing such transfers, such as whether the transfer is to be made in foreign currency and whether the transfer can be made promptly.[57] In most BITs, MTPs cover all 'transfers' or 'payments' related to investment.[58] Further, depending on the treaty language, MTPs cover both inflows and outflows of funds.[59] These 'transfers' include both current transfers (such as the transfer of income derived from investments)[60] and

[55] See Michael Waibel. 2009. 'BIT by BIT – The Silent Liberalization of the Capital Account', in *International Investment Law for the 21st Century: Essays in the Honour of Christoph Schreuer*, Christina Binder and others (eds). New York: Oxford University Press, p. 497; Salacuse, *The Law of Investment Treaties*, pp. 256–71; Abba Kolo and Thomas Wälde. 2008. 'Capital Transfer Restrictions under Modern Investment Treaties', in *Standards of Investment Protection*, August Reinisch (ed.). New York: Oxford University Press, p. 205.

[56] UNCTAD. 2000. 'Transfer of Funds', http://unctad.org/en/docs/psiteiitd20.en.pdf., p. 32, accessed on 17 March 2018.

[57] Salacuse, *The Law of Investment Treaties*, pp. 285–91.

[58] Salacuse, *The Law of Investment Treaties*, pp. 285–91.

[59] Salacuse, *The Law of Investment Treaties*, pp. 285–91.

[60] See the 2003 Indian Model BITthat allows for transfers of 'Net operating profits including dividends and interest in proportion to their share-holdings,' art. 7(1)(b) https://www.italaw.com/sites/default/files/archive/ita1026.pdf. Also

capital transfers (e.g. the transfer of proceeds of liquidation of foreign investment).[61]

Monetary Transfer Provisions are an integral part of the protection offered to foreign investment by host states in BITs. Monetary Transfer Provisions are important for foreign investors because they provide the freedom to transfer all funds related to investment for a number of business-related needs.[62] For example, a foreign investor may need to bring in additional capital to support the existing investment or might need to repatriate capital back to the home country in order to service debts or to pay dividends or to repatriate proceeds of the sale of investment, etc.[63] Restrictions on the transfer of funds related to an investment may result in investment not being made in the first place, because foreign investors will be deprived of the benefits accruing from the investment (such as repatriating profits) and will also not have the freedom to develop their investment (for example, bringing in additional capital to support the existing investment).[64] Thus, as a general matter, foreign investors tend to be free, at all times, to transfer funds in and out of the host country.

For the foreign investor to freely transfer funds out of the country, it is necessary to draw from the host country's foreign exchange reserve (for example, by converting earnings in the local currency into an international currency by drawing from the foreign exchange reserve).[65] However, the host country's foreign exchange reserve is finite and also serves other significant purposes, like paying for

---

see D. Zimmermann. 2013. *A Contemporary Concept of Monetary Sovereignty*. New York: Oxford University Press, p. 48 (hereinafter Zimmermann, *A Contemporary Concept of Monetary Sovereignty*).

[61] For example, the 2003 Indian Model BIT, art. 7(1)(f) provides an example of capital transaction–'Proceeds received by investors in case of sale or partial sale or liquidation'.

[62] Dolzer and Schreuer, *Principles of International Investment Law*, p. 212.

[63] Salacuse, The Law of Investment Treaties, p.150.

[64] Thomas Wälde and Abba Kolo. 2007. *Investor-State Disputes: The Interface between Treaty-Based International Investment Protection and Fiscal Sovereignty*, *Intertax* 35:424–49, 434.

[65] Vandevelde, *Bilateral Investment Treaties*, p. 316.

imports and maintaining the value of domestic currency.[66] Thus, if the freedom to transfer funds out of the country severely impacts the finite foreign exchange reserve of the host country, the country could impose restrictions on the conversion of local currency into foreign currency,[67] which, in turn, will impact the right of the foreign investor to transfer funds out of the country. Similarly, large infusions of capital by the foreign investor can have adverse macroeconomic consequences, such as the appreciation of the country's currency, the consequent reduction of export competitiveness, and the widening of the current account deficit; it can also result in inflation by increasing the monetary supply, which can have other adverse macroeconomic consequences.[68] These might also compel the host state to impose restrictions on inflows, which could impact the rights of foreign investors. Consequently, the critical question is whether regulatory measures like capital controls that restrict the transfer of funds breach a country's obligations under the MTPs in BITs.

Before we look at BITs, it is important to bear in mind that under international law states have a right to impose restrictions on transfer of funds across borders. For instance, Article VI.3 of the IMF Articles provides that member countries may impose controls as are necessary to regulate international capital movement.[69] According to Sir Joseph Gold, Article VI.3 was necessary 'because of the destabilising effects that flows of "hot money" had in the period before the IMF came into existence'.[70] However, member countries, while exercising control on international capital movement, have to ensure that these controls are not exercised in a manner that will restrict payments on current accounts, since the IMF Articles prohibit such restrictions. Article VIII.2 (a) of the IMF Articles provides that subject

[66] Vandevelde, *Bilateral Investment Treaties*, p. 316.

[67] Vandevelde, *Bilateral Investment Treaties*, p. 316.

[68] Salacuse, *The Law of Investment Treaties*, p. 256.

[69] Andreas F. Lowenfeld. 2008. *International Economic Law*, 2nd edition. New York: Oxford Univeristy Press, p. 608 (hereinafter Lowenfeld, *International Economic Law*).

[70] Joseph Gold. 1984. '"Exchange Contracts", Exchange Control, and the IMF Articles of Agreement: Some Animadversions on *Wilson, Smithett & Cope Ltd.* v. *Terruzzi*', *International & Comparative Law Quarterly* 33: 777, 778–9.

to certain provisions[71] no member country shall impose restrictions on the payment of transfers for current international transactions.[72] Article VIII.2 (a) covers only outflows.[73] If a member country has to impose restrictions on current account restrictions, it will have to obtain permission from the IMF.[74]

In context of BITs, the answer to the above question would depend on many factors including the language of the MTP in the treaty. We will now discuss this for Indian BITs and FTA investment chapters.

5.2.1 India's Standalone BITs

Article 7 (l) of the 2003 Indian Model BIT provides that each country 'shall permit all funds of an investor of the other Contracting Party related to an investment in its territory to be freely transferred, without unreasonable delay and on a non-discriminatory basis'. Further, it provides that such funds may include:

(a) Capital and additional capital amounts used to maintain and increase investments;

[71] These provisions are – Article VIII.3(b) and Article XIV.2 of the IMF Articles (n 17). Also important to note that once a country notifies to the IMF its willingness to accept the obligations contained in Article VIII, there is no going back; see Lowenfeld, *International Economic Law*, p. 607.

[72] IMF Articles (n 17) Article VIII (2) (a) provides: 'Subject to the provisions of Article VII, Section 3(*b*) and Article XIV, Section 2, no member shall, without the approval of the Fund, impose restrictions on the making of payments and transfers for current international transactions.' A majority of membership of IMF is now under Article VIII regime; see Asif H. Qureshi and Andreas R. Zeigler. 2011. *International Economic Law*. London: Sweet & Maxwell, p. 205. For a detailed analysis of the IMF Articles and capital and current account transactions see Joseph Gold. 1971. 'The Fund's Concepts of Convertibility', Pamphlet Series of the International Monetary Fund No 14, Washington; Richard W. Edwards. 1985. *International Monetary Collaboration*. New York: Transnational Publishers; Qureshi and Ziegler, *International Economic Law*, n 25, pp. 202–25; Lowenfeld, *International Economic Law*, n 41, pp. 606–22.

[73] Zimmermann, *A Contemporary Concept of Monetary Sovereignty*, p. 50.

[74] IMF Articles (n 17) Article VIII.2.

(b) Net operating profits including dividends and interest in proportion to their share-holdings;
(c) Repayments of any loan including interest thereon, relating to the investment;
(d) Payment of royalties and services fees relating to the investment;
(e) Proceeds from sales of their shares;
(f) Proceeds received by investors in case of sale or partial sale or liquidation;

From the list it is clear that the 2003 Model covers both capital and current account transfers. Furthermore, Article 7 of the 2003 Model does not recognize any exceptions to the right of the investor to transfer funds.

A very large majority of Indian BITs contain similar language providing an unqualified right to foreign investors (not subject to exceptions) to transfer 'all funds related to investment'. This is followed by an inclusive list of funds that can be transferred, which means that even those funds that do not figure in the list can be transferred provided they are funds related to investment.[75] This large majority of Indian BITs do not make any reference to imposing restrictions on transfer of funds for any reason such as a balance of payment problem or for any other macroeconomic objective. Also, there is no reference to the IMF Articles in these BITs.

Interestingly, Indian law allows for imposing restrictions on capital account transactions under the Foreign Exchange Management Act (FEMA Act) enacted in 1999. Section 6(1) of the FEMA Act

[75] See India–Germany BIT art. 7; India–Denmark BIT art. 7; Agreement between The Government of The Republic of India and The Government of Turkmenistan for The Promotion and Protection of Investments (signed 20 September 1995, entered into force 27 February 2006) (India–Turkmenistan BIT) art. 7; India–Netherlands BIT art. 7; Agreement between The Government of The Republic of India and The Government of The Republic of Tajikistan for The Promotion and Protection of Investments (signed 13 December 1995, entered into force 23 November 2003) (India–Tajikistan BIT) art 7; India–Poland BIT art. 7; India–Sri Lanka art. 7; India–Vietnam BIT art. 7; Agreement between The Government of The Republic of India and The Government of The Republic of Austria for The Promotion And Protection of Investments (signed 8 November 1999, entered into force 1 March 2001) (India–Austria BIT) art. 6.

allows for capital account transactions; however, this is subject to section 6(2), which gives the power to RBI to specify, in consultation with the central government—any class or classes of capital account transactions which are permissible and the limit up to which foreign exchange shall be admissible for such transactions.[76] Also, section 6(3) gives power to the RBI to prohibit, restrict or regulate a number of capital account transactions.[77]

As a result, if India imposes restrictions on transfer of funds by foreign investors, especially on capital transfers,[78] does it imply a violation of India's obligations under the BIT, assuming that these restrictions are lawful under the Indian law and consistent with the IMF Articles on capital transfers? Somewhat related question arose in the *Continental Casualty* v. *Argentina* case,[79] which involved the interpretation of a broadly worded MTP in the US–Argentina BIT, similar to the ones found in large number of Indian BITs. Argentina imposed certain restrictions on the transfer of funds out of the country[80] due to a severe economic crisis.[81] These measures were

[76] Section 6(2)(b) of the Foreign Exchange Management Act 1999 (India).

[77] See Section 6(3), (a) to (j) of the Foreign Exchange Management Act 1999 (India).

[78] India cannot impose restrictions on current account transactions because on 20 August 1994, India accepted the obligations of Article VIII, Sections 2, 3, and 4 of the IMF Articles of Agreement. However, India maintains the following restrictions on the making of payments and transfers for current international transactions, which are subject to Fund approval under Article VIII, Section 2(a): restrictions related to the non-transferability of balances under the India–Russia debt agreement; restrictions arising from unsettled balances under inoperative bilateral payments arrangements with two Eastern European countries; and a restriction on the transfer of amortization payments on loans by non-resident relatives – See IMF Country Report No 11/50. 2011, http://www.imf.org/external/pubs/ft/scr/2011/cr1150.pdf, February, accessed on 17 March 2018.

[79] *Continental Casualty Company* v. *Argentine Republic*, ICSID Case No. ARB/03/9, Award (5 September 2008).

[80] Argentina issued Decree 1570 of 2001 (*Corralito*) which forbade withdrawals from banks and transfers of funds out of Argentina – Seepara 237.

[81] For a detailed description of the Argentine economic crisis, see Jim Saxton. 2003. 'Argentina's Economic Crisis: Causes and Cures', Joint Economic Committee, United States Congress, Washington, DC, <http://www.hacer.org/pdf/Schuler.pdf>, accessed on 17 March 2018.

challenged by the foreign investor[82] who alleged that they violated the MTP in the US–Argentina BIT.[83] The *Continental* Tribunal said that the MTP in the US–Argentina BIT was *lex specialis*[84] compared to the IMF regime, because the IMF Articles distinguish between current and capital transactions whereas such a formal distinction is missing in the MTP in US–Argentina BIT.[85] Morevoer, MTPs deal only with funds related to investment whereas IMF Articles deal with all kinds of cross-border transfers. In other words, by virtue of the *lex specialis* principle, MTPs will prevail over the conflicting IMF Articles.[86] This approach is in line with Muchlinski's view that, where the MTPs in BITs do not mention the IMF regime, the presumption is that countries wanted to keep the IMF regime outside the BIT.[87]

If a tribunal were to take the position adopted by the tribunal in *Continental Casualty* v. *Argentina*, then, India imposing restrictions on transfer of funds, even if lawful under Indian law and consistent with the IMF Articles, could still amount to a breach of the broad and unqualified MTPs contained in large number of Indian BITs. However, the outcome would be different in a small number of Indian BITs where the transfer of funds related to investment are subject to domestic laws and policies. For example, Article 7(1) of the India–Russia BIT states, 'Each contracting party shall, in accordance with the laws and regulations of its state, ensure to investors of the other contracting party, the free transfer of payment in relation

[82] *Continental Casualty* v. *Argentina* paras 62, 237.

[83] *Continental Casualty* v. *Argentina* paras 62, 237.

[84] According to this rule, *lex specialis* – one norm deals with the same subject matter more directly and precisely in comparison to another norm – prevails over the more general norm.

[85] See *Continental Casualty* v. *Argentina* paras 243–44. See also Annamaria Viterbo. 2012. *International Economic Law and Monetary Measures: Limitations to State's Sovereignty and Dispute Settlement*. Gloucestershire, UK: Edward Elgar, p. 281 (hereinafter Viterbo, *International Economic Law and Monetary Measures*).

[86] See also Viterbo, *International Economic Law and Monetary Measures*, p. 281.

[87] Peter T. Muchlinski. 2009. 'Trends in International Investment Agreements: Balancing Investor Rights and the Right to Regulate: The Issue of National Security', *Yrbk Intl Invest L& Pol.* 1:35, 60.

to investments...'.[88] Such language grants regulatory freedom to the host state to impose restrictions on transfer of funds without worrying about violating the MTP provided the restrictions are in accordance with domestic laws.

Similarly, the outcome would be different in another small set of Indian BITs that contain express exceptions to MTPs. For example, Article 6(3) of the India–Slovakia BIT, while permitting the investor to transfer funds related to investment, states that 'a contracting party may prevent or restrict transfer through equitable non-discriminatory and good faith application of its laws...'. The India–Slovakia BIT then provides that this restriction could be for adoption of safeguard measures in circumstances such as macroeconomic or serious BoP difficulties. The Bilateral Investment Treaty further provide that these restrictions are to be imposed for a limited duration and may not go beyond what is necessary to remedy the BoP situation.[89] Few Indian BITs require the restrictions imposed on transfer of funds for the purposes of BoP difficulties or for other macroeconomic difficulties to be consistent with the IMF Articles.[90]

5.2.2 Investment Chapters in India's FTAs

All investment chapters in India's FTAs contain a provision on monetary transfer. These provisions, like the provisions in India's standalone BITs, allow for transfers of all funds in and out of the country. However, these provisions, unlike the large majority of India's standalone BITs discussed earlier, subject the right of foreign investors to transfer funds to certain conditions.

[88] India–Israel BIT art. 7.1; India–Italy BIT art. 7.1; and India–Argentina BIT art. 7.1.

[89] Article 6.4 of the India–Slovakia IIA. Similar or related provisions subjecting MTPs to specific exceptions are present in the following Indian BITs: India–Iceland art. 7.4; India–Mexico art. 8.4; Agreement between The Government of The Republic of India and The Government of The Republic of Bulgaria for The Promotion and Protection of Investments (signed 26 October 1998, entered into force 23 September 1999) India–Bulgaria Ad art. 7.4; India–Romania Ad art. 7.4; and India–Czech Republic Ad art. 2.

[90] India–Mexico BIT art. 8.4(a); India–Colombia BIT art. 5.4.

For example, Article 94(1) of the India Japan FTA provides for all transfers or funds relating to investments. Each Party shall ensure that all transfers relating to investments in its area of an investor of the other Party may be made freely into and out of its area without delay. However, Article 94 is subject to Article 97, which allows India to adopt or maintain measures not in conformity with article 94—

a) in the event of serious balance-of-payments and external financial difficulties or threat thereof; or
b) in cases where, in exceptional circumstances, movements of capital cause or threaten to cause serious difficulties for macroeconomic management in particular, monetary and exchange rate policies.[91] Article 97 further states that such measures should be maintained in a manner that is consistent with the IMF Articles.[92]

Similarly, in all the investment chapters of these FTAs, the rights to transfer funds relating to investment are also subject to some other non-monetary conditions such as:

a) bankruptcy, insolvency, or the protection of the rights of creditors;
b) issuing, trading, or dealing in securities, futures, options, or derivatives;
c) criminal or penal offences, and the recovery of proceeds of crime;
d) ensuring the satisfaction of judgments, orders or awards in adjudicatory proceedings such as judicial and quasi-judicial proceedings; or
e) social security, public retirement or statutory savings schemes, including provident funds, retirement gratuity programmes, and employees insurance programmes.[93]

[91] See India Japan FTA arts 97(1) (a) and (b). Also see India–Singapore FTA art 6.7 and India–Korea FTA art. 10.11 which is quite similar to Article 97 of India–Japan FTA, India–Malaysia FTA art. 10.8.3.

[92] See India–Japan FTA art. 97 (2) (a) and also (b) to (e) for other conditions that should be complied with while imposing these measures.

[93] India–Singapore FTA art. 6.6(2); Also see India–Korea FTA art. 10.10(4); India–Malaysia FTA art 10.8 (3); and India–Japan FTA art 94(3).

Consequently, India's FTA investment chapters and very few India's standalone BITs provide exceptions to MTPs.

5.3 Non-Precluded Measures Provisions or General Exception Clauses

Non-Precluded Measures (NPM) provisions in a BIT, also known as General Exceptions clause (starting with words like—'*nothing in this agreement precludes …*') provide the regulatory latitude to host countries to deal with threats to important national interests.[94] Non-Precluded Measures provisions provide flexibility to countries to deviate from the substantive obligations in certain circumstances that warrant giving preference to non-investment policy goals over investment protection. Given the debate on the conflict between investment protection and host countries' regulatory power, NPM provisions in BITs are useful tools that allow a host country to adopt measures for the pursuit of non-investment objectives without incurring any liability under international law.

Non-Precluded Measures provisions in BITs were put to test when a spate of arbitration cases was brought against Argentina for adopting measures aimed at addressing an economic crisis in early 2000.[95] For example, US investors claimed that the regulatory measures adopted by Argentina violated many provisions of the US–Argentina BIT, whereas Argentina relied on the NPM provision given in Article XI of the BIT[96] as a defence for these claims. Article XI of the US–Argentina BIT provides that '[t]his treaty shall not preclude the application by either party of measures necessary for the maintenance of public order, the fulfilment of its obligations with respect

[94] Salacuse, *The Law of Investment Treaties*, p. 343; Andrew Newcombe. 2011. 'General Exceptions in International Investment Agreements', in *Sustainable Development in World Investment Law*, Marie-Claire C. Segger, M. Gehring, and Andrew Newcombe, and Andrew Newcombe (eds), pp. 356–7. Netherlands: Kluwer International.

[95] For more on the Argentine economic crisis and subsequent IIA disputes see – Alvarez and Khamsi, 'The Argentine Crisis and Foreign Investors'.

[96] US–Argentina BIT provides US–Argentina BIT, Alvarez and Khamsi, 'The Argentine Crisis and Foreign Investors', art. XI.

to the maintenance or restoration of international peace or security, or the protection of its own essential security interests.' These cases, despite similar facts and law, have resulted in conflicting decisions with some ISDS tribunals concluding that Argentina's action cannot be condoned under Article XI[97] whereas some have held otherwise.[98]

A Non-Precluded Measures provision has two main elements: first, the permissible objectives, and second, the nexus requirement. Permissible objectives mean those objectives mentioned in the NPM provision for which the host state can deviate from its treaty obligations. So, for example, if we take Article XI of the US–Argentina BIT as an example of a NPM provision, then 'public order' and 'essential security interest' can be described as permissible objectives. It is important to note that a host state will be able to deviate from its BIT obligations, relying on the NPM provision, only for those objectives that are contained in the NPM provision and not for other objectives.[99] Nexus requirement in an NPM provision is

[97] CMS Award, (n 8); Enron Award, (n 8); Sempra Award, (n 8).

[98] LG&E Award, (n 8); Continental Casualty Award, (n 8). Also see Urbaser S.A. and Consorcio de Aguas Bilbao Biskaia, Bilbao Biskaia Ur Partzuergoa v. Argentine Republic (ICSID Case No. ARB/07/26), Award, 8 December 2016, paras 712–724.

[99] For more discussion on this, see William Burke-White and Andreas von Staden. 2008. *Investment Protection in Extraordinary Times: The Interpretation and Application of Non-Precluded Measures Provisions in Bilateral Investment Treaties*, VA. *Journal of International Law* 48: 314. For a discussion on NPM provision in Indian BITs see. Prabhash 2012. 'Non-Precluded Measures in Indian International Investment Agreements and India's Regulatory Power as a Host Nation', *Asian Journal of International Law* 2(1): 29 (hereinafter Ranjan, 'Non Precluded Measures in Indian International Investment Agreements and India's Regulatory Power as a Host Nation'); Amit Kumar Sinha. 2016. 'Non-Precluded Measures Provisions in Bilateral Investment Treaties of South Asian Countries', *Asian Journal of International Law* 7(2): 227–63. doi:10.1017/S2044251316000023 (hereinafter; Sinha, 'Non-Precluded Measures Provisions in Bilateral Investment Treaties of South Asian Countries'). For a different view point on the inclusion of General Exception clauses in BITs, see A. Newcombe. 2013. 'The Use of General Exceptions in IIAs: Increasing Legitimacy or Uncertainty?', in *Improving International Investment Agreements*, Armand de Mestral and Celine Lévesqueeds, p. 267. New York: Routledge.

the link between adopted measures and the permissible objective to be achieved through that measure. So, in Article XI of the US–Argentina BIT 'necessary' is the nexus requirement that acts as a link between the measures adopted to achieve the permissible objective. In other words, the State can adopt only those measures that are 'necessary' to achieve 'essential security interest'. The significance of the nexus requirement is in establishing the degree of connection between the adopted measure and the permissible objective sought to be achieved. The stricter the nexus requirement, stricter will be the degree of connection between the measure adopted and the permissible objective sought to be achieved. Thus, a nexus requirement like 'necessary' is stricter as against 'related to' or 'directed to'.[100] The threshold to prove that a measure is 'necessary' to achieve something is higher than the threshold to prove that a measure is merely 'related to' or 'directed to' achieving something.

5.3.1 India's standalone BITs

Article 12(2) of India's 2003 Model BIT provides that nothing in this Agreement precludes the host Contracting Party from taking action for the protection of its essential security interests or in circumstances of extreme emergency in accordance with its laws normally and reasonably applied on a non-discriminatory basis. This means that India will be able to invoke the NPM provision only in situations where it wishes to protect its 'essential security interests' or if there are situations of 'extreme emergency'.[101] Such NPM provision is present in many Indian BITs.[102] Arguably, 'essential security

[100] In this regard, see the WTO ruling in *United States – Standards for Reformulated and Conventional Gasoline*, WT/DS2 and 4, Report of the Appellate Body, 29 April 1996, 17–18. Also see Chapter 6 on *Devas* v. *India*.

[101] Also see Ranjan, 'Non Precluded Measures in Indian International Investment Agreements and India's Regulatory Power as a Host Nation', p. 21; Sinha, 'Non-Precluded Measures Provisions in Bilateral Investment Treaties of South Asian Countries', p. 227.

[102] India UK BIT art. 11(2); India–Poland BIT art. 12(2); India–Sri Lanka BIT art. 12(2); India–Vietnam BIT art. 12(2); India–Oman BIT art. 12(2); India–Egypt BIT art. 11(2); Agreement between The Government of The Republic of India and The Government of Kyrgyz Republic for The

interest' and 'circumstances of extreme emergency' has broad enough to cover many objectives. However, as this author argued earlier, the presence of words like 'essential' and 'extreme emergency' imply that the threshold should be significantly higher for India to successfully invoke the NPM provisions.[103]

The above interpretation of 'essential security interests' was affirmed by an ISDS tribunal in *Devas* v. *India*, which involved the interpretation of Article 11(3) of the India–Mauritius BIT. Article 11(3) provides: 'the provisions of this Agreement shall not in any way limit the right of either Contracting Party to apply prohibitions or restrictions of any kind or take any other action which is directed to the protection of its essential security interests…'. The tribunal held that the 'essential security interest' provision is not self-judging.[104] Further, the tribunal held that 'essential security interest' does not include *any* security interest, but only those security interests that are 'essential'.[105] The tribunal endorsed the view of the investors that prefixing 'security interests' with 'essential' means that the security interest must be vital or absolutely necessary or extremely important.[106] In other words, the threshold to satisfy the requirement of 'essential security interest' is quite high.

However, the tribunal held that in the determination of 'essential security interest', a 'wide measure of deference' shall be given to the host state.[107] It was held that 'an arbitral tribunal may not sit in judgement

---

Promotion and Protection of Investments (signed 16 May 1997, entered into force 12 May 2000) (India–Kyrgyz Republic BIT) art. 12(2); India–Romania BIT art. 12(2); India–Bulgaria BIT art. 12(2); India–Thailand BIT art. 12(2); India–Croatia BIT art. 12(2); India–Cyprus BIT art. 12(2); India–Finland BIT art. 12(2); India–Tajikistan BIT art. 12(2); Agreement between Government of The Republic of India and The Government of Ukraine for The Promotion and Protection of Investments (signed 1 December 2001, entered into force 12 August 2003) India–Ukraine BIT art. 12(2).

103 Ranjan, 'Non Precluded Measures in Indian International Investment Agreements and India's Regulatory Power as a Host Nation', pp. 36–42.

104 *Devas* v. *India*, paras 218–219. The fact that 'essential security interests' provision in Indian BITs.

105 *Devas* v. *India*, paras 235, 242, 243.

106 *Devas* v. *India*, paras 228, 243.

107 *Devas* v. *India*, para 244.

on national security matters ... national security issues relate to the existential core of a State'.[108] According to the tribunal, the burden of proof is on the investor who challenges a measure adopted by a state for safeguarding an 'essential security interest' to show that the measure has been adopted in bad faith or that the measure is not related to 'essential security interest'.[109] Very few of India's standalone BITs contain additional permissible objectives like 'public health'[110], 'public order',[111] etc. Some BITs contain a narrower 'public health' objective, namely, 'prevention of pests and diseases'.[112]

As regards the nexus requirement is concerned, some Indian BITs contain 'necessary' as the nexus requirement.[113] The critical question here is whether 'necessary' in these BITs should be interpreted using the customary international law defence of necessity.[114] The investor–state dispute settlement tribunals in *CMS* v. *Argentina, Enron* v. *Argentina*, and *Sempra* v. *Argentina* while interpreting 'necessary' in the NPM provision in the US–Argentina BIT read the customary law necessity defence given in Article 25 of the ILC Articles[115] into

[108] *Devas* v. *India*, para 245. Also see Chapter 6 for more on *Devas* v. *India*.

[109] *Devas* v. *India*, para 245. Also see Chapter 6 for more on *Devas* v. *India*.

[110] Agreement between The Government of The Republic of India and The Government of The Republic of Mauritius for The Promotion and Protection of Investments (signed 4 September 1998, entered into force 20 June 2000) (India–Mauritius BIT) art. 11(3).

[111] India–Portugal BIT art. 12(2); India–Saudi Arabia BIT art. 14.

[112] India–Kuwait BIT art. 14(2); India–Mauritius BIT art. 11(3); Agreement between The Republic of India and Bosnia and Herzegovina for The Promotion and Protection of Investments (signed 12 September 2006, entered into force 14 February 2008) (India–Bosnia Herzegovina BIT) art. 12; India–Spain BIT art. 13(2) provides '*circumstances of extreme emergency posing a threat to the life or health of human beings, animals or plants*'.

[113] See Article 15 India–Australia BIT; Article 13(5) India–Colombia BIT; Article 12 India–Denmark BIT. Also see Sinha. 'Non-Precluded Measures Provisions in Bilateral Investment Treaties of South Asian Countries', p. 227 at 242.

[114] See Article 25 of the ILC Articles of State Responsibility Also see S.P. Jagota. 1985. 'State Responsibility: Circumstances Precluding Wrongfulness', *Netherlands Yearbook of International Law* 16: 249.

[115] See Article 25 of the ILC Articles of State Responsibility Also see Jagota, 'State Responsibility', p. 249.

the treaty defence. The tribunals concluded that since Argentina's measures didn't satisfy Article 25, they were illegal.[116] However, the tribunal in *LG&E* v. *Argentina* followed a different method while interpreting 'necessary' in the same US–Argentina BIT. The LG&E tribunal first used Article XI (the NPM provision of the BIT) and subsequently, bizzarely, used Article 25 of the ILC articles on state responsibility to support its conclusion that the measures were consistent under Article XI.[117] The *CMS* annulment committee, the *Continental* tribunal, and the *Sempra* annulment committee emphasized on the difference between the two provisions and held that Article XI of the US–Argentina BIT differed in material respects from Article 25.[118]

The tribunal in *Continental Casualty* v. *Argentina* made it clear that the situations regulated by Article 25 of the ILC Draft Articles on State Responsibility are different from those regulated by the NPM provision in the US–Argentina BIT.[119] The tribunal viewed the strict conditions given in Article 25 of the ILC Articles as exceptional in nature because they can be invoked in any context against any international obligation.[120] Thus, the tribunal held that invocation of the NPM provision (in the US–Argentina BIT) limiting the general investment protection obligations is not necessarily subject to the

[116] *CMS Tribunal*, para 304 onwards; para 353–78; *Enron tribunal*, para 333–334, para 339; also see the discussion in Newcombe and Paradell (2009), 494–495; *Sempra Tribunal*, paras 375 & 378.

[117] See Kurtz, 'Adjudging the Exceptional at International Law', pp. 355–6 for criticism of the methodology adopted by the *LG&E* tribunal.

[118] *Sempra Annulment*, para 198; *Continental tribunal*, para 167; *CMS Annulment*, para 129. For a detailed discussion on how ISDS tribunals have interpreted 'necessary' in Article XI of the US Argentina BIT, see Prabhash Ranjan. 2016. 'Protecting Security Interests in International Investment Law', in *Security And International Law*, Mary Footer, Julia Schmidt, and Nigel D. White (eds). Hart Publishing: Oxford, pp. 273–99.

[119] *Continental Casualty* v. *Argentina*, para. 167. See also *Sempra Energy* v. *Argentina (Annulment Proceeding)*, paras 198–200 and Dolzer, above n 86, at 705.

[120] *Continental Casualty* v. *Argentina*, para. 167. See also *Sempra Energy* v. *Argentina (Annulment Proceeding)*, paras 198–200 and Dolzer, above n 86, at 705.

same conditions of application as the customary international law defence of necessity.[121] The tribunal also said that in such situations of grave crisis, a state must be accorded a significant margin of appreciation.[122] The *Continental Casualty* tribunal embraced the WTO jurisprudence on 'necessary' in Article XX of GATT 1994[123] to find the meaning of 'necessary' in Article XI of US–Argentina BIT.[124]

The World Trade Organization's necessity test represents a variant of the three-step proportionality analysis discussed before.[125] These steps are as follows. First, whether the measure is suitable for the legitimate public purpose—this will require a causal link between the measure and its object.[126] Second, whether the measure is necessary, that is, whether there is a less investment-restrictive alternative measure reasonably available that will achieve the same objective. The

[121] *Continental Casualty* v. *Argentina*, para. 167. See also *Sempra Energy* v. *Argentina (Annulment Proceeding)*, paras 198–200 and Dolzer, above n 86, at 705. For arguments in support of the approach adopted by the *Continental Casualty* tribunal to discover the legal nature of the NPM in US–Argentina BIT, see T. Gazzini. 2009. 'Foreign Investment and Measures Adopted on Grounds of Necessity: Towards a Common Understanding', *Transnational Dispute Management* 7(1): 17–18.

[122] *Continental Casualty*, para. 181.

[123] On WTO's jurisprudence on 'necessary' see Appellate Body Report, *Korea—Measures Affecting Imports of Fresh, Chilled and Frozen Beef*, WT/DS 161 and WT/DS169/AB/R, adopted 10 January 2001; Appellate Body Report, *Dominican Republic—Measures Affecting the Importation and Internal Sale of Cigarettes* WT/DS320/AB/R, adopted 19 May 2005; Appellate Body Report, *US—Measures Affecting the Cross-Border Supply of Gambling and Betting*, WT/DS/285/AB/R, adopted 20 April 2005; *Brazil—Measures Affecting Imports of Retreaded Tyres, Appellate Body Report*, WT/DS332/AB/R, 17 December 2007 (*Brazil – Tyres)*.

[124] *Continental Casualty*, paras. 192–195.

[125] Benedict Kingsbury and Stephan W. Schill. 2010. 'Public Law Concepts to Balance Investors' Rights with State Regulatory Actions in the Public Interest—the Concept of Proportionality', in *International Investment Law and Comparative Public Law*, Stephan W. Schill (ed.). Oxford: Oxford University Press, p. 75, at 85–88 (hereinafter Kingsbury and Schill, 'Public Law Concepts to Balance Investors' Rights with State Regulatory Actions in the Public Interest').

[126] Kingsbury and Schill, 'Public Law Concepts to Balance Investors' Rights with State Regulatory Actions in the Public Interest', p. 75, at 85–88.

third step will involve proportionality *stricto sensu*, that is, weighing and balancing the importance of the permissible objective sought to be achieved with the restriction on trade.[127] Although weighing and balancing in the WTO's necessity test is not the same as proportionality *stricto sensu*, it has been criticised by many because it allows the WTO adjudicator to replace the importing country's assessment with his/her own assessment.[128]

The *Continental Casualty* tribunal applied the WTO jurisprudence to determine whether Argentina's measures satisfied the test of 'necessity' by asking the following questions. Whether the measures contributed materially to the realization of essential security interests (the legitimate aim under Article XI)[129] and whether there existed alternative measures reasonably available to Argentina, 'which were less in conflict or more compliant with its international obligations, while providing an equivalent contribution to the achievement of the objective pursued'[130] (the less restrictive alternative test).

The tribunal answered the first question in the affirmative by stating that there is a genuine means-end relationship between the measures and the objective;[131] and the second question negatively[132] and thus came to the conclusion that measures adopted by Argentina were 'necessary' to protect its essential security interests. Important to note is the fact that the tribunal only undertook a 'means-end relationship' analysis but did not weigh and balance the significance of the objective with the restrictive impact on investment. This could be

[127] Kingsbury and Schill, 'Public Law Concepts to Balance Investors' Rights with State Regulatory Actions in the Public Interest', p. 75, at 85–8.

[128] See Jan Neumann and Elisabeth Türk. 2003. 'Necessity Revisited: Proportionality in World Trade Organization Law After *Korea – Beef, EC – Asbestos* and *EC – Sardines*', *Journal of World Trade* 37(1): 199, at 232–3; Peter Van den Bossche. 2008. 'Looking for Proportionality in WTO Law', *Legal Issues of Economic Integration* 35(3):283 at 284; For a different view on this see Michael Trebilcock, Robert Howse, and Antonia Eliason. 2013. *The Regulation of International Trade* 4th edition. London: Routledge, pp. 683–4.

[129] *Continental Casualty* v. *Argentina*, para. 196

[130] *Continental Casualty* v. *Argentina*, para. 198; see also Appellate Body, *Brazil-Tyres*, para. 156.

[131] *Continental Casualty* v. *Argentina*, para 197.

[132] *Continental Casualty* v. *Argentina*, paras 200–219.

explained by the reliance of the *Continental Casualty* tribunal on the 'margin of appreciation' standard to review Argentina's measure.[133]

'Necessary' in the NPM provisions in Indian BITs should be interpreted using the less restrictive alternative test laid down by the *Continental Casualty* tribunal. Nonetheless, important to underscore that given the varying approaches of ISDS tribunals, the interpretation of 'necessary' is subject to arbitral discretion.

Many Indian BITs contain weaker nexus requirement such as 'for',[134]'relating to',[135] and 'directed to' as given in Article 11(3) of the India–Mauritus BIT. In these BITs, even if a measure adopted is not 'necessary' to attain the permissible objective, it will still pass the muster as long as it is related to or directed to achieving the objective in question. In other words, the degree of connection between the measures adopted and the objective sought to be achieved depends on the nexus requirement given in the BIT. This was reaffirmed by the tribunal in *Devas* v. *India*. The nexus requirement in Article 11(3) of India–Mauritius BIT is 'directed to'. Given the text, the tribunal did not agree with the foreign investors who argued that the requirement of 'necessity' should be read into Article 11(3).[136] Thus, the tribunal concluded that India was not required to demonstrate that the actions it took were 'necessary' though it still had to meet the requirement of security interests being 'essential',[137] as already discussed.

A weak nexus requirement like 'for' implies that India will be able to adopt a large number of measures to achieve permissible objectives (provided it is able to show that there exists a permissible objective as per the NPM provision) even if such measures are not 'necessary'. However, the presence of 'for' as the nexus requirement creates a genuine apprehension that the NPM provision could be abused by India.

[133] *Continental Casualty* v. *Argentina*, paras 181 and 187. See Burke-White and Von Staden, *Investment Protection in Extraordinary* Times, n 58, pp. 326–7.

[134] See India–Cyprus BIT; India–Egypt BIT; India–Indonesia BIT; India–Isreal BIT.

[135] See India–Colombia BIT.

[136] *Devas* v. *India*, para 238.

[137] *Devas* v. *India*, para 243.

Also, India's standalone BITs do not contain separate general and security exceptions clause.

5.3.2 Investment Chapters in India's FTAs

Non-Precluded Measures provisions in the investment chapters of India's FTAs with Singapore, Korea, and Malaysia follow GATT Article XX structure. The Non-Precluded Measures provision in the investment chapter of India's FTA with Japan is based on Article XIV of GATS. Further, the NPM provisions in investment chapters of India's FTAs are divided in two categories—General Exceptions[138] and Security Exceptions.[139]

The Non-Precluded Measures provisions in the investment chapters of these FTAs, unlike India's stand alone BITs, contain a wide range of permissible objectives covering not just security interests but also other socio-economic objectives like environment and health. For example, Article 10.18 (1) (b) of the India–Korea FTA allows the host country to take measures necessary to protect environment. Apart from this, the same FTA also contains a permissible objective related to environment, which allows the host country to take measures necessary to conserve exhaustible natural resources [Article 10.18 (1) (e)]. The investment chapter in India–Singapore FTA, unlike the India–Korea FTA, does not contain 'protection of environment' as a specific permissible objective. Rather, it allows the host country to deviate from its treaty obligations by taking measures related to 'conservation of exhaustible natural resources'.[140] This formulation, though related to environmental protection, is narrower in scope in comparison to 'protection of environment'.

Furthermore, investment chapters in both India–Singapore and India–Korea FTAs have environment as one of the objectives in the provision titled 'measures in the public interest'.[141] Thus, under the

[138] India–Singapore FTA, art. 6.11; India–Japan FTA, art. 11(2); India–Korea FTA art. 10.18(1); India–Malaysia FTA art. 12.1.

[139] India–Singapore FTA art. 6.12; India–Japan FTA art. 11(2); India–Korea FTA art. 10.18(2).

[140] India–Singapore FTA art. 6.11(1)(e).

[141] India–Singapore FTA art. 6.10 and India–Korea FTA art. 10.16. These provisions allow countries to take measures for the protection of public health.

investment chapters of these FTAs, India can adopt an environmental measure if adopting such a measure is in public interest. The investment chapters in these FTAs also allow host state to deviate from their treaty obligations to pursue the objective of 'public order'.[142]

In investment chapters of all these FTAs, the chapter of the 'security' exception clause allows countries to adopt measures, which the countries consider as necessary for the protection of Essential Security Interests (ESI). Thus, the security exceptions in the investment chapters of all these FTAs are self-judging subject to a good faith review.

5.4 Investor State Dispute Settlement (ISDS)

Investor State Dispute Settelement is an integral part of protection for foreign investment within BITs.[143] It allows an individual foreign investor to directly bring a claim against the host state challenging her exercise of public power.[144] In the absence of an ISDS provision, the options for the foreign investor to settle disputes with the State would be to either directly negotiate with the host state[145] or use local courts[146] or diplomatic protection.[147] However, these options are not very attractive for the foreign investor for a variety of reasons. For instance, local courts of a country may lack necessary judicial independence or may be too slow in deciding cases. Likewise, diplomatic protection will be of limited value if the investor's home state is not willing to extend assistance to the foreign investor.[148]

Therefore, vast majority of BITs contain ISDS provisions, thus providing for adjudication of investment disputes before an international

[142] India–Korea FTA art. 10.18; India–Singapore FTA art. 6.11; India–Japan FTA art. 11; India–Malaysia FTA art. 12.1.

[143] For a detailed discussion on ISDS in BITs see Salacuse, *The Law of Investment Treaties*, pp. 392–435.

[144] See the discussion in Dolzer and Schreuer, *Principles of International Investment Law*, n 1, pp. 235–310; Salacuse, *The Law of Investment Treaties*, n 2, pp. 353–92.

[145] Salacuse, *The Law of Investment Treaties*, p. 396.

[146] Salacuse, *The Law of Investment Treaties*, p. 397. Also see Dolzer and Schreuer, *Principles of International Investment Law*, p. 235.

[147] Salacuse, *The Law of Investment Treaties*, pp. 398–9.

[148] Salacuse, *The Law of Investment Treaties*, p. 398.

tribunal. Most BITs allow foreign investors to bring claims against the host state even without exhausting local remedies.[149] It is important to bear in mind that the rule related to 'exhaustion of local remedies' is a long-standing rule of customary international law,[150] even pre-dating the existence of the modern international law.[151] However, countries in their BITs have followed different Models varying from express requirement of exhaustion of local remedies,[152] to making

[149] Dolzer and Schreuer, *Principles of International Investment Law*, p. 265. Also see *Helnan* v. *Egypt*, Decision on Annulment, 14 June 2010, paras 43–57; *Generation Ukraine, Inc* v. *Ukraine*, Award, 16 September 2003, para 13.4.

[150] *Case Concerning Elettronica Sicula S.p.A. (ELSI) (U.S.* v. *Italy)*, Judgement, 1989 I.C.J. Rep. 1989, para 31 (July 20); *Interhandel Case (Switzerland* v. *U.S.)*, Judgment, 1959 I.C.J. Rep. 1959, para 6 (Mar. 21); See also Theodor Meron. 1959. 'The Incidence of the Rule of Exhaustion of Local Remedies', *Brit. Y.B. Int'l. L* 83; A.A. CancadoTrindade. 1976. 'Origin and Historical Development of the Rule of Exhaustion of Local Remedies in International Law', *Belgian Rev. Int'l L.* 12: 499; Chittranjan Felix Amersinghe. 2004. *Local Remedies in International Law*, 2nd edition. Cambridge: Cambridge University; James R. Crawford and Thomas D. Grant. 2007. 'Exhaustion of Local Remedies', *Max Planck Encyclopedia of Public International Law*. Oxford: Oxford University Press.

[151] Matthew C. Potterfield. 2015. 'Exhaustion of Local Remedies in Investor-State Dispute Settlement: An Idea Whose Time Has Come?', *Yale J. Int'l. L.*41; See also, for the doctrine of exhaustion of local remedies in international investment law—Ursula Kriebaum. 2009. 'Local Remedies and the Standards for the Protection of Foreign Investment', *International Investment Law for the 21st Century: Essays in Honour of Christoph Schreuer*. New York: Oxford University Press; Mavluda Sattorova. 2012. 'Return to Local Remedies Rule in European BITs? Power (Inequalities), Dispute Settlement, and Change in Investment Treaty Law', *Legal Issues Econ. Integration* 39(2):223–48.

[152] For example, Agreement on economic cooperation between the Government of the Kingdom of the Netherlands and the Government of the Republic of Singapore, 16 May 1972, entered into force 7 September 1973 [Netherlands–Singapore BIT], 1972, art. XI:

The Contracting Party in the territory of which nationals of the other Contracting Party make or intend to make investments, *shall after the exhaustion of all local administrative and judicial remedies*, agree to any demand on the part of such nationals to submit, for arbitration or conciliation, to the Centre established by the Convention of Washington of 18 March 1965 on the settlement

no reference to exhaustion of local remedies,[153] to express rejection of the exhaustion principle in certain BITs.[154] Some BITs contain a 'fork in the road' provision in their BITs, which requires the investor to choose between litigating in local courts of the host state or before an international tribunal and that the choice once made is final.[155]

Another facet is that in large majority of BITs, the ISDS clauses offer unequivocal consent to arbitration to investors who are nationals of the other contracting state.[156] Whether the consent is unequivocal or not depends on the actual wording of the BIT. For example, phrases like contracting party 'hereby consents' or where the dispute 'shall be submitted' to arbitration implies an offer of unequivocal consent to arbitration.[157] This consent to arbitration, often, covers

---

of investment disputes between States and nationals of other States, any disputes that may arise in connection with the investments (emphasis added).

[153] Most of the BITs fall in this category. For example, see India–UK BIT, art. 10, which makes no reference whatsoever to the 'exhaustion principle'. Such absence is generally interpreted as the waiver of the requirement of exhaustion of local remedies.

[154] For example, see the Agreement Between the Government of the Republic of Croatia and the Government of The Kingdom of Cambodia on the Promotion and Reciprocal Protection of Investments, 18 May 2001, entered into force 15 June 2002 [Croatia–Cambodia BIT], art. 10.2(b):

In case of arbitration, each Contracting Party, by this Agreement irrevocably consents in advance, even in the absence of an individual arbitral agreement between the Contracting Party and the investor, to submit any such dispute to this Centre. *This consent implies the renunciation of the requirement that the internal administrative or judicial remedies should be exhausted* (emphasis added).

[155] See *Thunderbird* v. *Mexico*, Award, 26 January 2006, paras 111–8.

[156] Christoph Schreuer. 2008. 'Consent to Arbitrate', in *The Oxford Handbook of International Investment Law*, Peter Muchlinski, Federico Ortino, and Christoph Schreur (eds). Oxford: Oxford University Press, pp. 832 at 835–6. Also see Vandevelde, *Bilateral Investment Treaties*, pp. 433–9.

[157] See Article 8(1) of the Agreement Between the Government of United Kingdom of Great Britain and Northern Ireland and the Government of the Democratic Socialist Republic of Sri Lanka, 13 February 1980. Also see Dolzer and Schreuer, *Principles of International Investment Law*, p. 258; Jan Paulsson.1995. 'Arbitration Without Privity', *ICSID Review – Foreign Investment Law Journal* 10: 235; *RosInvest* v. *Russia*, Award on Jurisdiction, 1 October 2007, paras 56–75; *Millicom* v. *Senegal*, Decision on Jurisdiction, 16 July 2010, paras 56 and 61–66.

'any dispute concerning an investment', which is quite broad covering not just treaty breaches but also contractual breaches.[158] A foreign investor may accept this offer, for example, by instituting ICSID arbitral proceedings against the host state.[159] The unequivocal consent to arbitrate by the host states in large majority of BITs is a very important aspect from the perspective of international rule of law.[160] It ensures that states could be held accountable for the exercise of their public power by a third party, that is, an international tribunal, which will have the power to review the action of the host state—whether executive, judicial, or legislative.[161] On the other hand, questions have also been raised about the ISDS system pertaining to lack of transparency and an apprehension of bias.[162]

A broader ISDS provision, that is, one that does not require a foreign investor to exhaust local remedies before pursuing international arbitration, has a broad jurisdictional scope, does not contain a 'fork in the road' provision, and where the State has given an unequivocal consent to arbitration will be foreign investor friendly. It will give much space to the foreign investor to not just challenge many measures of the host state but also at a forum of his choice. Conversely,

[158] Vandevelde, *Bilateral Investment Treaties*, 433. Also see Article 9(1) of the Indian Model BIT; Article 9(1) of the Chinese Model BIT; Article VIII (1) of the Cambodia–Vietnam BIT.

[159] See *Generation Ukraine* v. *Ukraine*, Award, 16 September 2003, paras 12.2 and 12.3.

[160] For a discussion on international rule of law see James Crawford. 2003. 'International Law and the Rule of Law', *Adelaide Law Review* 24(3); Simon Chesterman 2008. 'An International Rule of Law?', *American Journal of Comparative Law* 56: 331; Nollkaemper, *National Courts and the International Rule of Law*, n 14; Stéphane Beaulac. 2009. 'The Rule of Law in International Law Today', in *Relocating the Rule of Law*, G. Palombella and N. Walker (eds), p. 197. Oxford: Portland, Or, Hart.

[161] Andreas Kulick. 2012. *Global Public Interest in International Investment Law*. Cambridge:New York: Cambridge University Press, p. 93. See also Schill, *The Multilateralization of International Investment Law*, p. 374.

[162] Van Harten, *Investment Treaty Arbitration, Procedural Fairness, and the Rule of Law*. See also Also see Vicki Been J.C. Beauvais. 2003. 'The Global Fifth Amendment?', *New York University Law Review* 78:30. Also see Chapter 1.

a restricted ISDS provision will narrow the scope of claims that a foreign investor can bring against the State.

5.4.1 Indian Standalone BITs

All Indian BITs contain investor–state dispute resolution mechanisms. Investors can bring disputes against India before international arbitral tribunals without exhausting the local remedies. However, it is important to mention that though Indian BITs provide for submission of disputes to ICSID, the investor cannot exercise this option because India is not a member of ICSID. Thus, the option available to the investor is to either use the ICSID Additional Facility Rules or to have an *ad hoc* arbitration tribunal based on the UNCITRAL Arbitration Rules.

Most of the BITs are silent on the relationship between different judicial forums, that is, between domestic courts and international arbitral forums, barring some BITs that provide for a 'fork in the road' provision.[163] In other words, a foreign investor can commence

[163] Agreement between The Government of The Republic of India And The Government of The Argentine Republic on The Promotion And Reciprocal Protection of Investments (Signed on 20 August 1999; Entry into force: 12 August 2002) (India–Argentina BIT); Agreement between The Government of The Republic of India And The Government of Republic of Belarus on The Promotion And Protection of Investments (Signed on 20 August 1999; Entry into force: 12 August 2002) (India–Belarus BIT); Agreement for the Promotion And Protection of Investments between the Republic of Colombia and Republic of India (Signed: 10 November 2009; Entry into Force: 2 July 2012) (India–Colombia BIT); Agreement Between The Government of The Republic of India And The Government of Czech Republic on The Promotion And Protection of Investments (Signed on 11 October 1996; Entry into force: 6 February 1998) (India–Czech Republic BIT); Agreement Between The Government of The Republic of India And The Belgium Luxemburg Economic Union on The Promotion And Protection of Investments (Signed on 31 October 1997; Entry into force: 8 January 2001) (India–BLEU BIT); Agreement between The Government of The Republic of India And The Government of Republic of Finland on The Promotion And Protection of Investments (Signed on 7 November 2002; Entry into force: 9 April 2003) (India–Finland BIT); Agreement Between The Government of The Republic of India And The Government of Republic of Indonesia on The Promotion And

judicial proceedings at both domestic and international levels. Likewise, the scope of ISDS provision in Indian BITs is quite broad. A large number of BITs cover any dispute relating to investment.[164] In other words, the foreign investor can use ISDS to sue India for contractual breaches as well as long as they relate to the investment made. In comparison to these treaties, the jurisdiction of an ISDS tribunal in some BITs is restricted to treaty claims only.[165] Similarly,

---

Protection of Investments (Signed: 10 February 1999; Entered into Force: 22 January 2004) (India–Indonesia BIT); Agreement between The Government of The Republic of India And The Government of Republic of Lithuania on The Promotion And Protection of Investments (Signed: 31 March 2011; Entered into Force: 1 December 2011) (India–Lithuania BIT); Agreement between The Government of United Mexican States and the Government of Republic of India for the Promotion and Protection of Investments (Signed: 21 May 2007; Entry into force: 23 February 2008) (India–Mexico BIT). Agreement between the Government of Republic of India and the Government of Kingdom of Thailand on Promotion and Protection of Investments (Signed 10 July 2000; Entry into Force: 13 July 2001) (India–Thailand BIT); Agreement between the Government of Republic of India and the Government of Ukraine on Promotion and Protection of Investments (Signed 1 December 2001; Entry into Force: 12 August 2003) (India–Ukraine BIT).

[164] India–Argentina BIT; India–Australia BIT; India–Bangladesh BIT; India–Belarus BIT; India–Czech Republic BIT; India–BLEU BIT; India–China BIT; India–France BIT; India–Germany BIT; Denmark–India BIT; India–Ghana BIT; India–Indonesia BIT; India–Republic of Korea BIT; India–Italy BIT; India–Malaysia BIT; India–Netherlands BIT; India–Austria BIT.

[165] India–Bulgaria BIT; Agreement for the Promotion And Protection of Investments between the Republic of Colombia and Republic of India (Signed: 10 November 2009; Entry into Force: 2 July 2012) (India–Colombia BIT); Agreement between Government of Republic of India and Government of Republic of Croatia for the Promotion and Protection of Investments (Signed: 4 May 2001; Entry into Force: 19 January 2002) (India–Croatia BIT); Agreement between Government of Republic of India and Government of Greece for the Promotion and Protection of Investments (Signed: 26 April 2007; Entry into Force: 10 April 2008) (India–Greece BIT); Agreement between Government of Republic of India and Government of the Arab Republic of Egypt for the Promotion and Protection of Investments (Signed: 9 April 1997; Entry into Force: 22 November 2000) (India–Egypt BIT); Agreement between The

most BITs give an implied or express consent to arbitration barring some.[166] Also, barring very few BITs,[167] Indian BITs do not contain a limitation period for submission of claims. In sum, Indian stand-alone BITs contain very broad ISDS provisions and thus are friendly to foreign investors.

Government of United Mexican States and the Government of Republic of India for the Promotion and Protection of Investments (Signed: 21 May 2007; Entry into force: 23 February 2008) (India–Mexico BIT); Agreement between Government of Republic of India and Government of Republic of Poland for the Promotion and Protection of Investments (Signed: 7 October 1996; Entry into Force: 31 December 1997) (India–Poland BIT); Agreement between Government of Republic of India and Government of State of Qatar for the Promotion and Protection of Investments (Signed: 7 April 1999; Entry into Force: 15 December 1999) (India–Qatar BIT); Agreement between Government of Republic of India and Government of The Federal Government of Federal Republic of Yugoslavia for the Reciprocal Promotion and Protection of Investments (Signed: 31 January 2003; Entry into Force: 10 April 2008) (India–Serbia BIT).

166 Some of the BITs that require case by case consent are: Agreement between The Government of The Republic of India And The Government of Australia on The Promotion And Protection of Investments (Signed on 26 February 1999; Entry into force: 4 May 2000) (India–Australia BIT); Agreement between The Government of The Republic of India And The Belgium Luxemburg Economic Union on The Promotion And Protection of Investments (Signed on 31 October 1997; Entry into force: 8 January 2001) (India–BLEU BIT); Agreement between Government of Republic of India and Government of the Arab Republic of Egypt for the Promotion and Protection of Investments (Signed: 9 April 1997; Entry into Force: 22 November 2000) (India–Egypt BIT); Agreement between the Government of Republic of India and the Government of Mongolia for the Promotion and Protection of Investments (Signed: 2 January 2001; Entry into force: 29 April 2002) (India–Mongolia BIT); Agreement between the Government of Kingdom of Morocco and the Government of Republic of India for the Promotion and Protection of Investments (Signed: 13 February 1999; Entry into force: 22 February 2001) (India–Morocco BIT); Agreement between the Government of Republic of India and the Government of Nepal for the Promotion and Protection of Investments (Signed: 21 October 2011) (India–Nepal BIT).

167 India–Colombia BIT; India–Hungary BIT; India–Mexico BIT.

5.4.2 India's FTA Investment Chapters

The Free Trade Agreement investment chapters do not contain such broad ISDS provisions. For example, the ASEAN–India agreement contains a choice of forum clause in Article 20.7.[168] If a treaty dispute between an investor and State has not been resolved within 180 days from the date of the written request made by the investor, through consultations and negotiations, then the investor will have the choice of submitting the dispute either to courts or administrative tribunals of the disputing party,[169] or to international arbitration under ICSID,[170] UNCITRAL Arbitration Rules[171] or any other arbitral institution.[172] Along with the choice of forum clause, the Indian-ASEAN investment agreement provides a 'fork in the road' provision by making it clear that an investor submitting a dispute to any court, administrative tribunal or to any arbitration tribunal shall exclude resort to other procedures.[173] Furthermore, India's FTA investment chapters contain limitation period for submission of claims[174] and cover only treaty claims.[175]

5.5 Summing up

Like the last chapter, this chapter also shows that Indian standalone BITs contain broad provisions such as an expansive expropriation

[168] ASEAN–India Investment Agreement, art. 20.7.

[169] ASEAN–India Investment Agreement, art. 20.7(a).

[170] ASEAN–India Investment Agreement, art. 20.7 (b) and (c).

[171] ASEAN–India Investment Agreement, art. 20.7 (d).

[172] For instance, London Centre for International Arbitration (LCIA) Arbitration Rules (2014); Singapore International Arbitration Centre (SIAC) Arbitration Rules 2016.

[173] Article 20(7) ASEAN–India Investment Agreement; India–Japan EPA; India–South Korea EPA.

[174] Agreement on Investment under the Framework Agreement on Comprehensive Economic Cooperation between the Association of Southeast Asian Nations and Republic of India (Signed 12 November 2014) (India–ASEAN BIT); India-Japan EPA; India–South Korea EPA; India–Malaysia FTA; India–Singapore EPA.

[175] India–ASEAN BIT; India–Japan EPA; India–South Korea EPA; India–Malaysia FTA; India–Singapore EPA.

provision, a broad ISDS provision. On the other hand, the general exception provision is narrower, meaning thereby that it provides the host state limited opportunities to deviate from their treaty obligations in order to address non-investment objectives such as public health. The other pattern, consistent with Chapter 4, is that India's FTA investment chapters represent a better balance of investment protection with the host state's right to regulate in comparison with India's standalone BITs. Consistent with Chapter 4, this chapter also shows that India was primarily a 'rule taker' in international investment law because most of these provisions are borrowed from the BITs that 'capital exporting' countries followed based on the laissez faire liberalism model. Also, consistent with Chapter 4, this chapter also shows how India moved away from the elements of CERDS and NIEO it tried developing in the 1970s. The adoption of ISDS is the most obvious example of this. While India, despite negotiating, didn't accede to the ICSID convention,[176] it provided a very foreign investor friendly ISDS provision in its BITs in the 'acceptance' phase.

[176] See Chapter 2.

provision, a broad ISDS provision. On the other hand, the general exception provision is narrower, meaning thereby that it provides the host state limited opportunities to deviate from their treaty obligations in order to address non-investment objectives such as public health. The other pattern, consistent with Chapter 4, is that India's FTA investment chapters represent a better balance of investment protection with the host states right to regulate in comparison with India's standalone BITs. Consistent with Chapter 4, this chapter also shows that India was primarily a rule taker in international investment law because most of these provisions are borrowed from the BITs that capital exporting countries followed based on the laissez faire neoliberal model. Also, consistent with Chapter 4, this chapter also shows how India moved away from the elements of CERDS and NIEO it had developing in the 1970s. The adoption of ISDS is the most obvious example of this. While India, despite negotiating, didn't accede to the ICSID convention,[126] it provided a very foreign investor friendly ISDS provision in its BITs in the acceptance phase.

[126] See Chapter 2.

PHASE III

BACKLASH

6

BITs Come Home to Roost but No Philip Morris Moment Yet!

This and the next two chapters examine the third phase of the Indian BIT programme which began in 2011. As mentioned in Chapter 3, India's economic policy to foreign investment did not change post 2010. The 2011 FDI policy declared that the objective and the intent of the government are to promote foreign direct investment through a transparent and predictable policy framework which reduces regulatory burden on foreign investors.[1] Taking its foreign investment initiative further, the Indian government took a number of steps to further liberalize foreign investment post 2011. For instance, in 2012, India liberalized the FDI norms in the retail sector, traditionally considered sensitive for the domestic economy, by allowing FDI up to 51 per cent under the approval route, that is, subject to the government's permission.[2]

[1] Department of Industrial Policy and Promotion, Ministry of Commerce and Industry, Government of India, Consolidated FDI Policy. 2011.http://dipp.nic.in/sites/default/files/FDI_Circular_012011_31March2011%20%205_0.pdf, p. 5, accessed on 24 February 2018.

[2] Government of India, Ministry of Commerce & Industry, Department of Industrial Policy & Promotion, (FC-I Section), Press Note No. 5 (2012 Series) http://dipp.nic.in/sites/default/files/pn5_2012_2.pdf, accessed on 24 February 2018; See Chapter 3 also for 'approval route'.

Narendra Modi, who became India's Prime Minister in May 2014, launched a major initiative called 'Make in India' to make India a manufacturing hub by attracting foreign investment.[3] India's intent and objective to attract and promote foreign direct investment in order to supplement domestic capital, technology, and skills, for accelerated economic growth was re-articulated as part of India's FDI policy in 2017.[4] The Modi government told the Parliament of India recently that the 'FDI policy is reviewed on an ongoing basis; with a view to making it more investor friendly and to ensure that India remains an increasingly attractive investment destination.'[5] The government further liberalized FDI norms in the retail sector in 2018 by permitting 100 per cent FDI in single brand retail trading under the automatic route.[6] Defence, another sensitive sector closed for foreigners, has also been opened to foreign investors allowing 49 per cent FDI under the automatic route and more than 49 per cent FDI under the approval route.[7]

In other words, India's economic policy to foreign investment, post 2010 is a further strengthening of the economic reforms agenda of 1991. Economically and politically, India has embraced foreign investment much more post 2010. However, as this and subsequent two chapters of the book show, there has been a noticeable break

[3] See for details, Make in India, http://www.makeinindia.com/about, accessed on 24 February 2018.

[4] Department of Industrial Policy and Promotion Ministry of Commerce and Industry, Government of India. 2017. 'Consolidated FDI Policy (Effective from 28 August 2017)', http://dipp.nic.in/sites/default/files/CFPC_2017_FINAL_RELEASED_28.8.17.pdf, 28 August, accessed on 24 February 2018.

[5] Government of India, Ministry of Commerce and Industry, Department of Industrial Policy and Promotion, Rajya Sabha, Starred Question No 53, 7 February 2018, http://dipp.nic.in/sites/default/files/rs53_0.pdf, accessed on 24 February 2018.

[6] Government of India, Ministry of Commerce and Industry, Department of Industrial Policy and Promotion, Press Note No.1, 2018, http://dipp.nic.in/sites/default/files/pn1_2018.pdf, accessed on 24 February 2018.

[7] Government of India, Ministry of Commerce and Industry, Department of Industrial Policy and Promotion, Rajya Sabha, 'Unstarred Question No. 287'(20 July 2016), http://dipp.nic.in/sites/default/files/ru287.pdf, accessed on 24 February 2018.

from the past in India's legal approach to foreign investment under international law. This, for the first time, has created a cleavage between India's economic policy to foreign investment and India's legal approach to foreign investment under international law.

The year 2011 was a watershed year for the Indian BIT programme. In 2011, the first publicly known BIT arbitral award was issued against India in the case *White Industries* v. *India.*[8] The award was followed by a number of foreign companies, in 2012 and afterwards, issuing ISDS arbitral notices to India. In complete contrast to the period of acceptance (from 1994 to 2010), the number of ISDS claims against India increased substantially from 2011 onwards, both in numbers and scope. According to UNCTAD, since 2011, 13 ISDS claims have been filed against India (Table 6.1).[9] However, UNCTAD's records only show those ISDS cases that are currently active, that is, those in which an ISDS arbitral tribunal has been formed. Several arbitral notices were not pursued by foreign investors.[10] As it was predicted,[11]

[8] White Industries Case *[White Industries Australia Limited* v. *Republic of India]*, UNCITRAL, Final Award (30 November 2011) [hereinafter, White Industries].

[9] UNCTAD. 'India – As Respondent State', http://investmentpolicyhub.unctad.org/ISDS/CountryCases/96?partyRole=2, accessed on 24 February 2018, updated on 31 July 2018.

[10] See the following documents to know about the ISDS cases filed/ISDS arbitral notices against India—Government of India, Ministry of Finance, Lok Sabha, 'Unstarred Question No. 4819' (4 May 2012), Bilateral Pacts Questionhttp://164.100.47.194/Loksabha/Questions/QResult15.aspx?qref=122495&lsno=15, accessed on 24 February 2018; Government of India, Ministry of Commerce and Industry, Lok Sabha, 'Unstarred Question No. 6133' (14 May 2012), http://164.100.47.194/Loksabha/Questions/QResult15.aspx?qref=122714&lsno=15, accessed on 24 February 2018; Government of India, Ministry of Finance, Lok Sabha, 'Unstarred Question No. 4322' (22 March 2013), http://164.100.47.194/Loksabha/Questions/QResult15.aspx?qref=137667&lsno=15, accessed on 24 February 2018; Government of India, Ministry of Finance, Lok Sabha, 'Unstarred Question No. 2391' (25 July 2014), http://164.100.47.194/Loksabha/Questions/QResult15.aspx?qref=2274&lsno=16, accessed on 24 February 2018. Apart from what the government has reported to the Parliament, it has not revealed much information or details voluntarily about the ISDS claims that have been brought against India say on the website of the finance ministry. For example, no information has been made

the White Industries award and the rising ISDS claims altered India's approach towards BITs compelling the government to rethink about BITs and triggering a backlash against BITs and ISDS, as discussed in Chapters 7 and 8.

A major indicator of India's changed approach to BITs is the decreasing number of BITs signed during this period. From 1994 to 2010, India signed 79 BITs and two FTAs containing investment chapters,[12] whereas 2011 onwards India signed only four BITs[13], two FTAs containing investment chapters[14] and an investment agreement with ASEAN.[15] In other words, from 1994 to 2010, India signed, on

available regarding stages at which each of these claims are or the amount of damages have been claimed.

[11] Prabhash Ranjan. 2012. 'The White Industries Arbitration: Implications for India's Investment Treaty Program', *Investment Treaty News Quarterly* 3(2): 12 at 14 (hereinafter Ranjan, 'The White Industries Arbitration').

[12] Comprehensive Economic Cooperation Agreement between the Republic of India and the Republic of Singapore (signed 8 April 2003) (India–Singapore FTA); Comprehensive Economic Cooperation Agreement between the Republic of India and the Republic of Korea (signed 7 August 2009) (India–Korea FTA).

[13] Agreement between the Republic of India and the Lithuania on the Reciprocal Promotion and Protection of Investments (signed 31 March 2011, entered into force 1 December 2011) (India–Lithuania BIT); Agreement between the Republic of India and the Lithuania on the Reciprocal Promotion and Protection of Investments (signed 21 October 2011) (India–Nepal BIT) Agreement between the Republic of India and the Republic of UAE on the Reciprocal Promotion and Protection of Investments (signed 12 December 2013, entered into force 21 August 2014) (India–UAE BIT); Agreement between the Republic of India and the Republic of Slovenia on the Reciprocal Promotion and Protection of Investments (signed 14 June 2011) (India–Slovenia BIT).

[14] Comprehensive Economic Cooperation Agreement between the Republic of India and the Republic of Malaysia (India–Malaysia FTA) (signed 1 July 2011); Comprehensive Economic Cooperation Agreement between the Republic of India and the Republic of Japan (signed 1 August 2011) (India–Japan FTA).

[15] This is According to the UNCTAD, see UNCTAD. http://investmentpolicyhub.unctad.org/IIA/CountryBits/96#iiaInnerMenu, accessed on 24 February 2018 and UNCTAD. http://investmentpolicyhub.unctad.org/IIA/CountryOtherIias/96#iiaInnerMenu, accessed on 24 February 2018.

an average, five investment treaties every year, this number fell to one investment treaty per year from 2011 to 2018. Interestingly, of the seven treaties signed by India in this phase, five were signed in 2011 itself and negotiations for most of these treaties would have been over by the time India lost the White Industries case. In other words, although these treaties were signed in 2011, they are reflective of the approach followed by India during the 'acceptance' phase.

This chapter studies the ISDS claims brought against India. The investor–state dispute settlement claims have been divided based on the reason, for which the claim has been brought against India such as judicial delays (Section 6.1); cancellation of telecom licenses (Section 6.2); cancellation of spectrum licenses (Section 6.3); amendment in tax laws retrospectively (Section 6.4); actions of state governments impacting foreign investment (Section 6.5). Through the study of these cases we will assess the core reason behind these claims. In other words, are these cases an instance of foreign investors using BITs to challenge India's regulatory measures aimed at protecting say the environment or public health? Do these cases present the pathologies of BITs and ISDS system by encroaching upon India's sovereign right to regulate? Or are these ISDS claims examples of foreign investors challenging abuse of India's exercise of public power?

6.1 Judicial Delays in Enforcement of Arbitral Awards: The White Industries Case

The White Industries was the first and the most prominent ISDS claim brought against India for judicial delays.[16] This case involved challenging judicial delays in enforcing an international commercial arbitration award as a violation of the India–Australia BIT (see Table 6.1).[17]

[16] *White Indus. Austl. Ltd.*, at 139–40. Also see Prabhash Ranjan and Deepak Raju. 2014. 'Bilateral Investment Treaties and Indian Judiciary (with Deepak Raju as the second author)', *The George Washington International Law Review* 46 (4): 809–47 (hereinafter Ranjan and Raju, 'Bilateral Investment Treaties and Indian Judiciary').

[17] *White Industries* v. *Australia* at 45.

Table 6.1 ISDS Claims Against India since 2011

No.	Year of Initiation	Name of the Case	Reason for the Claim	Outcome of Original Proceedings	Home State of Investor
1.	2017	Vodafone v.India (II)	Imposition of taxes retrospectively	Pending	United Kingdom
2.	2016	Astro and South Asia Entertainment v.India	Alleged unfair and bias criminal investigation by the government relating to suspecting bribery by the claimants of Indian government officials	Pending	United Kingdom Mauritius
3.	2016	RAKIA v.India	Alleged non-fulfilment and subsequent cancellation of a MoU between Indian state of Andhra Pradesh and the claimant	Pending	United Arab Emirates
4.	2016	Strategic Infrasol and Thakur Family Trust v.India	Government's alleged non-investigation of allegations of forgery and criminal actions by an Indian construction company	Pending	United Arab Emirates
5.	2016	Vedanta v.India	Claims arising out of a tax bill of approximately $3.29 billion, imposed by the Government on Cairn India Limited in 2015, for the alleged failure to pay taxes on capital gains arising from Cairn's operations in 2006-2007.	Pending	United Kingdom

6.	2015	Cairn v.India	Claims arising out of a draft assessment order issued by the Indian Income Tax Department addressed to the claimant's subsidiary, Cairn UK Holdings Limited, in respect of fiscal year 2006/7 in the amount of USD 1.6 billion plus any applicable interest and penalties	Pending	United Kingdom
7.	2014	LDA v.India	Claims arising out of a series of measures by the Indian Government that allegedly prevented the effective implementation of a joint venture related to a port modernization project at Haldia, in the city of Kolkota, in which the claimant held stakes; including allegedly failing to provide protection and security to the project	Pending	France
8.	2014	Vodafone v. India (I)	Imposition of taxes retrospectively	Pending	Netherlands
9.	2013	Deutsche Telekom v. India	Claims arising out of the Government's cancellation of a contract concluded with Devas, a company in which the claimant held interests, concerning the provision of broadband services to Indian consumers.	Decided in favour of the investor	Germany
10	2013	KHML v.India	Claims arising out of the cancellation by India's Supreme Court of a telecoms licence held by a company in which the claimant had invested	Pending	Mauritius

(Cont'd)

Table 6.1 *(Cont'd)*

No.	Year of Initiation	Name of the Case	Reason for the Claim	Outcome of Original Proceedings	Home State of Investor
11	2012	Devas v. India	Claims arising out of the alleged Government's cancellation of an agreement to lease capacity in the S-Band, part of the electromagnetic spectrum, for claimants' subsidiary to launch two satellites to provide multimedia services to mobile users across India.	Decided in favour of the investor	Mauritius
12	2012	Tenoch Holdings v. India	Claims arising out of the withdrawal by Indian authorities of an approval to grant frequency allocation licences to claimants' local telecoms company By Cell, after it had previously obtained clearance from India's Foreign Investment Board.	Pending	Russian Federation Cyprus
13	2011	White Industries v. India	Claims arising out of alleged judicial delays by the Government of India that left the claimant unable to enforce an ICC award for over nine years concerning a contractual dispute with Coal India, a State-owned mining	Decided in favour of the Investor	Australia

Source: UNCTAD. n.d. 'Investment Policy Hub', http://investmentpolicyhub.unctad.org/ISDS/CountryCases/96?partyRole=2, updated as of 31 July 2018.

An arbitration tribunal, operating under the International Chamber of Commerce (ICC) rules, in a contractual dispute between White Industries and Coal India (an Indian public sector company), on 27 May 2002 ruled in favor of White Industries.[18] White Industries was entitled to an award of A$4.08 million. Subsequently, on 6 September 2002, Coal India applied to the High Court of Calcutta to have the commercial award set aside under the relevant sections of the Indian Arbitration and Conciliation Act 1996)[19] (set-aside proceedings). Interestingly, White Industries was not made aware of this application until early October 2002.[20] On 11 September 2002, White Industries sought the enforcement of the award in India before the Delhi High Court[21] (enforcement proceedings). Both the proceedings experienced substantial delays. Finally, the enforcement proceedings were stayed pending the decision in the set-aside proceedings.[22] The matter finally went to the Supreme Court of India.[23]

With both, the enforcement and set-aside, proceedings still pending before the courts of India, White Industries initiated a BIT arbitration against India in 2010[24] under the India–Australia BIT.[25] White Industries claimed, *inter alia*, that the inordinate delay in judicial proceedings amounted to a violation of the fair and equitable treatment standard on account of two factors: (1) a denial of justice, and (2) a breach of White Industries' legitimate expectation that India would adhere to the New York Convention's standards on enforcement of

[18] *White Industries* v. *Australia* at 45.

[19] *White Industries* v. *Australia* at 45, p.19.

[20] *White Industries* v. *Australia* at 45, p. 19.

[21] *White Industries* v. *Australia* at 45, p. 19.

[22] *White Industries* v. *Australia* at 45, p. 19, para 11.4.4(v).

[23] For full procedural history of this case see *White Industries* v. *Australia* (n 8) pp. 19–24.

[24] See Ranjan, 'The White Industries Arbitration, p. 13; *See also,*Manu Sanan. 2012. 'The White Industries Award—Shades of Grey', *Journal of World Investment & Trade,* 13:661, 673–4 (hereinafter Sanan, 'The White Industries Award').

[25] Agreement Between the Government of Australia and the Government of the Republic of India on the Promotion and Protection of Investments, (Australia–India) (6 February 1999) 2116 U.N.T.S. 145 [hereinafter Austl.–India BIT Agreement].

foreign arbitral awards.[26] White Industries further argued that it was entitled to 'effective means of asserting claims and enforcing rights,' and that the conduct of the Indian courts had breached that standard.[27] White Industries also alleged that the delay on the part of the Indian courts amounted to an expropriation of its rights under the award.[28]

The tribunal, after examining prior investment arbitration jurisprudence, concluded that the ICC award represented a crystallization of White Industries' rights under a contract and hence could be characterized as part of White Industries' original 'investment' in India.[29] The tribunal dismissed White Industries' claim of a 'legitimate expectation' about Indian courts not entertaining an application to set aside a foreign award, noting that entertaining an application to set aside a foreign award was a regular practice in the Indian legal system, one of which White Industries should have been aware.[30] The tribunal also dismissed White Industries' claim of legitimate expectation that an award would be enforced without delay, citing the report of the law commission of India on delays in the Indian judicial system.[31] The tribunal also dismissed White Industries' allegation of denial of justice after examining all the factors, including India's assertion that the Indian judiciary was overextended due to its large population.[32] In this regard, the tribunal held that while the delays were unsatisfactory, they did not meet the high standards required for establishing a claim of denial of justice.[33] Additionally, the tribunal rejected White Industries' claim of expropriation, noting that the award had not yet been 'taken' or set aside.[34]

6.1.1 The 'Effective Means' standard

The tribunal held India responsible for not providing *White industries* with an 'effective means of asserting claims and enforcing rights'.

[26] See *White Indus. Austl. Ltd.*, at 91–2.
[27] See *White Indus. Austl. Ltd.*, at 105–08.
[28] See *White Indus. Austl. Ltd.*, at 119–21.
[29] See *White Indus. Austl. Ltd.*, at 31–2.
[30] See *White Indus. Austl. Ltd.*, at 94–6.
[31] See *White Indus. Austl. Ltd.*, at 94–6.
[32] See *White Indus. Austl. Ltd.*, at 98–105.
[33] See *White Indus. Austl. Ltd.*, at 105.
[34] See *White Indus. Austl. Ltd.*, at 121.

Although this requirement is not given in the India–Australia BIT, the tribunal held that by virtue of the MFN clause in the India–Australia BIT,[35] White industries could invoke the 'effective means' standard accepted by India under the India–Kuwait BIT.[36] Article 4(5) of the India–Kuwait BIT gives the 'essential means' standard as follows:

> Each Contracting State shall in accordance with its applicable laws and regulations provide effective means of asserting claims and enforcing rights with respect to investments and ensure to investors of the other Contracting State the right of access to its courts of justice, administrative tribunals and agencies, and all other bodies exercising adjudicatory authority ...[37]

In determining the content of the 'effective means' standard, the tribunal relied on the case of *Chevron-Texaco* v. *Ecuador.*[38] The tribunal in *Chevron* had held that under the 'effective means' standard, a distinct and potentially less demanding test is applicable in comparison to denial of justice under customary international law.[39] The tribunal then applied the 'effective means' standard to *White's* claim and came to the conclusion that the inability of the Indian Judiciary to decide *White's* jurisdictional claim (that is, the set-aside proceedings) in over nine years amounts to undue delay.[40] This undue delay, according to the tribunal, breached India's treaty obligation to

[35] Article 4(2) of the India–Australia BIT provides the MFN provision according to which, 'a contracting party shall at all times treat investments in its territory on a basis no less favourable than that accorded to investments or investors of any third country'.

[36] Article 4(2) of the India–Australia BIT provides the MFN provision according to which, 'a contracting party shall at all times treat investments in its territory on a basis no less favourable than that accorded to investments or investors of any third country', paras 11.2.2–11.2.8. Also see discussions in Chapter 4.

[37] India–Kuwait BIT. 'Agreement between The State of Kuwait and The Republic of India for The Encouragement and Reciprocal Protection of Investment' (signed 27 November 2001, entered into force 28 June 2003) art. 4.5.

[38] *Chevron Corporation and Texaco Petroleum Corporation* v. *Ecuador*, UNCITRAL, Partial Award on Merits (30 March 2010).

[39] Id, para 244.

[40] *White Industries* v. *India*, paras 11.4.16 to 11.4.20.

provide to foreign investors 'effective means' of asserting rights and enforcing claims.[41] However, important to note, the tribunal ruled that the delays in enforcement proceedings was not a breach of the effective means standard because White had not exhausted all means available to it to avoid such a delay.[42]

Fali Nariman, one of India's leading jurists, has critiqued the *White Industries* award.[43] Nariman argues that the tribunal, while incorporating the 'effective means' standard given in Article 4(5) of the India–Kuwait BIT overlooked or ignored the following words also given in Article 4(5): 'in accordance with its applicable laws and regulations.'[44] According to Nariman these words mandated 'the tribunal to apply Indian law'; and 'that under India's legal system established under India's written Constitution there is no right or cause of action for any litigant to claim damages for delays in the hearing of cases in Courts'.[45] White Industries award has also been critiqued for its problematic application of the standard laid down in *Chevron* v. *Ecuador*.[46]

Nonetheless, it can be safely said that had White Industries not faced such judicial delays in Indian courts to enforce its legal rights, this case would not have arisen. Judicial interference in arbitration

[41] *White Industries* v. *India*, paras 11.4.16 to 11.4.20. Also see, Jessica Wirth. 2013. '"Effective Means" Means? The Legacy of Chevron v. Ecuador', *Columbia Journal of Transnational Law* 52(1): 326 at 342–5 (hereinafter Wirth, '"Effective Means" Means? The Legacy of Chevron v. Ecuador').

[42] *White Industries* v. *India*, paras 11.4.4 and 11.4.5. Also see, L. Yves Fortier. 2015. *Investor-State Tribunals and National Courts: A Harmony of Spheres? in Practising Virtue: Inside International Arbitration*. Oxford: Oxford University Press, p. 292 at 306.

[43] Fali S. Nariman. 2014. 'Investment Arbitration under the Spotlight – What Next for Asia', https://law.smu.edu.sg/sites/default/files/law/CEBCLA/HSF_Lecture_4_Nov_Lecture_notes_Final_0.pdf, accessed on 24 February 2018 (hereinafter Nariman, 'Investment Arbitration under the Spotlight').

[44] Nariman, 'Investment Arbitration under the Spotlight', p. 39.

[45] Nariman, 'Investment Arbitration under the Spotlight', p. 39.

[46] Nariman, 'Investment Arbitration under the Spotlight', pp. 39–41; Wirth, '"Effective Means" Means?', pp. 348–55; Sanan, 'The White Industries Award'; Sumeet Kachwaha. 2013. 'The White Industries Australia Limited – Indian BIT Award – A Critical Assessment', *Arbitration International* 29: 275–93.

proceedings leads to significant delays in the arbitration process, and eventually negates the benefits of arbitration; and this has been recognized by the law commission of India (LCI) in its 246th report in 2014.[47] The LCI offered two reasons for such delays:

> First, the [Indian] judicial system is over-burdened with work and is not sufficiently efficient to dispose cases, especially commercial cases, with the speed and dispatch that is required. Second, the bar for judicial intervention (despite the existence of section 5 of the [Arbitration and Conciliation] Act) has been consistently set at a low threshold by the Indian judiciary, which translates into many more admissions of cases in Court which arise out of or are related to the Act.[48]

The LCI report then went on to make recommendations for amending the Indian Arbitration and Conciliation Act 1996 so as to ensure that international commercial arbitral awards involving foreign parties are dealt with expeditiously by the Indian courts.[49] As the report shows, the outcome of the White Industries case weighed heavily on LCI's minds in making the above recommendation.[50] The LCI report observed that the White Industries case 'serves as a reminder to the Government to urgently implement reforms to the judicial

[47] Government of India, Law Commission of India, Report No. 246, Amendments to the Arbitration and Conciliation Act 1996, 2014, http://lawcommissionofindia.nic.in/reports/report246.pdf, p. 15, August, accessed on 24 February 2018. The commission was entrusted with the task of reviewing the provisions of the Arbitration and Conciliation Act of 1996.

[48] Government of India, Law Commission of India, Report No. 246, Amendments to the Arbitration and Conciliation Act 1996, 2014, http://lawcommissionofindia.nic.in/reports/report246.pdf, p. 15, August, accessed on 24 February 2018, pp. 15–16.

[49] Government of India, Law Commission of India, Report No. 246, Amendments to the Arbitration and Conciliation Act 1996, 2014, http://lawcommissionofindia.nic.in/reports/report246.pdf, p. 15, August, accessed on 24 February 2018, p. 16.

[50] Government of India, Law Commission of India, Report No. 246, Amendments to the Arbitration and Conciliation Act 1996, 2014, http://lawcommissionofindia.nic.in/reports/report246.pdf, p. 15, August, accessed on 24 February 2018, p. 16. Also important to note that the Arbitration and Conciliation Act 1996 was amended.

system in order to avoid substantial potential liabilities that might accrue from the delays presently inherent in the system'.[51] On the basis of the LCI report, it can be safely said that the White Industries case played a critical role in mainstreaming the problem of judicial delays in dealing with foreign arbitral awards and also ushered in reforms at the domestic level in dealing with this problem.

6.2 ISDS Claims Due to Cancellation of Telecom Licenses

A host of ISDS claims were filed against India for the cancellation of telecom licenses.[52] This relates to the grant of Unified Access Service License (UAS) with second-generation (2G) spectrum (telecom licenses) to telecom companies by the Indian Government in 2008–9. These telecom licenses were not auctioned but were granted by the government on 'first-come-first-serve' basis. A writ petition was filed in the Supreme Court of India arguing that the granting of licenses following the 'first-come-first serve' policy was arbitrary and unconstitutional.[53] The Supreme Court agreed with the petitioners and held that 'there is a fundamental flaw in the first-come-first-serve-policy' because it allows people with access to the power-corridor to benefit over those who don't have such access.[54]

[51] Government of India, Law Commission of India, Report No. 246, Amendments to the Arbitration and Conciliation Act 1996, 2014, http://lawcommissionofindia.nic.in/reports/report246.pdf, p. 15, August, accessed on 24 February 2018, p. 16. Also important to note that the Arbitration and Conciliation Act 1996 was amended.

[52] UNCTAD. n.d. 'India – As Respondent State', http://investmentpolicyhub.unctad.org/ISDS/CountryCases/96?partyRole=2, accessed on 24 February 2018.

[53] This writ petition was filed by the Centre for Public Interest Litigation. See *Centre for Public Interest Litigation and Others* v. *Union of India and others* (2010) Writ Petition Civil No. 423/2010 in the Supreme Court of India 57–59. The argument of the petitioners was that granting licenses following the 'first come first serve' policy violates the principle of equality given in Article 14 of the Indian Constitution.

[54] This writ petition was filed by the Centre for Public Interest Litigation. See *Centre for Public Interest Litigation and Others* v. *Union of India and others* (2010) Writ Petition Civil No. 423/2010 in the Supreme Court of India 57–59.

The Court held that the grant of 2G licenses by the Indian government was 'arbitrary and unconstitutional' and hence all the licenses were illegal.[55] Consequently, the Supreme Court quashed all the 122 2G licenses granted on or after 20 January 2008 by the Department of Telecommunication.[56]

This order not only resulted in the cancellation of telecom licenses owned by Indian telecom companies but also the licenses owned by foreign telecom companies who did not participate in the initial allocation of telecom licenses on a 'first-come-first-serve basis'. For example, Telenor, a Norwegian company whose licenses were cancelled, bought these licenses from an Indian company, Unitech, and played no role either in the policy of allocating licenses or in the license-awarding process.[57] Unitech, after obtaining licence for Rs 1651 crores, sold 60 per cent of equity stake in favour of Telenor Asia, a part of Telenor Group (Norway) for Rs 6,120 crores between

---

The argument of the petitioners was that granting licenses following the 'first come first serve' policy violates the principle of equality given in Article 14 of the Indian Constitution, p. 85.

[55] This writ petition was filed by the Centre for Public Interest Litigation. See *Centre for Public Interest Litigation and Others* v. *Union of India and others* (2010) Writ Petition Civil No. 423/2010 in the Supreme Court of India 57–59. The argument of the petitioners was that granting licenses following the 'first come first serve' policy violates the principle of equality given in Article 14 of the Indian Constitution, p. 85.

[56] This writ petition was filed by the Centre for Public Interest Litigation. See *Centre for Public Interest Litigation and Others* v. *Union of India and others* (2010) Writ Petition Civil No. 423/2010 in the Supreme Court of India 57–59. The argument of the petitioners was that granting licenses following the 'first come first serve' policy violates the principle of equality given in Article 14 of the Indian Constitution, p. 85. See generally, Ranjan and Raju, 'Bilateral Investment Treaties and the Indian Judiciary', pp. 812–13.

[57] Siddharth. 2012. 'Telenor Seeks Arbitration, Claims Damages of $14 Billion from Government in 2G Case', *The Times of India*, 27 March, New Delhi, http://timesofindia.indiatimes.com/business/india-business/Telenor-seeks-arbitration-claims-damages-of-14bn-from-govt-in-2G-case/articleshow/12420404.cms, accessed on 24 February 2018 (hereinafter Siddharth, 'Telenor Seeks Arbitration').

March 2009 and February 2010.[58] Thus, Telenor argued that its investment should not be jeopardized on account of arbitrariness of the Indian State.[59] However, Telenor's lawfully obtained license was also cancelled by the Supreme Court.

The Supreme Court issued the judgment on 2 February 2012 and just six days later, it was predicted that the decision might trigger BIT claims against India.[60] Indeed, subsequent to the cancellation of the 2G licenses many foreign investors issued ISDS claims against India challenging the decision to cancel their spectrum licenses. For instance, in March 2012, it was reported that Telenor issued an ISDS notice to India alleging that cancellation of its licenses by the Supreme Court violates the investment chapter of the India–Singapore FTA.[61] However, later, Telenor announced that it won't pursue ISDS claim against India because the Indian government has allowed Telenor a set-off of 'Rs 16 billion (US$260 million) on payments due under its new spectrum licences by way of credit for the previously cancelled licences'.[62]

Similarly, Sistema, a Russian firm, whose 21 licenses were cancelled, also served a notice to India to commence ISDS proceedings under the India–Russia BIT.[63] In the notice, Sistema argued that

[58] *Centre for Public Interest Litigation and Others* v. *Union of India and others*, Writ Petitions (C) No. 423 of 2010 With No. 10 of 2011, para 44 (ii).

[59] See *Centre for Public Interest Litigation and Others* v. *Union of India and others*, Writ Petitions (C) No. 423 Of 2010 With No. 10 Of 2011, para 44 (ii).

[60] Prabhash Ranjan. 2012. 'Abroad Spectrum', *Indian Express*, 8 February, New Delhi, http://indianexpress.com/article/opinion/columns/abroad-spectrum/, accessed on 24 February 2018.

[61] http://www.thehindubusinessline.com/industry-and-economy/info-tech/article3155481.eceHINDU BUS. LINE Arun S. & Thomas K. Thomas, *2G Mess: Telenor May Invoke India-Singapore Bilateral Pact*; See Siddharth, 'Telenor Seeks Arbitration'.

[62] Herbert Smith Freehills. 2014. 'A BIT More Indian Investment Arbitration', https://hsfnotes.com/arbitration/2014/05/16/a-bit-more-indian-investment-arbitration/, 16 May, accessed on 24 February 2018.

[63] Fe Bureau. 2012. 'Fix Dispute in 6 months or face arbitration, Sistema Tells India', *Financial Express*, 29 February, New Delhi, http://www.financialexpress.com/news/fix-dispute-in-6-months-or-face-arbitration-sistema-tells-india/918076/0, accessed on 25 February 2018 (hereinafter Bureau, 'Fix

cancellation of its licenses following the investment of billions of dollars in the Indian telecommunication sector is contrary to India's obligations under the India–Russia BIT, including obligations like the non-expropriation of investments and the provision of full protection and security for the investment.[64]

Khaitan Holdings Mauritius Limited (KHML), another foreign investor whose 21 licenses were cancelled by the Supreme Court, issued an arbitration notice to India challenging the cancellation of its telecommunication licenses under the India–Mauritius BIT[65] (see Table 6.1). Khaitan Holdings Mauritius Limited has claimed a compensation of US$1400 million from the India.[66] Khaitan Holdings Mauritius Limited and India have nominated an arbitrator. However, the president of the tribunal has still not been appointed.[67]

These ISDS notices by telecom companies triggered a discussion in the Indian government on the interface between Indian BITs and India's judiciary.[68] The then attorney general of India stated that

---

Dispute in 6 months or face arbitration, Sistema Tells India'); Shauvik Ghosh. 2012. 'Sistema Sends a Notice to Govt', *Live Mint*, 29 February, New Delhi, http://www.livemint.com/Home-Page/Z1vlvjEkWXCj52YBjRapQJ/2G-Licences-Sistema-sends-notice-to-govt.html, accessed on 25 February 2018 (hereinafter Ghosh, 'Sistema Sends a Notice to Govt').

[64] Ghosh, 'Sistema Sends a Notice to Govt'. Specifically on Sistema's ISDS claim against India. See Sanya Malhotra. 2013. 'Cancellation ofTelecom Licenses in the 2G Case: Claim for Indirect Exprorpaition' *NUJS Law Review* 6 (2): 335.

[65] Bureau, 'Fix Dispute in 6 months or face arbitration, Sistema Tells India'; PTI. 2013. '2G Scam: Loop Investor Files International Arbitration Against Centre', New Delhi, https://www.thehindu.com/business/Industry/2g-scam-loop-investor-files-intl-arbitration-against-centre/article5189682.ece, 1 October, accessed on 25 February 2018; Shauvik Ghosh. 2012. 'Sistema Sends a Notice to Govt', http://www.livemint.com/Home-Page/Z1vlvjEkWXCj52YBjRapQJ/2G-Licences--Sistema-sends-notice-to-govt.html, 29 February, accessed on 25 February 2018.

[66] *KHML* v. *India*, 2013, http://investmentpolicyhub.unctad.org/ISDS/Details/553, accessed on 25 February 2018.

[67] *KHML* v. *India*, 2013, http://investmentpolicyhub.unctad.org/ISDS/Details/553, accessed on 25 February 2018.

[68] *KHML* v. *India*, 2013, http://investmentpolicyhub.unctad.org/ISDS/Details/553, accessed on 25 February 2018.

foreign telecommunication companies cannot claim damages from the Indian government under various BITs for losses emanating out of Supreme Court orders because court orders do not constitute a cause of action against the government.[69] It was also argued that the claim of damages by foreign investors is based on a complete misunderstanding of the constitutional provision prevailing in India, which recognizes separation of powers between the executive, judiciary, and legislature.[70] In other words, the attorney general made two related arguments: first, only executive actions, not judicial actions, can violate a BIT; second, one can have recourse to the domestic legal system to find out whether an international legal claim can be made. However, some in the Indian government did not agree with the former attorney general on this point. For example, the Indian Ministry of External Affairs argued that, for the purposes of international law, the Indian State is one entity: that is, actions of any organ of the state are attributable to India.[71]

[69] Thomas K. Thomas, 2012. 'Foreign Players Cannot Invoke Bilateral Treaties: Attorney-General', *Hindu Business Line,* http://www.thehindubusinessline.com/industry-and-economy/info-tech/article3764819.ece, 13 August, accessed on 25 February 2018.

[70] *Report of the Commission to the General Assembly on the Work of its Fifty-Third Session, Draft Articles on Responsibility of States for Internationally Wrongful Acts,* 56 U.N. GAOR Supp. No. 10, art. 4(1), U.N. Doc.A/56/10 (2001), *reprinted in* [2001] 2 Y.B. INT'L L. COMM'N 26, U.N. Doc.A/CN.4/SER.A/2001/Add.1 [hereinafter *Draft Articles on Responsibility*].

[71] Anandita Singh Mankotia. 2012. 'Notice by Sistema Not Relevant As SC Cancelled Licences, Not Government, Says AG, *Financial Express*, 23 May, New Delhi, http://www.financialexpress.com/news/notice-by-sistema-not-relevant-as-sc-cancelled-licences-not-govt-says-ag/952533, accessed on 24 February 2018; Joji Thomas Philip. 2012. 'AG Reiterates That 2G Investors Can't Seek Damages Under BIPA', *Economic Times*, 5 December, New Delhi, http://economictimes.indiatimes.com/news/news-by-industry/telecom/ag-reiterates-that-2g-investors-cant-seek-damages-under-bipa/articleshow/17496788.cms, accessed on 25 February 2018. At a conceptual level, this line of argument might also suggest that judicial actions of courts are not part of the actions of the Indian State. This would be quite misleading, however, because the Indian Constitution, although it does not expressly vest judicial power in the Supreme Court or other courts, clearly recognizes the division of three main functions of the state with the judicial power of the Indian state vesting in India's courts.

The general rule in international law is that conduct of the organs of the state or of those who have acted under the direction, instigation, or control of those organs ('agents' of the state) is attributable to a state.[72] Article 4(1) of the ILC Draft Articles on State Responsibility states as follows: The conduct of any state organ shall be considered an act of that state under international law, whether the organ exercises legislative, executive, judicial, or any other functions, whatever position it holds in the organization of the state, and whatever its character as an organ of the central government or of a territorial unit of the state.[73]

The International Law Commission thereby brings judicial organs within the purview of those organs, the conduct of which can result in the violation of a state's international obligations.[74] This codifies a broadly recognized principle of customary law.[75] The commentary on the ILC Articles of State Responsibility clearly states that the reference to 'state' in Article 4 is not limited to the organs of the central

---

Kumar v. India, (1997) 2 S.C.R. 1186; see also Singh, Mahendra Pal, V.N. Shukla's Constitution of India 472 (stating that judicial power of the state vests in the courts or the judiciary). As a result, exercise of judicial power by the courts is an exercise of state power by the Indian state. 'Foreign Telcos Can't Claim Damages from Government in 2G Case: AG', NDTV PROFIT, 5 December 2012, 8:36 PM, http://profit.ndtv.com/news/corporates/article-foreign-telcos-cant-claim-damages-from-government-in-2g-case-ag-314309.

[72] Ian Brownlie. 1983. *System of the Law of Nations: State Responsibility: Part 1*. Oxford: Oxford University Press, pp. 132–3.

[73] *Report of the Commission to the General Assembly on the Work of its Fifty-Third Session, Draft Articles on Responsibility of States for Internationally Wrongful Acts*, 56 U.N. GAOR Supp. No. 10, art. 4(1), U.N. Doc.A/56/10 (2001), *reprinted in* [2001] 2 Y.B. INT'L L. COMM'N 26, U.N. Doc.A/CN.4/SER.A/2001/Add.1 (hereinafter *Draft Articles on Responsibility*).

[74] *Report of the Commission to the General Assembly on the Work of its Fifty-Third Session, Draft Articles on Responsibility of States for Internationally Wrongful Acts*, 56 U.N. GAOR Supp. No. 10, art. 4(1), U.N. Doc.A/56/10 (2001), *reprinted in* [2001] 2 Y.B. INT'L L. COMM'N 26, U.N. Doc.A/CN.4/SER.A/2001/Add.1 (hereinafter *Draft Articles on Responsibility*).

[75] Malcolm N. Shaw. 2008. *International Law*, 6th edition. Cambridge: Cambridge University Press, pp. 786–7.

government.[76] It also specifies that the reference to 'state' in Article 4 'extends to organs of government of whatever kind or classification, exercising whatever functions, and at whatever level in the hierarchy, including those at provincial or even local level. No distinction is made for this purpose between legislative, executive or judicial organs.'[77] This clearly shows that the actions of the judiciary are very much a part of the actions of the state, and hence the judiciary can also be the source of an internationally wrongful act.[78] Indeed, there have been several instances of claims being brought against the conduct of a State's judicial organs, both under general international law and under international investment, before international courts and tribunals.[79]

Thus, the Attorney General, as opposed to the ministry of external affairs, was incorrect in arguing that foreign telecom companies could not challenge actions of the Indian judiciary under BITs. Another interesting aspect of the Supreme Court's decision on the 2G case is that there is nothing in the decision to show that the apex court considered India's BIT obligations before reaching its decision. The outcome of some of the BIT claims is awaited.

[76] *Draft Articles on State Responsibility.*

[77] *Draft Articles on State Responsibility.*

[78] *Draft Articles on State Responsibility.* Also see Difference Relating to Immunity from Legal Process of a Special Rapporteur of the Commission on Human Rights, Advisory Opinion, 1999 I.C.J. 62, 87 (29 April); Certain German Interests in Polish Upper Silesia (*Ger.* v. *Pol.*), 1926 P.C.I.J. (ser. A) No. 7, at 19 (25 May); Rosa Gelbtrunk (El Sal./U.S.), 15 R.I.A.A. 455, 477 (1902). Ian Brownlie. 2008. *Principles of Public International Law*, 7th edition. p. 451. Oxford: Oxford University Press.

[79] *S.S. Lotus (France* v. *Turkey),* 1927 P.C.I.J. (ser. A) No. 10, *Barcelona Traction Light and Power Company (Belgium* v. *Spain),* (New Application: 1962, Second Phase), 1970 ICJ REP.3; *Saipem Spa* v. *The People's Republic of Bangladesh,* ICSID Case No ARB/05/07 (Decision on Jurisdiction), para. 143; *Azinian* v. *Mexico,* Award of November 1, 1999, 5 ICSID Rep. 269, paras 97–105 (2002); *Middle East Shipping Cement Ltd* v. *Egypt,* 7 ICSID Rep 178, para 139. See also *Rumeli* v. *Kazakhstan,* ICSID Case No. ARB/05/16, Award, 29 July 2008 para 704. Also see Ranjan and Raju, 'Bilateral Investment Treaties and the Indian Judiciary'.

6.3 ISDS Cases Due to Cancellation of Spectrum Licenses

Two ISDS claims, *Devas* v. *India*[80] and *Deutsche Telekom* v. *India*[81], were brought against India for the cancellation of an agreement concerning the provision of broadband services to consumers in India. Specifically, the *Devas* v. *India*[82] dispute arose when the government cancelled an agreement signed in 2005 between Antrix, the marketing arm of the ISRO, a government entity, with Devas Multimedia, a multimedia services provider.[83] As per this agreement, Antrix was supposed to provide 70 MHz of S-band satellite spectrum to Devas for providing multimedia services to mobile users across India.[84] On 16 March 2006, CC/Devas and Telcom Devas made a first round of investment of approximately US$ 7.5 million each.[85] A second round of investment, of approximately the same amount, was made on 18 June 2007.[86] Soon Devas also secured the licences to deliver internet services throughout India.[87] As per the agreement between Devas and Antrix, the statelites were to be launched by June 2009. However, Antrix failed to meet the deadline but promised that the launch would take place by the end of 2009 or early 2010.[88] Notwitstanding these delays, the claimants continued meeting their financial obligations and other requirements.[89] However, on 2 July 2010, the Indian Space Commission decided to annul the agreement

[80] *CC/Devas (Mauritius) Ltd., Devas Employees Mauritius Private Limited, and Telcom Devas Mauritius Limited* v. *Republic of India,* PCA Case No. 2013-09 (Devas v India, PCA). For more on this case also see *Devas* v. *India,* http://investmentpolicyhub.unctad.org/ISDS/Details/484, accessed on 25 February 2018.

[81] *Deutsche Telekom* v. *India* (2013) http://investmentpolicyhub.unctad.org/ISDS/Details/550, accessed on 25 February 2018.

[82] Also see Chapters 4 and 5.

[83] See *Devas* v. *India,* http://investmentpolicyhub.unctad.org/ISDS/Details/484, accessed on 25 February 2018.

[84] *Devas v. India,* http://investmentpolicyhub.unctad.org/ISDS/Details/484, accessed on 25 February 2018.

[85] *Devas* v. *India,* para 107.

[86] *Devas* v. *India,* para 108.

[87] *Devas* v. *India,* para 109.

[88] *Devas* v. *India,* para 110.

[89] *Devas* v. *India,* para 111.

in view of the alleged increasing need of the military for the S Band spectrum.[90] This decision to annul the contract was announced by ISRO on 8 February 2011.[91] Finally, on 17 February 2011, the cabinet committee on security[92] (CCS) annulled the Antrix-Devas contract.[93]

Interestingly, the decision of the Space commission to annul the contract, taken on 2 July 2010 was not conveyed to the claimants, despite many meetings, between the government officials and Devas' representatives.[94] The claimants learnt about the decision only on 8 February 2011, when it was publicly announced.[95] The press release said,

> taking note of the fact that Government policies with regard to allocation of spectrum have undergone a change in the last few years and there has been an increased demand for allocation of spectrum for national needs, including for the needs of defence, para-military forces, railways and other public utility services as well as for societal needs, and having regard to the needs of the country's strategic requirements, the Government will not be able to provide orbit slot in S band to Antrix for commercial activities, including for those which are the subject matter of existing contractual obligations for S band. In the light of this policy of not providing orbit slot in S Band to Antrix for commercial activities, the 'Agreement for the lease of space segment capacity on ISRO/Antrix S-Band spacecraft by Devas Multimedia Pvt. Ltd.' entered into between Antrix Corporation and Devas Multimedia Pvt. Ltd. on 28th January, 2005 shall be annulled forthwith.[96]

[90] *Devas* v. *India*, PCA, para 468.

[91] *Devas* v. *India*, PCA, para 142.

[92] CCS is a select Cabinet committee that, among other matters, deals with all defence-related issues and comprises the prime minister, the minister of home affairs, the minister of external affairs, the minister of finance, and the minister of defence of the Indian government.

[93] Press Information Bureau, Government of India, Cabinet. 2011. 'CCS Decides to Annul Antrix-Devas Deal', http://pib.nic.in/newsite/PrintRelease.aspx?relid=69856 (Devas Press Release), 17 February, accessed on 25 February 2018 (hereinafter Press Information Bureau, 'CCS Decides to Annul Antrix-Devas Deal').

[94] Press Information Bureau, 'CCS Decides to Annul Antrix-Devas Deal'.

[95] Press Information Bureau, 'CCS Decides to Annul Antrix-Devas Deal'.

[96] Press Information Bureau, 'CCS Decides to Annul Antrix-Devas Deal'.

In other words, as the Devas tribunal held, from 2 July 2010 till 8 February 2011, the claimants were 'completely left in the dark' about the space commission's decision and the alleged growing needs of the military about the spectrum and its potential impact on the agreement.[97] The Devas Multimedia tribunal held that India's conduct constitutes a clear breach of the simple good faith required under international law and under the FET provision of the India–Mauritius BIT.[98] Therefore, the tribunal held that India is liable for this wrongful behaviour and must compensate the claimants for damages suffered from 2 July 2010 to 17 February 2011, the date of the CCS decision.[99]

The tribunal by majority held that the CCS decision of 2011 that reserved a part of the spectrum for defence and para military forces can be classified as being 'directed to the protection of its essential security interests'.[100] Though, according to the tribunal by majority, the same cannot be said about the decision to take back the spectrum for public utility services and other societal needs that are not 'essential security interests'.[101]

However, one arbitrator, David Haigh, dissented.[102] Arbitrator Haigh held that the CCS did not make a decision as to who would get the spectrum that was to be taken back from Devas.[103] This was to be decided by another body called the INSAT Co-ordination Committee (ICC).[104] As the press release of 17 February 2011 shows the reason offered to take the spectrum back ranged from needs of defence and para-military forces to public utility services and societal needs. Thus, according to Arbitrator Haigh, since the eventual

[97] Thomas K. Thomas. 2016. 'Antrix-Devas Case: Words that Lost India the Battle of The Hague', *The Hindu Business Line*, 6 September, New Delhi, http://www.thehindubusinessline.com/news/antrixdevas-case-words-that-lost-india-the-battle-of-the-hague/article9077293.ece, accessed on 25 February 2018.

[98] *Devas* v. *India*, PCA para 470.

[99] *Devas* v. *India*, PCA para 470. Also see Chapters 4 and 5.

[100] *Devas* v. *India*, para 354. Also see Chapter 5.

[101] *Devas* v. *India*, para 354. Also see Chapter 5.

[102] *Devas* v. *India*, Dissenting Opinion of David R. Haigh.

[103] *Devas* v. *India*, Dissenting Opinion of David R. Haigh, para 95.

[104] *Devas* v. *India*, Dissenting Opinion of David R. Haigh, para 89.

purpose of taking back the spectrum was either undertermined or was for multiple purposes, the CCS decision was not 'directed to' attaining the objective of 'essential security interest'.[105] Moreover, Arbitrator Haigh held that even three-and-half years after the CCS took the decision to withdraw the spectrum from and annul the agreements, no decision has been taken about the use of the spectrum, that is, whether it will be used for defence purposes, or for other societal needs.[106]

This case shows that the reason behind the adverse ISDS award against India was India's failure to follow due process in taking decisions and to act transparently vis-à-vis the foreign investor—a behaviour that adversely impacted the foreign investors. The fact that India acted in 'wilful disregard of due process of law' was also the conclusion that the tribunal in *Deutshe Telekom* v. *India*, deciding on similar facts, reached.[107]

6.4 ISDS Cases Due to Imposition of Taxes Retrospectively

Some foreign corporations such as Vodafone and Cairn Energy have brought cases against India due to imposition of taxes retrospectively (see Table 6.1). We discuss the cases brought by both these corporations one by one.

6.4.1 *Vodafone* v. *India*

In December 2006, Vodafone BV International (Vodafone's Netherland entity) entered into an agreement with Hutchison Telecommunications International Ltd (HTIL—a Cayman Island company) to buy HTIL's share of 67 per cent interest in an Indian company Hutchison Essar Ltd (HEL) for US$ 11 billion.[108] Subsequent to this transaction, the Indian tax authorities slapped a

[105] *Devas* v. *India*, Dissenting Opinion of David R. Haigh, para 98.

[106] *Devas* v. *India*, Dissenting Opinion of David R. Haigh, para 92.

[107] *Deutsche Telekom* v. *India*, para 389.

[108] T.P. Oswal and Manoj Solanki. 2010. 'The Vodafone Tax Dispute – A Landmark Judgment of the Bombay High Court', November, http://wwww.bcasonline.org/articles/artin.asp?961, accessed on 27 February 2018.

capital gains tax of US$ 2.2 billion on Vodafone.[109] Vodafone contended that the transactions did not involve a capital asset situated in India and hence no capital gains tax was payable. Whereas the Indian tax authorities contended that Vodafone's income is taxable under Section 9 of the Indian Income Tax Act, 1961 that makes income deemed to accrue or arise in India taxable.

The matter went to the Bombay High Court, which decided the case against Vodafone in 2010.[110] Vodafone challenged the decision of the Bombay High Court in the Supreme Court of India. The Supreme Court reversed the Bombay High Court ruling and held that Vodafone didn't owe any tax to the Indian government.[111] The Supreme Court held that the transfer of shares of a Cayman Islands company would not be subject to capital gains tax in India, under Section 9 of the Income Tax Act, as it stood then, since the shares of the Cayman Islands company were not located in India.[112] The Supreme Court also held that Section 195 of the Income Tax

[109] 2014. 'Vodafone Seeks Arbitration in India Tax Dispute', BBC News, 8 May, http://www.bbc.com/news/business-27321208, accessed on 27 February 2018. Also see Mahdev Mohan. 2016. 'Asian Perspectives on Investment Agreements and Arbitration', in *Yearbook on International Investment Law and Policy 2014*-15, Andrea K. Bjorklund (ed.), p. 317 at 333. Oxford: Oxford University Press.

[110] *Vodafone International Holdings B.V.* v. *Union of India (3 December 2008). Writ Petition No 2550 of 2007* https://indiankanoon.org/doc/1190473/, accessed on 27 February 2018. For more information related to the application of the Indian tax law on Vodafone BV, see Kumkum Sen. 2010. 'Vodafone Ruling: A Step Back in Investor Relations, *Business Standard* 13 September, http://www.business-standard.com/india/news/vodafone-rulingstep-back-in-investor-relations/407859/, accessed on 27 February 2018.

[111] *Vodafone International Holdings BV* v. *Union of India*, Civil Appeal No. 733 of 2012, 20 January 2012, In the Supreme Court of India, https://indiankanoon.org/doc/115852355/ (*Vodafone* v. *Union of India*, Supreme Court, 2012), accessed on 27 February 2018.

[112] *Vodafone International Holdings BV* v. *Union of India*, Civil Appeal No. 733 of 2012, 20 January 2012, In the Supreme Court of India, https://indiankanoon.org/doc/115852355/ (*Vodafone* v. *Union of India*, Supreme Court, 2012), accessed on 27 February 2018 (hereinafter *Vodafone International Holdings* v. *India*).

Act, as it stood then, was not applicable to the transaction between Vodafone and HTIL.[113] Section 195 puts an obligation on a payer to deduct tax at source from the payments made to non-residents if such payment is taxable under the Act.[114] The court held that since the transaction between Vodafone and HTIL was a case of 'outright sale' between two non-residents for a capital asset situated outside India, there was no obligation to deduct tax at source.[115] Accordingly, the court concluded that the Indian tax authority 'had no territorial tax jurisdiction to tax the said offshore transaction'.[116]

Interestingly, the Supreme Court gave a subtle but clear message to the Indian government on the importance of certainty and stability in the fiscal system for foreign investors. The court observed that 'FDI flows towards location with a strong governance infrastructure which includes enactment of laws and how well the legal system works. Certainty is integral to rule of law. Certainty and stability form the basic foundation of any fiscal system. Tax policy certainty is crucial for taxpayers (including foreign investors) to make rational economic choices in the most efficient manner'.[117]

After the ruling of the highest court of the land, it was believed that the last word had been said on this prolonged and complex tax battle. However, the battle had just begun. No sooner had the Supreme Court given its decision, the government of the day moved a bill in the parliament to amend the Income Tax Act.[118] The bill

[113] *Vodafone* v. *Union of India*, Supreme Court, 2012.

[114] Section 195(1) of the Income Tax Act, states: Any person responsible for paying to a non-resident, not being a company, or to a foreign company, any interest (not being interest referred to in section 194LB or section 194LC) or section 194LD or any other sum chargeable under the provisions of this Act (not being income chargeable under the head 'Salaries') shall, at the time of credit of such income to the account of the payee or at the time of payment thereof in cash or by the issue of a cheque or draft or by any other mode, whichever is earlier, deduct income-tax thereon at the rates in force.

[115] *Vodafone* v. *Union of India*, Supreme Court, 2012.

[116] *Vodafone* v. *Union of India*, Supreme Court, 2012.

[117] *Vodafone* v. *Union of India*, Supreme Court, 2012.

[118] The Finance Bill, 2012, Bill No. 11 of 2012, as Introduced in the Lok Sabha, http://164.100.24.219/BillsTexts/LSBillTexts/asintroduced/Finance%20Bill,%20Eng.pdf, accessed on 27 February 2018, (hereinafter Finance Bill, 2012).

amended Sections 9 and 195 of the Income Tax Act, not just to clarify that Vodafone-kind of offshore transactions are taxable, but also to make this clarification have retrospective application from 1 April 1962, that is, from the date on which the Indian Income tax had been enacted.[119] The bill, making an indirect but clear reference to the Supreme Court's Vodafone decision, said that some judicial pronouncements have created doubts about the scope and purpose of sections 9 and 195 of the Income Tax Act.[120] Therefore, the finance bill 2012 said that 'there is a need to provide clarificatory retrospective amendment to restate the legislative intent in respect of scope and applicability of sections 9 and 195 and also to make other clarificatory amendments for providing certainty in law'.[121] It was quite evident that these amendments were aimed at achieving two objectives: first, overrule the Supreme Court decision's on Vodafone; second, target Vodafone to pay taxes,[122] which even the highest court of the land believed, it didn't owe. The retrospective application of Sections 9 and 195 legalized the tax demand on Vodafone that was struck down by the apex court.

This retrospective legislative change attracted considerable attention and criticism,[123] with some commentators using terms like 'tax terrorism' to describe amendment of tax laws retrospectively.[124] An

[119] See Clause 4, Explanation 5 of the Finance Bill 2012 aimed at amending the Indian Income Tax Act, available at http://indiabudget.nic.in/ub2012-13/fb/bill31.pdf. The Finance bill 2012 added Explanations 4 and 5 to Section 9(1)(i), Explanation 2 to Section 2(47), and Explanation 2 to Section 195(1) of the Income Tax Act, 1961 to make the application of the laws retrospective in nature.

[120] Finance Bill, 2012, p. 19.

[121] Finance Bill, 2012, p. 19.

[122] Prabhash Ranjan. 2012. 'Measured Steps', 16 April, *Indian Express*, http://indianexpress.com/article/opinion/columns/measured-steps/, accessed on 27 February 2018.

[123] Gurcharan Das. 2012. 'The Government is not above the Rule of Law', https://blogs.timesofindia.indiatimes.com/men-and-ideas/the-government-is-not-above-the-rule-of-law/, 8 April, accessed on 27 February 2018.

[124] Surjit Bhalla. 2015. 'No Proof Required: Legacy of Tax Terrorism', 15 May, *Indian Express*, http://indianexpress.com/article/opinion/columns/no-proof-required-legacy-of-tax-terrorism/.

economic commentator criticising the government's efforts to amend the tax laws retrospectively observed very appropriately as follows:

> The nadir of the Manmohan Singh government's regime was reached when it finally decided to destroy India's reputation as a country ruled by laws, not by whimsical tyrants. Having lost a case in the supreme court, the government retrospectively amended a tax law laughably and untruthfully arguing that the new attempt at fiscal plunder was actually the intent of the parliamentarians of 1961![125]

Worried about the fallout of this legislative change, the then Prime Minister of India, Manmohan Singh, constituted an expert committee, under the leadership of Parthasarathi Shome, to look into the language and scope of the amendments.[126] This move was quite bizarre as it was Prime Minister Singh's finance minister, Pranab Mukherjee, who had mooted the amendments discussed above in his budget. Sanjaya Baru, Prime Minister Singh's press secretary, claims that the Prime Minister, till the day before Pranab Mukherjee was to present the budget proposing amendment to tax laws retrospectively, was not even aware of this move that would have disastrous consequences for investor sentiment.[127]

The Shome committee too was critical of the retrospective change and observed that 'the legislation with retrospective application in particular obviating an earlier Supreme Court decision on the matter of indirect transfer was not expected and thus perceived in negative light'.[128] The committee said that retrospective application of tax law should occur in rarest of rare cases and only after exhaustive and transparent consultations with stakeholders who would be affected.[129]

[125] Jaithirth Rao. 2017. 'Whither India's Economic Reforms?', in *India Now and in Transition*, Atul K. Thakur (ed.). New Delhi: Niyogi Books, p. 215 at 220.

[126] Draft Report on Retrospective Amendments Relating to Indirect Transfer Expert Committee. 2012.http://www.incometaxindia.gov.in/Lists/Press%20Releases/Attachments/21/Draft_Report.pdf (Shome Committee 2012), accessed on 27 February 2018.

[127] Sanjaya Baru. 2014. *The Accidental Prime Minister*. New Delhi: Penguin.

[128] Shome Committee 2012.

[129] Shome Committee 2012.

6.4.1.1 *Vodafone* v. *India (I)*

As soon as the government proposed an amendment to the Income tax law, Vodafone, on 17 April 2012, issued a notice to the Indian government announcing its intent to challenge the changes in the tax laws retrospectively under the India–Netherlands BIT.[130] Since the conciliatory proceedings between Vodafone and the Indian government failed, on 17 April 2014, Vodafone served a notice of arbitration to India under the India–Netherlands BIT alleging that the retrospective application of tax laws violates India's obligations under the treaty.[131] India dragged its feet on the appointment of arbitrators contending that taxation matters are outside the jurisdiction of BIT arbitration tribunals. Finally, after Vodafone requested the International Court of Justice (ICJ) to intervene,[132] an arbitration tribunal was constituted in June 2016,[133] which is currently hearing jurisdictional objections raised by India.[134] The administering institution is the Permanent Court of Arbitration, which is hearing the case under the UNCITRAL arbitration rules.[135]

When India elected a new government in May 2014, under the leadership of Prime Minister Narendra Modi of the Bharatiya Janta Party (BJP) with a clear majority in the parliament, it was widely believed that the new government will dump the retrospective changes made to the Income Tax act by the previous government. Indeed, the BJP, in its election manifesto for the 2014 general elections, had

[130] 2017. 'Vodafone Announces Results for the Year Ended on 31 March 2017', 16 May (Vodafone), http://www.vodafone.com/content/dam/vodafone/investors/financial_results_feeds/preliminary_results_31march2017/dl_prelim2017.pdf, p. 22.

[131] 'Vodafone Announces Results for the Year Ended on 31 March 2017'. Vodafone International Holdings BV v. India, (PCA Case No. 2016-35), UNCTIRAL (17 April 2014) http://investmentpolicyhub.unctad.org/ISDS/Details/581 (*Vodafone* v. *India* (I)).

[132] Vodafone moves ICJ over tax arbitration with India, (29 March, 2016) https://www.thehindu.com/business/Industry/Vodafone-moves-ICJ-over-tax-arbitration-with-India/article14181636.ece.

[133] Vodafone (2017); *Vodafone* v. *India* (I).

[134] Vodafone (2017).

[135] *Vodafone* v. *India* (I).

criticised the Manmohan Singh government for unleashing 'tax-terrorism', which had negatively impacted investor sentiment.[136]

Prime Minister Modi's finance minister, Arun Jaitely, in his budget speech of 10 July 2014 said the following on retrospective taxation:

> The sovereign right of the Government to undertake retrospective legislation is unquestionable. However, this power has to be exercised with extreme caution and judiciousness keeping in mind the impact of each such measure on the economy and the overall investment climate. This Government will not ordinarily bring about any change retrospectively which creates a fresh liability. Hon'ble Members are aware that consequent upon certain retrospective amendments to the Income Tax Act 1961 undertaken through the Finance Act2012, a few cases have come up in various courts and other legal fora. These cases are at different stages of pendency and will naturally reach their logical conclusion. At this juncture I would like to convey to this August House and also the investors community at large that we are committed to provide a stable and predictable taxation regime that would be investor friendly and spur growth.[137]

In other words, while the Modi government said that extreme caution and judiciousness should be exercised in amending tax laws retrospectively, it stopped short of amending the law and making Sections 9 and 195 of the Income Tax Act prospective in nature. Instead, it has relentlessly pursued the case demanding money from Vodafone[138] and even from HTIL.[139]

[136] BJP. 2014. 'BJP, Election Manifesto', http://www.bjp.org/images/pdf_2014/full_manifesto_english_07.04.2014.pdf, page 27, accessed on 27 February 2018.

[137] Arun Jaitely. 2014. 'Budget Speech 2014-15', 10 July, http://www.indiabudget.gov.in/budget2014-2015/ub2014-15/bs/bs.pdf, page 4, accessed on 27 February 2018.

[138] PTI. 2016. 'Vodafone gets I-T Reminder to Pay Up Rs 14,200-crore Tax Dues', *The Indian Express*, 16 February, http://indianexpress.com/article/india/india-news-india/vodafone-income-tax-department-modi/, accessed on 27 February 2018.

[139] ET Bureau. 2017. 'Income Tax Department Seeks Rs 32,320 crore from Hutchison over Vodafone Deal', *The Economic Times*, 30 August, https://economictimes.indiatimes.com/news/economy/policy/income-tax-department-imposes-rs-7900-crore-penalty-on-vodafone-for-tax-dues/articleshow/60273810.cms, accessed on 27 February 2018

In the 2016 budget, the Modi government, once again, reiterated its commitment to provide a stable and predictable taxation regime,[140] but, again, stopped short of amending the law to do away with the changes made by the Finance Act, 2012. Instead, the government offered an olive branch to companies like Vodafone: a one-time scheme of dispute resolution.[141] As part this scheme government said that it would not raise a tax demand subject to companies like Vodafone and Cairn Energy agreeing to withdraw ongoing ISDS claims; and settle the case by paying only the tax arrears, and that if they so, then, interest liability and penalty shall be waived.[142] A proposal such as this shows that, on the one hand, the Modi government claims that it does not believe in retrospective taxation in principle, on the other hand, it won't mind collecting the money due from the application of tax law retrospectively. However, Vodafone rejected this offer as it believes that it didn't owe any tax, as the law stood, when it bought 67 per cent stake in HEL from HTIL—a belief that was attested by the highest court of India.[143]

6.4.1.2 Vodafone v. *India (II)*

While the BIT arbitration under the India–Netherlands BIT was still pending, Vodafone, served a notice of dispute on 15 June 2015 followed by a notice of arbitration on January 24, 2017, under the India–UK BIT challenging the imposition of the same multi-billion dollar tax bill arising out of the retrospective amendment.[144] Upon receiving the notice, the Indian government knocked the doors of the Delhi High Court, seeking an order to restrain Vodafone

[140] Arun Jaitely. 2016. 'Budget Speech 2016-17', 29 February, http://www.indiabudget.gov.in/budget2016-2017/ub2016-17/bs/bs.pdf page 31, accessed on 27 February 2018 (hereinafter Jaitely, 'Budget Speech 2016-17').

[141] Jaitely, 'Budget Speech 2016-17'.

[142] Jaitely, 'Budget Speech 2016-17'.

[143] Suchetana Ray. 2016. 'Vodafone ignores tax settlement offer, to continue arbitration', *Hindustan Times*, 28 May, https://www.hindustantimes.com/business/vodafone-ignores-tax-settlement-offer-to-continue-arbitration/story-egoIcgPb18bppD7VuHO70J.html, accessed on 27 February 2018.

[144] *Vodafone Group Plc and Vodafone Consolidated Holdings Limited* v. *India (II)* (2017) http://investmentpolicyhub.unctad.org/ISDS/Details/819, accessed on 27 February 2018.

from initiating a parallel BIT proceeding on the same issue before another BIT tribunal citing 'abuse of process'. As Emmanuel Gaillard argues, 'abuse of process' in BIT arbitration 'does not violate any hard and fast legal rule' but 'nonetheless causes significant prejudice to the party against whom it is aimed and can undermine the fair and orderly resolution of disputes by international arbitration'.[145] For example, a foreign investor filing multiple arbitral proceedings against a country, on the same issue, before different arbitral tribunals in order to maximize her chances of success could amount to 'abuse of process';[146] or when a foreign investor seeks to secure jurisdiction of a BIT arbitration tribunal when a dispute is foreseeable but may not have crystalized.[147]

The Delhi High Court obliged the government by issuing an *ex parte* interim order on 22 August 2017, restraining the Vodafone Group from pursuing arbitration under the India–UK BIT.[148] This was followed by an order of Delhi High Court on 26 October 2017,[149] clarifying that the representatives/counsel for the parties were free to participate in the proceedings for appointment of a presiding arbitrator. The Indian government challenged this order of the Delhi High Court in the Supreme Court. The Apex court on

[145] Emmanuel Gaillard. 2017. 'Abuse of Process in International Arbitration', *ICSID Review - Foreign Investment Law Journal* 32 (1): 17–37.

[146] See *Ampal American Israel Corporation and Others* v. *Arab Republic of Egypt,* ICSID Case No ARB/12/11; *Mr Yosef Maiman and other* v. *Egypt* (UNCITRAL); See also, UNCTAD. 2017. 'IIA Issue Note – Investor-State Dispute Settlement: Review of Developments in 2016', p. 10, http://investmentpolicyhub.unctad.org/Upload/Documents/diaepcb2017d1_en.pdf, May, accessed 20 June 2018; Orascom TMT Investments S.àr.l. v. People's Democratic Republic of Algeria, ICSID Case No. ARB/12/35, Final Award, 31 May 2017.

[147] See *Philip Morris Asia Ltd* v. *The Commonwealth of Australia*, UNCITRAL PCA Case No. 2012-12, Award on Jurisdiction and Admissibility (17 December 2015).

[148] *Union of India* v. *Vodafone Group Plc United Kingdom & Anr, Delhi High Court*, CS(OS) 383/2017, Order (22 August 2017) ['*India* v. *Vodafone (22nd August Interim Order)*'].

[149] *Union of India* v. *Vodafone Group Plc United Kingdom and Anr,* CS(OS) 383/2017, Interim Order (26 October 2017) <https://www.italaw.com/sites/default/files/case-documents/italaw9704.pdf> accessed 20 June 2018.

14 December 2017 affirmed the 26 October 2017 order of the Delhi High Court. However, the apex court did not make any observations on the merits of the contentions since the final arguments were to be heard by the Delhi High Court. Finally, on 7 May 2018, the Delhi High Court dismissed the plea of the Indian government seeking an anti-arbitration injunction against Vodafone from proceeding under the India–UK BIT arbitration. In this process, the Delhi High Court dealt with several legal issues involving BIT arbitration of the kind that has not arisen before. We briefly discuss here the following issues—jurisdicxtion of Indian courts over BIT arbitration; applicability of the Arbitration and Concilliation (A&C) Act 1996 to BIT arbitration; and abuse of process.

Jurisdiction of National Courts over BIT Arbitrations

An important question before the court was whether Indian courts inherently lacked jurisdiction to hear any dispute arising out of a BIT. The Delhi HC held that there is no threshold bar or inherent lack of jurisdiction in the Court to deal with BIT arbitrations. The court provided the following reasons for its decision. First, the court held that there is no statutory bar or a case law relating to treaty obligation that ousts jurisdiction of Indian courts in relation to BIT arbitration. Second, India has not signed the ICSID Convention that, according to the court, 'completely negates the role of national courts'. Therefore, it was held that India has not acceded to ouster of jurisdiction of domestic courts over BIT arbitration. While it is true that India has not signed the ICSID convention, it is not quite correct that the ICSID convention completely negates the role of domestic courts. Article 26 of the ICSID Convention allows a state to make exhaustion of local remedies, a condition of consent to arbitration under the ICSID convention. Third, the court held that if the argument of lack of jurisdiction is accepted, then the court will be powerless to execute a BIT award if a foreign investor were to approach the domestic court.

Applicability of the A&C Act 1996 to BIT Arbitrations

A major conclusion of the court is that the Arbitration and Conciliation (A&C) Act 1996 does not *propriovigore* (by its own force or independently) apply to BIT arbitrations. In its interim order of August 2017, the Delhi HC had seemingly presumed that the A&C Act applied to BIT arbitration. The approach of the Delhi HC was same as that of the Calcutta HC in *Board of Trustees of the Port of Kolkata* v. *Louis Dreyfus*. Although the facts of the case before the Calcutta HC were different from the Vodafone case, an anti-arbitral injunction was sought from and granted by the Calcutta HC against a BIT arbitration initiated by Louis Dreyfus Armaturs SAS, a French foreign investor under the India–France BIT.[150] Without any explanation the Calcutta HC presumed that the A&C Act extends to a BIT arbitration.

The reason offered by the Delhi HC for the non-applicability of the A&C Act to BIT arbitration is that BIT arbitration is fundamentally different from international commercial arbitration (ICA). The 'cause of action' for BIT arbitration is not commercial in nature but based on state guarantees or treaty obligations undertaken by the state. Thus, BIT arbitration has its roots in public international law. While this distinction between BIT arbitration and ICA, globally, is quite well known and some Indian international investment lawyers have regularly talked and written about this,[151] yet it is not very well understood in India. This is because the BIT arbitration landscape in India, especially among law firms and practitioners, is dominated by lawyers having a background in commercial arbitration/private law without adequate training in public international law. Thus, BIT arbitration is often approached with the same mindset as commercial arbitration

[150] Louis Dreyfus Armateurs SAS v. The Republic of India (PCA Case No. 2014-26) http://investmentpolicyhub.unctad.org/ISDS/Details/600. France's Louis Dreyfus Armateurs (LDA) has brought a case against India under the India–France BIT challenging a series of measures adopted by the Indian government that allegedly prevented the implementation of a joint venture project to modernize the port in Haldia in Kolkata, India. Also see Bhushan Satish and Shreyas Jayasimha. 2015. 'Indian Courts First Blush with Investment Treaty Arbitration: Taking Some Lessons from the Calcutta High Court', http://kluwerarbitrationblog.com/2016/03/16/indian-courts-first-brush-with-investment-treaty-arbitration-taking-some-lessons-from-the-calcutta-high-court, 16 March, accessed 27 February 2018.

[151] P. Ranjan and D. Raju. 2011. 'The Enigma of Enforceability of Investment Treaty Arbitration Awards in India', *Asian Journal of Comparative Law* 6:1.

leading to many conceptual and normative problems. Hopefully, the conceptual clarification given by the Delhi HC will ensure that difference between the two is now well appreciated in India.

The Delhi HC held that given the non-applicability of the A&C Act to BIT arbitration, the national courts of India have the inherent power to restrain BIT arbitration which are oppressive, vexatious, inequitable, or constitute an abuse of the legal process. However, the court also said that where the subject matter of the dispute is governed by a dispute settlement clause of a BIT, the national courts should exercise self-restraint, except if there are compelling circumstances and the court has been approached in good faith, and no other efficacious remedy is available.

Abuse of Process

Another important contribution the case has made is on the question of abuse of process in BIT arbitration. As mentioned before, the Indian government's main contention was that filing multiple claims by entities in the same vertical corporate chain pertaining to same measure is per se an abuse of the legal process or is vexatious. The Delhi HC didn't agree with the government. The court said that if there are substantial reasons to bring two sets of proceedings simultaneously, they will not be vexatious. The court also said that since the Indian government has consistently claimed that the BIT arbitration under India–Netherlands BIT is without jurisdiction, invocation of another treaty by the parent company cannot be regarded as abuse per se.

Another factor that weighed heavily on the mind of the court to dismiss government's plea of abuse of process was the offer made by Vodafone to consolidate the two BIT proceedings. The court held that such an offer and undertaking is sufficient to placate India's concerns regarding double relief which may be granted by two tribunals in respect of the same matter. Further, the court stated simply because it would be expensive or inconvenient for the government to litigate before an arbitral tribunal do not make the proceedings oppressive. However, the court gave the government liberty to raise the abuse of process argument before the India–UK BIT, which would be the right forum to do so.

The detailed facts reported in the Delhi HC judgement show that the conduct of the Indian government in dealing with Vodafone leaves much to be desired. Right from amending the tax laws retrospectively with the specific objective to overrule the SC's decision to dragging its feet in the ISDS proceedings to running to domestic courts to stop Vodafone from pursuing BIT arbitration, raises a number of questions about the conduct of the Indian State. In fact, even after the 7 May 2018 ruling, the Indian government has challenged the ruling before the Delhi HC's division bench.[152] So, India is still trying its best to avoid being held accountable for its actions before an international tribunal.

6.4.2 *Cairn Energy* v. *India*

In 2015, Cairn Energy sued India under the India–UK BIT for a retrospective taxation measure.[153] The facts of this case are as follows: Cairn India Holdings Limited (CIHL) was incorporated in Jersey in August 2006 as a wholly owned subsidiary of Cairn UK Holdings Limited (CUHL).[154] Cairn UK Holdings Limited is a holding company established in the United Kingdom in June 2006.[155] Cairn UK Holdings Limited and Cairn India Holdings Limited entered into an agreement, under which the former transferred shares constituting the entire issued share capital of nine subsidiaries of the Cairn

[152] PTI. 2018. 'Centre Appeals in Delhi High Court against Vodafone's International Arbitration', 31 May, https://telecom.economictimes.indiatimes.com/news/centre-appeals-in-delhi-high-court-against-vodafones-international-arbitration/64406194.

[153] *Cairn Energy PLC and Cairn UK Holdings Limited* v. *The Republic of India* (PCA Case No. 2016-7) http://investmentpolicyhub.unctad.org/ISDS/Details/691 (*Cairn Energy* v. *India* 2015), accessed on 27 February 2018.

[154] Ishaan Vyas and Meyyappan Nagappan. 2017. 'Retrospective Capital Gains Tax on Indirect Transfers: The Ghost of the Vodafone case Revisits Cairn (UK)', 20 March, http://www.nishithdesai.com/information/news-storage/news-details/article/retrospective-capital-gains-tax-on-indirect-transfers-the-ghost-of-the-vodafone-case-revisits-cairn.html, accessed on 27 February 2018 (hereinafter Vyas and Nagappan, 'Retrospective Capital Gains Tax on Indirect Transfers').

[155] Vyas and Nagappan, 'Retrospective Capital Gains Tax on Indirect Transfers'.

group, held directly and indirectly by CUHL, engaged in the oil and gas sector in India.[156] Thereafter, Cairn India Limited (CIL) was incorporated in August 2006 in India as a wholly owned subsidiary of CUHL.[157] Following this, shares constituting the entire issued share capital of CIHL were transferred to CIL.[158] The consideration for this transaction between CIHL and CIL was partly in cash and partly in the form of shares of CIL.[159] Subsequent to this transaction, CIL divested 30.5 per cent of its shareholding by way of an initial public offering (IPO)and received approximately US$ 931 million.[160]

Many years later, in March 2015, the income tax department, armed with the changes made to Section 9 of the income tax Act in 2012 and applied retrospectively, issued a draft assessment order to CUHL (Cairn Energy) demanding US$ 1.6 billion in taxes for the transaction that happened in 2006.[161] Subsequently in January 2016, a final tax assessment order was sent to Cairn Energy.[162] Cairn Energy challenged the tax order in India's Income Tax Appellate Authority (ITAT) arguing that its tax liability should be assessed as per Section 9 of the Income Tax Act as it stood in 2006 and that retrospective changes made to the income tax Act were bad in law.[163] The Income Tax Appellate Authority held that it was not the right

[156] Vyas and Nagappan, 'Retrospective Capital Gains Tax on Indirect Transfers'.

[157] Vyas and Nagappan, 'Retrospective Capital Gains Tax on Indirect Transfers'.

[158] Vyas and Nagappan, 'Retrospective Capital Gains Tax on Indirect Transfers'.

[159] Vyas and Nagappan, 'Retrospective Capital Gains Tax on Indirect Transfers'.

[160] Vyas and Nagappan, 'Retrospective Capital Gains Tax on Indirect Transfers'.

[161] *Cairn Energy* v. *India* 2015.

[162] Vyas and Nagappan, 'Retrospective Capital Gains Tax on Indirect Transfers'.

[163] *Cairn UK Holdings Limited* v. *Deputy Commissioner of Income Tax*, Income Tax Appellate Tribunal, ITA No. 1669 /Del/2016, 9 March 2017 https://www.italaw.com/sites/default/files/case-documents/italaw8776.pdf page 8, accessed on 27 February 2018 (hereinafter *Cairn* v. *Commissioner of Income Tax*).

forum to decide on the constitutionality of the retrospective taxation.[164] The Income Tax Appellate Authority upheld the tax demand on Cairn Energy. However, on the question of levy of interest on the tax payable, the ITAT noted that since the taxpayer's tax liability has 'arisen because of retrospective amendment made by the Finance Act, 2012' to the income tax laws, the tax payer couldn't have visualized its liability for payment of advance in the year of transaction.[165] Thus, the ITAT held that the taxpayer need not pay interest on the tax.[166] This also shows that the ITAT implicitly accepted that the tax liability on Cairn Energy was because of the changes made in the law retrospectively. In other words, as the Indian Income Tax Act stood in 2006–7, that is, when the transaction took place, there was no tax liability on Cairn Energy.[167]

When Cairn brought the dispute against India, in March 2015, under the India–UK BIT India argued that the BIT does not provide for arbitration of taxation matters.[168] Thus, India didn't appoint an arbitrator despite the clear legal requirement, as per Article 9(3)(c)(i) of the treaty, to do so within two months from the date when Cairn informed the government of its intention to bring the dispute. Consequently, Cairn, under Article 9(3)(c)(ii), was forced to request the President of the International Court of Justice (ICJ) to intervene. Following the ICJ intervention, India named a Singapore-based lawyer J. Christopher Thomas as its arbitrator.[169]

Moreover, India's contention that tax matters are outside the jurisdiction of the India–UK BIT is not supported by the text of

164 *Cairn* v. *Commissioner of Income Tax*, p. 133.

165 *Cairn* v. *Commissioner of Income Tax*, p.165.

166 *Cairn* v. *Commissioner of Income Tax*, p.166.

167 Also see Vyas and Nagappan, 'Retrospective Capital Gains Tax on Indirect Transfers'.

168 PTI. 2015. 'Will Appoint Arbitrator to Resolve Cairn Tax Row: India to ICJ', *The Hindu Business Line*, 25 October, https://www.thehindubusinessline.com/companies/will-appoint-arbitrator-to-resolve-cairn-tax-row-india-to-icj/article7802608.ece, accessed on 27 February 2018.

169 PTI. 2015. 'Government Appoints Christopher Thomas as Arbitrator in Cairn Tax Case', 13 November, http://www.livemint.com/Politics/BJpufgXAwwOi1CyEBiC07O/Government-appoints-Christopher-Thomas-as-arbitrator-in-Cair.html, accessed on 27 February 2018.

the treaty. As per the India–UK BIT, tax matters are an exception to the provisions on national treatment and MFN.[170] Taxation is not an exception to any other substantive obligation such as the FET or expropriation. Further Article 9 of the India–UK BIT clearly states that 'any dispute between an investor of one Contracting Party and the other Contracting Party in relation to an investment' is a subject matter of the treaty.

Like the Vodafone arbitration, the Cairn Energy arbitration is also on and it would be interesting to see how it unfolds.

6.5 ISDS Claims Due to Actions of the State Government

There have been at least couple of ISDS claims that have been brought against India due to the actions of the state governments. This underlines the point that BITs can trigger liability against the Indian state even for actions of the provincial governments.[171] Here we discuss two such cases that have come to light—*Ras Al-Khaimah Investment Authority (RAKIA)* v. *India*[172] and *Nissan* v. *India*.[173]

6.5.1 *Rakia* v. *India*

The *RAKIA* v. *India* dispute stems from certain actions of the government of Andhra Pradesh (a southern state in India) that allegedly

[170] Agreement between the Republic of India and the Government of United Kingdom on the Reciprocal Promotion and Protection of Investments (signed 14 March 1994, entered into force 6 January 1995) (India–United Kingdom BIT) art. 4(3)(b).

[171] Also see the discussion on this issue in Chapter 7.

[172] *Ras-Al-Khaimah Investment Authority (RAKIA)* v. *India* (2016), UNCTAD available at http://investmentpolicyhub.unctad.org/ISDS/Details/767 (*RAKIA* v. *India* 2016), accessed on 27 February 2018.

[173] Aditi Shah. 2017. 'Exclusive: Nissan Sues India over Outstanding Dues; Seeks Over $770 Million', 1 December, https://in.reuters.com/article/nissan-india-arbitration/exclusive-nissan-sues-india-over-outstanding-dues-seeks-over-770-million-idINKBN1DV3N5 (Aditi Shah 2017), accessed on 27 February 2018.

have adversely impact RAKIA's investment in India, that is, an aluminium refinery-cum-power plant in Andhra Pradesh.[174]

In 2007, Anrak Aluminium Ltd. (Anrak)—a special purpose vehicle—established jointly by Penna cement industries Ltd., an Indian company, and RAKIA, an investment body of Ras Al-Khaimah which constitutes one of the seven emirates of the UAE, was incorporated in India.[175] Anrak was to install an alumina and aluminium refinery and smelter in Andhra Pradesh.[176] The memorandum of understanding entered into by the governments of Andhra Pradesh and Ras Al-Khaimah for this purpose, on 14 February 2007, *inter alia,* stated that the refinery plant would be backed by bauxite supplies from the Andhra Pradesh Mining Development Corporation (APMDC—an entity of the AP government), sourced from the Jerrela Group of Deposits in Visakhapatnam district.[177] In 2008, the AP Government gave its approval to the bauxite supply agreement (BSA) between APMDC and Anrak.[178] Subsequently, Anrak obtained SEZ status from the Indian government to commence its operations.[179]

[174] *RAKIA* v. *India* 2016, *Ras-Al-Khaimah Investment Authority (RAKIA)* v. *India* (2016), UNCTAD available at http://investmentpolicyhub.unctad.org/ISDS/Details/767 (*RAKIA* v. *India* 2016), accessed on 27 February 2018.

[175] See *Anrak Aluminium Ltd. & Ors.* v. *State Bank of India & Ors.* (*Anrak* v. *SBI*), CP(IB) No. 127/10/HDB/2017, decided by the National Company Law Tribunal, Hyderabad Bench (31 August 2017), 5–6, available at http://164.100.158.181/Publication/Hyderabad_Bench/2017/Others/148.pdf, accessed on 27 February 2018.

[176] See *Anrak Aluminium Ltd. & Ors.* v. *State Bank of India & Ors.* (*Anrak* v. *SBI*), CP(IB) No. 127/10/HDB/2017, decided by the National Company Law Tribunal, Hyderabad Bench (31 August 2017), 5–6, available at http://164.100.158.181/Publication/Hyderabad_Bench/2017/Others/148.pdf, accessed on 27 February 2018.

[177] Government of Andhra Pradesh, Industries and Commerce (M-II) Department. 2016. 'Mines and Minerals – Bauxite Mining – Cancellation of Bauxite supply agreement made between M/s APMDC Ltd and M/s ANRAK Aluminium Limited – Orders – Issued' 6 April, 3, http://apgoa.in/wp-content/uploads/2016/04/GO-NO-MS-44.pdf (Government of Andhra Pradesh 2016), accessed on 27 February 2018 (hereinafter Government of Andhra Pradesh, 'Mines and Minerals').

[178] Government of Andhra Pradesh, 'Mines and Minerals'.

[179] *Anrak* v. *SBI* para 6.

The bauxite mining area of Jerrela deposits falls entirely within the area of reserved forest and notified tribal areas.[180] Owing to stiff socio-political and environmental opposition by the tribals residing in this area, APMDC failed to supply bauxite to Anrak.[181] Consequently, on 6 April 2016, the AP Government rescinded the BSA.[182] The official reason for the BSA's cancellation was that several terms in the draft BSA were unfavourable to APMDC, and must be amended for better implementation as well as to augment APMDC's revenue.[183] The AP government did not mention stiff opposition from the tribals or environmental purposes for annulling the contract. Consequently, Anrak could not commence commercial operations—despite having completed construction of the refinery at a heavy expense[184]—and the refinery has since remained idle over the past four years.[185]

Whilst hearing Anrak's petition challenging the AP government's move, the High Court of AP & Telangana passed an interim order questioning the AP Government's powers to intervene in such a manner.[186] Nevertheless, despite the stay granted by the high court, APMDC also cancelled the BSA on 21 November, 2016.[187]

[180] *Anrak* v. *SBI*, para 3.

[181] *Anrak* v. *SBI*, para. 6.

[182] Government of Andhra Pradesh, 'Mines and Minerals', 3, para 12.

[183] Government of Andhra Pradesh, 'Mines and Minerals', paras 9–12; Special Correspondent. 2016. 'AP Govt Cancels Bauxite Supply Deal with Anrak', 24 March, Hyderabad, *The Hindu,*http://www.thehindu.com/news/cities/Hyderabad/ap-cancels-bauxite-supply-deal-with-anrak/article8020624.ece, accessed on 27 February 2018.

[184] TNN. 2016. 'AP Govt Cancels Bauxite Supply Deal with Anrak', 9 April, *The Times of India,* https://timesofindia.indiatimes.com/city/visakhapatnam/AP-govt-cancels-bauxite-supply-deal-with-Anrak/articleshow/51752189.cms., accessed on 27 February 2018.

[185] Dipanwita Gupta (ed.). 2017. 'UAE Serves Indian Govt Arbitration Notice for Failing on Bauxite Supplies for Andhra Alumina Project', *Al Circle.com,* https://www.alcircle.com/news/bauxite/detail/26773/uae-serves-indian-govt-arbitration-notice-for-failing-on-bauxite-supplies-for-andhra-alumina-project, 12 January, accessed on 27 February 2018.

[186] The matter has been posted for further hearing. See *Anrak* v. *SBI*.

[187] *Anrak* v. *SBI*, para 6.

On 8 December 2016, RAKIA served an ISDS notice under Article 10(5)(b) of the India–UAE BIT (2013)[188] to the India[189] for the alleged failure of the AP government to honour its commitment to direct the APMDC to supply bauxite, required for the operation of their investment. The notice sought mainly to either require APMDC to honour its contractual obligation under the BSA, or to require both the central and the AP governments to pay RAKIA compensatory damages on its total investment of US$ 44.71 million in Anrak.[190] The request[191] made to Ministry of Mines to make this notice available was denied citing Section 8 (1)(a) of the RTI Act.[192] Section 8(1)(a) states that any information that may prejudicially affect the sovereignty and integrity of the country shall not be shared with any citizen. It is not clear how sharing an ISDS arbitral notice shall affect India's sovereignty or India's economic interests or relations with friendly countries.

[188] The clause stipulates that if the dispute cannot be settled amicably within six months from the date of receipt of notice of dispute, the dispute may be submitted to inter alia 'an arbitral tribunal established under the Arbitration Rules of the United Nations Commission on International Trade Law (UNCITRAL) in force at the time of the commencement of the dispute.…' The trigger notice for dispute settlement had been served by RAKIA on 29 April 2016.

[189] Government of India, Ministry of Mines. 2017. 'Office Memorandum Constitution of Inter-Ministerial Group to Handle All Matters Pertaining to the Notice of Arbitration Served by Ras-AI-Khaimah Investment Authority (RAKIA), UAE under the India-UAE, BIPA', 5January, available at http://mines.nic.in/writereaddata/UploadFile/ConsitutionofIMGforArbitration2.pdf., accessed on 27 February 2018 (hereinafter Government of India, 'Office Memorandum').

[190] Government of India, 'Office Memorandum'.

[191] Information Sought under RTI Act, Registration Number MINES/R/2018/50116 (on file with the author).

[192] Section 8(1)(a) states: Notwithstanding anything contained in this Act, there shall be no obligation to give any citizen, information, disclosure of which would prejudicially affect the sovereignty and integrity of India, the security, strategic, scientific or economic interests of the State, relation with foreign State or lead to incitement of an offence.

6.5.2 *Nissan* v. *India*

The latest addition to the long list of foreign investors is the Japanese automaker Nissan Motor,[193] which sent a legal notice to the Indian government in July 2016 for alleged violations of the India–Japan Comprehensive Economic Partnership Agreement (CEPA). The notice was issued to the Prime Minister of India on 7 July 2016, thus providing a period of 90 days for an amicable resolution of the dispute.[194] Since no settlement was reached, it commenced arbitration proceedings on 27 February 2017.[195]

In its legal notice, Nissan stated that it had not received the tax incentives promised by government of Tamil Nadu (another southern state in India) in return for the establishment of a car manufacturing plant in Oragadam, near Chennai, as per the Memorandum of Understanding (MoU) signed in 2008. The Tamil Nadu government had promised Nissan that it would receive sales tax refund as an investment promotion subsidy, which were to be spread over a 21-year period with a cap of 115 per cent of investments.[196] In its notice, Nissan claimed approximately US$ 770 million in damages.[197] According to media reports, prior to the notice, Nissan

[193] Aditi Shah. 2017. 'Nissan Sues India Over Outstanding Dues; Seeks Over $770 Million', *Reuters*, https://www.reuters.com/article/us-nissan-india-arbitration-exclusive/exclusive-nissan-sues-india-over-outstanding-dues-seeks-over-770-million-idUSKBN1DV3MP, 1 December, accessed on 29 January 2018 (hereinafter Shah, 'Exclusive: Nissan Sues India over Outstanding Dues').

[194] Mohamed Imranullah S. 2018. 'Nissan Questions State's Stand Against International Arbitration', http://www.thehindu.com/todays-paper/tp-national/tp-tamilnadu/nissan-questions-states-stand-against-international-arbitration/article2249404, 23 January, accessed on 29 January 2018 (hereinafter Imranullah, 'Nissan Questions State's Stand Against International Arbitration').

[195] Imranullah, 'Nissan Questions State's Stand Against International Arbitration'.

[196] R. Balaji. 2017. 'TN Disputes Nissan's $770-m Claim', 1 December, *The Hindu*, http://www.thehindubusinessline.com/companies/tn-disputes-nissans-770m-claim/article9979531.ece, last accessed on 29 January 2018.

[197] ET Bureau. n.d. 'Nissan Sues India Over Outstanding Dues Seeks Over $770 Million', *Economic Times*, https://economictimes.indiatimes.com/

officials had made repeated requests to the government officials of the Tamil Nadu government for payment and even after the notice, several meetings took place between the representatives of Nissan and state and federal government officials where Nissan was repeatedly assured that it would receive the overdue payments. Finally, tired of these false assurances, Nissan asked India to appoint its arbitrator by August 2017 and the first hearing was slated to be held in mid-December 2017.

When the media broke the story on 1 December 2017 about the arbitration proceedings initiated by Nissan,[198] the Tamil Nadu government refuted the claim and immediately filed an application before the Madras High Court seeking an interim injunction to restrain Nissan from proceeding in the arbitration proceedings.[199] In the application, the government argued that Nissan had not approached the appropriate forum by initiating arbitration under the CEPA and instead, it should have availed itself of the remedy available under the MoU,[200] as the Government of Tamil Nadu is a party to the MoU and not the CEPA. The High Court ordered for notice to be served on *inter alia* Nissan and the central government.

In response, Nissan approached the arbitral tribunal comprising Kaj Hober, Jagdish Singh Kehar and Jean E. Kalicki for urgent interim relief. The order issued by the Tribunal in accordance with

---

industry/auto/news/nissan-sues-india-over-outstanding-dues-seeks-over-770-mln/articleshow/61875710.cms, accessed on 29 January 2018, updated on 1 December 2017.

[198] Shah, 'Exclusive: Nissan Sues India over Outstanding Dues'.

[199] TNN. 2017. 'Nissan Vs India: TN Seeks to Stop Arbitration', *The Times of India,* https://timesofindia.indiatimes.com/city/chennai/nissan-vs-india-tn-seeks-to-stop-arbitration/articleshow/61921731.cms, 6 December, accessed on 29 January 2018.

[200] The 2008 MoU contains a dispute resolution clause according to which any dispute that cannot be resolved amicably through negotiations among the parties should be decided by arbitration under the Indian Arbitration and Conciliation Act, 1996, the venue of the arbitration being Chennai. See https://timesofindia.indiatimes.com/city/chennai/nissan-vs-india-tn-seeks-to-stop-arbitration/articleshow/61921731.cms, accessed on 29 January 2018.

the UNCITRAL Arbitration Rules was subsequently produced by the Counsel for Nissan Motor before the Madras High Court.

In the order, the Tribunal stated that under Article 96 (21) of the CEPA, an arbitral tribunal constituted under the CEPA has the power to rule on jurisdictional objections and India had already raised a *ratione materiae* objection.[201] Additionally, since Nissan was concerned of the application filed by the Tamil Nadu Government, the Tribunal directed the Government of India, as well as Nissan, to take all necessary steps to ensure that the High Court does not issue an injunction against the arbitration proceedings under the India–Japan FTA investment chapter at least until the preliminary issue of jurisdiction was resolved.[202]

Post the order of the Arbitral Tribunal, the central government filed its counter affidavit in response to the petition filed by the Tamil Nadu government before the Madras High Court, wherein it informed the state government that the latter did not have the locus standi to challenge the arbitration proceedings initiated by Nissan as it is not a party to the CEPA or the dispute.[203]

The central government also submitted that it intended to challenge the jurisdiction of the arbitral tribunal on the basis of the fork-in-the-road clause in Article 96 (6) of the CEPA.[204] It stated that

[201] Mohamed Imranullah S. 2017. 'Nissan Motor moves Arbitral Tribunal', *The Hindu,* http://www.thehindu.com/news/national/nissan-motor-moves-arbitral-tribunal/article21291928.ece, 7 December, last accessed on 29 January 2018 (hereinafter Imranullah, 'Nissan Motor moves Arbitral Tribunal').

[202] Imranullah, 'Nissan Motor moves Arbitral Tribunal'.

[203] Gireesh Babu. 2018. 'Tamil Nadu has No Locus Standi in Nissan Global Dispute: Centre to Court', *Business Standard,* http://www.business-standard.com/article/economy-policy/tamil-nadu-has-no-locus-standi-in-nissan-global-dispute-centre-to-court-118010200964_1.html, 3 January, accessed on 29 January 2018.

[204] Article 96 (6) of the India–Japan CEPA provides: 'No investment dispute may be submitted to international conciliation or arbitration referred to in paragraph 4 if the disputing investor has initiated any proceedings for the resolution of the investment dispute before courts of justice or administrative tribunals or agencies. However, in the event that those proceedings are withdrawn within 30 days from the date of filing the case, the disputing investor may submit the investment dispute to such international conciliations or arbitrations.'

Nissan had already approached the Indian courts and, therefore, was barred from raising the investment dispute before the arbitral tribunal.[205] This was with reference to the writ petitions filed by Nissan and Renault in 2016, challenging the retrospective amendments made to the Tamil Nadu Value Added Tax Act (2006), which in the opinion of the central government is also the subject matter of the investment arbitration. These writ petitions are still pending before the Madras High Court.

In the hearing before the Madras High Court on 22 January 2017, Nissan filed its counter-affidavit and submitted that the Tamil Nadu government cannot object to the proceedings between Nissan and the Government of India and, further, it emphasized that Tamil Nadu had approached the court as late as 10 months after the company commenced the arbitration in February 2017 in its capacity as a foreign investor under the CEPA.[206]

To sum up, it would be interesting to see how these cases unfold. Both these cases show that two state governments had given certain assurances to foreign investors to lure them to investment. Once the investment was made, both the governments went back on their assurances.

6.6 Summing up

The closer study of the ISDS claims brought against India demonstrates five things. First, cases like *White Industries* v. *India* and *Devas Multimedia* v. *India* expose the broad and vague language of BIT provisions such as the MFN and FET provisions incorporated in Indian BITs. This outcome is consistent with the analysis done in Chapters 4 and 5.

Second, and equally important, is the fact that these cases show that none of the claims have been brought against India because India

[205] *Deccan Chronicle*. 2018. 'TN Govt has No Locus Standi in Nissan Case: Centre to Madras High Court', https://www.deccanchronicle.com/nation/current-affairs/030118/tn-govt-has-no-locus-standi-in-nissan-case-centre-to-madras-high-court.html, 3 January, accessed on 29 January 2018.

[206] Imranullah, 'Nissan Questions State's Stand Against International Arbitration'.

exercised her sovereign public power in good faith in order to attain an important public policy goal such as protection of the environment or promotion of public health, etc. None of these claims show that foreign investors used ISDS to encroach upon India's sovereign right to regulate—the dominant narrative of virulent critics of BITs and ISDS.

All these claims have arisen against India because either the Indian judiciary moved too slowly and or because the Indian executive was held to have acted in bad faith (such as cancelling spectrum licenses without following due process) or because the Indian executive and the legislative actions were considered problematic in so far as as amending income tax law in 2012 and making it applicable retrospectively from 1961 or because some of the state governments did not stand by the assurances they provided to attact investments once the investors moved in. In other words, most of these cases are outcome of central and state regulation, that prima facie, appear to be abusive and arbitrary. Indeed, the very purpose of a BIT is to protect foreign investment from such regulations not valid under law.

The discussion in the chapter shows that there are legitimate reasons for these cases ending up in ISDS.[207] Of course, one is fully conscious of the fact that there may be instances where foreign investors might abuse ISDS. Nonethless, every use of ISDS by a foreign investor should not be equated to encroachment upon the host state's right to regulate. This also shows that finding fault with the language of BITs alone, as the Indian government seems to have done, for the multiple ISDS claims against India is incorrect.

Third, these ISDS claims also show the failure of the organs of the Indian State to be sufficiently sensitive to India's BIT obligations. This failure is at all levels—judiciary (delays in enforcing foreign awards, issuance of anti-arbitral injunctions), the executive (central government and the state governments), and the legislature. There is very little evidence to show that these different organs of the Indian State fully understand the ramifications of BITs and often act as if

[207] Schill makes the similar point with resepct to some high-profile ISDS cases like Vattenfall, Philip Morris and Bilcon – See Schill, 'In Defense of International Investment Law'.

they are oblivious of India's international law obligations contained in BITs.[208]

Fourth, a closer study of these cases especially of the cases brought by Vadofaone and Cairn energy shows India's hostile attitude towards ISDS. This was reaffirmed recently when it was said that India won't accept the rulings of the ISDS tribunals if they ruled that deciding on taxation matters is within their jurisdiction.[209] India continues to belive that taxation matters are outside the jurisdiction of ISDS tribunals.[210]

Fifth, the cases brought by Vodafone and Cairn Energy show that despite the two foreign investors using a threat to start ISDS proceedings, India was not deterred from adopting the regulatory measures. Despite Vodafone's threat to sue India, India went ahead and amended the Income tax act retrospectively. Likewise, despite the ISDS threat issued by Cairn Energy, India went ahead and issued the draft income tax assessment order to Cairn Energy relying upon the amended law with retrospective affect. In simpler terms, these cases are examples to show that the threat chill as conceptualized by Tienhara,[211] had no chilling effect on India's regulatory power.

[208] See the section on internalization of BITs in Chapter 7.

[209] PTI. 2018. 'India May Not Accept Arbitration Orders Annulling Cairn, Vodafone Tax Demands', 22 May, economictimes.indiatimes.com/articleshow/64271201.cms?utm_source=contentofinterest&utm_medium=text&utm_campaign=cppst (hereinafter PTI, 'India May Not Accept Arbitration Orders Annulling Cairn, Vodafone Tax Demands').

[210] PTI, 'India May Not Accept Arbitration Orders Annulling Cairn, Vodafone Tax Demands'.

[211] See Chapter 1.

7

Mapping the Backlash

Once BITten Many Times Shy!

The White Industries arbitral award and the subsequent slapping of ISDS notices against India, as discussed in Chapter 6, took the Indian government by surprise. It presented a scenario not envisaged by members of the Indian government. For instance, the negotiators of the Indian BIT never expected the MFN provision in the BITs could be interpreted in such a broad manner.[1] Further, many in the Indian government didn't expect that a BIT claim would be brought against India for the actions of the Indian judiciary.[2] These ISDS claims against India led to a greater awareness about BITs in India. All-important stakeholders such as the Parliament, the academia, and the civil society started examining BITs critically (Section 7.1).

[1] Interview with an Official of the Ministry of Finance (name withheld), May 2012. Also see T. Wälde. 2009. 'Interpreting Investment Treaties: Experiences and Examples' in *International Investment Law for the 21st Century: Essays in Honour of Christopher Schreuer*, Christina Binder, Ursula Kriebaum, August Reinisch, and Stephan Wittich (eds), pp. 724, 737. Oxford: Oxford University Press.

[2] Interview with officials of the ministry of finance and commerce (names withheld), May 2012.

This paved the way for the review of Indian BITs by the government (Section 7.2). The review led to three critical outcomes—adoption of the 2016 Model BIT, termination of BITs with 50 plus countries and the proposal to issue joint interpretative statement (JIS) with another 25 countries (Section 7.3). It remains to be seen whether this attention to BITs rising from increasing ISDS claims have led to any internalization of BITs in India, that is, whether there is evidence to show that BITs are being considered while making national or regulatory policies or other decisions[3] (Section 7.4).

7.1 Involvement of Stakeholders

The increasing ISDS claims against India galvanized all key stakeholders such as, the parliament, the civil society including the academia, and the government. Some started demanding that India should revisit and review its BITs.[4] In totality, these stakeholders responded in their own ways putting the spotlight on Indian BITs.

7.1.1 Parliament

Since the Indian Parliament has no role in the ratification of treaties, it rarely deliberated upon BITs as discussed in Chapter 3. However, the loss of the ISDS claim against White Industries galvanized the Parliament and turned its focus on BITs and BIT connected arbitration. Concerns were expressed in the Parliament about the White Industries award. It was said, referring to the *White case,* that the 'arbitration tribunal criticized the Indian Supreme Court, in particular, and the Indian judicial system, in general, and made the Government of India liable to compensate for the lapse on the part

[3] See Mavluda Sattarova. 2014. 'The Impact of Investment Treaty Law on Host State Behaviour: Some Doctrinal, Empirical and Interdisciplinary Insights', in *The Role of State in Investor State Arbitration*, Shaheeza Lalani and Rodrigo Polanco Lazo (eds), p. 62. Leiden: Brill/Martinus Nijhoff.

[4] Prabhash Ranjan. 2015. 'Most Favoured Nation Principle in Indian Bilateral Investment Treaties: A Case for Reform', *Indian Journal of International Law*, 55(1): 39–64 (hereinafter, *MFN in Indian BITs*).

of our Judiciary'.[5] It was further said that 'this [arbitral award] is an attack on the sovereignty of the Indian Judiciary. The judicial functioning is one of the major sovereign functions of a State. Therefore, it is an attack on the sovereignty of the country'.[6]

Another indicator of greater attention posited on BITs are the noticeably critical discussions carried out in Parliament since the *White Industries* Award as against the period from 1994–2010. Opposition political parties have questioned BITs on the floor of the house, a phenomenon evident only after the *White Industries* case. For example, a Member of Parliament, in May 2012, asked the government to supply the details of all the BITs that India had entered into and whether the texts of these BITs were publicly available.[7] Similarly, another Member of Parliament, in September 2012, asked the government whether any panel had been constituted to oversee the BIT disputes brought against India.[8] Questions have also been asked about the ISDS claims that have been brought against India as

[5] Statement by P. Rajeeve, Member of Parliament (India). 2012. 'Transcript of the Proceedings of the Rajya Sabha', 22 May, http://164.100.47.5/newdebate/225/22052012/Fullday.pdf, p. 53, accessed 14 February 2018.

[6] Rajeeve, 'Transcript of the Proceedings of the Rajya Sabha'; For another critique of the *White* award, as to how it went beyond its mandate see Sanan, 'The White Industries Award', p. 661.

[7] Government of India, Ministry of Finance, 'Unstarred Question No. 5870, Bilateral Investment Treaties' (11 May 2012), http://164.100.47.194/Loksabha/Questions/QResult15.aspx?qref=123034&lsno=15, accessed 14 February 2018; Also see Government of India, Ministry of Commerce and Industry, Lok Sabha, 'Unstarred Question No. 6248, Bilateral Investment Treaties' (6 May 2013), http://164.100.47.194/Loksabha/Questions/QResult15.aspx?qref=140786&lsno=15, accessed 14 February 2018.

[8] Government of India, Ministry of Finance, Lok Sabha, 'Unstarred Question No. 3926, Bilateral Investment Pacts (5 September 2012), http://164.100.47.194/Loksabha/Questions/QResult15.aspx?qref=129086&lsno=15, accessed 14 February 2018 (hereinafter, Lok Sabha, Unstarred Question No. 3926); Government of India, Ministry of Finance, Lok Sabha, 'Unstarred Question No. 365, Bilateral Investment Promotion and Protection Agreement' (11 July 2014) http://164.100.47.194/Loksabha/Questions/QResult15.aspx?qref=824&lsno=16, accessed 14 February 2018 (hereinafter, Lok Sabha, Unstarred Question No. 365).

discussed in Chapter 6;[9] whether India has decided to review, renegotiate, and/or decided to terminate its BITs;[10] and whether India has adopted a new Model BIT.[11]

7.1.2 Academia and Civil Society

Within the Indian academic community, before the *White Industries* award, BITs did not attract much attention barring a few exceptions.[12] This academic disregard altered post the *White Industries* Award.[13] The existence of pro-investor obligations within the Indian BITs and its

[9] Government of India, Ministry of Finance, Lok Sabha, 'Unstarred Question No. 2391, Review of BIPA' (25 July 2014), http://164.100.47.194/Loksabha/Questions/QResult15.aspx?qref=2274&lsno=16, accessed 14 February 2018 (hereinafter, Lok Sabha, Unstarred Question No. 2391).

[10] Lok Sabha, Unstarred Question No. 365; Lok Sabha, Unstarred Question No. 2391.

[11] Government of India, Ministry of Commerce and Industry, Department of Industrial Policy and Promotion, Lok Sabha, 'Unstarred Question No. 1290, Bilateral Investment Treaties' (25 July 2016), http://164.100.47.190/loksabhaquestions/annex/9/AU1290.pdf, accessed 14 February 2018 (hereinafter, Lok Sabha, Unstarred Question No. 1290)

[12] Rao, 'Bilateral Investment Promotion Agreements'; Krishan, 'India and International Investment Law'; Prabhash Ranjan. 2008. 'International Investment Agreements and Regulatory Discretion: Case Study of India', *Journal of World Investment and Trade* 9(2): 209 (hereinafter, Ranjan, *Regulatory Discretion-Case Study of India*); Prabhash Ranjan. 2008. 'Medical Patents and Expropriation in International Investment Law – with Special Reference to India', *Manchester Journal of International Economic Law*, 5(3): 72 (hereinafter, *Medical Patents and Expropriation*)

[13] Ranjan, 'India and Bilateral Investment Treaties – A Changing Landscape', pp. 419–58; Prabhash Ranjan. 2015. 'Comparing Investment Provisions in India's FTAs with India's Stand Alone BITs: Contributing to the Evolution of New Indian BIT Practice', *Journal of World Investment & Trade* 16: 899 (hereinafter, *Comparing India's FTA and BITs*); *MFN in Indian BITs*, n 4; Biswajit Dhar, Reji Joseph, and T.C. James. 2012. 'India's Bilateral Investment Agreements: Time to Review', *Economic & Political Weekly* 47(52): 113 (hereinafter, Dhar, Joseph, and James, *India's BITs*); Smitha Francis and Murli Kallummal. 2013. 'India's Comprehensive Trade Agreements: Implications for Development Trajectory', *Economic & Political Weekly* 48(31): 109 (hereinafter, Smitha

adverse effects on India's regulatory space were discussed extensively.[14] For instance, in the case of *White Industries* v. *India*, it was argued that since the White award was an indictment for judicial delays, it encroached upon India's judicial sovereignty.[15] Similarly, while some academics demanded that India should review its BITs even before the *White Industries* case,[16] these demands gained further traction after the case and the issuance of ISDS notices against India.[17]

Francis and others, *India's Comprehensive Trade Agreements*); Aniruddha Rajput. 2016. 'India's Shifting Treaty Practice: A Comparative Analysis of the 2003 and 2015 Model BITs', *Jindal Global Law Review* 7(2): 201–26 (hereinafter, Rajput, *India's Shifting Treaty Practice*); Hanessian and Duggal. 2015. 'The 2015 Indian Model BIT: Is This Change the World Wishes to See', *ICSID Review- Foreign Investment Law Journal* 30(3): 729 (hereinafter, Hanessian & Duggal, *Is this the Change the World Wishes to See* (2015)); Grant Hanessian and Kabir Duggal. 2017. 'The Final 2015 Indian Model BIT: Is This the Change the World Wishes to See', *ICSID Review- Foreign Investment Law Journal* 32(1): 216–26 (hereinafter Hanessian and Duggal, 'The Final 2015 Indian Model BIT'); Garg, Tripathi, and Roy, 'The Indian Model Bilateral Investment Treaty, p. 69; Kavaljit Singh. 2016. 'An Analysis of India's New Model Bilateral Investment Treaty', in *Rethinking Bilateral Investment Treaties: Critical Issues and Policy Choices,* Kavaljit Singh and BurghardIgle (eds), p. 81. Amsterdam, New Delhi: Both Ends, Madhyam, SOMO (hereinafter, Kavaljit Singh, *Analysis of India's New Model BIT*); Nish Shetty and RomeshWeeramantary. 2016. 'India's New Approach to Investment Treaties', *Asian Dispute Review* 18(4): 189; Azernoosh Bazarafkan. 2016. 'The (R)evolution of Indian Model Bilateral Investment Treaty: Escaping Liability without Mitigating Risks', *Jindal Global Law Review* 7(2): 245–61; Deepak Raju. 2016. 'General Exceptions in the Indian Model BIT: Is the "necessity" test workable?', *Jindal Global Law Review* 7(2): 227–43.

[14] Dhar, Joseph, and James, *India's BITs*, n 13.

[15] P.K. Suresh Kumar. 2012. 'Globalisation and Judicial Sovereingty of India', *Economic and Political Weekly* XLVII: 49. Also see J. Ghosh. 2012. 'Worrying Trend', *Frontline* 29(5, 10–23 March), http://www.frontline.in/static/html/fl2905/stories/20120323290511500.htm, accessed 14 February 2018.

[16] Ranjan, *Regulatory Discretion-Case Study of India*.

[17] See, Ranjan, 'Comparing Investment Provisions in India's FTAs with India's Stand Alone BITs'; Dhar, Joseph, and James, "India's Bilateral Investment Agreements'; Francis and Kallummal, *India's Comprehensive Trade Agreements*.

Similarly, civil society organizations, in the aftermath of *White Industries* case and the ISDS notices against India, urged caution in ratifying new BITs. For instance, in a letter written by a 'forum against FTAs' to Manmohan Singh, then Prime Minister of India, tried to attract the government's attention to some of the problems existent in BITs.[18] The letter also argued that BITs curtailed India's policy space.[19] The civil society groups argued that the threat of BIT arbitrations 'will have a chilling effect on the ability of different ministries (of the Indian government) to regulate different social and economic needs.'[20] The Forum thus demanded that India should review its BITs and abstain from entering into new BITs.[21]

7.1.3 The Indian Government

Before the White Industries award, there was very little critical discussion in the Indian government on BITs. However, things changed quite dramtically after the White Industries award and as more and more foreign investors started suing India. Rattled by these ISDS claims, the Ministry of Commerce recommended removal of ISDS provisions from future BITs to protect India's sovereign measures from challenge before international arbitration tribunals.[22] Some in

[18] Forum against FTAs. 2013. 'We Call Upon the Government to Review and Rescind Its Decision to Sign BIT/ BIPA With the USA', *Open letter to the Indian Prime Minister, Dr Manhoman Singh*, 26 September, http://www.bilaterals.org/IMG/pdf/lettter_forum_ag_ftas_us_india_bits_26_sept.pdf, accessed 14 February 2018 (hereinafter, Forum Against FTAs).

[19] Forum Against FTAs, 'We Call Upon the Government to Review and Rescind Its Decision to Sign BIT/ BIPA With the USA'.

[20] M.R. Santosh. 2012. 'Concerns Regarding Proposed US-India Bilateral Investment Treaty', 13 June, https://donttradeourlivesaway.files.wordpress.com/2012/06/civil-society-letter-on-us-india-bit.pdf, accessed 14 February 2018.

[21] See Forum Against FTAs, 'We Call Upon the Government to Review and Rescind Its Decision to Sign BIT/ BIPA With the USA', n 19.

[22] A.R. Mishra. 2012. 'India May Exclude Clause on Lawsuits from Trade Pacts', *Livemint*, 29 January, http://www.livemint.com/Home-Page/dTXmHa0mYUyRrFko4HbiLP/India-may-exclude-clause-on-lawsuits-from-trade-pacts.html, accessed 14 February 2018; Garg, Tripathi, and Roy, 'The Indian Model Bilateral Investment Treaty', pp. 71–2.

the Indian government also suggested renegotiation of existing BITs to drop ISDS provision.[23]

The thinking of the government on BITs was most evident in the paper titled 'International Investment Agreements Between India and other Countries' issued by the Department of Industrial Policy And Promotion (DIPP) of the Ministry of Commerce in 2011.[24] This paper represented the first-ever comprehensive effort within the government to critically discuss Indian BITs. The paper, unfortunately, is not publicly available and was obtained by the members of nongovernmental organizations through the Right to Information Act (RTI). Some salient aspects of the paper are discussed here:

7.1.3.1 BITs and Foreign Investment Inflows to India

The paper discussed the lack of relationship between BITs and the increase in foreign investment. The paper suggested, purportedly based upon global evidence, that India should 'rethink the role of BITs in attracting foreign investment in India'.[25] The paper further stated that 'while IIAs may be a desirable objective, they are neither necessary nor sufficient for promoting FDI'. It may be noted that the position taken in the paper is not based on any empirical study of Indian BITs and foreign investment but on selective reading of the global literature looking at linkage between BITs and FDI inflows.

7.1.3.2 Indian BITs and India's Regulatory Power

The paper further recognized that 'when developing countries enter into BITs, a balance between investor's rights and domestic policy

[23] Subhomoy Bhattacharjee. 2012. 'India seeks Treaty Revision to Deal with Corporate Suits', *The Indian Express*, 4 April, http://archive.indianexpress.com/news/india-seeks-treaty-revisions-to-deal-with-corporate-suits/932195/, accessed 14 February 2018; Also see Garg et al., 'The Indian Model Bilateral Investment Treaty', pp. 71–2.

[24] Government of India, Ministry of Commerce, 'International Investment Agreements between India and Other Countries' (on file with author) (hereinafter, Commerce Ministry Paper). The paper is not publicly available, but was obtained by members of an NGO through India's Right to Information Act, 2005.

[25] Commerce Ministry Paper, p. 6.

must be ensured'. The paper stated that 'other legitimate public concerns must not be subordinated to investment protection issues.' In this regard, the paper identified a number of areas of concern in the Indian BITs such as an expansive definition of investment; an undefined fair and equitable treatment provision that could be subject to broad and expansive interpretations; a broad provision on expropriation without any reservations and exceptions; and a wide leverage to investors to freely transfer funds.[26] These broad and unqualified BIT provisions, according to the paper, could result in situations where India's exercise of regulatory power could be unduly compromised. The paper gives specific examples of situations where foreign investors could use broad provisions like the FET standard to bring an ISDS claim against India when a license granted to a foreign investor is 'cancelled on grounds of public policy'[27] or when 'significant changes' are made 'in tax regimes or the administration of taxes'[28] or when 'a foreign company' is denied 'environmental clearance, when such clearance has been granted to another company'.[29] The paper also discussed situations wherein foreign investors could use the broad MFN provisions to circumvent narrower FET provisions of a BIT, that is, a FET provision not linked to customary international law (given in the investment chapter of India–Korea FTA where FET is linked with customary international law) by borrowing a broad FET provision, that is, an autonomous FET provision[30] (given in the India–Mauritius BIT).[31] In another example, the paper recognized that since issuance of compulsory licenses on patented drugs is not excluded from the purview of expropriation, there could be situations where a patent holder may file a BIT claim against India for issuance of compulsory licenses.[32] Finally, the paper argued the possibility of

[26] Commerce Ministry Paper, p. 6.

[27] Commerce Ministry Paper, p. 11.

[28] Commerce Ministry Paper, p. 11.

[29] Commerce Ministry Paper, p. 11.

[30] For a discussion on broader and narrower FET provisions, see Chapter 4.

[31] Commerce Ministry Paper, p. 10.

[32] This issue in the context of Indian BITs has also been raised earlier—Ranjan, 'Medical Patents and Expropriation in International Investment Law', n 12; Ranjan, 'Pharmaceutical Patents and Expropriation in Indian Bilateral Investment Treaties'.

foreign investors using the transfer of funds provisions to bring ISDS claims against India if India faced 'a balance of payment crisis' 'and capital controls are imposed by the RBI'.[33] While these concerns are true in theory, the empirical evidence as discussed in Chapter 6 shows that most ISDS cases have not been brought against India for exercise of genuine right to regulate in public interest.

7.1.3.3 Critical of ISDS

The paper, overall, is extremely critical of the ISDS system[34] questioning the 'impartiality and the objectivity of the present international arbitration'.[35] The paper states that the ISDS system creates perverse incentives, where 'a growing number of the arbitration firms take cases on a commission basis' where 'a percentage of the final claim is agreed upon as fees', which, in turn, according to the paper, 'increases the incentive for litigation amongst potential clients'.[36] Further, the paper alleges that 'there is a growing international business in third party financing of arbitration claims, with private companies making a profit from those cases that are then won'.[37] The paper then goes on to conclude that the factors mentioned above 'fuelled by a growing awareness of the litigation potential of some of the key clauses in the investment agreements have led to a rapid increase in the number of investment treaty claims'.[38]

While some arguments presented in the paper are exaggerated, this paper was the first official acknowledgement by India that Indian BITs do not strike a balance between investment protection and India's ability to exercise regulatory power. The paper, thus, concluded that India should review its existing BITs by evaluating the benefits and risks of concluding such treaties. Further, on the issue of investment protection in BITs and providing regulatory space to India after review, the paper notes 'if after review, it is decided to

[33] Commerce Ministry Paper, p. 13.
[34] Commerce Ministry Paper, pp. 15–18.
[35] Commerce Ministry Paper, p. 17.
[36] Commerce Ministry Paper, pp. 17–18.
[37] Commerce Ministry Paper, pp. 17–18.
[38] Commerce Ministry Paper, pp. 17–18.

continue to enter into IIAs, then the rights and obligations of investors vis-à-vis India should be rebalanced and economic and public policy objectives like security, public health, and environment protection should be introduced into these agreements'. Thus, the paper recognized that the 'capital-exporting' country BIT model followed by India did not balance investment protection with India's ability to exercise regulatory power.

Another critical aspect of the paper was the revelation of the poor understanding and awareness of BITs within the Indian government. For example, this paper cited the UNCTAD database to report the number of BITs India had signed.[39] It is a telling commentary that a department of the Indian government was unaware of the number of BITs signed by India and had to rely on the statistics maintained by an international intergovernmental organization. Moreover, the paper, citing the *Dabhol* case, mentioned that 'neither the amount paid to the claimants nor the clauses of the IIA under which the claims were filed is known to this Department'[40], that is, the DIPP within the ministry of commerce. Lastly, the paper observed that 'there is no government department' that monitors BIT cases filed against India.[41]

7.1.3.4 Factors That Influenced Commerce Ministry's Thinking on BITs

The analytical and careful reading of the paper manifests three factors that impacted the thinking of the government. First, the works of major international organizations like UNCTAD, reflective from the heavy reliance made to the UNCTAD's World Investment Report. Second, the situation in states like South Africa, Brazil, and Latin America. The paper quotes the decision of South Africa to review its BITs as a basis for recommending a review by India. Third, the paper, despite not acknowledging the role of India academics, shows a clear impact of their work to recommend a review of Indian BITs. For instance, an article published in 2010, expressed concern about India entering

[39] Commerce Ministry Paper, p. 16.

[40] Commerce Ministry Paper, p. 16.

[41] Commerce Ministry Paper, p. 16.

into BITs and FTAs containing an investment chapter with the same country without the latter treaty containing any provision on how the two investment provisions will be streamlined.[42] The same concern is also expressed in the ministry of commerce paper, which states, 'a view needs to be taken in cases of countries where a BIPA exists and a CECA has been entered into or is proposed. How should coherence and compatiblilty between the BIPA and CECA be ensured?'

7.2 Review of BITs and Background to the New Model BIT

A greater involvement and demand by stakeholders combined with an analogous stand of the government to review existing BITs induced the process of revising Indian BITs.[43] In September 2012, the government decided to constitute a committee of secretaries (a secretary to the Indian government is the administrative head of the ministry or department and the principal adviser to the minister on all matters of policy and the administration within the ministry/department)[44] to be chaired by the cabinet secretary of India (the topmost executive official and senior most civil servant) to oversee all issues arising out of BITs and FTA investment chapters.[45] This

[42] Prabhash Ranjan. 2010. 'Conflicting Signals', *Business Standard*, 28 May, http://www.business-standard.com/article/opinion/-conflicting-signals-110052800026_1.html, accessed 14 February 2018.

[43] Garg, Tripathi, and Roy, 'The Indian Model Bilateral Investment Treaty', p. 71; Department of Economic Affairs, Ministry of Finance, Government of India. 2016. 'Transforming the International Investment Agreement Regime: The Indian Experience', http://unctad-worldinvestmentforum.org/wp-content/uploads/2015/03/India_side-event-Wednesday_Model-agreements.pdf, accessed 14 February 2018. (India's presentation in a Side Event at World Investment Forum 2016) (hereinafter, Department of Economic Affairs, GoI, *The Indian Experience*).

[44] Government of India, 2015. *Central Secretariat Manual of Office Procedure*, 14th edition. New Delhi: Ministry of Personnel Public Grievances and Pensions, https://darpg.gov.in/sites/default/files/CSMOP_0_0.pdf, accessed 14 February 2018.

[45] Lok Sabha, Unstarred Question No. 3926; Also see Hanessian and Duggal, *Is this the Change the World wishes to See*; Also see Government of India,

committee of secretaries was constituted in April 2013.[46] This committee, in turn, constituted a working group under the chairmanship of secretary, department of economic affairs of the ministry of finance, with representatives from different ministries such as commerce, telecommunications, coal, revenue, external affairs, law and justice, etc.[47] This working group was mandated *inter alia* to prepare a draft revised model text of the India BIT; to examine and harmonize the provisions of Indian BITs with those in India's FTA investment chapters; and to provide a detailed roadmap for the renegotiation of 82 Indian BITs.[48] Another important objective of the review, as claimed by the Indian government, was to'understand and identify the legal/policy challenges from the existing treaties'.[49] An inter-ministerial group (IMG) was also constituted to handle various ISDS disputes brought against India.[50] Simultaneously, the government announced in March 2013 its decision to put all BIT negotiations on hold.[51]

The manner in which the Indian government carried out the review of its BITs and how it came up with new model BIT remains

---

Ministry of Commerce and Industry, Lok Sabha, 'Unstarred Question No. 6248' (6 May 2013), http://164.100.47.194/Loksabha/Questions/QResult15.aspx?qref=140786&lsno=15, accessed 14 February 2018.

[46] Government of India, Cabinet Secretariat, Rashtrapati Bhawan, New Delhi (5 April 2013).

[47] Government of India, Ministry of Finance, Department of Economic Affairs, New Delhi. 2013. *Office Memorandum*, 26 March; Also see Kavaljit Singh, *Analysis of India's New Model BIT*.

[48] Government of India, Ministry of Finance. 2013. *Office Memorandum*. New Delhi: Department of Economic Affairs, 26 March; Alsosee Lok Sabha, Unstarred Question No. 3926.

[49] UNCTAD. 2014. 'Statement by India at the World Investment Forum 2014', http://unctad-worldinvestmentforum.org/wp-content/uploads/2014/10/Mayaram.pdf, 16 October, accessed 14 February 2018 (hereinafter, UNCTAD, 'Statement by India at the World Investment Forum 2014').

[50] Government of India, Ministry of Finance, Lok Sabha, 'Unstarred Question No. 4322, BIPPA with Countries' (22 March 2013), http://164.100.47.194/Loksabha/Questions/QResult15.aspx?qref=137667&lsno=15, accessed 14 February 2018 (hereinafter, Lok Sabha, Unstarred Question No. 4322); Also see Lok Sabha, Unstarred Question No. 2391.

[51] Lok Sabha, Unstarred Question No. 4322.

shrouded in secrecy.[52] While it is known that the process was led by the Ministry of Finance, it is not known whether detailed and well-publicized stakeholder consultations with industry, civil society, and the academia were held.[53] However, the Finance Ministry reportedly sought inputs from four international institutions.[54] Moreover, Finance Ministry officials, writing in their personal capacity in 2016, reported that the drafting of the model BIT involved 'rigorous and thoughtful debates within central government ministries and organisations'.[55] This confirms that the process of drafting the Model BIT was largely internal. The Indian government did not consider it appropriate to seek inputs from experts and institutions based in India.[56]

This largely internal review of BITs by the Indian government was completely different from other developing states such as South Africa.[57] South Africa reviewed its BITs by including more than hundred stakeholders from business, labour, local and international institutions.[58] These stakeholders were roped in to inform and update the South African executive about the legal consequences and effects of BITs on the developmental agenda of South Africa.[59]

[52] Mihaela Papa and Aditya Sarkar. 2017. 'Rising India in Investment Arbitration: Shifts in the Legal Field and Regime Participation', in *The Indian Legal Profession in the Age of Globalisation*, David B. Wilkins, Vikramaditya S. Khanna, David M. Trubek (eds), pp. 705 at 723. Cambridge: Cambridge University Press (hereinafter Papa and Sarkar, 'Rising India in Investment Arbitration').

[53] Papa and Sarkar, 'Rising India in Investment Arbitration', pp. 705 at 723.

[54] Papa and Sarkar, 'Rising India in Investment Arbitration', pp. 705 at 723; Singh, 'An Analysis of India's New Model Bilateral Investment Treaty', pp. 82–3.

[55] Garg, Tripathi, and Roy, 'The Indian Model Bilateral Investment Treaty', p. 71.

[56] Singh, 'An Analysis of India's New Model Bilateral Investment Treaty', p. 83.

[57] Mohammad Mossalam. 2015. 'Process Matters: South Africa's Experience Exiting its BITs', GEG Working Paper 2015/97, https://www.geg.ox.ac.uk/sites/geg/files/GEG%20WP_97%20Process%20matters%20-%20South%20Africas%20experience%20exiting%20its%20BITs%20Mohammad%20Mossallam.pdf, accessed 14 February 2018 (hereinafter Mossalam, 'Process Matters').

[58] Mossalam, 'Process Matters'.

[59] Mossalam, 'Process Matters'.

This review process led to two important public admissions being made by the Indian government. First, as also evident from the paper by the Commerce Ministry, that Indian BITs were not well-drafted as they contained broad and vague provisions open to wide interpretation by ISDS tribunals.[60] The government conceded in Parliament that India's earlier BITs 'contained many provisions which can be subjected to broad and ambiguous interpretations'.[61] India's 2014 statement during UNCTAD'S World Investment Forum, specifically mentioned that the FET and MFN provisions in Indian BITs were vague.[62] Explicitly, India said that MFN 'has been expanded to include rights beyond what is granted by a treaty'.[63] This concern arose directly from the *White Industries* case.[64] Likewise, India identified the FET provision in BITs as another candidate susceptible to wide interpretation.[65]

Second, India admitted that its BITs containing broad and vague provisions could encroach upon the host state's regulatory power.[66]

60 Department of Economic Affairs, GoI, Transforming the International Investment Agreement Regime', n 44; GargTripathi, and Roy, 'The Indian Model Bilateral Investment Treaty', pp. 76–7.

61 Government of India, Ministry of Finance, Lok Sabha, 'Unstarred Question No. 1754' (10 March 2017), http://164.100.47.194/Loksabha/Questions/QResult15.aspx?qref=47888&lsno=16, accessed 14 February 2018; Also see Government of India, Ministry of Commerce and Industry, Lok Sabha, 'Unstarred Question No. 169' (17 July 2017), http://164.100.47.194/Loksabha/Questions/QResult15.aspx?qref=53095&lsno=16, accessed 14 February 2018 (hereinafter, Lok Sabha, Unstarred Question No. 169).

62 UNCTAD. 'Statement by India at the World Investment Forum 2014'.

63 UNCTAD. 'Statement by India at the World Investment Forum 2014'.

64 See *White Industries Australia Limited* v. *Republic of India*, UNCITRAL, Final Award (30 November 2011).

65 UNCTAD. 'Statement by India at the World Investment Forum 2014'. As already discussed in Chapter 4, the FET provision in large number of Indian BITs do not provide any normative content and therefore subject to wide interpretations.

66 Government of India, Ministry of Commerce and Industry, Rajya Sabha, Question No. 1122.2017.26 July, http://dipp.nic.in/sites/default/files/ru1122_0.pdf, accessed 14 February 2018; UNCTAD. 'Statement by India at the World Investment Forum 2014'; Department of Economic Affairs, GoI, *The Indian Experience* (n 44).

Specifically, on the basis of *White Industries* award and other ISDS notices served on India, India said that the 'current investment treaty regime' 'can be viewed as unfair for States in the exercise of their regulatory power'.[67]

This admission came more than two decades after India started signing BITs. In the 'acceptance' phase, as discussed in Chapter 3, there was negligible discussion on whether the provisions in India's BITs were broad and whether they were susceptible to wide interpretations despite overwhelming global evidence. It is quite evident that had India not faced a slew of ISDA cases in the aftermath of the *White Industries* case the government would have continued overlooking the effect of the language of BITs on its regulatory powers. Nonetheless, as discussed in Chapter 6, many of these ISDS claims against India are an outcome of bad regulation or regulatory abuse by the Indian State. So, while it is good that India admitted to the problems associated with the broad and vague language of Indian BITs, it would be incorrect to put all the blame entirely on the broad and vague language of Indian BITs for these ISDS claims. Unfortunately, the review process did not focus on this aspect and thus perhaps only partly diagnosed the problem.

Broadly speaking, India's behaviour is consistent with the reactionary approach of several other states that also ignored the risk posed by BITs until they were hit by a flood of ISDS claims.[68]

7.3 Outcome of the Review Process

The review process launched in 2012 led to three outcomes: First, India adopting the Model BIT in 2016; second, India issuing notices of BIT termination to 58 countries; and third, India requesting 25 of its BIT partner states to issue joint interpretative statements in order to resolve, what India described as 'uncertainties and ambiguities that may arise regarding interpretation and

[67] UNCTAD. 'Statement by India at the World Investment Forum 2014'.
[68] Lauge N.S. Poulsen and Emma Aisbett. 2013. 'When the Claims Hit: Bilateral Investment Treaties and Bounded Rational Learning', *World Politics* 65(2): 273 at 276.

application of the standards contained' in India's BITs.[69] Let us discuss each of these outcomes.

7.3.1 Adoption of the 2016 Model BIT

The most significant outcome of the BIT review process was the adoption of a new Model BIT in December 2015, formally published on 14 January 2016,[70] which replaced India's 2003 Model BIT. However, before the adoption of the final Model BIT, the finance ministry circulated a draft version of the Model BIT[71] for comments.[72] The government stated that the objective of the Model BIT 'is to provide appropriate protection to foreign investors in India and Indian investors in the foreign country, while maintaining a balance between the investor's rights and the Government obligations'.[73]

The 2015 draft Model BIT attracted considerable attention.[74] The Model contained many pro-state provisions, which tilted the

[69] Government of India, Ministry of Finance, Department of Economic Affairs. 2016. 'Office Memorandum - Regarding Issuing Joint Interpretative Statements for Indian Bilateral Investment Treaties',8 February, http://indiainbusiness.nic.in/newdesign/upload/Consolidated_Interpretive-Statement.pdf, accessed 14 February 2018 (hereinafter JIS Note).

[70] See Prabhash Ranjan, Harsha Vardhana Singh, Kevin James and Ramandeep Singh, 'India's Model Bilateral Investment Treaty: Is India Too Risk Averse?', August 2018, Brookings India, https://www.brookings.edu/wpcontent/uploads/2018/08/India%E2%80%99s-Model-Bilateral-Investment-Treaty-2018.pdf

[71] Government of India. 2015. 'Draft Model Text for the Indian Bilateral Investment Treaty', https://www.mygov.in/sites/default/files/master_image/Model%20Text%20for%20the%20Indian%20Bilateral%20Investment%20Treaty.pdf, accessed 14 February 2018 (hereinafter, 2015 Draft Indian Model BIT).

[72] Government of India. 2015. 'Comments on the 2015 Draft Indian Model BIT', https://www.mygov.in/group-issue/draft-indian-Model-bilateral-investment-treaty-text/, accessed 14 February 2018 (hereinafter Government of India, 'Comments on the 2015 Draft Indian Model BIT').

[73] Government of India, 'Comments on the 2015 Draft Indian Model BIT'.

[74] Hanessian and Duggal, 'The 2015 Indian Model BIT'; Mahdev, 'Asian Perspectives on Investment and Arbitration', pp.317–48; Lise Jhonson, Lisa Sachs, and Sudhanshu Roy. 2015. 'Next Generation Treaty', *The Indian Express*, 12 November, http://indianexpress.com/article/opinion/columns/

balance in favour of the host state's regulatory power and away from investment protection.[75] For instance, first, the draft contained a 'self-judging' general exception clause. A 'self-judging' clause means that the BIT grants discretion to state to unilaterally deviate from its BIT obligation to protect certain interests based on its assessment.[76] Article 16.1 of the 2015 draft stated 'nothing in this Treaty precludes the Host State from taking actions or measures ... which it considers necessary' to protect public morals, public order, public health, environment, etc. The words, 'which it considers necessary' in Article 16.1 gave the discretion to the host state to self-judge, that is, to take any action, which, in the assessment of the state, was necessary for the protection of its interests. The adjudicator shall therefore have to grant significant deference to the state invoking such exception.[77] While a self-judging 'security exception' is found in numerous investment treaties,[78] a self-judging 'general exception' measure aimed at protecting environment

---

best-investment-treaty/, accessed 14 February 2018. Ranjan, 'Comparing Investment Provisions in India's FTAs with India's Stand Alone BITs'; 2015. 'A BIT of an Overreaction', *The Financial Express*, 4 April, http://www.financialexpress.com/opinion/column-a-bit-of-an-overreaction/60348/, accessed 14 February 2018.

[75] Also see Hanessian and Duggal, 'The 2015 Indian Model BIT'; Anirudh Krishnan. 2015. 'A Bit for the State, a Bit for the Investor', *The Hindu*, 8 September, http://www.thehindu.com/opinion/op-ed/a-bit-for-the-state-a-bit-for-the-investor/article7625893.ece, accessed 14 February 2018 (hereinafter, Krishnan, *A Bit for the State, a Bit for the Investor*).

[76] For more on such clauses see Stephan Schilland Robyn Briese. 2009. 'If the State Considers: Self-Judging Clauses in International Dispute Settlement', in *Max Planck Yearbook of United Nations Law*. Vol. 13, A. von Bagdandy and R. Wolfrum (eds), pp. 61–140. Leiden: Martinus Nijhoff.

[77] JürgenKurtz. 2010. 'Adjudging the Exceptional at International Investment Law: Security, Public Order and Financial Crisis', *International Comparative Law Quarterly* 59(2): 325 at 348.

[78] See Agreement for the Promotion and Protection of Investments Between the Republic of Colombia and the Republic of India (signed on 10 November 2009, entered into force 2 July 2012) ('India–Colombia BIT') art. 13.4 – 'Nothing in this Agreement precludes either Contracting Party from taking action, *which it considers necessary* for the protection of its essential security interests or in circumstances of extreme emergency in accordance with its laws normally, and reasonably applied on a non-discriminatory basis'; Also see Article XXI of GATT.

or public order and morality can be abused by the host state. In short, a 'self-judging' general exception provisions clearly gave precedence to the host state's regulatory power over investment protection.

Second, the 2015 Draft Model BIT stated that investment meant 'enterprise' in the host state that was constituted, organized, and operated in compliance with the laws of the host state.[79] Further, Article 1.2 of the treaty clarified that for an entity to be an 'enterprise' it shall have its management and 'real and substantial business operations' in the host state's territory.[80] For an enterprise to have 'real and substantial business operations' it should satisfy all the following conditions: made a substantial and long-term commitment of capital in the host state; engaged a substantial number of employees in the territory of the host state; assumed entrepreneurial risk; made a substantial contribution to the development of the host state through its operations along with transfer of technological knowhow, where applicable, and carried out all its operations in accordance with the law of the host state.[81]

Requiring a foreign enterprise to cumulatively satisfy all these requirements to be eligible for treaty protection would have made it extremely onerous for foreign corporations to make any effective use of the treaty protection. For example, how many employees should a foreign enterprise employ to satisfy the requirement of engaging a 'substantial number of employees'[82]—a phrase not defined in the 2015 draft Model BIT? It is well known that the number of employees engaged may vary significantly depending on whether the investment is capital-intensive or labour-intensive. Consequently, a capital-intensive investment engaging lesser number of employees would be denied treaty protection even if the investment assumed substantial entrepreneurial risk and made substantial contribution in terms of bringing new technology. Such a stringent definition of investment would have pushed large number of foreign enterprises outside the ambit of treaty protection, which, in turn, would have reduced considerably the opportunities of the host state's regulatory measures being held accountable under the BIT.

[79] See 2015 Draft Model BIT, art. 1.6.
[80] See 2015 Draft Model BIT, art. 1.2(ii).
[81] See 2015 Draft Model BIT, art. 1.2.1.
[82] See 2015 Draft Model BIT, art. 1.2.1 (ii).

Third, the 2015 draft Model BIT did not contain an MFN clause. Absence of an MFN provision meant that the host state's regulatory measures discriminatory towards one foreign investor vis-à-vis another foreign investor, could not be challenged under the treaty.[83] Fourth, the draft Model BIT did not contain a provision on 'full protection and security', which, as discussed in Chapter 4, is a key provision to provide physical protection and security to foreign investment.

Fifth, Article 2.4 of the 2015 draft Model BIT stated that 'nothing in this Treaty shall be interpreted to restrict the rights of either Party to formulate, modify, amend, apply or revoke its Law in good faith'. Thus, the host state could enact a new law or change an existing law, even if it violated a treaty provision, as long as this enactment or change had been made in good faith. Proving a state's bad faith can be an extremely difficult task for the foreign investor.[84] A provision such as this clearly put the interest of the host state way above investment protection. Finally, while the 2015 draft Model BIT retained ISDS provision, it provided for a complex and multi-step procedure for resolving disputes between the investor and the state.[85] This multi-step procedure reduced the appeal of the ISDS mechanism for foreign investors considerably. For example, the 2015 draft Model BIT barred an ISDS tribunal from exercising jurisdiction over 'any legal issue which has been finally settled by any judicial authority of the host State'.[86] Further, Article 14.3 provided that the foreign investor has to first exhaust all local remedies, and after exhausting local remedies and further satisfying many other procedural requirements, will be able to submit the dispute to international arbitration.[87] As one commentator observed, it is hard to envisage too many situations where an investor would fulfil the requirement to exhaust local remedies and yet overcome the jurisdictional restriction imposed by the draft Model BIT.[88] In other words, the draft Model BIT made the ISDS provisions redundant.

[83] Even the Final Model BIT does not contain an MFN clause. For more discussion on this, see Chapter 8.

[84] Salacuse, *The Law of Investment Treaties*. p. 243.

[85] Hanessian and Duggal, 'The 2015 Indian Model BIT'.

[86] See 2015 Draft Model BIT, art. 14.2(ii)(a).

[87] See 2015 Draft Model BIT, art. 14.3.

[88] Krishnan, 'A Bit for the State, a Bit for the Investor'.

The Law Commission of India had some concerns with the draft Model BIT, and thus, decided to take up the draft Model BIT for study.[89] It is critical to note that the LCI that works under the aegis of the Ministry of Law and Justice did not undertake the task of analysing the draft Model BIT on the recommendation of the finance ministry or on the recommendation of any other ministry/department. The decision to study the 2015 draft Model BIT was made by the LCI voluntarily. The Law Commission of India communicated this decision to the finance ministry on 8 April 2015.[90] In order to study the 2015 draft Model BIT, the LCI constituted a subcommittee of experts, of which this author was a member.[91] The subcommittee, after studying the draft Model BIT, came up with specific suggestions on several provisions of the draft Model BIT, which formed the basis of the LCI report submitted to the law minister of India on 27 August 2015.[92] The Law Commission of India's report aimed to 'assist the government in achieving a balanced negotiating text, that takes into consideration the protection of Indian investors investing abroad, as well as safeguarding the regulatory powers of the State'.[93] In other words, the report clearly recognized that the 2015 draft Model BIT, contrary to the government's claim, did not balance investment protection with the state's right to regulate. The report made many recommendations such as inclusion of an MFN Clause; not have a 'self-judging' general exception provision; dropping the restriction imposed on the jurisdiction of the ISDS provision to examine a legal issue settled by a domestic court, etc.[94] The purpose behind these recommendations was to improve the draft Model BIT by balancing investment protection with the host state's right to regulate.

89 Government of India, Law Commission of India, Report No. 260. 2015. 'Analysis of the 2015 Draft Model Bilateral Investment Treaty', p. ii, http://lawcommissionofindia.nic.in/reports/Report260.pdf, accessed 14 February 2018 (hereinafter, Law Commission of India, *Report No. 260*).

90 Law Commission of India, *Report No. 260*, p. 4.

91 Law Commission of India, *Report No. 260*, p. ii.

92 Law Commission of India, *Report No. 260*, p. ii.

93 Law Commission of India, *Report No. 260*, p. 5.

94 Law Commission of India, *Report No. 260*.

India finally adopted a Model BIT scaling down some of the pro-state provisions present in the draft Model BIT.[95] For example, the final 2016 Model BIT does not provide for a 'self-judging' general exception clause.[96] However, it is not known whether the finance ministry took the LCI report in consideration while revising the draft Model BIT. Although the government informed the Parliament that some of the recommendations made by the LCI on issues such as exhaustion of local remedies were accepted.[97] Even if the finance ministry took LCI's report into consideration, it is quite evident that some key recommendations made by the LCI, such as including a restricted MFN provision, were not accepted.

The adoption of the 2016 Model BIT shows that, unlike countries like South Africa that have decide to move out of the BIT system,[98] India continues to repose faith in the system while substantially altering the terms of engagement. These altered terms of engagement codified in the 2016 Model BIT are discussed in Chapter 8.

7.3.2 Termination of BITs

Indian BITs, like several other BITs, include modalities for unilateral termination.[99] For example, Article 15(1) of the India–Croatia BIT

[95] Joel Dahlquist and Luke Eric Peterson. 2016. 'Analysis: In Final Version of its Model Investment Treaty, India Dials Back Ambition of Earlier Proposals – But Still Favours Some Big Changes', *Investment Arbitration Reporter*, 3 January, https://www.iareporter.com/articles/analysis-in-final-version-of-its-new-model-investment-treaty-india-dials-back-ambition-of-earlier-proposals-but-still-favors-some-big-changes/, accessed 14 February 2018; Also see, Amokura Kawharu and Luke R. Nottage. 2017. 'Models for Investment Treaties in the Asian Region: An Underview', *Arizona Journal of International and Comparative Law* (forthcoming).

[96] See Chapter 8 for a detailed comment on the 2016 Model BIT.

[97] See Government of India, Ministry of Finance, Department of Economic Affairs, Rajya Sabha, 'Unstarred Question No. 2635, Changes in the Draft Model Bilateral Investment Treaty', (22 December 2015), https://164.100.158.235/question/annex/237/Au2635.pdf.

[98] Engela C. Schlemmer. 2016. 'An Overview of South Africa's Bilateral Investment Treaties and Investment Policy', *ICSID Review - Foreign Investment Law Journal* 31(1): 167–93 (hereinafter, Schlemmer, 'An Overview of South Africa's Bilateral Investment Treaties and Investment Policy').

[99] An exception to this is the India–Korea BIT of 1996 that is silent on unilateral termination. On termination of treaties in international law see generally

provides that either contracting party can give '*a written notice of its intention to terminate*' the treaty and that the treaty shall stand terminated from the date of receipt of such notice.[100] However, Article 15(2) of the same BIT also provides that notwithstanding the termination of

---

Laurence Helfer. 2012. 'Terminating Treaties', in *The Oxford Guide to Treaties*, Duncan B. Hollis (ed.), pp. 634–49. Oxford: Oxford University Press. For a general discussion on denunciation and termination of BITs see Tania Voon and Andrew D. Mitchell. 2016. 'Denunciation, Termination and Survival: The Interplay of Treaty Law and International Investment Law', *ICSID Review - Foreign Investment Law Journal* 31(2): 413–33 (hereinafter, Voon and Mitchell, 'Denunciation, Termination and Survival'); James Harrison. 2012. 'The Life and Death of BITs: Legal Issues concerning Survival Clauses and the Termination of Investment Treaties', *Journal of World Investment and Trade* 13: 928–50.

[100] See Agreement between the Republic of India and the Republic of Croatia on the Reciprocal Promotion and Protection of Investments (signed 4 May 2001, entered into force 19 January 2002) ('India–Croatia BIT') art. 15(1); Also see Agreement between the Republic of India and the Republic of Armenia on the Reciprocal Promotion and Protection of Investments (signed 23 May 2003, entered into force 30 May 2006) ('India–Armenia BIT') art. 16; Agreement between the Republic of India and the Government of Australia on the Reciprocal Promotion and Protection of Investments (signed 26 February 1999, entered into force 4 May 2000) ('India–Australia BIT') art. 17; Agreement between the Republic of India and the Republic of Austria on the Reciprocal Promotion and Protection of Investments (signed 8 November 1999, entered into force 1 March 2001) ('India–Austria BIT') art. 13; Agreement between the Republic of India and the Republic of Bahrain on the Reciprocal Promotion and Protection of Investments (signed 13 January 2004, entered into force 5 December 2007) ('India–Bahrain BIT') art. 15; Agreement between the Republic of India and the Republic of Bangladesh on the Reciprocal Promotion and Protection of Investments (signed 9 February 2009, entered into force 7 July 2011) ('India–Bangladesh BIT') art. 15; Agreement between the Republic of India and the Republic of Belarus on the Reciprocal Promotion and Protection of Investments (signed 27 November 2002, entered into force 23 November 2003) ('India–Belarus BIT') art. 15; Agreement between the Republic of India and the Republic of Bosnia and Herzegovina on the Reciprocal Promotion and Protection of Investments (signed 12 September 2006, entered into force 13 February 2008) ('India–Bosnia and Herzegovina BIT') art. 15; Agreement

the treaty, it shall continue to be effective for a further period of 15 years from the date of termination for investments made or acquired before the date of termination.[101] Such sunset or survival clauses, routinely found in most BITs, are present in Indian BITs providing for 10[102]

---

between the Republic of India and the Republic of Bulgaria on the Reciprocal Promotion and Protection of Investments (signed 29 October 1998, entered into force 23 September 1999) ('India–Bosnia and Bulgaria BIT') art. 15; Agreement between the Republic of India and the Republic of China on the Reciprocal Promotion and Protection of Investments (signed 21 November 2006, entered into force 1 August 2007) ('India–China BIT') art. 16; India–Columbia BIT, art. 17; Agreement between the Republic of India and the Republic of Croatia on the Reciprocal Promotion and Protection of Investments (signed 4 May 2001, entered into force 19 January 2002) ('India–Croatia BIT') art. 15; Agreement between the Republic of India and the Republic of Cyprus on the Reciprocal Promotion and Protection of Investments (signed 9 April 2002, entered into force 12 January 2004) ('India–Cyprus BIT') art. 16; Agreement between the Republic of India and the Republic of Czech Republic on the Reciprocal Promotion and Protection of Investments (signed 11 October 1996, entered into force 6 February 1998) ('India–Czech Republic BIT') art. 16; Agreement between the Republic of India and the Republic of Denmark on the Reciprocal Promotion and Protection of Investments (signed 6 September 1995, entered into force 28 August 1996) ('India–Denmark BIT') art. 18; Agreement between the Republic of India and the Republic of Egypt on the Reciprocal Promotion and Protection of Investments (signed 9 April 1997, entered into force 22 November 2000) ('India–Egypt BIT') art. 18; Agreement between the Republic of India and the Republic of Finland on the Reciprocal Promotion and Protection of Investments (signed 7 November 2002, entered into force 9 April 2003) ('India–Finland BIT') art. 15.

[101] India–Croatia BIT, art. 15(2).

[102] See Agreement between The Government of The Republic of India and The Government of The Argentine Republic on The Promotion and Reciprocal Protection of Investments (signed 20 August 1999, entered into force 12 August 2002) ('India–Argentina BIT') art. 15; India–Austria BIT, art. 10 and art. 13; India–Bangladesh BIT, art. 9 and art. 15; India–Bulgaria BIT, art. 9 and art. 15; India–Colombia BIT art. 9 and art. 17; India–Egypt BIT art. 15; India–Greece BIT; India–Kazakhstan BIT art. 14(6); India–Macedonia BIT art. 15(1); India–Malaysia BIT, art. 14(3); India–Mauritius BIT art. 13(2); Agreement between The Government of the Republic of India and The Government of the United Mexican

or 15[103] or even 20[104] years of protection to existing investments.

States On the Promotion and Protection of Investments (signed 21 May 2007, entered into force 23 February 2008) ('India–Mexico BIT') art. 32(4); India–Mongolia BIT art. 16(1); Agreement between The Government of The Republic of India and The Government of The Kingdom of Morocco for The Promotion and Protection of Investments (signed 13 February 1999, entered into force 22 February 2001 ('India–Morocco BIT') art. 15(2); India–Qatar BIT, art. 14(1); Agreement between The Government of The Republic of India and The Federal Government of The Federal Republic of Yugoslavia for The Reciprocal Promotion and Protection of Investments (signed 31 January 2003, entered into force 24 February 2009) ('India–Serbia BIT') art. 15(1); India–Slovakia BIT, art. 14(3).

[103] See India–Armenia BIT, art. 16(1); India–Australia BIT, art. 17(2); India–Bahrain BIT, art. 15(2); India–Bosnia & Herzegovina BIT art. 15(1); Agreement between The Government of The Republic of India and The Government of His Majesty The Sultan and Yang Di-Pertuan of Brunei Darussalam on The Reciprocal Promotion and Protection of Investments (signed 22 May 2008, entered into force 15 February 2009) ('India–Brunei BIT') art. 16(1); India–China BIT art. 16(1); India–Czech Republic BIT; India–Denmark BIT art. 18(1); India–Finland BIT art. 15(2); India–France BIT; India–Germany BIT; India–Ghana BIT art. 15(1); India–Hungary BIT art. 15(1); Agreement Between The Government of The Republic of India and The Government of The Republic of Iceland for The Promotion and Protection of Investments (signed 29 June 2007, entered into force 16 December 2008) ('India–Iceland BIT') art. 16(1); Agreement between The Government of the Republic of India and The Government of the Italian Republic for the Promotion and Protection of Investment (signed 23 November 1995, entered into force 26 March 1998) ('India–Italy BIT') art. 14(1); India–Jordan BIT, art. 15(1); Agreement between The State of Kuwait and The Republic of India for The Encouragement and Reciprocal Protection of Investment (signed 27 November 2001, entered into force 28 June 2003) ('India–Kuwait BIT') art. 16(1); Agreement between The Government of The Republic of India and The Government of The Lao People's Democratic Republic for The Promotion And Protection of Investments (signed 9 November 2000, entered into force on 5 January 2003) ('India–Lao PDR BIT') art. 16(1); Agreement between The Government of The Republic of India and The Government of The Republic of Latvia for The Promotion And Protection of Investments (signed 18 February 2010, entered into force 27 November 2010 ('India–Latvia BIT') art. 15(1); India–Libya BIT, art. 15(1); India–Lithuania BIT, art. 18(2).

[104] India–Saudi Arabia BIT, Art.16 (1); India–Oman BIT, Art.15(1).

A critical outcome of the review process was that the Indian government, following the footsteps of South Africa[105] and Indonesia,[106] decided to terminate all existing BITs whose initial validity had expired.[107] Consequently, the Indian government submitted to the Indian Parliament that India has issued notices of BIT termination to 58 countries.[108] UNCTAD's International Investment Agreements (IIAs) database confirms that India has terminated BITs with the following countries: Argentina, Australia, Austria, Croatia, Denmark, Egypt, Germany, Hungary, Indonesia, Italy, Malaysia, Netherlands, Oman, Switzerland, and Spain.[109] The termination of these BITs is to be complimented by the renegotiation of new BITs on the basis of the 2016 Model BIT.[110] Due to the sunset or survival clauses in these BITs, existing investment from these countries or any existing Indian investment into these countries will continue to enjoy protection for a stipulated period of protection. However, any new investment from these countries in India or Indian investment in these countries will not enjoy treaty protection till a new BIT is negotiated. This mega-termination of BITs, in many ways, has taken India back to the pre-1991 era of 'refusal' discussed in Chapter 2.

[105] See Schlemmer, 'An Overview of South Africa's Bilateral Investment Treaties and Investment Policy'.

[106] See Crockett, 'Indonesia's Bilateral Investment Treaties', pp. 437–48.

[107] Government of India, Ministry of Finance, Department of Economic Affairs. 2016. 'Major policy initiatives/ achievements/highlights of the year 2016', December, http://dea.gov.in/sites/default/files/Year%20End%20Review%20Final%20.pdf,, p. 16, accessed 14 February 2018 (hereinafter Department of Economic Affairs, *Major Policy Initiatives*).

[108] Lok Sabha, Unstarred Question No. 1290; Government of India, Ministry of Finance, Lok Sabha, 'Unstarred Question No. 4834' (31 March 2017), http://164.100.47.194/Loksabha/Questions/QResult15.aspx?qref=51410&lsno=16, accessed 14 February 2018.

[109] UNCTAD, *India*. Also see Annex of the Book.

[110] Department of Economic Affairs, *Major Policy Initiatives*, n 111, p.16; Ministry of Finance (Budget Division). 2017. 'Annual Report 2016-17', p. 28, http://dea.gov.in/sites/default/files/Annual%20Report-2016-17-E.pdf, 7 April, accessed 14 February 2018 (hereinafter, Ministry of Finance, *Annual Report 2016-17*).

The unilateral mode of termination of BITs is not the only method of terminating BITs. Article 54(b) of the VCLT allows contracting parties to terminate a treaty at any time by consent of all the parties after consultation with the other contracting states.[111] Thus, BITs can also be terminated by consensus, that is, both countries mutually agreeing to terminate the treaty. It is not known whether India explored the option of convincing its treaty partners to terminate BITs by consensus.[112] Arguably, from the perspective of the host state, mutual termination of BITs has the advantage of negating the survival clause.[113] Since the survival clause kicks in only if a BIT is terminated unilaterally, a mutual termination would render the survival clause inapplicable.[114] India could have also negotiated for amending the survival clause before mutually terminating the BIT.[115]

The first BIT India has been able to negotiate after the adoption of the new Model BIT is with Cambodia.[116] While the text of the BIT

[111] Also see Anthony Aust. 2007. *Modern Treaty Law and Practice*. 2nd edition. Cambridge: Cambridge University Press, p. 292.

[112] For example, although Indonesia terminated most of its BITs unilaterally, the Indonesia–Argentina BIT was extinguished by a mutual agreement – see Luke Eric Peterson. 2015. 'Indonesia ramps up termination of BITs – and kills survival clause in one such treaty – but faces new $600 mil. claim from Indian mining investor', *bilaterals.org*, 20 November, http://bilaterals.org/?indonesia-ramps-up-termination-of, accessed 14 February 2018.

[113] See Catherine Titi. 2016. 'Most-Favoured-Nation Treatment: Survival Clauses and Reform of International Investment Law', *Journal of International Arbitration* 33(5): 425–40 at 436–7 (hereinafter Titi, 'Most-Favoured-Nation Treatment').

[114] Titi, 'Most-Favoured-Nation Treatment', pp. 425–40 at 436–7; Also see Voon and Mitchell, 'Denunciation, Termination and Survival', n 103.

[115] Czech Republic has done this—see Luke Eric Peterson. 2011. 'Czech Republic Terminates Investment Treaties in Such a Way as to Cast Doubt on Residual Legal Protection for Existing Investments', *Investment Arbitration Reporter* 4(2).

[116] Press Information Bureau, Government of India. 2016. 'Cabinet approves Bilateral Investment Treaty between India and Cambodia to Boost Investment', 27 July, http://pib.nic.in/newsite/PrintRelease.aspx?relid=147849, accessed 14 February 2018 (hereinafter Press Information Bureau, 'Cabinet approves Bilateral Investment Treaty between India and Cambodia to Boost Investment').

is not yet publicly available, the Indian government claims that this BIT is in accordance with the text of the 2016 Indian Model BIT.[117] After the adoption of the new Model BIT, India has also signed a BIT with Brazil.[118] While the text of the India–Brazil BIT has not been released, reportedly, the BIT does not contain an ISDS provision,[119] which is a clear departure from the 2016 Indian Model BIT. In accordance with the Indian Model BIT, the India–Brazil BIT, it is claimed, also does not contain an FET and an MFN provision.[120]

The government claims that some developing countries have shown interest in renegotiating BITs with India based on the new Model BIT.[121] These countries are: Tajikistan, Turkmenistan, Kyrgyz Republic, Oman, Qatar, Belarus, Thailand, Armenia, and Zimbabwe.[122] A statement of interest in renegotiating BITs, however, does not imply a concomitant interest in the Indian Model BIT. Further, it may be noted that India is a net capital-exporter to many of these countries and, therefore, protecting Indian investment in these countries assumes great importance. India wants to enter into a BIT with Israel.[123] However, there are many differences between the

[117] Press Information Bureau, 'Cabinet approves Bilateral Investment Treaty between India and Cambodia to Boost Investment'.

[118] Robert G. Volterra and Giorgio Francesco Mandelli. 2017. 'India and Brazil: Recent Steps Towards Host State Control in the Investment Treaty Dispute Resolution Paradigm', *Indian Journal of Arbitration Law* 6(1): 90 (hereinafter, Volterra and Mandelli, 'India and Brazil'); Herbert Smith Freehills. 2016. 'India and Brazil Conclude Negotiations of Bilateral Investment Treaty', 5 December, https://hsfnotes.com/arbitration/2016/12/05/india-and-brazil-conclude-negotiations-of-bilateral-investment-treaty/, accessed 14 February 2018.

[119] Volterra and Mandelli, 'India and Brazil', p. 109.

[120] Volterra and Mandelli, 'India and Brazil', p. 109.

[121] Government of India, Ministry of Finance, Department of Economic Affairs, Rajya Sabha, 'Unstarred Question No. 2927', (28 March 2017), http://164.100.47.4/newrsquestion/ShowQn.aspx; Lok Sabha, Unstarred Question No. 169.

[122] Government of India, Ministry of Finance, Department of Economic Affairs, Rajya Sabha, Unstarred Question No. 2927 (28 March 2017) (http://164.100.47.4/newrsquestion/ShowQn.aspx) (fn 121).

[123] Ministry of External Affairs. 2017. 'India-Israel Joint Statement During the Visit of Prime Minister to Israel', 5 July, http://www.mea.gov.in/

Israeli and the Indian Model BITs, which would make the negotiations difficult.[124]

What is interesting to note is that none of the major capital-exporting countries to India have shown much interest in the Indian Model BIT. For example, Canada wants India to tighten investment protection norms in the Model BIT.[125] Similarly, the US has expressed concerns regarding the non-inclusion of an MFN Clause in the new Indian Model BIT.[126] In fact, there are many differences between the Indian and the US Model BITs, which make future negotiations difficult.[127] The European Union (EU) has expressed displeasure at the unilateral termination of BIT's with EU member states by India.[128] The EU trade commissioner Cecilia Malmstrom said in 2017 that 'India's unilateral decision to terminate these BITs is very unfortunate and has important consequences for the rights

---

bilateral-documents.htm?dtl/28593/IndiaIsrael+Joint+Statement+during+the+visit+of+Prime+Minister+to+Israel+July+5+2017, accessed 14 February 2018.

[124] Prabhash Ranjan. 2017. 'BITs and pieces of trade with Israel', *The Hindu*, 20 July, http://www.thehindu.com/todays-paper/tp-opinion/bits-and-pieces-of-trade-with-israel/article19311072.ece, accessed 14 February 2018.

[125] Amiti Senand Surabhi. 2016. 'Canada to India: Tighten investment protection norms in new model treaty', *The Hindu BusinessLine*, 23 October, http://www.thehindubusinessline.com/economy/canada-to-india-tighten-investment-protection-norms-in-new-model-treaty/article9258701.ece, accessed 14 February 2018 (hereinafter Sen and Surabhi, 'Canada to India').

[126] Surabhi and Nayanima Basu. 2016. 'India-US investment treaty may not be signed in June', *The Hindu Businessline*, 25 May, http://www.thehindubusinessline.com/economy/policy/indiaus-investment-treaty-may-not-be-signed-in-june/article8646381.ece, accessed 14 February 2018; For a detailed commentary on the 2016 Indian Model BIT, see Chapter 8.

[127] Prabhash Ranjan. 2016. 'BIT of a Bumpy Ride', *The Hindu*, 2 June, http://www.thehindu.com/opinion/op-ed/Bit-of-a-bumpy-ride/article14378406.ece, accessed 14 February 2018.

[128] Asit Mishra. 2017. 'India Reluctant on EU Bid for High-level Dialogue on Contentious Issues', *Livemint*, 15 May, http://www.livemint.com/Politics/GJn2AGAFYZxb7lFmRQVpvK/India-cool-to-EU-bid-for-highlevel-dialogue-on-contentious.html, accessed 14 February 2018 (hereinafter Mishra, 'India Reluctant on EU Bid for High-level Dialogue on Contentious Issues').

and protection afforded to European investors in India. In particular, new European investors are facing a period of legal uncertainty, with inherent additional costs and risks associated with investing in India'.[129]

7.3.3 Issuing Joint Interpretations

Article 31(3)(a) of the VCLT provides that while interpreting a treaty, 'there shall be taken into account, together with the context any subsequent agreement between the parties regarding the interpretation of the treaty or the application of its provisions'.[130] In other words, an agreement regarding the meaning or interpretation of the terms of a treaty, after its conclusion, requires the treaty interpreter to take such agreements into account, together with the context of the treaty.[131] In the context of investment treaties, it has been argued that one of the ways a state can influence the interpretation of investment treaties is

[129] Mishra, 'India Reluctant on EU Bid for High-level Dialogue on Contentious Issues'. Aditi Shah. 2018. 'India's Proposed Investment Treaty Terms Leave Foreign Partners Cold', *Reuters*, 19 January, https://in.reuters.com/article/india-investment-treaty/indias-proposed-investment-treaty-terms-leave-foreign-partners-cold-idINKBN1F80J4, accessed 14 February 2018.

[130] For a commentary on Article 31(3)(a) of the VCLT see, Richard K. Gardiner. 2008. *Treaty Interpretation*. Oxford: Oxford Univeristy Press, pp. 216–25 (hereinafter, Gardiner, *Treaty Interpretation*); M.E. Villiger, 2009. *Commentary on the 1969 Vienna Convention on the Law of Treaties*. Leiden: Martinus Nijhoff; Hervé Ascensio. 2016. 'Article 31 of the Vienna Conventions on the Law of Treaties and International Investment Law', *ICSID Review-Foreign Investment Law Journal* 31(2): 366–87.

[131] Yearbook of the International Law Commission. 1966. A/CN.4/SER.A/1966/Add.1, Vol. 2, p. 221, para 14; Gardiner, *Treaty Interpretation*, n 134, p. 216; Romesh Weeramantary. 2012. *Treaty Interpretation in Investment Arbitration*. Oxford: Oxford University Press, pp. 80–1. (hereinafter, Weeramantary, *Treaty Interpretation*); Roberts, 'Power and Persuasion in Investment Treaty Interpretation', pp. 179–225 (hereinafter, Roberts, 'Power and Persuasion in Investment Treaty Interpretation'); Also see J.R. Crawford. 2013. 'A Consensualist Interpretation of Article 31(3) of the Vienna Convention on the Law of Treaties', in *Treaties and Subsequent Practice*, G. Nolte (ed.), p. 29. Oxford: Oxford University Press.

by reaching joint interpretations with other treaty parties.[132] Similarly, it has been argued that issuing joint binding interpretations, relying on Article 31(3)(a) of the VCLT, is one of the ways by which states can reassert control over BITs given the inconsistent and contradictory manner in which ISDS tribunals interpret these treaties.[133]

A good example of countries issuing binding joint interpretation is that of the three North American Free Trade Agreement (NAFTA) states, that is, the US, Canada and Mexico, issuing a joint interpretive statement under the auspices of the FTC.[134] This binding joint interpretation was issued in response to the ostensibly expansive interpretations offered by many NAFTA tribunals of the FET.[135] The joint interpretative statement issued by the NAFTA countries provides that the concept of FET does not require treatment in addition to or beyond what is required by the customary international law minimum standard of treatment of aliens.[136] Same clarification was also issued for the full protection and security provision.[137] North American Free Trade Agreement tribunals have taken the FTC interpretative note on board while interpreting the FET provisions,[138]

[132] Roberts, 'Power and Persuasion in Investment Treaty Interpretation', p. 194.

[133] Eleni Methyamaki and Antonios Tzanakopoulos. 2017. 'Masters of Puppets? Reassertion of Control through Joint Investment Treaty Interpretation', in *Reassertion of Control over the Investment Treaty Regime*, A. Kulick (ed.). Cambridge: Cambridge University Press (hereinafter, Methyamaki and Tzanakopoulos, 'Masters of Puppets?').

[134] North American Free Trade Agreement. 2001. 'Notes of Interpretation of Certain Chapter 11 Provisions', NAFTA Free Trade Commission, 31 July, http://www.international.gc.ca/trade-agreements-accords-commerciaux/topics-domaines/disp-diff/NAFTA-Interpr.aspx?lang=eng, accessed 14 February 2018 (hereinafter, NAFTA FTC Note).

[135] Roberts, 'Power and Persuasion in Investment Treaty Interpretation', p. 180.

[136] NAFTA FTC Note.

[137] NAFTA FTC Note.

[138] *ADF Group Inc.* v. *United States of America*, ICSID Case No. ARB (AF)/00/1, Award (9 January, 2003) para 177, 18 ICSID Rev. 195 (2003); *Methanex* v. *United States*, NAFTA Ch. 11/UNCITRAL Arb. Trib, Jurisdiction and Merits (3 August 2005), pt. IV, ch. C, para 22 (http://www.state.gov/s/l/c3741.htm) accessed 14 February 2018.

although other ISDS tribunals have not made much use of Article 31(3) of the VCLT in interpreting BIT provisions.[139]

India, as per the third critical outcome of the review process, decided to write to 25 countries, pending the expiry of the initial duration of the BIT, to issue a JIS.[140] India hopes to issue a JIS recognizing the uncertainties and ambiguities that may arise in the interpretation of BITs signed with these 25 countries.[141] India believes that a JIS under Article 31(3)(a) and (b) of the VCLT would curtail uncertainties by complimenting the process of treaty interpretation.

Let us briefly examine some of the provisions of India's proposed JIS. Firstly, at the outset, the JIS states that the interpretative note shall be read together with the treaty and shall form an integral part of the treaty.[142] It also states upfront that

> interpretation of this agreement shall be done in accordance with the high level of deference international law accords to states with regard to their development and implementation of domestic policies. Interpretation and application of the agreement shall also reflect strong presumption of legitimacy and regularity international law provides to domestic legislative, administrative and judicial determinations made by the contracting parties.[143]

This language shows that India wants the ISDS tribunals to grant a high deference to states in certain aspects while interpreting the treaty. A part of this language has been incorporated in Article 23.1 of the 2016 Indian Model BIT.[144]

[139] O.K. Fauchald. 2008. 'The Legal Reasoning of ICSID Tribunals: An Empirical Analysis', *European Journal of International Law*19: 301, 332–3; Weeramantary, 'Treaty Interpretation', n 135, p. 80.

[140] JIS Note.

[141] JIS Note; These 25 countries are: Bahrain, Kuwait, Finland, Saudi Arabia, China, Jordan, Libya, Iceland, Macedonia, Myanmar, Mozambique, Latvia, Bangladesh, Serbia, Sudan, Turkey, Lao PDR, Bosnia and Herzegovina, Trinidad and Tobago, Mexico, Syria, Senegal, Lithuania, Colombia, Brunei Darussalam.

[142] See JIS Note, art. 1(1).

[143] JIS Note, art.1(3).

[144] See the discussion in Chapter 8.

Second, Article 4 (3) of the JIS states that for an asset to qualify as investment, the following minimum characteristics have to be satisfied: the lasting contribution of capital or other resources; the expectation of gain or profit; the assumption of risk; and significance for the development of the host country.[145] The requirement that investment be of significance for the development of the host state to enjoy treaty protection, also reflected in Article 1.4 of the 2016 Model BIT and discussed in Chapter 8 in detail, is quite subjective. It is often difficult to objectively ascertain whether an investment has been significant for the host state's development.[146] This is especially so when the text does not give any guidance on how to assess 'significance' for the host state.[147]

Third, Article 5 of the JIS note states that 'in treaties which are silent on inclusion or exclusion of taxation measures from the scope, it is implied that such treaties do not apply to any law or measure regarding taxation including measures taken to enforce taxation obligations'.[148] A complete exclusion of taxation measures from the ambit of the BIT, as also incorporated in Article 2.4(ii) of the 2016 Model BIT,[149] is a clear reaction to the ISDS claims brought by Vodafone and Cairn Energy for changing taxation laws retrospectively.[150] As discussed in Chapter 8, the omission of taxation measures from the purview of BITs would pave the way for abuse of the power of taxation by the host state without any remedy available to the investor under the BIT.

Fourth, Article 6 of the JIS Note offers a number of clarifications on the scope of the FET provision. Like the NAFTA FTC note, it states that the concept of FET does not require treatment in addition to or beyond that which is required by the customary international law minimum standard of treatment of aliens.[151] Another major clarification given in Article 6.3 of the JIS Note is that the FET

[145] JIS Note, art. 4(3).
[146] See Section 8.1 of Chapter 8.
[147] See Section 8.1 of Chapter 8.
[148] JIS Note, art. 5(1).
[149] See section 8.8.1 of Chapter 8.
[150] See Chapter 6.
[151] See JIS Note, art. 6(1).

standard 'does not require compensation for "measures" designed or applied to further [certain] public policy objectives'.[152] The note specifies that these public policy objectives includes protection or improvement of natural resources and environment;[153] protection or improvement of human, animal or plant life or health;[154] protection or improvement of human capital, conditions of work and human rights;[155] protection or improvement of economic conditions and the integrity of the financial system;[156] implementation of fiscal policy measures, including taxation.[157] Article 6.4 further clarifies that 'measures' include new laws and regulations, changes in interpretation and application of existing laws, provided such changes are consistent with the law of the host state adopting such measures.[158]

It is not clear what is the meaning of the words 'does not require compensation for "measures" designed or applied to further [certain] public policy objectives' in Article 6.3. Does it mean that the foreign investor cannot challenge these measures as violations of the FET standard? Or does it mean that while these measures adopted to pursue public policy objectives can be challenged as violations of the FET provision, the host state is under no obligation to compensate the foreign investor even if it is found that the state breached the FET obligation? Either way, it immunizes a large number of the host state's regulatory measures from accountability under the BIT. Further, in order to escape liability, host states may classify all regulatory measures as pursuing public policy objectives notwithstanding their effect on foreign investment. This could open up the possibilities of regulatory abuse by host states. In many ways, this interpretative clarification amounts to rewriting the FET provision in most Indian BITs.

Fifth, the JIS note also states that legislative, executive, regulatory, administrative, and judicial measures of general applicability aimed at achieving public policy objectives shall not constitute expropriation

[152] JIS Note, art. 6(3).
[153] JIS Note, art. 6.3(a).
[154] JIS Note, art. 6.3(b).
[155] JIS Note, art. 6.3(c).
[156] JIS Note, art. 6.3(d).
[157] JIS Note, art. 6.3(e).
[158] JIS Note, art. 6.4.

in the context of FET.[159] In other words, a regulatory measure for the implementation of fiscal policy measures including taxation shall not constitute expropriation whatever be the effect of the regulatory measure on foreign investment.[160]

Sixth, the JIS note provides important clarifications to the MFN provision. Article 9.1 states that the MFN provision is designed to protect against illegitimate and 'intentional' discrimination against a foreign investment or a foreign investor. Consequently, a foreign investor must establish 'intent' to discriminate on part of the host state.[161] Furthermore, Articles 9.2 (a) and (b) clarify that the MFN provision cannot be used to alter the substantive content of the treaty by incorporating provisions found in other treaties; and that the MFN provision does not apply to dispute settlement or to other procedural and jurisdictional provisions.

In sum, the following points can be made about the proposed JIS. First, the language of some of the provisions in the JIS, such as the clarification on definition of investment are examples of re-assertion of control over interpretation of BITs by India, as argued by Methymaki and Tzanakopoulos[162] as well as by Roberts.[163] Arguably, the re-assertion of control, as reflected in the definition of investment, could be to reconcile investment protection with the host state's right to regulate.

Second, the language of some of the provisions in the JIS, such as excluding tax measures altogether or endeavouring to create a safe haven for regulatory measures that pursue public policy objectives from the FET provision, are illustrative of backlash against investment treaties. This backlash is not aimed at recalibrating the system to balance rights of investors and states. It is aimed at diluting considerably the efficacy of BITs to hold states accountable for their regulatory conduct that may impinge on the rights of foreign investors. Third, and related to the above two points, many provisions in

[159] JIS Note, art. 10.3.

[160] JIS Note, art. 10.3(e).

[161] JIS Note, art. 9.1.

[162] Methyamaki and Tzanakopoulos, 'Masters of Puppets?', n 137.

[163] Roberts, 'Power and Persuasion in Investment Treaty Interpretation', n 135.

the JIS are host state friendly and tilt the balance heavily in favour of the host state's regulatory power.

Barring a few countries like Bangladesh,[164] it is not known if other countries have accepted India's proposed JIS note. Given the very pro-state nature of India's JIS and given the fact that India is a major capital exporter to Bangladesh, these developments are more suitable to Bangladesh as a host country than to Indian companies who have or wish to invest in Bangladesh. Further, a unilateral termination of these BITs upon completion of the initial duration cannot be ruled out in the absence of the adoption of the JIS.

7.4 Tentative Steps towards Internalizing BITs

Post the ISDS claims; while there has been greater awareness about BITs in India, not much evidence exists to show the extent to which the Indian government has internalized BITs. Here we document two recent instances to show that some tentative steps have been taken towards internalizing BITs. The first step pertains to signing a 'centre–state investment agreement' and the second one pertains to the proposals made by a high-level committee on arbitration constituted by the ministry of law and justice. We discuss both these developments separately.

[164] Press Information Bureau, Government of India. 2017. 'Cabinet Approves Joint Interpretative Notes on the Agreement between India and Bangladesh for Promotion and Protection of Investments', 12 July, http://pib.nic.in/newsite/PrintRelease.aspx?relid=167345, accessed 14 February 2018; Also see Joint Interpretative Declaration between the Republic of India and the Republic of Colombia Regarding the Agreement For the Promotion and Protection of Investments between India and Colombia, Signed on 10 November 2009, available at: https://dea.gov.in/sites/default/files/JID%20with%20Colombia.pdf.2017. 'Signing of Joint Interpretative Note (JIN) to Bilateral Investment Agreement between India and Bangladesh', 4 October, http://dea.gov.in/sites/default/files/Signed%20Copy%20of%20JIN.pdf, accessed 14 February 2018. A similar JIS has been signed with Colombia recently – 'Joint Interpretative Declaration between the Republic of India and the Republic of Colombia Regarding the Agreement for the Promotion and Protection of Investments between India and Colombia', signed on 4 October 2018, https://dea.gov.in/sites/default/files/JID%20with%20Colombia.pdf.

7.4.1 Centre–State Investment agreement

The 2016 general budget document of the finance ministry states that in order to ensure effective implementation of Indian BITs, a Centre State Investment Agreement (CSIA) be introduced.[165] It was claimed that such an agreement will 'ensure fulfilment of the obligations of the State governments under these treaties' and that States which opt to sign this agreement will be seen as more attractive destinations by foreign investors'.[166] State governments will have the option of signing this agreement with the centre and if any state government does not sign this agreement then it will be informed to all BIT treaty partner countries.[167]

The critical objective behind introducing the CSIA is to sensitize state governments about India's BIT obligations. This sensitization might lead to state governments considering BITs while adopting laws or other regulatory measures to ensure that their laws and regulations are consistent with India's BITs. Such internalization is critical considering many regulations of state governments directly impact foreign investors as the cases of *Rakia* v. *India* and *Nissan* v. *India*, discussed in Chapter 6 demonstrate.

However, in response to a query filed under the RTI Act, the finance ministry informed that this idea was shelved in 2017.[168] According to the finance ministry, in view of the comments received

[165] ArunJaitley. 2016. 'Budget Speech 2016-2017',29 February, http://www.indiabudget.gov.in/budget2016-2017/ub2016-17/bs/bs.pdf, accessed 14 February 2018.

[166] Jaitley, 'Budget Speech 2016-2017'; Ministry of Finance, *Annual Report 2016-17*, n 114, p. 29; Government of India, Ministry of Finance, Department of Economic Affairs, Rajya Sabha, 'Unstarred Question No. 4369, Bilateral Investment Treaty with State government' (11 April 2017), https://164.100.158.235/question/annex/242/Au4369.pdf.

[167] See and Jay ManojSanklecha.2016. 'Sensitise States, Don't Intimidate Them', *The Hindu*, 26 April, http://www.thehindu.com/opinion/columns/Sensitise-States-don%E2%80%99t-intimidate-them/article14257240.ece, accessed 14 February 2018.

[168] Information Sought under RTI Act, Registration Number, MOOCD/R/2018/50035. Reply of Department of Economic Affairs (DEA), finance ministry (on file with the author).

on draft CSIA from concerned ministries/department, it was felt that entering into CSIA with states may have unforeseen and potentially undesirable consequences.[169] Consequently, the finance ministry that mooted this proposal withdrew it on 6 June 2017.[170]

While the finance ministry did not disclose the 'unforseen and potentially undesirable consequences' of the CSIA, it is not too difficult to imagine the problems with such an agreement. Assume that a state government does not sign an agreement with the centre. Further, through omission or commission this particular government infringes the rights enjoyed by a foreign investor under the BIT. If the investor were to challenge this as a violation of the BIT, can the central government, while responding to the claim, argue that the alleged violation was because of a state government's measure and thus the central government is not liable?

The answer to this question is a resounding 'no'. As laid down by the Supreme Court of India in *Azadi Bachao Andolan* v. *Union of India*[171], a combined reading of Entry 14 of the Union List of the Indian Constitution, which provides for entering into treaties, and Article 73, which extends the power of the central government to matters in the Union list, shows that the central government has the power to enter into treaties on behalf of the Indian republic.[172] This includes, but is not limited to, BITs. Once the central government has acceded to the terms of a treaty on behalf of the republic, the

[169] Information Sought under RTI Act, Registration Number, MOOCD/R/2018/50035. Reply of Department of Economic Affairs (DEA), finance ministry (on file with the author).

[170] Information Sought under RTI Act, Registration Number, MOOCD/R/2018/50035. Reply of Department of Economic Affairs (DEA), finance ministry (on file with the author).

[171] (2004) 10 SCC.1.

[172] The Supreme Court in *Maganbhai Ishwarbhai Patel* v. *Union of India* said that '[t]he executive is qua the State competent to represent the State in all matters international and may by agreement, convention or treaties incur obligations which in international law are binding upon the State' - 7 (1970) 3 SCC 400 [80]; Also see National Commission to Review the Working of the Constitution. 2001. 'A Consultation Paper on the Treaty Making Power under our Constitution', 8 January, http://lawmin.nic.in/ncrwc/finalreport/v2b2-3.htm, accessed 14 February 2018.

international obligations assumed thereunder, generally speaking, bind the entire country, including its constituent states, under international law. This is irrespective of whether the central government has entered into an agreement with the state governments regarding the implementation of the said treaty. As far as India's international law obligations are concerned, the central government, cannot justify the non-compliance of its BIT obligations by invoking 'provisions of its municipal law, or because of any special features of its governmental organization or its constitutional system.' This is consistent with the unitary conception of a sovereign nation under international law, where distribution of sovereign powers among its constituent-states is deemed to be an internal matter, not regulated by international law. In other words, the CSIA will not have much legal significance at least under international law.

Further, such an agreement especially in a multi-party democracy like India where the central and state governments are often politically non-aligned might undermine the centre–state relations and cooperative federalism for two reasons. First, the state governments will not like the shifting of the blame for violation of a BIT from New Delhi to state capitals. Second, the non-signatory state governments would not accept their characterization as an unprotected destination for foreign investment.[173]

If the objective of the central government is to sensitize states about BITs, then instead of entering into a CSIA, the central government should consider institutionalizing the involvement of state governments in the process of treaty-making.[174] This would enable the state government to build their internal capacity to deal with challenges that BITs pose. A forum such as the newly set up National Institute for Transforming India (NITI) Aayog,[175] which has the

[173] Also see Prabhash Ranjan and Jay Manoj Sanklecha. 2016. 'Sensitise States, Don't Intimiditate them', *The Hindu*, 26 April.

[174] Rekha Saxena. 2007. 'Treaty Making Powers: A Case for Federalisation and Parliamentarisation', *Economic and Political Weekly* 42(1): 24. Prabhash Ranjan. 2009. 'Treaties on Trade and Investment and the Indian Legal Regime', *Australian Journal of Asian Law* 11(1): 56–81 at 73–6.

[175] NITI Aayog, Government of India (http://niti.gov.in/content/overview) accessed 14 February 2018.

chief ministers of all states as members of the governing council,[176] could be used to create a centre–state consultative process on negotiating and signing BITs.

7.4.2 High-Level Committee on Arbitration

In December 2016, the Ministry of Law and Justice of Indian government constituted a high-level committee, under the leadership of Justice B.N. Srikrishna, to review effectiveness of arbitration in India and to prepare a roadmap to make India a hub of international arbitration.[177] The committee had retired and serving judges, practising lawyers, industry representatives, and an official of the ministry of law as its members.[178] No academic or an expert in international arbitration was appointed to serve as a member of the committee. One of the tasks given to the Srikrishna committee was to 'focus on the role of arbitrations in matters involving the Union of India, including bilateral investment treaties (BIT) arbitrations and make recommendations where necessary'.[179] Notwithstanding this, no official from the ministry of finance (the nodal body that deals with BITs in India) was appointed to serve on the committee.

The committee submitted its report to the law minister in July 2017 recommending many changes in Indian arbitration law and institutional mechanisms to promote arbitration in India.[180] The

[176] NITI Aayog. 2015. 'Composition of Governing Council', http://niti.gov.in/writereaddata/files/Composition%20of%20Governing%20Council%20of%20NITI%20Aayog.pdf, 16 February, accessed 14 February 2018.

[177] Press Information Bureau, Government of India. 2016. 'Constitution of High Level Committee to Review Institutionalization of Arbitration Mechanism in India', 29 December, http://pib.nic.in/newsite/PrintRelease.aspx?relid=155959 (hereinafter Press Information Bureau, 'Constitution of High Level Committee to Review Institutionalization of Arbitration Mechanism in India').

[178] Press Information Bureau, 'Constitution of High Level Committee to Review Institutionalization of Arbitration Mechanism in India'.

[179] Press Information Bureau, 'Constitution of High Level Committee to Review Institutionalization of Arbitration Mechanism in India'.

[180] Justice B.N. Srikrishna (Chairman of committee). 2017. 'High Level Committee to Review Institutionalization of Arbitration Mechanism in India',

committee's recommendations are largely on the issue of managing and resolving BIT disputes. Here we focus on the committee's recommendations on BIT arbitration.

For better management of BIT disputes, the committee has recommended the creation of an inter-ministerial committee (IMC), which will have officials from the ministries of finance, external affairs, and law. The committee has also recommended hiring external lawyers having expertise in BIT arbitrations to boost the government's legal expertise; creating a designated fund to fight BIT disputes; appointing counsels qualified in BIT arbitration to defend India against BIT claims. As a step towards internalizing BITs, the committee recommended that

> there must be targeted capacity building measures within the government to help in policy formulation, decision-making and timeline management to help the state effectively deal with an investment treaty arbitration. Therefore, it may be worthwhile for the government to undertake a capacity building exercise, whereby mid-level and senior lawyers who appear for or advise the government, as well as senior bureaucrats and potential judges, are sent to attend appropriately tailored courses on investment law and investment treaty arbitration.[181]

The most significant recommendation of the committee is the creation of the post of an 'International Law Adviser' (ILA) to advise the government on international legal disputes particularly BIT disputes; and who will be responsible for the day-to-day management of a BIT arbitration.[182] The intent behind this suggestion is laudable, that is, augmenting the government's expertise on BITs and designating a single authority for dealing with all BIT arbitrations. However,

---

30 July, http://legalaffairs.gov.in/sites/default/files/Report-HLC.pdf, accessed 14 February 2018 (hereinafter Srikrishna, 'High Level Committee to Review Institutionalization of Arbitration Mechanism in India').

[181] Srikrishna, 'High Level Committee to Review Institutionalization of Arbitration Mechanism in India', p. 105.

[182] Srikrishna, 'High Level Committee to Review Institutionalization of Arbitration Mechanism in India', p. 110.

this recommendation will amount to duplicating an already existing arrangement to offer advice on international law, including BITs, to the government.

The legal and treaties (L&T) division of the external affairs ministry is mandated to offer legal advice to the government on all international law matters including BIT arbitrations.[183] Instead of creating a new office for dealing with BIT arbitrations, which would only deepen the red-tape and departmental turf-wars between ministries, the L&T division should be strengthened and upgraded. The legal and treaties division is currently understaffed,[184] which hampers its working. Given the vast experience and expertise in dealing with international law dipsutes and matters before different international tribunals, the L&T division should be made the designated authority to deal with all BIT arbitrations and, thus act as the coordinator of the proposed IMC. Furthermore, the IMC should have a member from the commerce ministry as well. Commerce ministry, while dealing with India's trade agreements—that also cover investment protection—works in tandem with the finance ministry. Thus, it is only prudent that both be part of an IMC on BIT dispute management.

On resolving BIT disputes, the committee made some useful interventions such as mentioning the possibility of establishing a BIT appellate mechanism and a multilateral investment court. However, committee's conclusion that the investor–state dispute settlement (ISDS) mechanism, given in Article 15 of the Indian Model BIT, provides an effective mechanism for settling BIT disputes between an investor and state is problematic.[185] The ISDS mechanism in the Model BIT is discussed in Chapter 8. It is not known whether

[183] Ministry of External Affairs, Legal and Treaties Division, http://www.mea.gov.in/treaty.htm, accessed 14 February 2018.

[184] A query was raised in the Indian parliament about the existence of vacancies in the L&T Division in 2017 – Government of India, Ministry of External Affairs, Lok Sabha, 'Unstarred Question No. 5163, Vacancies in Legal and Treaties Division' (5 April 2017), http://www.mea.gov.in/lok-sabha.htm?dtl/28320/QUESTION+NO5163+VACANCIES+IN+LEGAL+AND+TREATIES+DIVISION, accessed 14 February 2018.

[185] Also see Prabhash Ranjan. 2017. 'A BIT of Critique', *The Hindu*, 24 August, http://www.thehindu.com/opinion/op-ed/a-bit-of-critique/article19547578.ece, accessed 14 February 2018.

the government has accepted all recommendations of the committee and whether it has started working towards implementing these recommendations.

This report clearly points to the lack of consistency and coordination within different ministries of the Indian government in dealing with BITs in general and BIT arbitration in particular. In fact, none other than the finance minister of India, Arun Jaitley, in a letter written to the prime minister's office on 26 May 2017, recognizes these problems. The letter shows the various faultlines within the government on the issue of handling of BIT dipsutes, and is worth quoting in full:

> A former colleague from the legal fraternity has handed me a note which I am enclosing. It indicates that under various bilateral treaties, there are 23 arbitrations which are on, where Government of India is not being adequately represented. There are some which concern the Department of Revenue which I am bringing to the notice of Revenue Secretary for immediate action. There are others which are dealt by the Ministry of Mines [Rakia v. India] and Ministry of Heavy Industries [Nissan v. India]. These are illustrative cases only.
>
> In some cases we [Indian government] are defaulting in the matter of appointment of arbitrators. This will result in the international forum usurping our power to appoint the arbitrator. We have engaged lawyers who may not have adequate stature to create an impact on these arbitrations. Further, there is no coordinating Ministry which is following up on day to day basis. This needs to be addressed adequately'.[186]

7.5 Summing up

The discussion in this chapter shows how different actors or stakeholders such as the parliament, the government, civil society, and so on started reacting to India's BITs once India was flooded by ISDS claims. The reactions varied from asking the purpose of BITs, examining do BITs lead to greater FDI inflows, questioning the

186 *The Wire*. 2017. 'ArunJaitely's Letter to PMO on Vodafone Arbitration', 26 May, https://www.scribd.com/document/375590061/Arun-Jaitley-s-Letter-to-PMO-on-Vodafone-Arbitration-dated-May-26-2017#from_embed.

relationship between BITs and India's right to regulate. There was a much deeper engagement with BITs in this phase than we saw in the 'acceptance' phase. The period also saw some efforts to internalize BITs, that is, the process of ensuring that BITs are taken into account while reaching policy decisions. India launched the review of BITs in this phase and took certain decisions, which can be described as backlash against BITs. India terminated some of its BITs and also adopted a Model BIT that we discuss in the next chapter. The faith that India had shown towards BITs in the 'acceptance' phase stood shaken. However, it is also important to bear in mind that barring some non-governmental organizations, the backlash that we see against BITs and ISDS, especially emanating from the government is not a broader backlash against globalization. India continues to remain committeed to an open and liberal economy. This backlash is specific to the nature of BITs mainly due to the ISDS cases that have been brought against India.

8

The 2016 Indian Model BIT

Making the BIT Unworkable for Investors

Having discussed the developments leading to the adoption of the 2016 Model BIT in the last chapter, this chapter critically examines India's 2016 Model BIT.[1] As mentioned in the last chapter, the 2016 Model BIT shows the altered terms with which India wants to remain engaged within the BIT system. Unlike the 2003 Model BIT,[2] the 2016 Model BIT is very detailed and contains 38 Articles divided into seven chapters. While the 2016 Model BIT has been commented upon,[3] including

[1] Also see Prabhash Ranjan and Pushkar Anand. 2017. 'The 2016 Model Indian Bilateral Investment Treaty: A Critical Deconstruction', *Northwestern Journal of International Law and Business* 28 (1): 1.

[2] Government of India. 2003. 'Indian Model Text of Bilateral Investment Promotion and Protection Agreement', http://www.italaw.com/sites/default/files/archive/ita1026.pdf, accessed 9 January 2018.

[3] Prabhash Ranjan, 2017. 'Investment Protection and Host State's Right to Regulate in Indian Model Bilateral Investment Treaty 2016: Lessons for Asian countries', in International Law of Foreign Investment in Asia: Sustainability, Regionalization and Arbitration, Julien Chaisse, Tomoko Ishikawa, and Sufian Jusoh (eds), pp. 47–65. Singapore: Springer; Hanessian and Duggal, 'The Final 2015 Indian Model BIT', pp. 216–26, (hereinafter Hanessian & Duggal, *Is this the Change the World wishes to See*); Rajput, 'India's Shifting Treaty Practice',

quite uncritically[4] this chapter studies the Model BIT from the standpoint of two key objectives that the government claims seeks to achieve through the Model BIT. Firstly, the Model BIT purportedly seeks to provide 'appropriate protection to foreign investors in India' 'while maintaining a balance between investor's rights and the government's obligations'.[5] The submissions of the Government of India to the Indian Parliament stated that the 'new Indian Model Bilateral Investment Treaty text is aimed at providing appropriate protection to foreign investors in India and Indian investors in the foreign country, in the light of relevant international precedents and practices, while maintaining a balance between the rights of the investors rights and the obligations of the Government'.[6] Secondly, the Model BIT ostensibly aims to provide precise treaty provisions to minimize arbitral discretion.[7]

---

pp. 201–26 (hereinafter Rajput, *India's Shifting Treaty Practice*); Kawharu and Nottage, 'Models for Investment Treaties in the Asian Region'; Sharma, 'A Good Offence Is Not Always the Best Defence', pp. 203–7.

4 See various chapters in Rajput, *Protection of Foreign Investment in India and Investment Treaty Arbitration.*

5 Garg Tripathi, and Roy, 'The Indian Model Bilateral Investment Treaty'; Department of Economic Affairs, Ministry of Finance, Government of India. 2016. 'Transforming the International Investment Agreement Regime: The Indian Experience',http://unctad-worldinvestmentforum.org/wp-content/uploads/2015/03/India_side-event-Wednesday_Model-agreements.pdf, accessed 9 January 2018 (India's presentation in a Side Event at World Investment Forum 2016).

6 Department of Industrial Policy & Promotion, Ministry of Commerce & Industry, Government of India, Lok Sabha,'Unstarred Question No. 1290' (25 July 2016), http://164.100.47.190/loksabhaquestions/annex/9/AU1290.pdf, accessed 9 January 2018. Also see Ministry of Finance, Budget Division. 2017. *Annual Report 2016-17*, http://dea.gov.in/sites/default/files/Annual%20Report-2016-17-E.pdf, p. 28, 7 April.

7 Garg Tripathi, and Roy,'The Indian Model Bilateral Investment Treaty', pp. 76–7. For more on these reasons and justifications see Part II of the paper. The effort by India to minimize arbitral discretion can also been seen as an attempt to assert greater control over the investment treaty regime. On this, see generally–Kulick, *Reassertion of Control Over the Investment Treaty Regime.*

We will study the following key jurisdictional, substantive, and dispute resolution provisions in the 2016 Model BIT: definition of investment (Section 8.1), MFN (Section 8.2), fair and equitable treatment (Section 8.3), full protection and security (Section 8.4), expropriation (Section 8.5) monetary transfer provisions (Section 8.6), general exception clause (Section 8.7), other exceptions (Section 8.8), investor-state dispute settlement provision (Section 8.9), and termination of the BIT (Section 8.10) from two standpoints: firsly, whether the Model BIT balances investment protection with state's right to regulate and, secondly, whether the draft of the Model BIT can assist in reduing arbitral discretion as claimed by the Indian government.

8.1 Definition of Investment

As discussed in Chapter 4, the definition of investment in a BIT plays an important role in determining the scope of rights and obligations under the treaty and the establishment of the ISDS tribunal jurisdiction. Most Indian BITs provide a broad asset-based definition of 'investment' where every kind of asset with economic value established or acquired by the foreign investor amounts to an investment. In the 2016 Model BIT, India has sought to move away from broad asset-based definition of investment to an enterprise-based definition where an enterprise is taken together with its assets.[8] Therefore, only an enterprise that is legally constituted in India can bring a claim under the relevant BIT.[9] The transition from an asset-based

[8] See Government of India. 2014. 'Model Text for the Indian Bilateral Investment Treaty 2016', http://mof.gov.in/reports/ModelTextIndia_BIT.pdf (hereinafter '2016 Indian Model BIT'), 16 October. art 1.4 provides:

> 'investment' means an enterprise constituted, organised and operated in good faith by an investor in accordance with the law of the Party in whose territory the investment is made, taken together with the assets of the enterprise, has the characteristics of an investment such as the commitment of capital or other resources, certain duration, the expectation of gain or profit, the assumption of risk and a significance for the development of the Party in whose territory the investment is made...

[9] '2016 Indian Model BIT', art. 1.3 provides: enterprise means: (i) any legal entity constituted, organized and operated in compliance with the law of

approach to an enterprise-based approach aims to narrow the scope of protected investments and thus seeks to reduce the number of BIT claims that may be brought against India.[10]

In the 2016 Model BIT, investment means an enterprise that has been constituted, organized, and operated in good faith by an investor in accordance with the domestic laws of the country.[11] Article 1.4 also provides a non-exhaustive list of assets that an enterprise may possess.[12] Further, the enterprise must satisfy certain characteristics of investment such as commitment of capital and other resources, duration, the expectation of gain or profit, and the assumption of risk and significance for the development of the country where the investment is made. Article 1.4 does not clarify whether the characteristics of investment are to be satisfied by an enterprise or by its assets. This may be understood with the help of the following example: let us assume that a foreign pharmaceutical enterprise, legally constituted in India for last 10 years, gets a patent on a drug. After, say, just six months from the granting of the patent, the Indian government revokes the patent for some reason, and the enterprise wishes to challenge the revocation before an arbitral tribunal. Here, will the 'characteristics test' of investment be required to be satisfied by the asset (patent right), the enterprise, or both? If it is the patent right, then it might be difficult to satisfy the 'characteristics test' due to the short duration for which the asset has been in existence. If, on the other hand, the 'characteristics test' has to be satisfied by the enterprise, it would be easier to fall under the definition of 'investment' and the short duration for which the patent right has been in existence will be irrelevant.

The definition of investment does not also clarify the actual meaning of the characteristics that an enterprise or asset is expected to

---

a Party, including any company, corporation, limited liability partnership or a joint venture; and (ii) a branch of any such entity established in the territory of a Party in accordance with its law and carrying out business activities there.

[10] Srikar Mysore and Aditya Vora. 2016. 'Tussle for Policy Space in International Investment Norm Setting: The Search for a Middle Path?', *Jindal Global Law Review* 7(2): 135, 143.

[11] '2016 Indian Model BIT', art. 1.4.

[12] '2016 Indian Model BIT', art.1.4 (a) to (h).

possess. For instance, the definition does not specify how long the enterprise should be in existence to be part of the definition of investment and thus leaves this determination to the discretion of an ISDS tribunal. Similarly, the lack of guidance available to determine the meaning of 'significance for the development' of the country accords further discretion to ISDS tribunals. This requirement was inserted in the Model BIT to ensure that assets that do not contribute to the development of the host country do not enjoy treaty protection.[13] However, as the tribunal in *LESI SpA* v. *Algeria* held, it is difficult to ascertain whether an investment has contributed to the development of the host state.[14] For instance, it is not clear how sizeable or successful the investment should be to conclude that it has contributed to the development of the host state.[15] While some tribunals suggest that it is enough if the investment contributes in one way or another,[16] other tribunals have held that this contribution should be 'significant.'[17] The absence of precise benchmarks against which the 'significance' of contribution may be measured, leaves the same to be decided by the arbitral discretion of ISDS tribunal, the exact opposite of the government's intent of reducing arbitral discretion. Moreover, including this criterion to determine whether an investment has been made would also mean, as the Annulment Committee held in *Malaysian Historical Salvors* v. *Malaysia*,[18] that investments making

[13] Garg, Tripathi, and Roy, 'The Indian Model Bilateral Investment Treaty', 84. On broad asset-based definitions of foreign investment allowing for a large range of transactions to enjoy protection under the BIT see UNCTAD (2011), 9.

[14] *LESI SpA et Astaldi SpA* v. *Algeria*, ICSID Case No. ARB/05/3, Decision on Jurisdiction (French), 12 July 2006, para 72(iv).

[15] See *Mr. Patrick Mitchell* v. *The Democratic Republic of Congo*, ICSID Case No. ARB/99/7, Annulment proceeding, 9 February 2004, para 33 (hereinafter *Patrick Mitchell* v. *Congo*). See Ranjan and Anand 2017.

[16] *Patrick Mitchell* v. *Congo*. See Ranjan and Anand 2017.

[17] *Malaysian Historical Salvors* v. *Malaysia*, ICSID Case No. ARB/05/10, Award on Jurisdiction (17 May 2007) para 124.

[18] *Malaysian Historical Salvors* v. *Malaysia*, ICSID Case No. ARB/05/10, Decision on the Application for Annulment, 16 April 2009 (hereinafter *Malaysian Historical Salvors* v. *Malaysia*).

'small contributions, and contributions of a cultural and historical nature' shall not get treaty protection.[19] It tilts the balance in favour of the host state because treaty protection could be denied to foreign investments despite being lawful and despite making a commitment of capital or other resources on the subjective ground that it is not significant for the development of the host state.

8.2 Most Favoured Nation Treatment

In Chapter 4, we discussed the importance of the MFN provision in BITs. Post the White Industries setback,[20] India took the stand that use of the MFN provision by foreign investors to borrow beneficial substantive and procedural provisions from third country BITs, in order to replace or supplement the provisions of the primary BIT, disturbs the various strategic, diplomatic, and political reasons behind the negotiation of bilateral treaties.[21] Therefore, in order to ensure non-repetition of the White Industries situation, the Indian Model BIT 2016 does not include an MFN provision.[22]

However, not having an MFN provision in the BIT means exposing foreign investment to the risk of discriminatory treatment by the host state on two levels. First, the host state could offer preferential treatment to the foreign investor under one BIT without providing the same treatment to the foreign investor under another. Here is a simple example to illustrate this: Assume the BIT between countries A and B does not contain an FET provision, whereas the BIT between countries B and C does. Absence of an MFN provision in the A–B BIT would mean that while investors from C can enjoy

[19] *Malaysian Historical Salvors* v. *Malaysia* para 80 (b).

[20] *White Industries Australia Limited* v. *Republic of India*, UNCITRAL, Final Award (30 November 2011), discussed in Chapter 4.

[21] UNCTAD. 2014. 'Statement by India at the World Investment Forum 2014', http://unctad-worldinvestmentforum.org/wp-content/uploads/2014/10/Mayaram.pdf (hereinafter 'India's 2014 Statement'), 16 October, accessed 9 January 2018; Garg, Tripathi, and Roy, 'The Indian Model Bilateral Investment Treaty', pp. 75–6.

[22] Garg, Tripathi, and Roy, 'The Indian Model Bilateral Investment Treaty', p. 76.

FET protection in country B, country A's investors will not be able to borrow the FET protection into the A–B BIT and thus not enjoy FET protection in country B. Second, the host state could offer preferential treatment to foreign investors from one country and not offer the same treatment to foreign investors from another country in the application of domestic measures or regulations. For example, country B offers tax incentives to country C's investors and not to country A's investors. Absence of an MFN provision in the A–B BIT would mean that investors from country A cannot ask for the same tax concessions from country B.

A more balanced approach to abate India's concern to proscribe foreign investors from borrowing beneficial procedural and substantive provisions from a secondary BIT could have been addressed by limiting the scope of the MFN treatment in the BIT, rather than its outright removal. The EU–Canada Comprehensive Economic and Trade Agreement (CETA)[23] is a progressive example of the same. Article 8.7(1) of the EU–Canada CETA contains the MFN provision, which puts both sides under an obligation not to accord treatment less favourable to a foreign investor than that accorded in like situations to investors of a third country with respect to the establishment, acquisition, expansion, conduct, etc. This clearly means that host states cannot discriminate between foreign investors in the application of domestic regulatory measures (similar to the second situation discussed earlier). In order to limit the scope of the MFN provision so as to exclude first situation discussed earlier, Article 8.7(4) states that 'treatment' referred to in Article 8.4(1) does not include 'procedures for the resolution of investment disputes between investors and states provided for in other international investment treaties' and that 'substantive obligations in other international investment treaties and other trade agreements do not in themselves constitute "treatment" and thus cannot give rise to a breach of this Article [MFN]'

[23] Comprehensive Economic and Trade Agreement Between Canada, of the one Part, and the European Union and its Member States, of the Other Part, Oct. 30, 2016, 2016/0206 (NLE), Chapter 8 (Investment). (hereinafter 'EU–Canada CETA'), http://international.gc.ca/trade-commerce/trade-agreements-accords-commerciaux/agr-acc/ceta-aecg/text-texte/toc-tdm.aspx?lang=eng, accessed 9 January 2018.

unless a host state has adopted or maintained measures pursuant to those obligations.[24] This clarification ensures that investors cannot use the MFN provision to borrow beneficial procedural provisions or beneficial substantive provisions from a secondary BIT unless it can be shown that the host state has adopted or is maintaining a domestic measure in accordance with some substantive provision given in the BIT. Even the Law Commission of India[25] had recommended this balanced approach[26] to not do away with the MFN provision completely that exposes foreign investors to discriminatory treatment and tilts the balance in favour of the host state's regulatory power.

8.3 Fair and Equitable Treatment

The 2016 Model BIT does not contain an FET provision.[27] India decided not to include a provision on FET because ISDS tribunals have often interpreted this provision too broadly.[28] Instead, the Model BIT contains a provision entitled 'Treatment of Investments'.[29] Article 3.1 prohibits a country from subjecting foreign investments to measures that constitute a violation of customary international law 'through':

[24] Comprehensive Economic and Trade Agreement Between Canada, of the one Part, and the European Union and its Member States, of the Other Part, Oct. 30, 2016, 2016/0206 (NLE), Chapter 8 (Investment). (hereinafter 'EU–Canada CETA'), http://international.gc.ca/trade-commerce/trade-agreements-accords-commerciaux/agr-acc/ceta-aecg/text-texte/toc-tdm.aspx?lang=eng,accessed 9 January 2018,art. 8.7(4). See Ranjan and Anand, 'The 2016 Model Indian Bilateral Investment Treaty, pp. 22–5.

[25] Law Commission of India. 2015. *Analysis of the 2015 Draft Model Indian Bilateral Investment Treaty*, Report No. 260, p. 24, August,http://lawcommissionofindia.nic.in/reports/Report260.pdf, accessed 9 January 2018.

[27] See Rajput, 'India's Shifting Treaty Practice'. Ranjan and Anand, 'The 2016 Model Indian Bilateral Investment Treaty, 25–28.

[28] India's 2014 Statement, n 19.

[29] See 2015 Draft Model BIT, n 4, art. 3. 2015. 'Comments on the 2015 Draft Indian Model BIT', https://www.mygov.in/group-issue/draft-indian-Model-bilateral-investment-treaty-text/, accessed 9 January 2018 (hereinafter 2015 Draft Model BIT).

1) denial of justice, which covers both judicial and administrative proceedings; or
2) fundamental breach of due process; or
3) targeted discrimination on manifestly unjustified grounds such as gender, race, or religious belief or
4) manifestly abusive treatment such as coercion, duress, and harassment.[30]

The above Article is an attempt to provide normative content to the international minimum standard (IMS)[31] without a direct reference to the FET provision. This content, distinct even from the standard formulated under the 1926 *Neer* award,[32] also rejects the evolution of the IMS with respect to treatment of foreign investors, a stance taken by many NAFTA tribunals. For instance, the tribunal in *Mondev.* v. *USA*[33] held that the 'content of the minimum standard today cannot be limited to the content of customary international law as recognised in arbitral decisions in the 1920s'.[34]

Another possible reason for the absence of an FET provision from the Indian Model BIT is to remove the controversial concept of legitimate expectations, which many tribunals have held to be part of the FET provision.[35] It may be recalled that while some tribunals

[30] 2016 Model Bit, art. 3.1.

[31] For a discussion on IMS in context of the FET provision, see Section 4.2 of Chapter 4.

[32] *LFH Neer and PE Neer* v. *United Mexican States* (Docket No. 136), General Claims Commission – United States and Mexico, 4 UNRIAA 60 (15 October 1926), see Section 4.2 of Chapter 4; Hanessian and Duggal, 'The 2015 Indian Model BIT', p.729.

[33] *Mondev International Ltd.* v. *United States of America*, ICSID Case No. ARB(AF)/99/2, Award (11 October 2002)

[34] *Mondev International Ltd.* v. *United States of America*, ICSID Case No. ARB(AF)/99/2, Award (11 October 2002), para 123. Many other ISDS tribunals have expressed the same view – see *Gami Investments, Inc.* v. *The Government of the United Mexican States*, UNCITRAL Final Award (15 November 2004) para 95; *Merril* v. *Canada,* paras 205-13. Also see, Jonathan Bonnitcha. 2014. *Substantive Protection under Investment Treaties: A Legal and Economic Analysis*. Cambridge: Cambridge University Press, pp.151–2.

[35] See Section 4.2 in Chapter 4.

have interpreted the notion of legitimate expectations broadly,[36] other ISDS tribunals, like the tribunal in *Glamis Gold* v. *USA*, have narrowed the scope of legitimate expectations to situations where a host state's conduct 'creates reasonable and justifiable expectations on the part of an investor (or investment) to act in reliance on said conduct'.[37] A similar narrower definition of legitimate expectations is given in Article 8.10(4) of the EU–Canada CETA. Article 8.10(4) states that while judging the FET obligation, a tribunal may take into 'account whether a Party made a specific representation to an investor to induce a covered investment, that created a legitimate expectation, and upon which the investor relied in deciding to make or maintain the covered investment, but that the Party subsequently frustrated'. This narrower definition of legitimate expectations consists of three parts: firstly, whether the host state made a specific representation to the investor inducing her investment; secondly, whether the investor relied upon this representation in making the investment; and thirdly, whether the host state subsequently frustrated the representation. This approach reconciles the interests of the foreign investors as well as the state.

On the one hand, it avoids the broad definition of legitimate expectations followed by tribunals, such as in *Tecmed* v. *Mexico*, thereby allowing sufficient regulatory space to the host state. Thus, the change in laws and regulatory framework by a state would not amount to breach of legitimate expectations, unless specifically contracted between the state and the investor. On the other hand, the above definition also reassures foreign investors that their investments shall be protected if the host state renege on a promise to the investor for investing.[38] In short, legitimate expectations worded in

[36] See *S.A* v. *USA*; *PSEG Global Turkey*, paras 252–253; *Duke Energy* v. *Ecuador*, para 340. Also see the discussion in section 4.2 of Chapter 4.

[37] *Glamis Gold* v. *USA*, para 621; *Thunderbird* v. *Mexcio*, para 147.

[38] Henckels, in context of EU–Canada CETA, where such a meaning of legitimate expectations is given, writes that the text should also clarify the circumstances in which it would be permissible for the host state to deviate 'from legitimate expectations once established'—see Henckels, 'Protecting Regulatory Autonomy through Greater Precision in Investment Treaties', p. 38. (hereinafter Henckels, 'Protecting Regulatory Autonomy through Greater Precision in Investment Treaties').

this narrower form would place constraints upon the discretion of ISDS tribunals.[39] The Indian Model BIT should have included this narrower definition of legitimate expectations, instead of ousting the concept completely. The non-inclusion of legitimate expectations even in a narrower form tilts the scale in favour of the host state's regulatory power.

Another key omission in Article 3.1 of the Indian Model BIT is the removal of arbitrariness as a ground to challenge the host state's regulatory measure. Investor–state dispute settlement tribunals,[40] including the NAFTA tribunal, have held that if a state acts in a manifestly arbitrary manner, it breaches the IMS.[41] The ICJ, in the *ELSI* case,[42] provided some guidance regarding the meaning of arbitrary action. The World Court stated that arbitrariness 'is not so much something opposed to a rule of law, as something opposed to the rule of law … It is a wilful disregard of due process of law, an act which shocks, at least surprises, a sense of juridical propriety'.[43] Non-inclusion of 'manifest arbitrariness' in the Indian Model BIT leaves a gap in the protection of foreign investment. The inclusion of 'manifest arbitrariness' would have provided reasonable regulatory latitude to India while also ensuring protection to foreign investors from acts in bad faith or in an irrational or manifestly unreasonable manner.

[39] Henckels, in context of EU–Canada CETA, where such a meaning of legitimate expectations is given, writes that the text should also clarify the circumstances in which it would be permissible for the host state to deviate 'from legitimate expectations once established'—see Henckels, 'Protecting Regulatory Autonomy through Greater Precision in Investment Treaties').

[40] *Saluka Investments BV* v. *The Czech Republic,* UNCITRAL, Partial Award (17 March 2006) para 284; *Metaplar* v. *The Argentine Republic*, ICSID Case No. ARB/03/5,Award (6 January 2008) para 187; *AES Summit Generation Limited and AES-Tisza ErömüKft* v. *The Republic of Hungary*, ICSID Case No. ARB/07/22, Award (23 September 2010) para 9.3.40.

[41] *Thunderbird* v. *Mexico,* para 197; See also *Glamis Gold* v. *USA*, para 625; *Cargill* v. *Mexico*, ICSID Case No. ARB(AF)/05/2, Award (18 September 2009) para 298.

[42] *Elettronica Sicula SpA* (ELSI) (*U.S.* v. *Italy*), [1989] ICJ Rep. 15 (20 July 1989) [128].

[43] *Elettronica Sicula SpA* (ELSI) (*U.S.* v. *Italy*), [1989] ICJ Rep. 15 (20 July 1989) [128].

The absence of 'manifest arbitrariness' also results in increasing the discretion of the ISDS Tribunal. Whether a foreign investor could rely on 'customary international law' in Article 3.1 to invoke 'manifest arbitrariness' as a ground to challenge host state's regulatory conduct would depend entirely upon such discretion of the tribunal. Therefore, the removal of the ground of 'manifest arbitrariness,' in fact, defeats the overarching purpose of reducing discretionary powers. Also, the reference to 'fundamental breach of due process' in Article 3.1 means that a host state can be held liable only if a violation of due process reaches a particular threshold of severity and not otherwise. However, in the absence of any guidance in the text about the meaning of 'fundamental', it is again left to the discretion of ISDS tribunals to determine the threshold of severity.[44]

Therefore, while Article 3.1 of the Indian Model BIT imposes some limitations on the interpretative authority of ISDS tribunals by specifically trying to define the content of IMS, it is still open to question whether the reference to 'customary international law' could be used to bring in other elements into the equation. By not specifically mentioning FET in the Model BIT, India has avoided the problems pertaining to determining the content of the standard and its possibly expansive definition. However, the absence of grounds like manifest arbitrariness or narrowed formulation of legitimate expectations for judging the host state's regulatory conduct tilts the balance in favour of the state rather than the investor. Given the lack of specificity and expandable nature of the FET provision, some seem to be supportive of the Indian Model BIT not containing an FET provision.[45] However, this concern can be addressed by drafting an FET provision that clearly specifies its content. The FET provision in the EU–Canada CETA is a good example of such drafting.

[44] Henckels makes the same point for 'fundamental breach of due process' given in the FET provision of the EU–Canada CETA, see Article 8.10(2)(b). See, for example, Henckles, 'Protecting Regulatory Autonomy through Greater Precision in Investment Treaties'; See also Ursula Kriebaum. 2014. 'FET and Expropriation in the (Invisible) EU Model BIT', *Journal of World Investment and Trade* 15: 454, 474.

[45] See Rajput, 'India's Shifting Treaty Practice', pp. 102–8. Also see Ranjan and Anand, 'The 2016 Model Indian Bilateral Investment Treaty', pp. 31–6.

India could have borrowed the definition of the same from Article 8.10 of the EU–Canada CETA.

8.4 Expropriation

Article 5.1 of the Model BIT prohibits nationalization or expropriation either directly or through measures having an effect equivalent to expropriation, except for public purpose, in accordance with due process and on payment of adequate compensation.[46] The Model BIT explains that direct expropriation occurs either through nationalization or through a formal transfer of title or outright seizure.[47] Article 5.3 (a)(ii) of the Model BIT provides that indirect expropriation occurs if a country's measure or a series of measures has an effect 'equivalent to direct expropriation', that is, the effect should result in substantial or permanent deprivation of the fundamental attributes of property—rights of use, enjoyment, and disposal—of the investor's investment, without the formal transfer of title.[48] This is a clear reference to the *sole effects* doctrine combined with the 'substantial deprivation' test to determine indirect expropriation discussed in Chapter 4.

However, to muddy the waters, Article 5.3 (b) of the Model BIT provides: The determination of whether a measure or a series of measures have an effect equivalent to expropriation requires a case-by-case, fact-based inquiry, that takes into consideration:

[46] 2016 Indian Model BIT, art. 5.1 For a general discussion on the concept of expropriation in BITs, see Chapter 5.

[47] 2016 Indian Model BIT, art. 5.3(a)(i) provides:

The Parties confirm their shared understanding that: a) Expropriation may be direct or indirect: (i) direct expropriation occurs when an investment is nationalized or otherwise directly expropriated through formal transfer of title or outright seizure;

[48] 2016 Indian Model BIT, art. 5.3(a)(ii) provides:

> The Parties confirm their shared understanding that: a) Expropriation may be direct or indirect: (ii) indirect expropriation occurs if a measure or series of measures of a Party has an effect equivalent to direct expropriation, in that it substantially or permanently deprives the investor of the fundamental attributes of property in its investment, including the right to use, enjoy and dispose of its investment, without formal transfer of title or outright seizure.

(i) the economic impact of the measure or series of measures, although the sole fact that a measure or series of measures of a Party has an adverse effect on the economic value of an investment does not establish that an indirect expropriation has occurred;
(ii) the duration of the measure or series of measures of a Party;
(iii) the character of the measure or series of measures, notably their object, context, and intent; and
(iv) whether a measure by a Party breaches the Party's prior binding written commitment to the investor whether by contract, licence or other legal instrument.

In order to determine whether there is an 'effect equivalent to expropriation', the Article mandates an ISDS tribunal to adopt a case-by-case, fact-based inquiry, taking into account a number of factors, including the economic impact[49] of the measures; duration; character of the measures like their object and intent; and whether there has been a breach of prior written commitment to the investor.[50] So far as duration and economic impact are taken into consideration as factors to determine the effect of alleged measures, the scope of the Article is still in compliance with the sole effects doctrine.[51] However, the introduction of the character, object, and intent of the alleged measure test is a part of the proportionality analysis[52] for

[49] 2016 Indian Model BIT, art. 5.3 (b)(i) (explaining that the adverse economic impact on the investments does not establish the occurrence of indirect expropriation).

[50] 2016 Indian Model BIT, art. 5.3(b)(iv). Expropriation provision in some new BITs contain this kind of language see, EU–Canada CETA, annex 8-A; 2012 U.S. Model BIT, annex B (4)(a) (https://ustr.gov/sites/default/files/BIT%20text%20for%20ACIEP%20Meeting.pdf) accessed 9 January 2018; 2004 Canadian Model BIT, annex B.13(1) (http://www.italaw.com/documents/Canadian2004-FIPA-Model-en.pdf) accessed 9 January 2018; This kind of language is largely reflective of the test laid down in a leading US Case on regulatory takings – *Penn Central Transport* v. *City of New York*, 438 US 104 (1978) 123–125.

[51] For a discussion on the 'sole effects doctrine', see Chapter 5.

[52] For a discussion on the proportionality analysis in context of the expropriation provision in BITs, see Chapter 5.

determination of indirect expropriation. The language of the Model BIT raises two difficult questions: First, in determination of indirect expropriation, how does one reconcile the 'substantial deprivation test', which focuses only on the effect of regulatory measure and not on purpose behind the impugned regulatory measure, given in Article 5.3(a)(ii), with the proportionality test, given in Article 5.3 (b) (i–iv), where both effect and purpose have to be taken into account? Second, assuming that an ISDS tribunal decides to employ proportionality analysis, how will such tribunal, in the context of Article 5.3(b), decide the weight to be given to each factor? Should the economic impact of the measure on foreign investment be given more importance than the objective and intent behind the measure or vice-versa? The text does not answer these questions and thus vests sole and heightened discretion in the hands of ISDS tribunals.[53] This discretion shall allow the ISDS tribunals to second-guess the regulatory measures adopted by host states by weighing and balancing the benefit of these measures with the effect on foreign investment.[54] Such a determination would either result in foreign investment protection trumping over the host state's regulatory power or vice versa based on the subjective determination of the tribunal.[55]

Further, in addition to the sole effect test and the proportionality test, Article 5 also includes the police powers doctrine,[56] 'non-discriminatory regulatory measures or the awards of the judicial bodies of a host state that are designed and applied to protect legitimate public interest or public purpose objectives such as health, safety, and

[53] See Henckels, 'Protecting Regulatory Autonomy through Greater Precision in Investment Treaties', who offers similar critique for the EU–Canada CETA that contains similarly worded expropriation provision as the Indian Model BIT.

[54] See Han Xiuli. 2007. 'The Application of the Principle of Proportionality in Tecmed v. Mexico', *Chinese Journal of International Law* 6: 635, 636–7. See Chapter 5.

[55] See Prabhash Ranjan. 2014.'Using Public Law Concept of Proportionality to Balance Investment Protection with Regulation in International Investment Law: A Critical Appraisal', *Cambridge Journal of International and Comparative Law*3.

[56] For a discussion on the police powers doctrine in context of expropriation provision in BITs, see Chapter 5.

environment shall not constitute expropriation under this article.'[57] The formulation of the aforesaid exception is quite close to the language used by the *Methanex* tribunal in its pronouncement of the doctrine of police powers where it held that '... a non-discriminatory regulation for a public purpose, which is enacted in accordance with due process and, which affects, inter alios, a foreign investor or investment is not deemed expropriatory ...'[58]

Similarly worded provisions are also present in other treaties such as EU–Canada CETA.[59] However, in these treaties, such provisions are qualified by the following words: 'except in rare circumstances'. For example, Annex 8-A (3) of the EU–Canada CETA provides: 'for greater certainty, except in the rare circumstance when the impact of a measure or series of measures is so severe in light of its purpose that it appears manifestly excessive, non-discriminatory measures of a Party that are designed and applied to protect legitimate public welfare objectives, such as health, safety, and the environment, do not constitute indirect expropriations'. This provision, unlike Article 5.5 of the Indian Model BIT, recognizes that there may be situations where a host state's non-discriminatory measures designed and applied for public welfare purposes may amount to expropriation when the impact of a measure is manifestly excessive on foreign investment in light of its object and purpose.[60] Although it may be difficult to determine when measures are excessive in light of the regulatory purpose they seek to achieve,[61] language such as this at least provides an opportunity to balance investment protection with the host state's regulatory power. In the case of the Indian Model BIT, Article 5.5 does not afford any such opportunity. Thus, even

[57] 2016 Indian Model BIT, art. 5.5.

[58] *Methanex Corp.* v. *United States of America*, NAFTA-UNCITRAL, Award (3 August 2005).

[59] See EU–Canada CETA, Annex 8-A (3), Feb. 15, 2017; Trans-Pacific Partnership, Annex 9-B(3)(b) (4 February 2016) (https://ustr.gov/trade-agreements/free-trade-agreements/trans-pacific-partnership/tpp-full-text) accessed 9 January 2018.

[60] See EU–Canada CETA.

[61] See Henckels, 'Protecting Regulatory Autonomy through Greater Precision in Investment Treaties', pp. 42–3.

if the impact of the regulatory measures is manifestly excessive or disproportionate, the regulatory measure will not amount to expropriation as long as the measure satisfies the bare minimum threshold of being non-discriminatory and aiming to fulfil some public welfare measure. Even the usual benchmarks to check regulatory overreach such as ensuring that a measure is adopted in 'good faith' or followed 'due process' are not mentioned in Article 5.5. This leaves a major gap in protection of foreign investment because it allows the host state to completely shift the cost of a regulatory measure on foreign investors, which clearly tilts the balance in favour of the host state. A broad provision such as this, with limited checks, could also be prone to abuse by host states as sweeping regulatory measures could be undertaken by merely claiming large public benefit, which would compromise protection of foreign investment.[62]

One commentator who is supportive of the Indian Model BIT[63] seems to suggest that provisions such as Article 5.5 would allow India to counter claims of expropriation brought by foreign investors for suffering losses.[64] However, this argument wrongly presumes that when a state exercises so-called public welfare measures, the only adverse impact on the foreign investor would be inflicting losses of commercial nature. As discussed earlier, the impact of a regulatory measure on the foreign investor could be much more than just commercial losses. In certain situations, it could even be complete destruction of foreign investment. Can a state pass on such high cost for implementing a public welfare to a foreign investor and not compensate or follow other due-process requirements? Moreover, the concern that commercial losses suffered by foreign investors could be challenged as expropriation can be very well addressed by the application of the 'substantial deprivation' test as part of the sole effects doctrine. Mere commercial losses suffered by a foreign investor would not result in substantial deprivation of foreign investment and thus not amount to expropriation.

[62] Kenneth J. Vandevelde. 2009. *US International Investment Agreements.* Oxford: Oxford University Press, p. 296.

[63] Rajput, *Protection of Foreign Investment in India and Investment Treaty Arbitration.*

[64] Rajput, *Protection of Foreign Investment in India and Investment Treaty Arbitration*, 96–7.

In sum, the expropriation provision does not reduce the arbitral discretion. Whether the state's right to regulate will be balanced with investment protection, to a great extent, will depend on the ISDS tribunal interpreting the provision. With reference to the inclusion of the police powers doctrine, the provision is without fetters and provides unchecked powers to the host state.

8.5 Full Protection and Security

The 2016 Model BIT provides that foreign investment and investors shall be accorded full protection and security.[65] FPS is, however, restricted to physical security of the foreign investment and investors and does not extend to '*any other obligation whatsoever*'.[66] Given the arbitral maze on the actual scope of the FPS provision,[67] this clarity in the Indian Model BIT is welcome and would help curb arbitral discretion. It also reconciles investment protection with the host state's regulatory power. While the provision puts the host state under an obligation to provide physical security to foreign investment, it also ensures that the host state's adoption of regulatory measures impacting the business or legal environment cannot be challenged as a violation of FPS.

8.6 Monetary Transfer Provisions

The 2016 Model BIT recognizes the investor's right to transfer all funds related to investment such as contributions to capital, profits, dividends, interest payments, etc.[68] However, the right to transfer is subject to three restrictions. Firstly, Article 6.1 subjects the investor's

[65] See 2016 Indian Model BIT, art. 3.2. For a discussion on MTPs in BITs, see Chapter 5.

[66] 2016 Indian Model BIT, art. 3.2 provides: 'For greater certainty, 'full protection and security' only refers to a Party's obligations relating to physical security of investors and to investments made by the investors of the other Party and not to any other obligation whatsoever.'

[67] See section 4.3 of Chapter 4.

[68] 2016 Indian Model BIT, art. 6.1. See Chapter 5 for discussion on MTPs in BITs.

right to transfer funds to the domestic laws of the host state. Secondly, Article 6.3 provides that 'nothing in this treaty shall prevent' the host state the good faith application of its laws, including actions relating to bankruptcy, insolvency, compliance with judicial decisions, labour obligations and laws on taxation, etc.[69] Thirdly, Article 6.4 provides that the host state may temporarily restrict the investor's right to transfer funds in the event of serious BoP difficulties or in situations where movement of capital could cause or threaten to cause 'serious difficulties for macroeconomic management.' While this formulation provides a textual basis to balance the investor's right to transfer funds and the host state's regulatory power, the ground of serious BoP difficulty remains unclear.

The same exception for serious BoP difficulties and external financial difficulties is also found in the general exceptions clause in Article 32.2 (discussed in the following section). This will allow India to deviate from all substantive obligations (including MTPs) in order to remedy serious BoP problems, exchange-rate difficulties, and external financial difficulties.[70] Since these exceptions are already part of MTPs in Article 6, reiteration of the same in the general exception clause is redundant. Alternatively, if these exceptions are given in the general exception clause, then there is no need to have them as part of the MTP provision. Overall, the MTPs in the Model BIT protect the interest of foreign investors by allowing free transfer of funds. At the same time, by subjecting these transfers to certain conditions it allows the host state to exercise its right to regulate.

8.7 Non-Precluded Measures (NPM) Clauses or General Exceptions

The 2016 Model BIT contains a separate chapter on exceptions covering both general and security exceptions.[71] Article 32 contains

[69] 2015 Draft Indian Model BIT, art. 6.3, sub-items (i) to (xi). Comments on the 2015 Draft Indian Model BIT, (https://www.mygov.in/group-issue/draft-indian-model-bilateral-investment-treaty-text/) accessed 9 January 2018.

[70] 2015 Draft Indian Model BIT, art. 16.1 (iii).

[71] See Chapter 5 for a discussion on NPMs or General Exceptions in BITs.

general exceptions with a long list of permissible objectives, which includes protection of public morals;[72] maintenance of public order;[73] protection of human, animal, or plant life or health;[74] protection and conservation of the environment;[75] to ensure compliance with domestic laws that are not inconsistent with the provisions of the treaty.[76] The inclusion of these permissible objectives will provide opportunities to reconcile investment protection with the host state's right to regulate.

Another interesting aspect of the NPM provision is that it contains 'necessary' as the only nexus requirement for all the above-mentioned permissible objectives.[77] Footnote 6 of the Model BIT provides guidance for the determination 'necessary' measures.[78] Footnote 6 provides that in considering whether a measure is necessary, the tribunal shall take into account whether there was no less restrictive alternative measure reasonably available to the country or not. The author has previously argued for this interpretation of necessity to be put in the text.[79]

The meaning of necessary is partly inspired from the WTO jurisprudence, which has developed a two-tier test to determine the meaning of 'necessary' in Article XX of GATT.[80] The test involves, firstly, the proportionality or the weighing and balancing test. The

[72] 2016 Indian Model BIT, art. 32.1 (i).

[73] 2016 Indian Model BIT, art. 32.1 (i).

[74] 2016 Indian Model BIT, art. 32.1 (ii).

[75] 2016 Indian Model BIT, art. 32.1 (iv).

[76] 2016 Indian Model BIT, art. 32.1 (iii).

[77] For a discussion on nexus requirements like 'necessary' see Section 5.3 of Chapter 5.

[78] 2016 Indian Model BIT, art. 32.1.

[79] Also see Chapter 5. Also see Ranjan and Anand, 'The 2016 Model Indian Bilateral Investment Treaty', pp. 40–4.

[80] See Chad P. Bown and Joel P. Trachtman. 2009. 'Brazil – Measures Affecting Imports of Retreaded Tyres: A Balancing Act', *World Trade Review* 8(1): 85, 87. For WTO jurisprudence on 'necessary' in Article XX of GATT see Appellate Body Report, *Korea—Measures Affecting Imports of Fresh, Chilled and Frozen Beef*, WTO Doc. WT/DS 161 and 169/AB/R (adopted Dec. 11, 2000); Appellate Body Report, *Brazil—Measures Affecting Imports of Retreaded Tyres*, WTO Doc. WT/DS332/AB/R (adopted 3 December 2007).

test requires balancing different factors like the importance of the regulatory value pursued, the contribution made by the challenged measure to the regulatory value and the restrictive effect of the measure on international trade. The second stage of the test, assuming the measure is *prima facie* necessary, analyses the measure-undertaken vis-à-vis with least trade restrictive measure reasonably available to the importing country.[81] If an alternate less restrictive measure is available then the impugned measure is not necessary. The Indian Model BIT has adopted the second part of the two-tier test. Consequently, this will not allow for any weighing and balancing review, or, in other words, for subjective assessment to be made by an ISDS tribunal regarding whether a regulatory measure is significant vis-à-vis the cost imposed on foreign investment. A clear definition of necessary would help curtail arbitral discretion. At the same time, that least restrictive measures test would ensure that foreign investments are adequately protection.

The definition also ousts the defence of necessity under customary international law.[82] Arbitral tribunals have previously imported the customary international law definition of necessary to interpret the meaning of the term in a BIT.[83]

Nevertheless, a major textual flaw in Article 32 is the absence of a chapeau provision. Presently, the Model BIT only requires that measures should be applied on a 'non-discriminatory' basis.[84] A stronger protection could have been ensured through a chapeau clause specifying that there shall be no unjustifiable discrimination or that there shall be no disguised restriction, parimateriae Article XX of the GATT.[85] Such provision would have prevented a potential misuse or abuse of the NPM provisions.

[81] Andrew D. Mitchell and Caroline Henckels. 2013. 'Variations on a Theme: Comparing the Concept of "Necessity" in International Investment Law and WTO Law', *Chicago Journal of International Law* 14:93, 98.

[82] See Article 25 of the ILC Articles of State Responsibility and the discussion in Chapter 5.

[83] See the discussion in Chapter 5.

[84] See 2016 Indian Model BIT, art. 32.1.

[85] The significance of the chapeau in context of Article XX of GATT has been repeatedly asserted by the WTO Appellate Body. See Appellate Body Report, *United States—Standards for Reformulated and Conventional Gasoline,*

In conclusion, the general exception clause is precisely drafted and does impose constraints on the exercise of arbitral discretion. However, the absence of a full-fledged chapeau of the kind found in Article XX of GATT opens the possibility of a regulatory abuse by host states.

8.8 Other Exceptions

Apart from the NPM provisions or the general exception clauses, Article 2 of the 2016 Model BIT, while describing the scope and coverage of the treaty, specifically excludes certain regulatory measures from the purview of the treaty. We discuss two important regulatory measures here.

8.8.1 Taxation

Article 2.4 (ii) of the Model BIT states that the treaty shall not apply to 'any law or measure regarding taxation, including measures taken to enforce taxation obligations.' The article further provides that the host state's decision characterising a regulatory measure as related to taxation, whether made before or after the commencement of arbitral proceedings, shall be non-justiciable.[86] No arbitral tribunal shall be able to review such decision.[87]

As mentioned in Chapter 7, it is evident that India has decided to keep taxation measures outside the purview of the BIT in response to challenges made by Vodafone and Cairn to India's retrospective application of taxation law.[88] Allowing host states the sole and unfettered

---

WTO Doc. WT/DS2/AB/R (adopted 29 April 1996); Appellate Body Report, *United States: Import Prohibition of Certain Shrimp and Shrimp Products*, WTO Doc. WT/DS58/AB/R (adopted 12 October 1998); See also EU–Canada CETA, art. 28.3.

[86] 2016 Indian Model BIT, art. 2.4(ii).

[87] 2016 Indian Model BIT, art. 2.4(ii).

[88] Also see Chapter 6. Also see Julien Chaisse, Investor-State Arbitration in International Tax Dispute Resolution—A Cut above Dedicated Tax Dispute Resolution? Virginia Tax Review (2016) for a detailed discussion on relationship between investment treaties and taxation.

prerogative to characterize a regulatory matter as relating to taxation might lead to regulatory abuse. An ISDS tribunal in *EnCana* v. *Ecuador* has previously recognized the states capacity to abuse their power to tax by designing tax laws that are 'extraordinary, punitive in amount or arbitrary' which, in turn, could trigger a claim of indirect expropriation.[89] Similarly, the tribunal in *Burlington* v. *Ecuador* recognized that taxation can be confiscatory leading to indirect expropriation.[90] Excluding taxation measures altogether from the purview of the BIT is a disproportionate reaction especially when taxation is arguably part of a state's police powers and thus allows for non-compensation in cases of deprivation of foreign investment.[91] The absolute exemption of taxation measures from arbitral review limits the protection to foreign investment even through abuse of taxation powers.

8.8.2 Compulsory License

The Model BIT also excludes the issuance of compulsory licenses (CLs) provided that such issuance is consistent with the WTO treaty.[92] In other words, foreign investors can challenge the issuance of CLs for not being in accordance with the TRIPS Agreement.[93]

[89] *EnCana Corporation* v. *Republic of Ecuador*, LCIA Case No. UN3481, Award (3 February 2006) para 177.

[90] *Burlington Resources, Inc.* v. *Republic of Ecuador*, ICSID Case No. ARB/08/5, Decision on Liability (14 December 2014) para 395; See also *Occidental Exploration* v. *Ecuador*, para 85.

[91] Newcombe and Paradell, *Law and Practice of Investment Treaties*, p. 358. See also Brownlie, *Principles of Public International Law*, p. 532; Louis B. Sohn andR.R. Baxter. 1961. 'International Responsibility of States for Injuries to Aliens', *American Journal of International Law* 55: 545.

[92] 2016 Indian Model BIT, art. 2.4(iii) (providing that the treaty shall not apply to 'the issuance of compulsory licenses granted in relation to intellectual property rights, or to the revocation, limitation or creation of intellectual property rights, to the extent that such issuance, revocation, limitation or creation is consistent with the international obligations of Parties under the WTO Agreement.')

[93] See Christopher Gibson. 2010. 'A Look at the Compulsory License in Investment Arbitration: The Case of Indirect Expropriation', *American University International Law Review* 25(3): 357, 421; Bryan Mercurio. 2012.

Consequently, an ISDS tribunal, with limited or no expertise in the WTO law,[94] is empowered to make a substantive determination as to whether the issuance of CL is consistent with TRIPS.[95] Thus, this provision too, like many other provisions discussed so far, fails to reduce arbitral discretion, one of the key objectives sought to be achieved by the Model BIT.

8.9 Investor–State Dispute Settlement

As discussed in Chapter 5, the ISDS provision in BITs are a redressal mechanism offered by the host state to investors to challenge breach of the substantive obligations under that BIT.[96] The Indian Model BIT provides for ISDS; however, qualifies the same in three ways.[97] This section will also discuss two other important features of the ISDS chapter in India's Model BIT—appointment of arbitrators and the standard of review.

'Awakening the Sleeping Giant: Intellectual Property Rights in International Investment Agreements', *Journal of International Economic Law* 15(3): 871, 905–06 (hereinafter Mercurio, 'Awakening the Sleeping Giant').

94 Mercurio, 'Awakening the Sleeping Giant', n 88, p. 905. Also see Ranjan, 'Pharmaceutical Patents and Expropriation in Indian Bilateral Investment Treaties'.

95 Ranjan, 'Pharmaceutical Patents and Expropriation in Indian Bilateral Investment Treaties'.

96 Eric De Brabandere. 2014. *Investment Treaty Arbitration as Public International Law: Procedural Aspects and Implications*. pp. 50–1. Cambridge: Cambridge University Press. (hereinafter Brabandere, *Investment Treaty Arbitrationas Public International Law*)

97 See Hanessian and Duggal, "The Final 2015 Indian Model BIT', n 2, p. 226. Also see Prabhash Ranjan and Pushkar Anand. 2018. 'Investor State Dispute Settlement in the 2016 Indian Model Bilateral Investment Treaty: Does it Go Too Far?', in *International Investment Treaties and Arbitration Across Asia,* Luke Nottage et al. (eds), pp. 579–611. Leiden: Brill/Nijhoff; Julien Chaisse. 2017. 'The State of Investor-State Arbitration—A Reality Check of the Issues, Trends, and Directions in Asia-Pacific, *The International Lawyer* 51(1):151–99.

8.9.1 Jurisdictional Qualification

The Indian Model BIT limits the scope of ISDS to disputes arising out of the alleged breach of an obligation under Chapter II of the BIT and not under any other chapter.[98] In other words, a foreign investor can bring a claim against the host state only for the alleged violation of 'treatment of investments' that includes free protection and security (FPS), national treatment, expropriation, monetary transfer provisions and compensation for losses (a provision that obligates the host state to accord national treatment in terms of payment of compensation etc. when foreign investment suffers losses due to war or due to armed conflict, civil strife etc).[99] Specifically, any dispute arising due to the breach of the obligations contained in Articles 9 (Entry and Sojourn of Personnel) and 10 (Transparency) is excluded from the scope of ISDS.[100]

Another important jurisdictional limit is the restriction to disputes arising solely out of the breach of the BIT.[101] The Model BIT specifically excludes disputes arising solely out of the breach of contract between an investor and host state from the jurisdiction of an ISDS tribunal. These disputes must be resolved in the domestic courts or in accordance with the dispute resolution process provided within the concerned contract.[102] In other words, the Indian Model BIT does not contain any umbrella clause that elevates a contractual breach to the breach of BIT obligations by requiring host states to observe not just treaty, but 'any other obligations', it may owe to the foreign investors.[103] 'Any other

[98] 2016 Indian Model BIT, art. 13.2.

[99] 2016 Indian Model BIT, art. 7.

[100] 2016 Indian Model BIT, art. 7.

[101] 2016 Indian Model BIT, art. 13.2; Rajput, 'India's Shifting Treaty Practice', n 2.

[102] 2016 Indian Model BIT, art. 13.2.

[103] See, for example, the 2005 German Model BIT, art. 7.2; Swiss Model BIT, art. 10.2; see, Christoph Schreuer. 2004. 'Travelling the BIT Route: of Umbrella Clauses, and Forks in the Road', *Journal of World Investment & Trade* 5(2): 231 (hereinafter Schreuer, *Travelling the BIT Route*). See also generally, Stephan W. Schill. 2009. 'Enabling Private Ordering: Function, Scope and Effect of Umbrella Clauses in International Investment Treaties', *Minnesota Journal of International Law* 18(1): 32; Brabandere, *Investment Treaty Arbitration as Public International Law*, p. 38.

obligations' has been interpreted to allow investors to access ISDS even for contractual breaches.[104]

In addition to these limits, the Model BIT also imposes two other limitations on an ISDS tribunal. Firstly, an ISDS tribunal cannot exercise jurisdiction over any claim that is or has been subject to arbitration under chapter V of the treaty, which provides for state–state dispute settlement.[105] The ASEAN–India investment agreement does not contain any such provisions. Secondly, an ISDS tribunal shall not have the jurisdiction to review the 'merits' of a decision made by a domestic judicial authority.[106] It is not clear what 'merits' means. If 'merits' means that an ISDS tribunal should not question whether a domestic court correctly applied the domestic law, such an interpretation is reasonable, as treaty arbitration tribunals do not act as courts of appeal.[107] However, arguably, 'merits' in Article 13.5 could also be given an expansive interpretation to mean that an ISDS tribunal cannot question a domestic court decision even when the court decision violates a treaty obligation. Such an interpretation would exempt domestic judicial decisions from review for breach of BIT.[108] Further, foreign investors 'will be precluded from resorting to ISDS' on issues addressed by domestic courts as, arguably, any issue decided by a domestic court would be tantamount to issue decided on 'merits'.[109]

104 See Schreuer, 'Travelling the BIT Route', n 98. See *SGS Société Générale de Surveillance SA* v. *Islamic Republic of Pakistan*, ICSID Case No. ARB/01/13, Decision on Jurisdiction (6 August 2003); *Joy Mining Machinery Limited* v. *Arab Republic of Egypt*, ICSID Case No. ARB/03/11, Award on Jurisdiction (6 August 2004) (denying the applicability of Umbrella clauses); *Eureko BV* v. *Republic of Poland*, Ad Hoc, Partial Award (19 August 2005) (holding that the umbrella clause automatically transforms a contract violation into a treaty violation).

105 2016 Indian Model BIT, art. 13.5(ii).

106 2016 Indian Model BIT, art. 13.5 (i).

107 *Azinian* v. *Mexico*, ICSID Case No. ARB (AF)/97/2, Final Award (1 November 1999) para 99; *ADF* v. *United States*, ICSID Case No. ARB (AF)/00/1, Final Award (9 January 2003) para 190.

108 Jarrod Hepburn and Ridhi Kabra, 'India's New Model Investment Treaty: Fit for Purpose?', *Indian Law Review,* 1(2) (on file with the authors). Also, important to see, Article 4 of the ILC Articles of State Responsibility state that judiciary is part of State for the purpose of international law.

109 Sonia E.Rolland and David M Trubek. 2017. 'Legal Innovation in Investment Law: Rhetoric and Practice in South', *University of Pennsylvania*

Investor–state dispute settlement tribunals recognize that domestic court decisions may violate international law and trigger state liability[110] either by constituting denial of justice,[111] or for violating other BIT standards like providing foreign investors with 'effective means' of asserting claims and enforcing rights.[112] Excluding judicial decisions from the purview of BIT permits the host state' to preclude investment protection.

8.9.2 Exhaustion of Local Remedies

As discussed in Chapter 5, the rule of exhaustion of local remedies is a long-standing rule of customary international law.

In the 2016 Model BIT, India has qualified its consent to ISDS by requiring that a foreign investor should first exhaust local remedies at least for a period of five years before commencing international arbitration.[113] These five years are to be counted from the date when the foreign investor first acquired 'knowledge of the measure in question and the resulting loss or damage to the investment' or when the investor should have first acquired such knowledge.[114] The other critical element is that the foreign investor should submit the dispute to the local court within one year from the date on which the investor acquired the knowledge or should have acquired the knowledge about the measure.[115]

Journal of International Law (forthcoming), University of Wisconsin Legal Studies Research Paper No. 1406, https://papers.ssrn.com/sol3/papers.cfm?abstract_id=2934605, accessed 9 January 2018.

[110] See *Tokios Tokelés* v. *Ukraine*, ICSID Case No. ARB/02/18, Award (26 July 2007) para 133; *Loewen* v. *United States*, ICSID Case No. ARB(AF)/98/3, Award (26 June 2003) paras 121, 132.

[111] See *Dan Cake SA* v. *Hungary*, ICSID Case No. ARB/12/9, Decision of Jurisdiction & Liability (24 August 2015). See also Paulsson, January 2005. *Denial of Justice in International Law*. Cambridge: Cambridge University Press.

[112] See *Chevron* v. *Ecuador*, PCA Case No. 34877, Partial Award on the Merits (30 March 2010) para 379.

[113] 2016 Indian Model BIT, art. 15.1 and 15.2

[114] 2016 Indian Model BIT, art. 15.2.

[115] 2016 Indian Model BIT, art. 15.1.

The requirement to exhaust local remedies shall not be applicable 'if the investor can demonstrate that there are no available domestic legal remedies capable of reasonably providing any relief in respect of the same measure'.[116] Thus, the burden to show that there is no reasonably available relief falls on the foreign investor.[117] The Model BIT has another clarification attached to art 15.1, which precludes the investors from claiming that they have complied with the exhaustion requirement on the basis that the claim under this treaty is by a different party or in respect of different cause of action. A clarification of this nature will ensure that an investor cannot escape the requirement to exhaust local remedies if, for example, another corporate entity within the same group is making use of local remedies or by citing different cause of action (which is easy to show as the cause of action in domestic forum is formulated in domestic law terms which would be different from the cause of action formulated in treaty terms).[118]

8.9.3 Additional Qualifications

The Model BIT provides that the foreign investor, after exhausting all local remedies for five years, without reaching a satisfactory resolution, can commence the arbitral process by transmission of a notice of dispute to the host state.[119] This 'notice of dispute' will be accompanied by another six months of attempts by the investor and the state to resolve the dispute through meaningful negotiation,

[116] 2016 Indian Model BIT, art. 15.4.

[117] The burden of proof imposed by the formulation of 'futility exception' used in the Model BIT is lower than that imposed by the '*obvious futility*' rule but greater than '*absence of reasonable prospects of success*' rule. For further details see, the commentary to art. 15(a) of *Draft Articles on Diplomatic Protection with Commentaries*, II:2, Y.B. Int'l. L. Comm'n, pt. 3, at 76, UN Doc A/61/10 (2006).

[118] See comments of Gus van Harten on the text of 2015 Draft India Model Bilateral Investment Treaty Text (https://www.mygov.in/group-issue/draft-indian-Model-bilateral-investment-treaty-text/), accessed 9 January 2018. See also Hanessian & Duggal, 'The Final 2015 Indian Model BIT', n 2; *Occidental Exploration* v. *Ecuador*.

[119] 2016 Indian Model BIT, art. 15.2.

consultation or other third party procedures.[120] In the event that there is no amicable settlement of the dispute, the investor can submit a claim to arbitration,[121] subject to the following additional conditions:

- first, not more than six years have elapsed from the date on which the investor first acquired or should have acquired knowledge of the measure in question;[122] and/or,
- second, not more than 12 months have elapsed from the conclusion of domestic proceedings;[123]
- third, before submitting the claim to arbitration, a minimum of 90 days' notice has to be given to host state;[124]
- fourth, the investor must waive the 'right to initiate or continue any proceedings' under the domestic laws of the host state.[125]

Additionally, in cases where the claim is submitted by a foreign investor in respect of loss or damage to a juridical person owned or controlled by the investor, the juridical person must waive its right to initiate or continue any proceedings under the laws of the host state.[126]

The various limitations on the timeframe effectively reduce the window for submission of claim for arbitration to a meagre three-month time period. For example, assuming that a measure alleged to violate the BIT came to the knowledge to foreign investors on 1 May 2017, the foreign investor must first submit the dispute in the local courts within one year of such knowledge. Assuming that the investor submits the dispute on 1 May 2017 itself, domestic legal remedies should be exhausted at least for a period of five years, that is, until 30 April 2022, unless it can demonstrate the available domestic

[120] 2016 Indian Model BIT, art. 15.4.

[121] 2016 Indian Model BIT, art. 16.

[122] 2016 Indian Model BIT, art. 15.5(i).

[123] 2016 Indian Model BIT, art. 15.5(ii); also see Hanessian and Duggal, 'The Final 2015 Indian Model BIT', n 2, p. 7.

[124] 2016 Indian Model BIT, art. 15.5(v).

[125] 2016 Indian Model BIT, art. 15.5(iii).

[126] 2016 Indian Model BIT, art. 15.5(iv).

legal remedies cannot reasonably provide any relief. If the investor is not satisfied with the outcome of the domestic legal proceedings, it can submit a notice of dispute. Assuming that the 'notice of dispute' is filed without delay on 1 May 2022 itself, a further period of six months has to be spent by the investor trying to 'amicably settle the dispute with the host state', that is, until 31 October 2022. After this, the foreign investor can submit a 'notice of arbitration' to the host state. Only at the end of these further 90 days, that is, in January 2023, can the foreign investor actually submit a proper 'claim to arbitration'. However, this claim to arbitration must be submitted by April 2023, as the 'claim for arbitration' has to be submitted within 12 months from the conclusion of domestic proceedings, which in our example is 30 April 2022.

Thus, even when the foreign investor is extremely prompt, the maximum time period that it gets for the submission of 'claim for arbitration' to an ISDS tribunal is about three months only. The 2016 Model BIT has drastically curtailed the window for submitting a claim for arbitration by erecting a number of procedural barricades in the form of stringent time limits that are to be adhered to.

8.9.4 Appointment of Arbitrators

The Model BIT comprehensively lays down the arbitral procedure to be followed. The Model BIT provides for arbitration with three arbitrators having relevant expertise or experience in public international law, international trade, and investment law, or the resolution of disputes arising under international trade or investment agreements.[127] The arbitrators are required to be independent and not to be affiliated with or take instructions from either any disputing party or the government of any disputing party with regard to trade and investment matters.[128] Each party shall appoint one arbitrator.[129] The presiding arbitrator has to be appointed by the agreement of co-arbitrators and the disputing parties.[130] However, in case the arbitral

[127] 2016 Indian Model BIT, art. 18.1.
[128] 2016 Indian Model BIT, art. 18.1.
[129] 2016 Indian Model BIT, art. 18.2.
[130] 2016 Indian Model BIT, art. 18.2.

tribunal is not constituted, that is, if either of the arbitrators is not appointed by the parties, or the presiding arbitrator is not appointed in the manner prescribed, the Secretary General of the ICSID shall appoint such arbitrators if the arbitration is submitted under the ICSID Convention or ICSID Additional Facility Rules.[131] Where the arbitration is submitted under the UNCITRAL Rules, Secretary General of the Permanent Court of Arbitration shall be the appointing authority.[132]

There is no limitation as to the nationality of the third or the presiding arbitrator to be appointed. However, a limitation exists in respect of the appointing authority, where an arbitral tribunal has not been constituted within 120 days from the date of submission of claim of arbitration.[133] The appointing authority, whether in ICSID or UNCITRAL, should not be a national of either party. If their nationality is the same, the appointment of arbitrators is to be done by the president of ICJ, or vice-president, or the next most senior judge, who is not a national of either party.[134]

Conflict of Interest and Challenge to the Appointment of Arbitrators

Challenges to arbitrators in international arbitrations have become recurrent in the last few years. As the number of ISDS cases has increased, there is a lack of comparable increase in the 'pool of arbitrators' to decide such cases, resulting in 'real or perceived conflicts' and ultimately leading to increase in the challenges to appointment of arbitrators on various grounds.[135] The new Model BIT has a detailed provision relating to the prevention of conflict of interest of arbitrators and challenges to their appointment.[136] The BIT gives a

[131] 2016 Indian Model BIT, art. 18.3 (a).

[132] 2016 Indian Model BIT, art. 18.3(b).

[133] 2016 Indian Model BIT, art. 18.3.

[134] 2016 Indian Model BIT, proviso to art. 18.3.

[135] Chiara Giorgetti. 2016. 'Challenge of Arbitrators in International Disputes: Two Tribunals Reject the 'Appearance of Bias', *ASIL Insights*, 16(20), https://www.asil.org/insights/volume/16/issue/20/challenges-arbitrators-international-disputes-two-tribunals-reject-, accessed 9 January 2018.

[136] 2016 Indian Model BIT, art. 19, art. 19.3.

wide scope to parties to challenge the appointment of arbitrators and is reflective of the scepticism that India attaches to the impartiality and independence of ISDS arbitrators. Article 19.2 imposes a positive duty on an arbitrator to disclose in writing, on an ongoing basis, any circumstance that might give rise to justifiable doubts regarding the independence, impartiality or freedom from conflicts of interest in the eyes of the disputing parties.[137] The presence of information raising a justifiable doubt in the public domain, or the ability of those individuals to access that information independently, does not relieve the arbitrators of the affirmative duty to make such disclosure.[138]

The Model BIT provides a comprehensive list of the circumstances in which justifiable doubts are deemed to exist.[139] These factors include:

- interest of the arbitrator or his/her associates or relatives in the outcome of the arbitration;[140]
- where the arbitrator is or has been a legal representative/advisor of the appointing authority or an affiliate of the appointing party in the preceding three years prior to commencement of arbitration;[141]
- where the arbitrator and the counsel belong to the same law firm, or the arbitrator acts concurrently with the lawyer or law firm of the one of the parties in another dispute;[142]
- where the law firm of the arbitrator is currently rendering or has rendered services, whereof it derives financial interests, to one of the parties or its affiliates;[143]
- where the arbitrator has received full briefing of the merits or the procedural aspects from the appointing party or his/her counsel thereof, prior to his/her appointment;[144]

137 2016 Indian Model BIT, art. 19.2.
138 2016 Indian Model BIT, art. 19.2.
139 2016 Indian Model BIT, art. 19.10.
140 2016 Indian Model BIT, art. 19.10.
141 2016 Indian Model BIT, art. 19.10.
142 2016 Indian Model BIT, art. 19.10.
143 2016 Indian Model BIT, art. 19.10.
144 2016 Indian Model BIT, art. 19.10.

- where the arbitrator is a manager, director, or member of the governing body, or has a similar controlling influence by virtue of shareholding or otherwise in one of the parties;[145]
- where the arbitrator has publicly advocated a fixed position regarding an issue on the case that is being arbitrated.[146]

While most of these grounds do not pose much problem, the one provided for in Article 19.10(h) deserves a closer look. In the *CC/Devas Mauritius Ltd and Ors* v. *Republic of India*,[147] India relied on the above-mentioned ground to challenge the appointment of the Presiding Arbitrator (Hon. Marc Lalonde) and Co-Arbitrator (Professor Francisco Orrego Vicuna) in the case of *Devas* v. *India*.[148] India argued that both arbitrators had served together on two tribunals[149] which took a position on a legal issue (the 'essential security interests' clause) expected to arise in the present proceedings and that Professor Vicuna repeated the same view in a third tribunal[150] and later defended his view in an article authored by him.[151] Therefore, according to India, the two arbitrators had a pre-existing view on an issue in dispute between the parties, which constituted

[145] 2016 Indian Model BIT, art. 19.10.

[146] 2016 Indian Model BIT, art. 19.10.

[147] *CC/Devas (Mauritius) Ltd, Devas Employees Mauritius Private Limited, and Telcom Devas Mauritius Limited* v. *Republic of India*, PCACase No. 2013-09, Award (25 July 2016).

[148] *CC/Devas (Mauritius) Ltd, Devas Employees Mauritius Private Limited, and Telcom Devas Mauritius Limited* v. *Republic of India*, PCACase No. 2013-09, Award (25 July 2016), [3]. See also, Romain Zamour. 2015. 'Issue Conflicts and the Reasonable Expectation of an Open Mind: The Challenge Decision in Devas v. India and its Impact', in *Challenges and Recusals of Judges and Arbitrators in International Courts and Tribunals*, Chiara Giorgetti (ed.), pp. 227–46. Leiden: Brill-Nijhoff.

[149] *CMS Gas Transmission Co.* Award; *Sempra Energy International* v. *The Argentine Republic*, ICSID Case No. ARB/02/16, Award (28 September 2007).

[150] *Enron Corporation* Award.

[151] Francisco Orrego Vicuna. 2011. 'Softening Necessity', in *Looking to the Future: Essays on International Law in Honor of W Michael Reisman*, Mahnoush H. Arsanjani, Jacob Katz Cogan, Robert D. Sloane, and Siegfried Wiessner (eds), pp. 741–51. Leiden: MartinusNijhoff.

an 'issue-conflict'.[152] Judge Peter Tomka of the ICJ who was the appointing authority in this case did not sustain India's challenge in the case of Marc Lalonde,[153] but upheld India's challenge as regards Professor Vicuna.[154] Judge Tomka held that 'being confronted with the same legal concept in this case arising from the same language on which he has already pronounced on the four aforementioned occasions [thrice as part of a tribunal and once in his article] could raise doubts for an objective observer as to Professor Orrego Vicuna's ability to approach the question with an open mind'.[155] In reaching this decision, Judge Tomka placed particular weight on the article authored by Professor Vicuna where he defended his view on 'essential security interest'.[156]

Therefore, while taking a certain position in a few cases is not enough to disqualify an arbitrator, repeatedly taking the same position and then publicly defending it can be a ground for disqualification.[157] This is a broader approach on the issue of conflict of interest than the existing case law.[158] For instance, in *Urbaser* v. *Argentina*, where the appointment of Professor McLachlan was challenged for the stand he took on MFN and necessity clause in his academic writings, the tribunal said:

[152] *CC/Devas,* para 52.

[153] *CC/Devas,* para 52, para 67.

[154] *CC/Devas,* para 52, para 64.

[155] *CC/Devas,* para 52, para 64.

[156] *CC/Devas,* para 52, para 64.

[157] Fernando A. Tupa. 2015. 'Arbitrator Challenges in Investment Arbitration: Is an Overhaul Needed?', in *Investment Treaty Arbitration and International Law*, Ian A. Laird, Borzu Sabahi, Frédéric G. Sourgens, and Todd J. Weiler (eds), p. 63. New York: Juris Publishing.

[158] Gavan Griffithand Daniel Kalderimis. 2015. 'Pure Issue Conflicts in Investment Treaty Arbitration', in *Practising Virtue: Inside International Arbitration*, David D. Caron, Stephan W. Schill, Abby Cohen Smutny, and Epaminontas E. Triantafilou(eds), p.611. Oxford: Oxford University Press. See also cases on issue conflicts such as *Urbaser SA and Consorcio de Aguas Bilbao Bizkaia, Bilbao Biskaia Ur Partzuergoa* v. *The Argentine Republic*, ICSID Case No. ARB/07/26, Decision on the Claimant's Proposal to Disqualify Professor Campbell McLachlan, Arbitrator (12 August 2010).

> [T]he mere showing of an opinion, even if relevant in a particular arbitration, is not sufficient to sustain a challenge for lack of independence or impartiality of an arbitrator. For such a challenge to succeed there must be a showing that such opinion or position is supported by factors related to and supporting a party to the arbitration (or a party closely related to such party), by a direct or indirect interest of the arbitrator in the outcome of the dispute, or by a relationship with any other individual involved, such as a witness or fellow arbitrator.[159]

Article 19.10(h) not only institutionalizes India's argument in *Devas* v. *India* but is worded so broadly that it would cover even situations similar to the *Urbaser* case. Consequently, the ground implies lack of independence and impartiality and denies an opportunity to an academic to serve as an arbitrator simply because the person concerned has 'publicly advocated a fixed position' on an issue under arbitration.[160] Such broad interpretation of the issue could lead to a chilling effect on academic writing by those who desire to be appointed as arbitrators, thus adversely impacting academic freedom, as well as the ongoing development of international investment law.[161] Article 19.10(h) also goes against the International Bar Association (IBA) guidelines on conflict of interest, which clearly provide that an arbitrator having previously expressed a legal opinion on an issue that also arises in the arbitration does not constitute a conflict of interest, provided the opinion of the arbitrator is not focused on the case.[162]

8.9.5 Standard of Review

Standard of review—the degree of deference granted by an international adjudicator to national decision-makers[163]—is an important

[159] *Urbaser* v. *Argentina* (n 156), para 45.

[160] Stephan Schill offers the same view on the impact of the *Devas* v. *India* ruling. See StephanSchill. 2014. 'Arbitrator Independence and Academic Freedom', *Journal of World Investment & Trade*, 15: 1.

[161] Schill, 'Arbitrator Independence and Academic Freedom', p. 1.

[162] Rule 4.1.1 read with para 7 of Part II of the IBA Guidelines on Conflict of Interest in International Arbitration, Adopted by the Resolution of the IBA Council (23 October 2014).

[163] See Jan Bohanes and Nicolas Lockhart. 2010. 'Standard of Review in WTO Law', in *The Oxford Handbook of International Trade Law*, Daniel

issue in ISDS, which has attracted considerable attention.[164] All ISDS tribunals are confronted with the following question while judging the legality of the host state's actions vis-à-vis the BIT: whether to accord a high level of deference to the host state or whether to strictly review the actions of the host state.[165] Investment treaties generally do not provide much information or guidance on intensity with which ISDS tribunals ought to scrutinize the actions of the host state.[166] Some BITs or FTA investment chapters contain self-judging security provisions.[167] The words 'which it considers necessary'

Bethlehem, Isabelle Van Damme, Donald McRae, and Rodney Neufeld (eds), p. 379. Oxford: Oxford University Press.

[164] On the issue of deference and standard of review in international investment law, see Henckels, 'Indirect Expropriation and the Right to Regulate', p. 223; Caroline Henckels. 2013. 'Balancing Investment Protection and the Public Interest: The Role of the Standard of Review and the Importance of Deference in Investor-State Arbitration', *Journal of International Dispute Settlement* 4: 197 (hereinafter Henckels, 'Balancing Investment Protection and the Public Interest'); Stephan W. Schill. 2012. 'Deference in Investment Treaty Arbitration: Re-Conceptualizing the Standard of Review', *Journal of International Dispute Settlement* 3(3): 577–607 (hereinafter Schill, 'Deference in Investment Treaty Arbitration'); Valentina Vadiand Lukasz Gruszczynski. 2013. 'Standards of Review in International Investment Law and Arbitration: Multilevel Governance and the Commonwealth', *Journal of International Economic Law* 16(3): 613-33 (hereinafter Vadi and Gruszczynski, 'Standards of Review in International Investment Law and Arbitration'); Julian Arato. 2014. 'The Margin of Appreciation in International Investment Law', *Virginia Journal of International Law* 54(3): 545 (hereinafter Arato, 'The Margin of Appreciation in International Investment Law'); Luke Nottage. 2016. 'Rebalancing Investment Treaties and Investor-State Arbitration: Two Approaches', *Journal of World Investment & Trade* 17(6): 1015–40; Esme Shirlow. 2014. 'Deference and Indirect Expropriation Analysis in International Investment Law: Observations on Current Approaches and Future Analysis', *ICSID Review- Foreign Investment Law Journal* 29: 595 (hereinafter Shirlow, 'Deference and Indirect Expropriation Analysis in International Investment Law').

[165] See Arato, 'Margin of Appreciation'.

[166] Vadi and Gruszczynski, 'Standards of Review in International Investment Law and Arbitration', p. 615; Arato, 'Margin of Appreciation'.

[167] Article 11(3) of the Comprehensive Economic Partnership Agreement between Republic of India and Japan (signed 16 February 2011, entered into

means that an ISDS tribunal, while interpreting such a provision, should be more respectful or deferential to the host state's choice of action in comparison to a situation where such a clause is absent in the treaty.[168] In the presence of such a self-judging clause, the task of an ISDS tribunal is restricted to undertaking a good faith review, that is, whether the host state invoked the clause in good faith.[169]

However, if a BIT is silent on this question, then it is left to ISDS tribunals to determine the standard of review. This could potentially stretch from '*de novo* review of the state actions', on the one hand to 'total deference to the states', on the other.[170] The actual determination of standard of review can vary. For instance, the tribunal will grant greater deference to host states in matters pertaining to the making of factual determinations considering that the domestic agencies of the host state, not the ISDS tribunal, will have the expertise to do the same.[171] Similarly, ISDS tribunal shall grant greater deference

---

force 1 October 2011), provides 'nothing in this agreement shall be construed to prevent a Party from taking any action *which it considers* necessary for the protection of its essential security interests ...'. See also 2016 Indian Model BIT, art. 33.1.

[168] Schill, 'Deference and Indirect Expropriation Analysis in International Investment Law', p. 595.

[169] Schill, 'Deference and Indirect Expropriation Analysis in International Investment Law', p. 595; See *Case Concerning Certain Questions of Mutual Assistance in Criminal Matters (Djibouti* v. *France)*, I.C.J. Reports 2008, Judgment (4 June 2008) para 145.

[170] See *Whaling in the Antarctic (Australia* v. *Japan) (Merits)* [2014] ICJ Rep 226 [62-69]; WTO, *EC Measures Concerning Meat and Meat Products (Hormones)*, AB-1997-4, (16 January 1998); see Shirlow, 'Deference and Indirect Expropriation Analysis in International Investment Law', p. 600; Henckels, 'Balancing Investment Protection and the Public Interest'.

[171] Schill, 'Deference and Indirect Expropriation Analysis in International Investment Law', n 162, pp. 602–3. See also art. 17.6(i) of the WTO's Anti-Dumping Agreement, which provides that in assessment of 'facts of the matter', the panel shall determine whether establishment of facts by the anti-dumping authorities of a member state was proper and whether their evaluation of those facts unbiased and objective. If the establishment of the facts was proper and the evaluation was unbiased and objective, even though the panel might have reached a different conclusion, the evaluation shall not be overturned'.

to host states in determining what should be the appropriate level of environmental or health protection[172] or whether a measure serves public interest[173] or when domestic courts reach a decision based on interpretation of domestic law.[174] In contrast, ISDS tribunals shall grant a lesser degree of deference to the host state in certain situations such as retrospective application of domestic laws.[175] Another example to demonstrate differing standard of review is from the cases that were brought against Argentina, in the wake of severe financial crisis that Argentina faced. ISDS tribunals took contrary views on the emergency measures, with a few Tribunals refusing to grant deference to Argentina while examining the necessity of Argentinian emergency measures to safeguard essential security interest,[176] and the others paying deference to Argentinian response measures.[177]

172 Schill, 'Deference and Indirect Expropriation Analysis in International Investment Law', p. 601; Henckels, 'Balancing Investment Protection and the Public Interest', n 162, p. 246; Rahim Moloo and Justin Jacinto. 2011. 'Environmental and Health Regulation: Assessing Liability under Investment Treaties', *Berkley Journal of International Law* 29: 1. See also WTO, *EC Hormones* [124].

173 See Haretn, *Investment Treaty Arbitration and Public Law*, pp. 144–5; Burke-White and Staden, 'Private Litigation in a Public Law Sphere: Standard of Review in Investor-State Arbitrations', pp. 283, 342; Shirlow, 'Deference and Indirect Expropriation Analysis in International Investment Law', p. 619; ISDS tribunals have applied differing standards of review in reviewing 'public interest' – compare *Feldman* v. *Mexico*, ICSID Case No. ARB(AF)/99/1, Award (16 December 2002) para 116 with *CME* v. *Czech Republic*, UNCITRAL, Award (13 September 2001) para 533.

174 *Azinian* (n 103) para 99; *Mondev International Ltd.* (n 31) para 136; Schill, *Deference in Investment Treaty Arbitration* (n 162); Henckels, *Balancing Investment Protection and the Public Interest* (n 162).

175 Schill, *Deference in Investment Treaty Arbitration* (n 162) 601.

176 *CMS Gas Transmission Co* (n 78) paras 304–394; *Sempra* (n 147) paras 325–397; *Enron Corporation* Award (n 78) paras 288–345.

177 *LG&E Energy Corp., LG&E Capital Corp., and LG&E International, Inc.* v. *Argentine Republic*, ICSID Case No. ARB/02/1, Decision on Liability (3 October 2006) paras 201–266; *Continental Casualty Company* v. *The Argentine Republic*, ICSID Case No. ARB/03/9, Award (5 September 2008) paras 160–236; *Total S.A.* v. *The Argentine Republic*, ICSID Case No. ARB/04/01, Decision on Liability (27 December 2010) paras 135–180.

Against this backdrop, let us examine Article 23.1 of the Indian Model BIT that requires an ISDS tribunal to interpret the treaty 'in the context of such high level of deference that international law accords to the States regarding their development and implementation of domestic policies'.[178] Article 23.1 provides that if the host state advances a treaty interpretation, which according to the state furthers its 'development' and enables implementation of 'domestic policies', the tribunal should grant 'high level of deference' to the state. This could lead to differing outcomes depending upon the composition of the ISDS tribunal. Let us try to understand this with the help of a hypothetical example. Assume India cancels the licenses given to all coal-based power projects, affecting operating foreign companies involved in power-generation, claiming it is necessary for environmental protection as mandated by its domestic and developmental policies. Article 32.1 of the Indian Model BIT (that allows host states to adopt measures to protect and conserve environment) provides the treaty defence of necessity and states in a footnote that 'in considering whether a measure is necessary, the Tribunal shall take into account whether there was no less restrictive alternative measure reasonably available to a Party'.[179] The following outcomes are possible. First, the tribunal may grant high deference to India's assessment and uphold the measure unless the investor proves regulatory abuse in the form of cancellation of licences without following due process. Alternatively, the tribunal may apply deference only in certain issues which together combine to make up the review. So, the tribunal may grant high deference to India that it adopted a measure to achieve a developmental objective in pursuit of domestic policy (cancellation of licenses for environmental protection); but it could still go on to review whether the measure (cancellation of licenses) violated the treaty (such as if there were alternative measures reasonably available to India to achieve the stated objective).

8.10 Termination of the BIT

As discussed in Chapter 7, it is usual for BITs to include modalities pertaining to termination of BITs. For example, BITs typically allow

[178] 2016 Indian Model BIT, art. 23.1.

[179] See fn 6 to article 32.1 of the 2016 Indian Model BIT.

a contracting party to unilaterally terminate the treaty after the expiry of a specific period of time subject to a notice period. Further, as mentioned in Chapter 7, the treaty provisions continue to operate for existing investments, even after unilateral termination, for a specific period of time. A good example of this is Article 22 of the US Model BIT. Article 22.1 provides that the treaty shall remain in force for a period of 10 years and shall continue in force thereafter unless terminated in accordance with Article 22.2. Article 22.2 provides that 'A Party may terminate this Treaty at the end of the initial ten-year period or at any time thereafter by giving one year's written notice to the other Party.'

The 2016 Indian Model BIT also includes similar modalities. However, it differs significantly from other BITs like the US Model BIT. Article 38.2 of the Model BIT provides that

> this treaty shall remain in force for a period of ten years and shall lapse thereafter unless the Parties expressly agree in writing that it shall be renewed'. Further, Article 38.2 provides the 'treaty may be terminated anytime after its entry into force if either Party gives to the other Party a prior notice in writing twelve (12) months in advance stating its intention to terminate the Treaty. The Treaty shall stand terminated immediately after the expiry of the twelve (12) month notice period.

The significant differences are as follows: First, unlike the US Model BIT, there is no automatic renewal of the Indian BIT after the initial period of first 10 years. The default setting is that the BIT shall lapse after the initial 10-year period unless both the countries agree in writing to renew the treaty. Second, unlike the US Model BIT, the Indian BIT can be unilaterally terminated any time after the treaty comes into force by giving a one-year notice. There is no need to wait for the initial 10-year period to end as it the case with most BITs.

Furthermore, Article 38.3 of the Indian Model BIT states that: 'in respect of investments made prior to the date when the termination of this Treaty becomes effective, the provisions of this Treaty shall remain in force for a period of five years'. A combined reading of Articles 38.2 and 38.3 reveal that if a country wants to get rid of its BIT obligation, say in the latter half of its initial 10-year period, instead of unilaterally terminating the BIT, the country may simply refuse to renew the BIT at the end of the tenth year. This way, the country will be able to get rid of the treaty commitments without the sunset or the survival clause of five years kicking in for existing investments.

The provisions pertaining to termination of the BITs are heavily pro-state and against foreign investment.

8.11 Summing up

Based on the discussion in this chapter, one can conclude that barring some of the provisions like FPS and MTPs, the Model BIT has not succeeded in reconciling the interests of foreign investors with the regulatory right of host states. The Model BIT contains a narrow definition of investment, an extremely narrow FET-type provision, excludes MFN clause and taxation measures from the purview of the BIT. Furthermore, the expropriation provision in the Model BIT blurs the line between lawful and unlawful expropriation, provides for an NPM provision without a chapeau, contains a complicated and sequential ISDS and makes it easier for the state to terminate BITs. Thus, while the Model BIT scaled down pro-state provisions given in the 2015 draft Model BIT, the presence of these provisions still makes the Model BIT lean in favour of the host state friendly with limited rights provided to foreign investors. Furthermore, although the attempt of the Model BIT is to reduce arbitral discretion, as the discussion shows, many provisions still remain undefined and vague, thereby continuing to grant significant discretion to ISDS arbitral tribunals. Thus, contrary to the Indian government's claims, the Indian Model BIT neither balances investment protection with the host state's right to regulate nor does it reduce arbitral discretion.

A close examination of the provisions of the 2016 Indian Model BIT in this chapter show that these provisions have been drafted with the aim to protect the host state's accountability from being tested by independent international tribunals. India's purpose behind the Model BIT seems to be to immunize itself from future BIT claims. If the objective, as it appears, is to immunize India from BIT claims for protectionist purposes, then the government ought to specifically acknowledge the same and not hide behind the façade of protecting foreign investment. A more truthful approach would then be to walk out of the BIT system altogether, instead of having your cake and eating it too! While the purpose to narrow down the broader laissez faire liberalism language of India's BITs (documented in Chapters 4 and 5) is praiseworthy, the actual translation of that intent has gone wrong.

9

Conclusion

Throw the Bathwater, but Keep the Baby!

The story of Indian BITs is quite riveting. In the first phase, that is, during the 'refusal' phase, India's approach to BITs was closely tied to India's overall policy towards foreign investment. In this phase, although India did not shut its door to foreign investment, it followed an economic model that was based on self-reliance and import-substitution industrialization. Foreign investment, at best, played a peripheral role. During the 'refusal' phase, India's approach to foreign investment, relatively, was liberal from 1947 till 1965 instead of the period from 1966 to 1980. Nehru's economic pragmatism ensured that India stayed away from the tendencies of nationalising foreign investment that dominated many post-colonial states. Despite following a planned economy development model based on a socialistic paradigm, in Nehru's India foreign investment was welcomed if it helped in India's economic development. In the late 1960s and in the 1970s, under Prime Minister Indira Gandhi, India made a decisive shift towards adopting populist socialistic policies which included nationalization and adopting a not-so-welcoming attitude to foreign investment and private businesses. This discouraging attitude towards foreign investment started to change in the 1980s.

India did not reject international law on foreign investment during this period. However, along with other developing countries, India did contest some principles espoused by developed countries on questions of treatment to aliens, compensation for expropriation and so on. India also tried to shape the formation of international law on foreign investment through regular interventions at many forums. An important element of these interventions was that questions such as compensation for expropriation should be decided under domestic laws. India's contestation of some principles of international investment law was stronger at the multilateral level in comparison to the bilateral level. In other words, there was no dualism in India's approach towards international investment law when compared with India's overall policy towards foreign investment during this period. The fact that India did not enter into BITs in this period, despite many developing countries doing so, reveals this consistency.

This consistency or lack of dualism between economic policy on foreign investment and international investment law continued in the 'acceptance' phase also though in a different order. As realization dawned on Indian policymakers that import-substitution industrialization and a socialistic paradigm of economic development had not yielded results that were largely anticipated, India in late 1980s and early 1990s started to change gears. The massive BoP crisis in 1991, under the astute leadership of Prime Minister Narasimha Rao, was converted into an opportunity to usher in a new economic paradigm that showed greater trust, not suspicion, in markets and businesses. India, slowly but surely, started to move away from economic nationalism it had practised for four decades towards economic liberalism. An integral part of this movement towards economic liberalism was 'embracing' foreign investment. To deepen the agenda of attracting foreign investment, India started embracing BITs as a tool to promote and protect foreign investment. In other words, BITs became a tool to codify and communicate the policy of investment promotion and protection to the foreign investors and capital-exporting countries. In this period, India signed many BITs mainly adopting BIT models of developed countries based on laissez faire liberalism. These BITs contained broad provisions providing substantive protection to foreign investors with scant regard for the host state's right to regulate.

India's loss to the White Industries in 2011 and being sued by many foreign corporations thereafter marked the beginning of the third phase of the Indian BIT story—the phase of 'backlash'. Rattled by these ISDS claims, India started reviewing its BITs and concluded that the BITs it had signed thus far contained broad provisions that gave much discretion to ISDS tribunals. Consequently, as a matter of backlash against BITs, India unilaterally terminated 58 of them and adopted a new Model BIT in 2016 that is pro host state, providing limited rights to foreign investors. This marked a 180-degree turn from BITs modelled on laissez faire liberalism that India signed from 1994 till 2010 towards a BIT modelled on economic nationalism.

While India was correct in reaching the conclusion it did, the fact that has been ignored is that many of these disputes have arisen due to India exercising regulation considered bad in law. As the discussion in Chapter 6 shows, most of the ISDS claims brought against India deserved to be brought given the alleged abuse of public power by the Indian State. This abuse of public power has taken many forms—cancellation of spectrum licenses without following the due process, judicial delays in dealing with commercial arbitral awards, changing tax laws retrospectively, going back on the alleged assurances that induced foreign investment. In fact, these claims show the significance of BITs and ISDS to safeguard the interests of foreign investors in view of a state abusing its public power.

These ISDS claims are quite different from the Philip Morris type of claims where the state's regulatory measures pertaining to public health were challenged. The ISDS claims against India should have made India to think carefully about its own exercise of public power and about the conduct of the various organs of the Indian State while dealing with foreign investors in the interests of good governance. While some introspection has happened, largely these genuine ISDS claims have become a ground to attack BITs and ISDS to the extent that India wants to throw the baby out with the bathwater!

It is clear that India's opposition to ISDS cannot be linked to foreign investors using BITs and ISDS to challenge sovereign regulatory measures of the state enacted to pursue public interest. This, of course, does not mean that a Philip Morris kind of ISDS claim against India cannot be brought or that there cannot be a genuine conflict between investment protection and India's right to regulate in public interest. However, empirically it is yet to happen with India.

In other words, India's opposition to BITs and ISDS has got more to do with India's reluctance to be held accountable before an international tribunal forum for a claim brought by a foreign investor and then paying monetary damages to the foreign investor. Prima facie, this is bizarre given India has been entering into BITs with ISDS provisions since 1994. However, as the discussions in Chapters 6 and 7 show, India did not quite realize the actual import of ISDS till it lost the White Industries case.

India has strongly reacted against the BIT and the ISDS regime, which goes beyond what some scholars argue as reasserting control[1] over the system. The pendulum has swung from one extreme to another. For all practical purposes, India has walked out of the BIT system, even if it continues to pretend, unlike South Africa, that it is still invested in the system.

At times, much is made of developing countries like India being a 'rule maker' (that is, creating new investment rules) and not being a 'rule taker' (that is, borrowing investment rules made by western countries). Some elements of the Indian Model BIT such as provisions requiring 'high deference' in treaty interpretation whenever the host state cites developmental reasons or cites implementation of domestic policies; a clause that rules out the appointment of individuals as arbitrators for simply advocating a view on issues that might arise in a particular ISDS case arguably are examples of India emerging as a 'rule maker' in international investment law. However, the real issue is not whether India is now a 'rule maker' or a 'rule taker'. The real issue is whether the new model BIT will help India in achieving the twin objectives of protecting and promoting investment, and safeguarding the state's right to regulate. There is no harm in India being a 'rule taker' in international investment law as long as it can achieve the twin objectives. The analysis in the book shows that India has not been able to achieve these twin objectives simultaneously.

There is another paradox that has crept into India's BIT programme. Unlike the 'refusal' and the 'acceptance' phase, we find dualism in the 'backlash' phase. There is a disconnect between India's

[1] See Kulick, *Reassertion of Control over the Investment Treaty Regime.*

economic policy on foreign investment and India's approach governing BITs. India's foreign investment policy has become more liberal since 1991. However, India's approach towards BITs and international investment law, from 2011 onwards, has become quite illiberal. This backlash against BITs has put the clock back and, in many ways, has taken India back to the pre-1991 era. Today, any new foreign investment coming from the 50 plus countries with whom India has terminated the BIT will not enjoy the same protection as the investment already made before the termination of the BIT. Likewise, any new Indian investment to these 50 plus countries shall not enjoy any treaty protection. This, in turn, will expose foreign investment to regulatory risks. As the examples from Zimbabwe demonstrate, absence of BITs and ISDS might put the smaller and medium-sized enterprises at greater risk.[2]

Way Forward

Indian BIT practice needs to evolve keeping two things in mind. First, India's desire to increase foreign investment inflows especially under projects like 'Make in India'. While the role of BITs in attracting foreign investment should not be exaggerated, there is evidence to show that BITs in India have played an important role in attracting foreign investment. The significance of BITs for foreign investors in India also assumes importance because India does not enjoy the reputation of being a friendly place to do business. For instance, India's rank in World Bank's ease of doing business is abysmal at 100 out of 190 nations.[3] When it comes to specific factors that are critical for foreign investors, such as starting a business, dealing with construction permits and enforcing contracts, India's ranks are 156, 181, and 164, respectively.[4]

[2] Nikos Lavranos. 2017. 'The Proven Benefits of ISDS and BITs –Even for SMEs and Small Claims', http://arbitrationblog.kluwerarbitration.com/2017/10/24/proven-benefits-isds-bits-even-smes-small-claims/.

[3] World Bank. 2018. 'Doing Business 2018: Reforming to Create Jobs'. Washington DC: World Bank Group, p. 4 (hereinafter World Bank, 'Doing Business 2018'). Although India's rank improved from 130 in 2017 to 100 in 2018.

[4] World Bank, 'Doing Business 2018', p. 92.

In recent times, there have been many instances where sudden and drastic changes have been made, negatively impacting businesses such as the Modi government's decision to suddenly withdraw 86 per cent of the currency in circulation,[5] or the decision to interfere in the business of companies like Monsanto[6] and Amazon.[7] These undue regulatory interventions create an atmosphere of uncertainty for foreign investors. A pro-state BIT with limited protection to foreign investment will not be of much interest to those countries that are major exporters of capital to India. Indeed, after the adoption of the new Model BIT India has not been able to sign any BIT based on the new Model barring few countries (see Annex of the book). India's negotiations with the US, Canada[8], and EU Member countries[9] are stuck due to disagreements over the new Model.

Second, today, India is not just an importer but also an exporter of capital. India's overseas FDI has increased from less than US$ 1 billion in 2000–1 to more than US$ 21 billion in 2015–16.[10] A BIT that tilts towards the host state's regulatory power will reduce protection for Indian companies abroad. The significance of BITs for Indian companies can be gauged from three recent instances. First, an Indian investor, Flemingo Duty-free Shop Private Limited (FDF) successfully sued Poland under the India–Poland

[5] 'How Demonetization Has Impacted Key Sectors', *Livemint*, 9 Decemberhttp://www.livemint.com/Politics/a0Fk7NwHWsKcxiu4A3i4tK/How-demonetisation-has-impacted-key-sectors.html.

[6] Mayank Bhardwaj, Rupam Jain, and Tom Lasseter. 2017. 'Seed Giant Meets its Match as Hindu Nationalists Assert Power in Modi's India', 28 March, http://www.reuters.com/investigates/special-report/monsanto-india/.

[7] Aditya Kalra. 2017. 'India Privately took Amazon to Task Over Insulting Flag Doormat', 31 March, http://in.reuters.com/article/amazon-com-india-politics-idINKBN17208G.

[8] Amiti Sen and Surabhi. 'Canada to India'.

[9] Indivjal Dhasmana. 2017. 'India-EU ties Stumble Over Keeping Tax Out of Bilateral Investment Treaty', *Business Standard*, 10 April, http://www.business-standard.com/article/economy-policy/india-eu-ties-stumble-over-keeping-tax-out-of-bilateral-investment-treaty-117041000416_1.html.

[10] See Reserve Bank of India. n.d. 'Data on Overseas Investment', https://www.rbi.org.in/Scripts/Data_Overseas_Investment.aspx.

BIT, winning damages of € 17.9 million.[11] The tribunal found that Poland, by illegally terminating a series of lease agreements enjoyed by FDF's indirect Polish subsidiary, had expropriated FDF's investment and denied fair and equitable treatment to it under the India–Poland BIT. Second, an Indian mining company, Indian Metals & Ferro Alloys Ltd. (IMFA), has sued Indonesia under the India–Indonesia BIT at the Permanent Court of Arbitration, The Hague, claiming US$ 599 million in damages, for regulatory problems pertaining to the claimant's coal mining permits.[12] Third, an Indian investor has sued Macedonia under the India–Macedonia BIT for the alleged expropriation of mining concessions awarded to the Indian investor.[13]

International Rule of Law Infused with the Normativity of Embedded Liberalism

Apart from these economic justifications in favour of BITs, India also needs to look closely at rule of law and governance-related justifications for BITs.[14] As some scholars have argued BITs and ISDS further the interests of the international community as a whole by establishing a legal infrastructure that governs international investment relations.[15] In 2005, the United Nations General Assembly (UNGA) adopted the 2005 World Summit outcome, which recognized the need for universal observance to and implementation of the rule of law at both national and international levels.[16] This triggered scholarly debates

[11] Flemingo Duty Free Shop Private Limited v. the Republic of Poland, UNCITRAL, Award (12 August 2016).

[12] *Indian Metals & Ferro Alloys Limited (India)* v. *The Government of the Republic of Indonesia, PCA Case No. 2015-40.*

[13] Allison Ross, 'Indian couple threatens claim against Macedonia', *Global Arbitration Review* (Nov. 11, 2016), http://globalarbitrationreview.com/article/1073304/indian-couple-threatens-claim-against-macedonia. Also see Ranjan and Anand 2017, 52–54.

[14] Schill and Djanic,'Wherefore Art Thou?', p. 29 at 32.

[15] Schill and Djanic,'Wherefore Art Thou?', p. 29 at 32.

[16] '2005 World Summit Outcome' UN Doc A/RES/60/1 (24 October 2005) para 134. See also UN Doc A/RES/63/128 (15 January 2009).

endeavouring to delineate the meaning of the international rule of law.[17] Most scholars understand the rule of law at the international level in the formal sense and not in the substantive sense.[18] For instance, it is argued that the international rule of law needs to be distinguished from the international rule of *good* law and that at the international level it should be understood narrowly.[19] Accordingly, attempts have been made to examine whether the formal core values of the rule of law are to be found in the international legal system.[20] It has been argued that across cultures and political systems it is the formal notion of the rule of law that is applicable and accepted, which is consistent with 'how' the rule of law is articulated at international forums.[21]

The following elements are generally considered to be central to the formal version of the rule of law. First, exercise of public power must be controlled by law and should be based upon authority conferred by law;[22] second, the requirement of formal legality, such as

[17] James Crawford. 2003. 'International Law and the Rule of Law', *Adelaide Law Review* 3: 24; Simon Chesterman. 2008. 'An International Rule of Law?', *American Journal of Comparative Law* 56 331 (hereinafter Chesterman, 'An International Rule of Law?'); André Nollkaemper. 2011. *National Courts and the International Rule of Law*.Oxford; New York, Oxford University Press, p. 1 (hereinafter Nollkaemper, *National Courts and the International Rule of Law*); Stéphane Beaulac. 2009. 'The Rule of Law in International Law Today', in *Relocating the Rule of Law*, G. Palombella and N. Walker (eds), p. 197. Oxford; Portland, Or, Hart (hereinafter Beaulac 'The Rule of Law in International Law Today').

[18] Beaulac, 'The Rule of Law in International Law Today', p. 201; Chesterman, 'An International Rule of Law?', 333; Mattias Kumm. 2003. 'International Law in National Courts: The International Rule of Law and the Limits of the Internationalist Model', *Virginia Journal of International Law* 44: 19 (hereinafter Kumm, 'International Law in National Courts'). On 'formal' and 'substantive' rule of law, see Paul Craig, 'Formal and Substantive Conceptions of the Rule of Law: An Analytical Framework' (1997) *Public law* 467.

[19] Kumm, 'International Law in National Courts', p. 22.

[20] Beaulac 'The Rule of Law in International Law Today'.

[21] Chesterman, 'An International Rule of Law?', p. 342.

[22] Nollkaemper, *National Courts and the International Rule of Law*, p. 3; Chesterman, 'An International Rule of Law?', n 14, p. 342; Kumm, 'International Law in National Courts', p. 22; Beaulac, 'The Rule of Law in International Law Today', pp. 204–5.

rules, must be set out and applied in a manner that meets a certain threshold of predictability and clarity;[23] third, public powers cannot set or change the law at will—they have to act within the powers conferred by law;[24] and fourth, there must be a process of independent adjudication in order to ensure accountability of exercise of public power.[25]

Bilateral Investment Treaties meet some of the formal requirements of international rule of law. For example, BITs impose limits on the host state's exercise of public power so as to restrict the state's undue interferences with the rights of foreign investor's. Thus, a national treatment provision ensures that host state's right to favour domestic investments is subject to extending the same treatment to foreign investment in the same sector. Likewise, the host state's right to expropriate foreign investment is linked to following the requirements of due process, public purpose and due compensation. Similarly, BITs through the ISDS mechanism can hold the host state's accountable for the exercise of their public power.

However, the existence of BITs cannot be justified merely by using the language of international rule of law. Even the first-generation BITs modelled on laissez faire liberalism contained these characteristics. Yet, most countries including India contested these treaties because they found BITs imposing too many constraints on their public power and because they were not convinced how fair and impartial the dispute settlement system is. Therefore, for wider acceptability and sustainability of BITs as tools that advance international rule of law, they need to be remodelled using the normativity of embedded liberalism.[26] Else, states will keep contesting BITs based

[23] Beaulac, 'The Rule of Law in International Law Today', pp. 205–6.

[24] Nollkaemper, *National Courts and the International Rule of Law*, p. 4. See also Gianluigi Palombella. 2009. 'The Rule of Law Beyond the State: Failures, Promises, and Theory', *International Journal of Constitutional Law* 7:442, 442–67.

[25] Chesterman, 'An International Rule of Law?', p. 342; Beaulac, 'The Rule of Law in International Law Today', pp. 204–5; Nollkaemper, *National Courts and the International Rule of Law*, p. 5.

[26] See Catharine Titi. 2016. 'Embedded Liberalism and IIAs: The Future of the Right to Regulate, with Reflections on WTO Law', in *20 Years of Domestic*

on laissez faire liberalism as forces of hyper globalization that take away many areas of public policy out of democratic contestation. In order to smoothen the rough edges of undemocratic liberalism, the compromise of embedded liberalism, that has given stability to the WTO system, needs to be reflected in BITs as well.

The normativity of embedded liberalism will require that BITs should reconcile investment protection with the host state's right to regulate. Thus, while BITs may impose limits on the host state's exercise of public power for the protection of foreign investment, at the same time, should allow the host state to deviate from their investment protection obligations for compelling public policy reasons such as protection of public health and environment. Likewise, BITs should continue to hold the host state's accountable for the exercise of their public power through ISDS or any other international dispute settlement forum (including a multilateral investment court if countries agree). However, for states to readily submit themselves to the jurisdiction of such tribunals, the working of the tribunals should be fair and transparent. Further, states should be convinced that the adjudicators in such a system do not suffer from any systemic bias in favour of foreign investors.

Given the global debate on international investment law, BITs that reflect such compromise would be more acceptable to a broad range of stakeholders. Such BITs shall be acceptable to states because it would restore some power back to them which they feel has been transferred to international tribunals. Thus, countering the perception that forces of globalization have gone too far. Capital owners will also favour such BITs, because, as Piketty reminds us, capital owners cannot have more people (including states) grow disaffected with globalization[27] (including investment treaties). In simpler terms, for BITs to be acceptable, they should not be perceived as being part of

---

Policy Under WTO Law: The Embedded Liberalism Compromise Revisited, Gillian Moon and Lisa Toohey (eds), 7 November. Cambridge University Press, 2018. forthcoming. Available at SSRN: https://ssrn.com/abstract=2865840.

[27] Piketty, Thomas. 2014. *Capital in the 21st Century*, translated by Arthur Goldhammer. Cambridge, Massachusetts: The Belknap Press of Harvard University Press, p. 180.

a global economic system where distribution of benefits and burdens are skewed in favour of foreign investors and against host states and their people. The normativity of embedded liberalism reflected in the text of BITs could go a long way in restoring the confidence of states and civil society into investment treaties being useful tools to advance international rule of law. This changed approach to BITs is necessary because as India's greatest Prime Minister Nehru had said close to 60 years back: 'International law, if it is to be effective has to be related to the realities of international life; otherwise it becomes merely an academic exercise of some professor or pandit sitting in an university.'[28]

In recent years, many states have started recalibrating their investment treaties that reflect the compromise of embedded liberalism. The investment chapter in the EU–Canada Comprehensive Economic and Trade Agreement (CETA) is a good example of this. India's FTA investment chapters, to some extent, present this compromise as the discussions in Chapters 4 and 5 demonstrate. Instead of adopting an inward-looking and a protectionist or a defensive attitude to BITs, the Indian BIT practice needs to emerge in a manner that protects and promotes foreign investment without compromising India's right to regulate. India's FTA investment chapters could be a good starting point for this. This will have several advantages. First, it will signal to foreign investors, capital-exporting countries and others that India is willing to protect their investments in accordance with international law. Second, the public policy exceptions will explicitly recognize India's right to regulate in public interest. Third, it will protect the interests of Indian investment abroad, which is a growing reality as India emerges as an exporter of capital.

Fourth, it will renew India's commitment to international law and global norms in accordance with Nehru's vision that 'the objectives of [India's] foreign policy are the preservation of world peace and enlargement of human freedom'.[29] We live in times where unilateralism in

[28] Jawahar Lal Nehru. 1960. 'Inaugural Address at the Indian Society of International Law', *Indian Journal of International Law* 1: 6.

[29] Jawahar Lal Nehru. 1954. '"Discovery of America", Address to the East and West Association, New York, October 10, 1949', *Nehru, Jawaharlal Nehru Speeches 1949-1953*. New Delhi: East and West Publishers, pp. 124–5.

international relations and populism is on the rise. Some countries wish to abandon international institutions and international law at the altar of their narrow and short-term self-interest often for populist reasons. As economic history shows, such unilateralism is self-defeating but not before it has pounded the global order and made it chaotic. The ongoing trade war is the most evident symptom of this global chaos led by unilateralism. At times such as these, responsible democracices like India who have always championed the cause of a just global order based on mutual respect (the principles of Panchsheel that Nehru laid down) should step up to the plate. It is critical for India to re-pledge its commitment towards playing an active role in building a stable global economic order. India needs to conduct its international investment relations with other countries in accordance with rules laid down in investment treaties that balance interests of all stakeholders. This will not only enlarge individual freedom, as Nehru had envisaged, but will also demonstrate India's commitment to international rule of law and economic liberalism premised on a pro-market, not pro-business, approach. Such an approach of India will be in accordance with its liberal democractic constitutional order based on rule of law.

Borrowing from the policy-oriented approach of the New Haven School, India's new policy should be distributing the value of foreign investment protection and promotion without compromising on the host state's right to regulate. India should then use BITs as a process to communicate to the audience (foreign investors and all countries) that this policy enjoys authority. India should agree to a fair and transparent investor–state dispute settlement system that's workable for foreign investors to show the willingness to make the preferred expression effective. Whether India will do all this, we will have to wait and watch!

Annexure

Current Status of BITs Signed by India

Table A.1 BITs That India Has Terminated

Serial No.	Name of the BIT	Date of Agreement	Date of Enforcement	Date of Termination
1.	India–United Kingdom	14 March, 1994	6 January, 1995	22 March, 2017
2.	India–Russian Federation	24 December, 1994	5 August, 1996	22 March, 2017
3.	India–Germany	10 December, 1995	13 July, 1998	22 March, 2017
4.	India–Malaysia	3 August, 1995	12 April, 1997	22 March, 2017
5.	India–Denmark	6 September, 1995	28 August, 1996	22 March, 2017
6.	India–Turkmenistan	20 September, 1995	27 February, 2006	22 March, 2017
7.	India–Netherlands	6 November, 1995	5 December, 1996	22 September, 2016

(*Cont'd*)

Table A.1 (*Cont'd*)

Serial No.	Name of the BIT	Date of Agreement	Date of Enforcement	Date of Termination
8.	India–Italy	23 November, 1995	26 March, 1998	22 March, 2017
9.	India–Tajikistan	13 December, 1995	23 November, 2003	22 March, 2017
10.	India–South Korea	26 February, 1996	7 May, 1996	22 March, 2017
11.	India–Poland	7 October, 1996	31 December, 1997	22 March, 2017
12.	India–Czech Republic	11 October, 1996	6 February, 1998	22 March, 2017
13.	India–Kazakhstan	9 December, 1996	26 July, 2001	22 March, 2017
14.	India–Sri Lanka	22 January, 1997	13 February, 1998	22 March, 2017
15.	India–Vietnam	8 March, 1997	1 December, 1999	22 March, 2017
16.	India–Oman	2 April, 1997	9 December, 2015	22 March, 2017
17.	India–Switzerland	5 April, 1997	16 February, 2000	22 March, 2017
18.	India–Egypt	9 April, 1997	22 November, 2000	22 March, 2017
19.	India–Kyrgyz Republic	16 May, 1997	12 May, 2000	22 March, 2017
20.	India–France	2 September, 1997	17 May, 2000	22 March, 2017
21.	India–Spain	30 September, 1997	16 October, 1998	22 March, 2017
22.	India–Belgium	31 October, 1997	8 January, 2001	22 March, 2017

Serial No.	Name of the BIT	Date of Agreement	Date of Enforcement	Date of Termination
23.	India–Romania	17 November, 1997	9 December, 1999	22 March, 2017
24.	India–Mauritius	4 September, 1998	20 June, 2000	22 March, 2017
25.	India–Bulgaria	26 October, 1998	23 September, 1999	22 March, 2017
26.	India–Morocco	13 February, 1999	22 February, 2001	22 March, 2017
27.	India–Indonesia	10 February, 1999	22 January, 2004	22 March, 2017
28.	India–Australia	26 February, 2009	4 May, 2000	22 March, 2017
29.	India–Qatar	7 April, 1999	15 December, 1999	22 March, 2017
30.	India–Uzbekistan	18 May, 1999	28 July, 2000	22 March, 2017
31.	India–Argentina	20 August, 1999	12 August, 2002	22 March, 2017
32.	India–Austria	8 November, 1999	1 March, 2001	22 March, 2017
33.	India–Portugal	28 June, 2000	19 July, 2002	22 March, 2017
34.	India–Sweden	4 July, 2000	1 April, 2001	22 March, 2017
35.	India–Thailand	10 July, 2002	13 July, 2001	22 March, 2017
36.	India–Lao PDR	9 November, 2000	5 January, 2003	22 March, 2017
37.	India–Mongolia	3 January, 2001	29 April, 2002	22 March, 2017
38.	India–Croatia	4 May, 2001	19 January, 2002	22 March, 2017

(*Cont'd*)

Table A.1 (*Cont'd*)

Serial No.	Name of the BIT	Date of Agreement	Date of Enforcement	Date of Termination
39.	India–Ukraine	1 December, 2001	12 August, 2003	22 March, 2017
40.	India–Cyprus	9 April, 2002	12 January, 2004	22 March, 2017
41.	India–Yemen	30 October, 2002	10 February, 2004	22 March, 2017
42.	India–Finland	7 November, 2002	9 April, 2003	31 July, 2019
43.	India–Belarus	27 November, 2002	27 November, 2003	22 March, 2017
44.	India–Taiwan	17 October, 2002	25 February, 2005	21 March, 2018
45.	India–Armenia	23 May, 2003	30 May 2006	22 March, 2017
46.	India–Hungary	3 November, 2003	2 January, 2006	22 March, 2017
47.	India–Saudi Arabia	25 January, 2006 in New Delhi	20 May, 2008	31 July, 2019
48.	India–Bosnia & Herzegovina	11 September, 2006 in New Delhi	14 February, 2008	31 July, 2019
49.	India–Slovak Republic	27 February, 2006 in Slovak	16 June, 2007	22 March, 2017
50.	India–China	21 November, 2006 in New Delhi	1 August, 2007	3 October, 2018
51.	India–Trinidad & Tobago	12 March, 2007 in New Delhi	7 September, 2007	15 August, 2018

Serial No.	Name of the BIT	Date of Agreement	Date of Enforcement	Date of Termination
52.	India–Hellenic Republic (Greece)	26 April, 2007 in Athens	12 April, 2008	22 March, 2017
53.	India–Iceland	29 June, 2007 Iceland	16 December, 2008	31 July, 2019
54.	India–Macedonia	17 March, 2008 in Skopje, Macedonia	7 October, 2007	31 July, 2019

Source: Department of Economic Affairs, Ministry of Finance, Government of India, https://dea.gov.in/bipa.

Table A.2 BITs India Has Terminated That Were Signed but Never Enforced

Serial No.	Name of the BIT	Date of Agreement	Date of Enforcement	Date of Termination
1.	India–Djibouti	19 May, 2003		22 March, 2017
2.	India–Ethiopia	5 July, 2007		22 March, 2017
3.	India–Ghana	5 August, 2002		22 March, 2017
4.	India–Uruguay	11 February, 2008		22 March, 2017
5.	India–Zimbabwe	10 February, 1999		22 March, 2017
6.	India–Seychelles	2 June, 2010		22 March, 2017
7.	India–Slovenia	14 June, 2011		22 March, 2017
8.	India–Nepal	21 October, 2011		22 March, 2017

Source: Department of Economic Affairs, Ministry of Finance, Government of India, https://dea.gov.in/bipa.

Table A.3 BITs India Has Not Terminated

Serial No.	Name of the BIT	Date of Agreement	Date of Enforcement
1.	India–Turkey	17 September, 1998	18 October, 2007
2.	India–Senegal	3 July, 2008 in Dakar, Senegal	17 October, 2009
3.	India–Mozambique	19 February, 2009 at New Delhi	23 September, 2009
4.	India–Latvia	8 February, 2010 at New Delhi	27 November, 2010
5.	India–Bangladesh	9 February, 2009	7 July, 2007
6.	India–Lithuania	31 March, 2011	1 December, 2011
7.	India–Brunei Darussalam	22 May, 2008 in New Delhi	15 January, 2009
8.	India–Syrian Arab Republic	18 June, 2008 in New Delhi	22 January, 2009
9.	India–Myanmar	24 June, 2008 in Myanmar	8 February, 2009
10.	India–Mexico	21 May, 2007 in New Delhi	23 December, 2008
11.	India–Libya	26 May, 2007 in Libya	25 March, 2009
12.	India–Jordan	1 December, 2006 in New Delhi	22 January, 2009
13.	India–Bahrain	13 January, 2004	5 December, 2007
14.	India–Serbia	31 January 2003	24 February 2009
15.	India–Sudan	23 October, 2003	18 October, 2003
16.	India–Kuwait	27 November, 2001	28 June, 2003
17.	India–Colombia	10 November 2009	Not known

Source: Department of Economic Affairs, Ministry of Finance, Government of India, https://dea.gov.in/bipa.

Table A.4 New BITs Signed by India after the 2016 Model BIT[1]

Serial Number	Name of the BIT	Date of Agreement
1.	India–Belarus[2]	24 September 2018
2.	India–Taiwan[3]	18 December 2018

Source: Department of Economic Affairs, Ministry of Finance, Government of India, https://dea.gov.in/bipa.

[1] These BITs are yet to be enforced.

[2] Treaty between Republic of Belarus and Republic of India, signed on 24 September 2018.

[3] Bilateral Investment Agreement between the India Taipei Association in Taipei and the Taipei Economic and Cultural Centre in India signed on 18 December 2018.

Table A.5 Countries with Whom India Has Issued a Joint Interpretative Note/ Declaration Regarding the Existing BITs

Serial Number	Name of the BIT	Date of Agreement	Date of Enforcement
1.	Joint Interpretative Note on India-Bangladesh BIT[1]	4 October 2017	4 October 2017
2.	Joint Interpretative Declaration on India-Colombia BIT[2]	4 October 2018	4 October 2018

Source: Department of Economic Affairs, Ministry of Finance, Government of India, https://dea.gov.in/bipa.

[1] Joint Interpretative Notes on the Agreement between the Government of the Republic of India and the Government of the People's Republic of Bangladesh for the Promotion and Protection of Investments signed on 4 October 2017.

[2] Joint Interpretative Declaration between the Republic of India and the Republic of Colombia Regarding the Agreement for the Promotion and Protection of Investments between India and Colombia signed on 10 November 2009.

Index

About the Author

Prabhash Ranjan teaches at the Faculty of Legal Studies, South Asian University, New Delhi, India. The author is a Chevening scholar. Ranjan has also been a Visiting Fellow at the Lauterpacht Centre for International Law, Cambridge University, United Kingdom, and a Visiting Scholar at Brookings India.